RESIDENTIAL ENERGY

COST SAVINGS AND COMFORT FOR EXISTING BUILDINGS

SIXTH EDITION

John Krigger

Visit our web site at *www.srmi.biz*

Please work safely when following the procedures outlined in this book. If you cannot safely complete any of the procedures suggested in this book, we recommend that you hire a professional to do the job, or skip the procedure altogether. Your failure to heed this warning could result in injury, death, or damage to your home. Please perform only those tasks for which you are willing to assume responsibility.

Published by Saturn Resource Management, Inc.
805 North Last Chance Gulch, Helena MT 59601

For more information about improving the efficiency of your home, visit:
www.srmi.biz

For ordering information or special discounts for bulk purchases, please contact Saturn Resource Management, (406) 443-3433.

Design by John Krigger and Darrel Tenter
Cover artwork by Bob Starkey
Other artwork and photos by Bob Starkey, John Krigger, Marty Lord, and Steve Hogan
This edition was compiled by Darrel Tenter using Adobe FrameMaker®. The text is set in Minion Pro and Myriad Pro.

The following names appearing in this book are registered trademarks: Air Krete®, Energy Star®, IECC®, International Energy Conservation Code®, Tyvek®, V-seal®.

Publisher's Cataloging-in-Publication
(Provided by Quality Books, Inc.)

Krigger, John.
    Residential energy : cost savings and comfort for
existing buildings / John Krigger . --
6th ed.
    p. cm.
    Includes bibliographical references and index.
    ISBN 978-1-880120-23-1

    1. Dwellings--Energy conservation--United States.
I. Dorsi, Chris. II. Title.

TJ163.5.D86K75 2013   696
              QBI12-600018

ACKNOWLEDGEMENTS

This publication relies on the ongoing work of many people. We're indebted to those who have contributed their knowledge and insight over the years to the constantly evolving field of building science.

We offer thanks to the DOE Weatherization Assistance Program, the DOE Existing Building Efficiency Research Program, and Pacific Gas and Electric Company for the original financing and conceptual guidance for this book.

We recognize the periodicals *Energy Design Update* and *Home Energy* for chronicling the residential energy conservation field so competently, and the Affordable Comfort Conference (ACI) for providing a forum for the building science community.

We thank the scientists, engineers, and support staff from these organizations for performing valuable original research, and for producing important information resources:

E-Source
Ecotope Inc.
Florida Solar Energy Center
Lawrence Berkeley Laboratory
National Renewable Energy Laboratory
Oak Ridge National Laboratory
PG&E Energy Training Center – Stockton

Thanks to these individuals who provided assistance through personal conversations, seminars, and publications:

Bob Davis, Seattle WA
R.W. Davis, Athens OH
Jim Fitzgerald, Minneapolis MN
Skip Hayden, Ottawa Canada
Joe Lstiburek, Chestnut Hill MA
Gary Nelson, Minneapolis MN
Dale Pickard, Bozeman MT
John Siegenthaler, Utica NY
John Tooley, Raliegh NC

Thanks to these individuals for suggestions, contributions, and technical review of this book:

Rana Belshe, Fairchild WI
David Butler, Sierra Vista, AZ
Anthony Cox, Christianburg, VA
Chris Dorsi, Habitat X, Helena, MT
Tony Gill, Augusta ME
Adam Gifford, Newport ME
Bruce Harley, Stamford VT
Bill Hill, Muncie IN
Bill Holloway, Stockton CA
Rick Karg, Topsham ME
Tim Lenahan, Columbus OH
Bruce Manclark, Goldendale, WA
Joe Miuccio, Liverpool NY
Charlie Richardson, Boulder CO
Russ Rudy, Kansas City, MO
Kendall Shannon, Leawood, KS
Ken Tohinaka, Burlington VT
Bill Van der Meer, Williamsport PA
Doug Walter, Manhattan KS
Larry Weingarten, Monterey CA

Thanks to these loyal customers and many others, whose support makes the sixth edition of this book possible:

Pearson Education
Conservation Services Group
CA Building Performance Contractors Assoc.
American Home Inspectors Training
NRCERT
COAD
Building Science Academy
Center for Employment Training
FSL Home Improvement
Colorado Governor's Energy Office

Thanks to these certification organizations for their support, guidance, and collaboration:

Residential Energy Services Network (RESNET)
Building Performance Institute (BPI)

PREFACE

Residential Energy is a cooperative project of Saturn Resource Management and our customers throughout North America. During *Residential Energy's* 20 year history, customers have offered valuable feedback to us that has improved this book substantially. With each edition of *Residential Energy*, we've updated the content to reflect the evolving best practices for the diagnosis, retrofit, maintenance, and energy management of residential buildings. We're striving to improve this book as you strive to understand and improve the buildings you work with.

A commitment to energy efficiency is critical in an environment where energy policy and opinion vary widely over time. Reducing the energy use of our buildings is vitally important, because buildings in the U.S. and Canada account for more than forty percent of North America's total energy consumption. U.S. and Canadian citizens, along with our building trades, governments, and utility companies, invest in energy conservation, which improves both our economy and our environment. With the threats of climate change and energy price volatility, our economy and environment both depend on us all to keep improving the energy efficiency of our buildings.

With this 6th edition of *Residential Energy*, we've updated the book to improve its reference and training information. Among the important changes in this 6th edition are these:

- Updated energy statistics
- Improved explanations of energy calculations
- A new section on LED lighting
- Important updates to insulation information
- Improved description of ASHRAE Standard 62.2 - 2013
- Additions to the glossary and appendices
- Incorporated suggestions from dozens of readers
- Editing to improve readability

Not every energy conservation measure is worth our investment. We need to perform realistic financial analyses to support our energy-efficiency proposals. Analysis continues to prove that insulation, air-sealing, efficient appliances, heating and cooling improvements, and energy-conserving behavior return our investments better than almost any other financial opportunity. The recognition that simple measures are the most effective is the approach we've championed in *Residential Energy*.

Home health and building durability are essential companions to building energy efficiency. We all have a role — whether as building scientists, designers, builders, homeowners, or building residents — to understand buildings as systems and to improve the health, safety, durability, and energy efficiency of our buildings. Buildings-as-systems is our mantra, and we at Saturn are proud to be a part of the building-science revolution. Thanks to all you customers for supporting us in this important work.

– John Krigger July 2013

A Quick Word on QR Codes

Throughout this book you will see QR or *Quick Reference* Codes. These images allow smart phone users to quickly access content by scanning 2D code image with a QR code reader app. These apps are available for most smart phone platforms. When you see one of these images in the book just scan it with your phone's QR scanner app and you'll be directed to additional content.

We hope you find these codes useful.

Home Page	Energy Blog	Public Forum
srmi.biz	blog.srmi.biz	forum.srmi.biz

Facebook	Twitter	LinkedIn
facebook.com/ saturn.resources	@SaturnOnline	linkedin.com/company/ saturn-resource-

E-mail	Toll Free	You Tube
saturn@srmi.biz	800-735-0877	youtube.com/ OnlineSaturn

CONTENTS

This chapter provides a general overview of residential energy use. It presents history, statistics, policy, energy-bill analysis, customer education, and energy-efficiency ratings.

Energy – Past and Present

Cultures around the world have used energy conservation principles and passive solar technologies for centuries. For instance, some Native American communities maximized winter heating by orienting their dwellings and villages to the south. Middle East natives used wind chimneys, whitewashed walls and roofs, and window shading for cooling.

Before the industrial revolution, residential heat was provided by wood fires. Artificial light was provided by candles and oil or gas lamps.

A little over 100 years ago, things began to change rapidly. In the early 1880s, Thomas Edison invented the incandescent light and built the world's first power station. By 1908, 8% of American homes had electricity. By 1925, 53% of homes were connected to the country's expanding electrical grid. By the 1930s, natural gas began to compete with wood and coal as a heating fuel. Today, natural gas provides over 50% of the energy used in residential buildings.

Over the past 50 years, Americans have embraced air conditioning, replacing earlier attempts at low-energy cooling. Evaporative coolers appeared in the 1920s and window air conditioners in the 1940s. Central air conditioning followed in the 1950s. Today, around 70% of existing homes and 80% of new homes have air conditioners. Televisions, stereos, computers, swimming pools, spas, and all types of electric gadgets make American homes the most energy consumptive in the world.

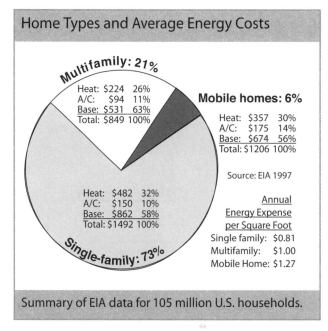

Home Types and Average Energy Costs

Multifamily: 21%

Heat:	$224	26%
A/C:	$94	11%
Base:	$531	63%
Total:	$849	100%

Mobile homes: 6%

Heat:	$357	30%
A/C:	$175	14%
Base:	$674	56%
Total:	$1206	100%

Source: EIA 1997

Heat: $482 32%
A/C: $150 10%
Base: $862 58%
Total: $1492 100%

Single-family: 73%

Annual Energy Expense per Square Foot
Single family: $0.81
Multifamily: $1.00
Mobile Home: $1.27

Summary of EIA data for 105 million U.S. households.

The Energy Picture Today

The United States represents about 5% of the world's population. Yet it consumes 25% of the world's energy supplies. The U.S. is the second behind China in total energy use and seventh in per capita energy use behind Canada and several smaller countries.

Buildings use about 40% of our total annual energy consumption. Energy is a principal commodity of our society, amounting to about 9% of the U.S. Gross National Product (GNP).

The benefits we receive from energy consumption are counterbalanced by environmental damage. With the exception of some renewable resources, energy consumption inevitably produces harmful by-products such as carbon dioxide, acid rain, and radioactive waste. Carbon dioxide is the most important cause of global warming, which is now an international problem and urgent priority.

Annual Average Household Energy Cost by Region (1997)

	Northeast		Midwest		South		West	
	$/yr	%	$/yr	%	$/yr	%	$/yr	%
Space heating	$689	39%	$575	39%	$329	23%	$253	22%
Space cooling	$78	4%	$85	6%	$211	15%	$134	12%
Water heating	$244	14%	$188	13%	$213	15%	$177	15%
Appliances & other	$752	43%	$645	42%	$662	47%	$590	51%
Total cost	$1763	100%	$1492	100%	$1415	100%	$1155	100%

Energy Information Administration: *A Look at Residential Energy Consumption in 1997.*

CO_2 Emission for Energy Sources

Type of energy	Typical use	Typical CO_2 emission
Natural gas	920 therms	11,000 lbs.
Fuel oil	660 gallons	14,500 lbs.
Electricity	10,800 kWh	16,300 lbs

From Energy Information Administration *A Look at Residential Consumption.*

Most scientists now agree that our unbridled energy use is warming the atmosphere through a process called the greenhouse effect. Gases, like carbon dioxide, that contribute to the greenhouse effect are called greenhouse gases. Recent climate changes, increasing forest fires, record droughts, melting polar ice, and other weather events, confirm that the earth is indeed warming. Unfortunately, U.S. greenhouse gas production increased by 17% between 1990 and 2007.

Energy consumption also produces undesirable economic side effects. Even with increased domestic production, the U.S. imported 50% of the oil it used in 2010, making oil our largest import. Importing oil creates about 50% ($25 billion) of our annual balance-of-trade deficit of about $50 billion per year.

Our foreign-oil dependence dominates our foreign policy and has precipitated expensive military intervention. Energy conservation can help reduce this reliance on fossil fuels, especially if we eliminate federal subsidies for fossil fuels.

Energy Sources Compared

Fossil energy is solar energy stored in ancient plant and animal remains. Fossil fuels, such as coal, oil, and natural gas, are very convenient to use and account for over 95% of energy used in homes. Supplies of fossil energy are limited and nonrenewable. Fossil fuels produce carbon dioxide—the main cause of global warming—and other air pollutants, which are a major worldwide cause of respiratory disease, environmental sensitivities, and neurological disorders.

Nuclear electricity harnesses energy released by the splitting of atoms and releases no carbon dioxide. At one time, experts predicted that nuclear electricity would become the world's cleanest and cheapest energy source—a prediction that has not yet materialized. Nuclear electricity is expensive, requiring large government subsidies. The nuclear industry's radioactive waste disposal process is a grave environmental, economic, socioeconomic, and political problem.

Past, Present, and Future Energy Consumption

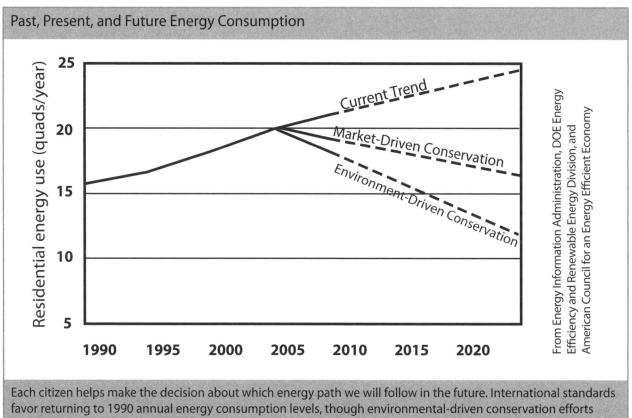

From Energy Information Administration, DOE Energy Efficiency and Renewable Energy Division, and American Council for an Energy Efficient Economy

Each citizen helps make the decision about which energy path we will follow in the future. International standards favor returning to 1990 annual energy consumption levels, though environmental-driven conservation efforts could result in even lower energy consumption.

Renewable energy is the same as solar energy, and includes wind power, direct solar energy, and biomass energy. As fossil-fuel supplies dwindle, renewable energy is becoming more widely used. The advantages of renewable energy are safety, environmental quality, and sustainability.

Energy efficiency and energy conservation must bridge the gap between the present fossil-fuel era and the future renewable-energy era. If high standards of residential comfort and convenience are to endure, energy efficiency and energy conservation must precede and support the implementation of renewable energy systems.

Understanding Home Energy Usage

Most of the energy statistics presented here come from the Department of Energy's Energy Information Administration (EIA). EIA reports energy consumption in dollars, millions of BTUs (MMBTU), or quads. A quad is one quadrillion British thermal units of energy—the equivalent of 40 million tons of coal or 182 million barrels of fuel oil.

The EIA recognizes three distinct housing types among the approximately 105 million American households: single-family, multifamily, and mobile homes. Householders in the U.S. spent about $150 billion for 20 quads of energy in 2000. By 2007, consumption rose to 22 quads, a 10% increase. Of this total energy in quads, 65% is electricity, 26% is natural gas, 7% is oil and propane, and the remaining 2% is renewable energy.

See "Calculating Energy Intensity" on page 24, for more information on energy intensity and energy indexes. See "Analyzing Annual Energy Costs" on page 277.

It's easy to get confused by percentages and pie charts unless you understand the relationship between electricity and natural gas—the leading energy sources. If you look at energy consumption, space heating consumes around half of the primary energy used in an average home. However, space heating is only about one-third of the $1400 average annual household energy cost, because natural gas, the main home-heating fuel, is less expensive than electricity.

Energy Intensity by Housing Type (Btu/ft²/yr)

Housing Type	Pre-1990	Post-1990
Single family	60,900	45,100
Multifamily (2–4 units)	94,400	50,400
Multifamily (> 4 units)	58,000	41,500
Mobile Home	92,200	50,600

For total delivered energy per square foot of floor area. Energy Information Administration: 1997

Electricity's higher cost reflects the fact that its generation and transmission is only about 30% efficient. On the other hand, electricity is typically around 100% efficient at the point of use when it's converted into heat for home or water heating. Natural gas, oil, and propane are only 40% to 90% efficient at heating a home or its hot water, but the fossil fuels are cheaper than electricity because they don't experience the generation and transmission losses. This makes direct comparisons of homes heated by fossil fuels and electricity tricky. Electrically heated homes may use less energy on site, but the energy costs more. The EIA resolves this problem by using dollars as a unit for energy consumed, and their dollar-based statistics include both fossil fuels and electricity.

Wise Energy Use

We know that our standard of living can endure with less energy, less money, and less environmental damage. For example, the year 2000 per capita energy consumption is about the same as it was in 1973, while per capita economic output has increased over 70% since 1973. Our increasing energy consumption has instead followed increasing population and increasing number of households.

From 1976 to about 1986, home-energy efficiency increased at an impressive rate, following the energy-price hikes of the mid-1970s. New buildings were more efficient than ever before. Owners of existing homes invested in insulation, storm windows, and better heating systems. Then around 1986, the cost of energy dropped, and the trend toward annual increases in energy efficiency stalled. From 1986 through 2005, energy concerns faded from public consciousness in the U.S. Then in 2008, energy shocks struck once more, caused by increasing worldwide energy demand and peaking oil supply. These shocks helped precipitate a worldwide financial crisis.

There are two major approaches to the wise use of energy in the future: energy efficiency and energy conservation. Although very similar, they aren't exactly the same. *Energy efficiency* is the more popular approach and focuses on maximizing the economic benefits of wise energy use. Energy efficiency often results in energy savings, as when you buy a new ENERGY STAR® qualified refrigerator to replace your inefficient old one.

The *energy-conservation* approach focuses more narrowly on reducing non-renewable energy use and its resulting environmental damage. Proponents of this approach are more willing to ask consumers for changes in behavior than the energy-efficiency approach.

A quad of electricity costs more than a quad of natural gas because around 70% of the fuel energy, used to make electricity, is lost in the generation and transmission processes. About 105 MMBTUs of electrical energy are consumed at the average home annually. However, an additional 155 MMBTUs of energy are wasted annually by the electric generation and transmission facilities for every household served. Electricity's premium price reflects these losses.

For many years, analysts considered energy consumption and GNP to be causally linked. A rising GNP and rising energy consumption were considered signs of progress, although this view does not consider that a home's energy efficiency may increase, giving more comfort and services for less money. Some economists and world leaders may now be ready to challenge the necessity of economic growth to achieve prosperity.

Many American policy-makers believe "efficiency" is a more positive word than "conservation." Nevertheless, North Americans are using energy at an unsustainable rate. We must now reduce energy consumption to preserve our prosperity, security, and environment. Energy efficiency is a term that describes our efforts to use energy more efficiently. Energy conservation means reducing energy consumption by eliminating energy waste. Energy efficiency and energy conservation provide the following benefits.

Efficiency of Use - Efficient homes maximize comfort, service, and value for each unit of energy.

Energy Security - Wasting less energy makes individuals and communities less dependent on energy and less vulnerable to price and supply fluctuations.

Environmental Restoration - Wasting less energy creates less environmental damage.

Sustainable Prosperity - Wasting less energy preserves fossil fuels for future generations and allows for diversity of energy generation options.

Potential for Energy Conservation

The lack of insulation and inefficient heating and cooling systems, among other problems, drives typical residential buildings to use one-and-a-half to two times as much energy as necessary to achieve comfort and convenience. This excess energy usage costs about $45 billion annually.

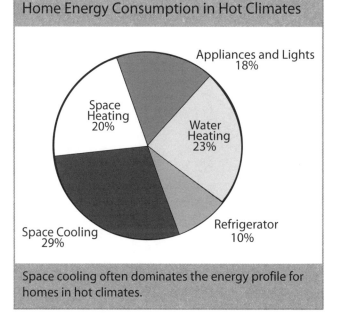

Home Energy Consumption in Hot Climates

Appliances and Lights 18%
Space Heating 20%
Water Heating 23%
Space Cooling 29%
Refrigerator 10%

Space cooling often dominates the energy profile for homes in hot climates.

The Department of Energy's Weatherization Assistance Program typically saves 10% to 30% of total household energy consumption, according to nationwide studies.

Residential energy conservation programs use four main strategies to achieve energy savings in residential buildings:

♦ Making thermal improvements to building shells.

♦ Replacing older heating systems, cooling systems, lighting, and other energy-using devices with new and efficient equipment.

♦ Repairing or adjusting existing energy-using equipment.

♦ Educating building occupants about energy-efficient practices.

The energy professional's most important challenge is to find the sources and causes of residential energy waste. These vary depending upon climatic conditions, building characteristics, and building operating procedures. For example, heating energy waste may dominate Minnesota single-family homes, while waste from cooling, water heating, and lighting may be the dominant problem in Texas high-rise residential buildings.

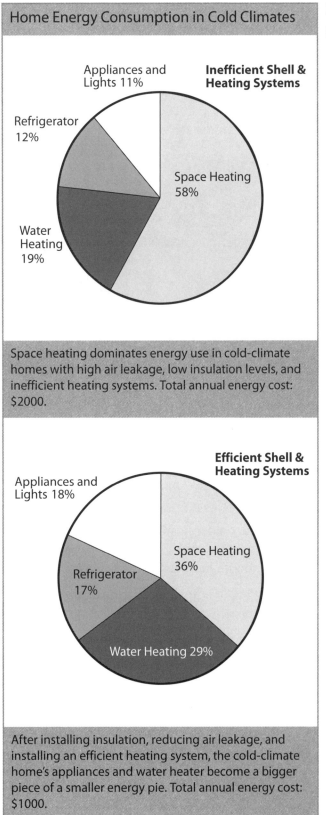

Home Energy Consumption in Cold Climates

Appliances and Lights 11%

Inefficient Shell & Heating Systems

Refrigerator 12%

Space Heating 58%

Water Heating 19%

Space heating dominates energy use in cold-climate homes with high air leakage, low insulation levels, and inefficient heating systems. Total annual energy cost: $2000.

Efficient Shell & Heating Systems

Appliances and Lights 18%

Refrigerator 17%

Space Heating 36%

Water Heating 29%

After installing insulation, reducing air leakage, and installing an efficient heating system, the cold-climate home's appliances and water heater become a bigger piece of a smaller energy pie. Total annual energy cost: $1000.

Inefficiency can be divided into the following general categories:

- Heating—Seasonal efficiencies for fossil-fuel-heating systems range from 30% to 90%. Most older systems operate at the mid-to-lower end of this scale.

- Heat losses—Depending on the thermal resistance of building shells, heat moves from indoors to outdoors through the shell during the heating season.

- Air leakage—Infiltrating air must be heated or cooled to a comfortable temperature, and heated or cooled air is lost when air leaks out of the building.

- Water heating—Energy losses in heating and storage of hot water can amount to 40% or more of that system's energy consumption.

- Cooling systems—Many cooling systems suffer from infrequent or improper maintenance. Simple adjustments and cleaning can increase typically low cooling efficiencies. Due to technological advances, newer cooling systems are much more efficient than older systems.

- Heat gains—Many homes use excessive cooling energy because of inadequate shading, excessive radiant heat gains from dark colored building materials, excessive air leakage, inadequate insulation, and internally generated heat.

- Distribution systems—Heated or cooled air leaking from ducts and uninsulated pipes in unconditioned spaces wastes a portion of the energy consumed by furnaces, boilers, air conditioners, and water heaters.

- Appliances and lighting—Refrigerators, lights, entertainment systems, computers, and other appliances use considerable electrical energy because of obsolete design, careless operation, or just the sheer number of electrical devices in a home.

- Resident behavior—The awareness and conscientiousness of a building's residents and managers has a significant influence on how much energy the building uses.

Cost-Effectiveness of Retrofits

Most government and utility programs require a retrofit to repay its initial investment within 10 years. If a retrofit achieves this or some other standard, we say it is cost-effective.

The cost-effectiveness of energy-efficient retrofits for residences depends on the following factors:

♦ Fuel usage—The more energy a home uses, the greater the potential for savings. Fuel usage helps to determine the level of cost-effective investments for a particular residence.

♦ Fuel cost—The more expensive the fuel, the more cost-effective any retrofit will be.

♦ Climate—The farther the outdoor temperature varies from a comfortable indoor temperature, the more energy is used for heating and cooling.

♦ Retrofit selection—The more skillfully an auditor assembles the optimal combination of retrofits, the more cost-effective the retrofit package will be.

♦ Materials costs and quality—An energy retrofit's ratio of savings to cost is dependent on skillful selection and purchasing of materials.

♦ Labor efficiency—Management, organization, and training have a large impact on whether retrofits will be cost-effective.

♦ Systems approach—The coordination of financing, energy auditing, work-orders, scheduling, and quality workmanship affects cost-effectiveness in a big way.

Priorities for Energy Efficiency

Energy retrofits employed without preliminary measurement or analysis can produce disappointing results. Therefore, energy professionals try to estimate a proposed retrofit's energy savings and prioritize the retrofits in descending order of their cost-effectiveness.

Comprehensive evaluations of government and utility energy-conservation programs have yielded surprising results. Some of the most important findings are listed below:

♦ Pre-retrofit fuel usage is a significant predictor of savings from energy retrofits; large users are large savers. Targeting large users increases average savings from the 10% to 20% range to the 20% to 30% range.

♦ Storm doors, storm windows, and window replacements are less cost-effective than insulation and air sealing because of their high cost per square foot.

♦ Thermal resistance of insulation is reduced by air flowing through and around the insulation.

♦ Densely packed, blown insulation can reduce air leakage when installed in building cavities.

♦ Leaky ducts can be a major source of energy waste, both by leaking conditioned air and by creating pressures that increase air leakage through the building shell.

♦ Preventable inefficiency in larger residential buildings is likely to be centered in the building's mechanical systems such as heating and cooling, water heating, and lighting.

♦ Winter heat loss and summer heat gain have somewhat different causes and require different retrofit strategies, although retrofits like attic and wall insulation reduce both heat loss and heat gain.

♦ Effective education and good quality management of energy specialists leads to more effective energy retrofits.

♦ Consumer education can produce measurable energy savings.

♦ Energy specialists who use equipment such as blower doors and heating-efficiency testers, produce more accurate assessments than those who don't use these testing devices.

An Energy Audit's Purpose

Energy auditors visit residential buildings and talk to owners and residents. They inspect, test, and measure to decide what energy-efficient retrofits are practical and cost-effective.

Specific purposes of an energy audit are to:

♦ Identify the type, size, condition, and rate of energy consumption for each major energy-using device.

♦ Recommend appropriate energy conservation, operation, and maintenance procedures.

♦ Estimate labor and materials costs for energy retrofits.

♦ Project savings expected from energy retrofits.

♦ Note current and potential health and safety problems and how they may be affected by proposed changes.

♦ Explain behavioral changes that will reduce energy waste.

♦ Provide a written record of decision making.

Computerized energy audits help set retrofit priorities by rating the cost-effectiveness of each retrofit, as well as analyzing the entire building retrofit proposal.

Quality Assurance Inspection

An energy professional's job doesn't end once priorities have been determined and retrofitting is authorized. Dollar savings and longevity of energy conservation measures are heavily dependent on proper installation. Inspecting every job helps ensure that the insulation, air sealing, space-conditioning, and baseload retrofits are done properly.

Changes are easier to implement if the job is still in progress. The best time for inspection is near project completion, while workers are still on the job.

The following are important elements of a quality-assurance inspection:

♦ Verifying compliance with specifications, job order, and energy audit.

♦ Providing feedback on performance of workers, both good and bad.

♦ Establishing procedures for correcting mistakes.

♦ Emphasizing the importance of maintenance procedures and conservation practices to residents.

♦ Arranging for future monitoring and evaluation, if appropriate.

The Energy Professional's Mission

The major goals of an energy specialist's work are to:

♦ Conserve energy, increase energy efficiency, and save money.

♦ Protect the environment by reducing harmful energy by-products.

♦ Increase comfort in residential buildings.

♦ Enhance health and safety of the building's residents.

♦ Increase public awareness of energy-saving products and procedures.

To accomplish their mission, energy auditors and technicians must:

♦ Understand basic energy principles. Once understood in theory, these principles can better be applied in practice.

♦ Recognize all of a building's important energy-saving opportunities and choose the most promising.

♦ Translate energy savings into dollars and compare projected savings with each energy conservation measure's cost.

♦ Evaluate and measure building performance before and after energy improvements.

♦ Know about incentives, rebates, and tax benefits available to customers.

♦ Explain conservation procedures and goals to building owners, fellow energy specialists, and technicians.

♦ Educate the building's residents about how they can use energy more efficiently and save money.

Energy and the Consumer

Consumers can control their energy consumption, within limits, if they are aware of energy-conserving habits and their benefits. Utility bills are a score card for both the energy specialist and the consumer to measure whether energy retrofits and behavior changes actually save energy.

Consumer Education

Consumer education can be one of the most cost-effective energy conservation measures. Households with equal-sized families and identical homes living next door to each other can have vastly different energy costs. Behavioral differences, comfort perceptions, and household operation and maintenance account for this variation.

Utility companies charge consumers for energy consumed within their living units. Educating consumers to adopt energy efficiency is an important part of the energy specialist's mission because behavior is such a major influence on energy consumption.

Setting priorities for occupant interactions is important because there's seldom time to discuss every potential savings opportunity. Consumer education methods succeed best when they consider a family's needs and education level. Customer acceptance depends on the energy-service provider's reputation, professional courtesy, and ability to communicate.

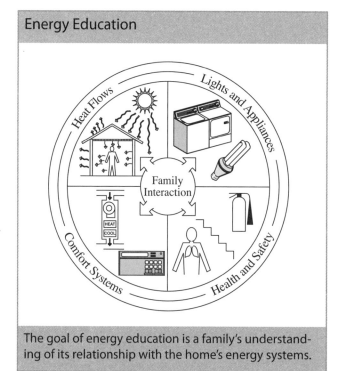

Energy Education

The goal of energy education is a family's understanding of its relationship with the home's energy systems.

Home Electricity Consumption

Indicator	Low	Medium	High
kWh/year	<4000	4000-8000	>8000
kWh/month	<320	320-670	>670
kWh/day	<10	10-20	>22
kWh/person/yr	<1700	1700-3400	>3400

Doesn't include heating, cooling, or water heating. Assumes 2.4 persons per household.

Making a good first impression is important for customer relations. Friendly, honest, and straightforward communication helps create an atmosphere where problems and solutions can be openly discussed.

The most important preconditions for changing residents' behavior are respecting and accepting them as they are. Tolerance and acceptance requires *active listening*—a set of courteous and effective listening habits, including:

♦ Paying attention and avoiding the urge to interrupt.

♦ Avoiding stereotyping or judging the speaker.

- Asking questions to clarify your understanding of their concerns.

- Paraphrasing and repeating the speaker's most important concerns to confirm your understanding.

- Empathizing with the speaker—putting yourself in his or her shoes.

The incentive for most learning is the expectation of benefits for the learner. Show customers how behavior changes will benefit them. Comparing the costs of current and alternative behaviors provides valuable information for informed choice. Informed consumers benefit from money savings, better comfort, improved health and safety, and a healthier environment.

Many retrofits provide a mixture of benefits—one or more may appeal to the consumer. For example, insulation and storm windows reduce energy costs, increase comfort, and reduce condensation. Articulating these benefits leads people to make correct decisions.

People learn best from their own experiences. Ideal learning opportunities occur when residents can make a decision, perform a task, or assist in an energy conservation procedure. For example, showing residents how to program their new automatic thermostat, set their water heater's temperature, or help them find air leaks during a blower door test, can stimulate their commitment to understanding and controlling their home's energy consumption.

Utility Bills

Utility bills are a useful tool to gauge a building's energy efficiency and measuring energy savings from retrofits. Both improvement in comfort and economic benefits from energy conservation are compared to the costs in order to set priorities and make decisions.

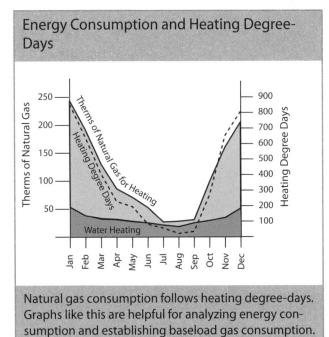

Energy Consumption and Heating Degree-Days

Natural gas consumption follows heating degree-days. Graphs like this are helpful for analyzing energy consumption and establishing baseload gas consumption.

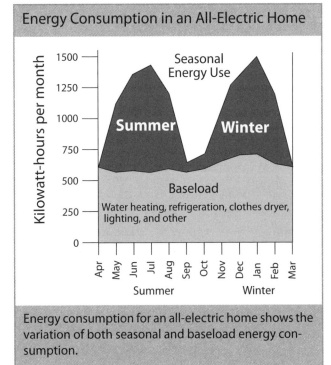

Energy Consumption in an All-Electric Home

Energy consumption for an all-electric home shows the variation of both seasonal and baseload energy consumption.

Electricity and natural gas, which comprise almost 90% of residential energy use, are distributed by central utilities that bill customers monthly for service. Utility bills contain a variety of information in addition to the payment

Utility Bill Anatomy

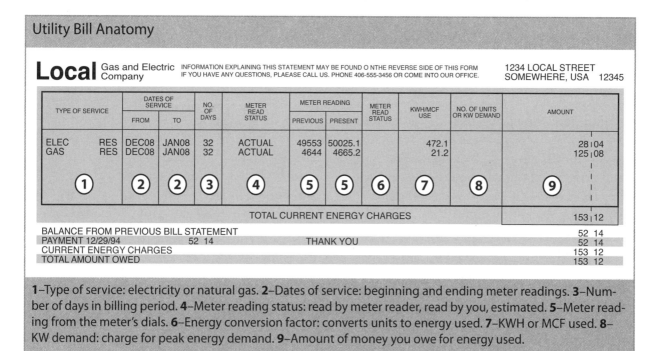

Local Gas and Electric Company | INFORMATION EXPLAINING THIS STATEMENT MAY BE FOUND O NTHE REVERSE SIDE OF THIS FORM IF YOU HAVE ANY QUESTIONS, PLAEASE CALL US. PHONE 406-555-3456 OR COME INTO OUR OFFICE. | 1234 LOCAL STREET SOMEWHERE, USA 12345

TYPE OF SERVICE	DATES OF SERVICE FROM	TO	NO. OF DAYS	METER READ STATUS	METER READING PREVIOUS	PRESENT	METER READ STATUS	KWH/MCF USE	NO. OF UNITS OR KW DEMAND	AMOUNT
ELEC RES	DEC08	JAN08	32	ACTUAL	49553	50025.1		472.1		28|04
GAS RES	DEC08	JAN08	32	ACTUAL	4644	4665.2		21.2		125|08
①	②	②	③	④	⑤	⑤	⑥	⑦	⑧	⑨

TOTAL CURRENT ENERGY CHARGES	153|12

BALANCE FROM PREVIOUS BILL STATEMENT — 52 14
PAYMENT 12/29/94   52 14   THANK YOU — 52 14
CURRENT ENERGY CHARGES — 153 12
TOTAL AMOUNT OWED — 153 12

1–Type of service: electricity or natural gas. **2**–Dates of service: beginning and ending meter readings. **3**–Number of days in billing period. **4**–Meter reading status: read by meter reader, read by you, estimated. **5**–Meter reading from the meter's dials. **6**–Energy conversion factor: converts units to energy used. **7**–KWH or MCF used. **8**–KW demand: charge for peak energy demand. **9**–Amount of money you owe for energy used.

amount owed to the utility company—energy consumption, rate information, the bill's time period, and other related information.

The energy consumption for heating and cooling is called *seasonal consumption*. The seasonal consumption varies from month to month depending on the outdoor conditions during the billing period. The remainder is called *baseload consumption*. Baseload varies little from month to month and forms a baseline on an annual energy-consumption chart as shown here in the chart. Sometimes auditors simply check the bill for three months when there was little heating or cooling to estimate the baseload consumption. However, baseload is usually a higher number than the average of the three lowest months. Baseload typically rises in the winter months. More artificial lighting, colder inlet water temperature for the water heater, and increased hot-water use during the winter can increase annual baseload 5–20%, depending on climate. An auditor, needing an accurate baseload, can install a meter on the heating or cooling system to isolate the seasonal consumption from the baseload consumption.

Energy units — Electrical energy is measured in *kilowatt-hours (kWh)*. Natural gas is measured in several ways: *hundred cubic feet (ccf)*, which is approximately equal to a *therm* (100,000 BTUs), or *thousand cubic feet (mcf)*, which is approximately equal to a *million BTUs (MMBTU)*.

In the year 2012, a therm or ccf of gas cost $0.50 to $1.40. A MMBTU or mcf is 10 times that amount or $5.00 to $14.00. A kilowatt-hour costs $0.06 to $0.15. Oil is $3.00 to $4.50 per gallon.

See "Equalized Heating Energy Cost Chart" on page 292 for a comparison of heating fuel costs.

Service codes, rate codes, and demand —

Utility customers pay different per-unit energy costs, depending on whether they are single-family or multifamily, urban or rural, commercial or residential, among other factors. Service codes identify these types of service.

The rate code is a group of numbers and/or letters recorded somewhere on the utility bill, referring to a particular written rate structure used to charge a particular type of customer. The code may specify one price for the first *block* of kWh or therms, and another unit price for the second block, and yet another for the third block. Some utility rates grant a cost reduction for successive blocks of energy consumption, while some levy a cost increase for successive blocks, to discourage customers from wasting energy.

Larger multifamily buildings may pay a demand charge. A demand charge is a separate service charge for the building's peak demand. The peak demand is the maximum amount of energy the building used during a 15-, 30-, or 60-minute interval during the billing month. Sometimes the demand charge is set by the building's maximum 15-minute consumption during an entire year.

Time period and meter reading — The utility bill shows the starting and ending date of the billing period. The meter reading at the beginning and end of the billing period is also shown. Some utilities show the energy consumption or energy cost per day. The time period information is important for comparison to similar periods in past years.

Energy-Efficiency Ratings of Buildings

Utility bills have their limitations as analytical tools for energy specialists because they are sensitive to changes in occupant behavior—and occupant behavior can cloud the effect of an energy retrofit. After the retrofit, utility bills take time to compile, and so it may be a year before the specialist knows if the retrofit had any effect.

Short-Term Energy Monitoring

Short-term energy monitoring can give energy specialists quicker information to evaluate their work. Most fuel-driven devices in residences use energy at a consistent measurable rate. If you know how long an energy-using device operates and its power rating, you can calculate energy consumption by multiplying power by time. For example, a 100-watt (power) light bulb burning for 10 hours uses 1000 watt-hours or one kilo-watt-hour of energy. A 100,000 BTUH (power) boiler operating for 10 hours uses one million BTUs (energy).

Two activities are essential to short-term energy monitoring: measuring power and measuring operating time. You can buy a recording watt meter, which measures both power and time, and connect it to the circuit for the refrigerator, clothes dryer, or electric water heater. Measuring the power of a natural gas furnace involves timing the revolutions of the gas meter's dials and multiplying the number of cubic feet per minute times the BTUs per cubic foot of the region's natural gas. An elapsed-time meter can measure the gas appliance's on-time. Some programmable thermostats also record furnace on-time.

Calculating Energy Intensity

A building's energy consumption divided by its floor area measures its energy intensity—a valuable indicator of the building's energy-saving potential. Two factors derived from a residential building's energy consumption are commonly used to gauge its energy efficiency based on the building's area of floor space.

The first factor, used for homes and smaller multifamily buildings in cold and temperate climates, is expressed in BTUs per square foot per heating degree-day ($BTU/ft^2/HDD$). This factor—often called the *Home Heating Index (HHI)*—gives a means of comparing buildings with different sizes, climate, and energy prices. The home heating index varies from HHI-2 in very efficient homes to HHI-20 or more in the most inefficient existing homes.

Three other energy indexes are used for homes in warm climates, electrically heated homes, and larger residential buildings. These indexes are expressed in annual BTUs per square foot (BTU/ft^2), dollars per square foot, or kilowatt-hours per square foot (kWh/ft^2). These indexes are more useful for buildings whose energy costs are not dominated by heating and not so directly related to heating degree-days. Extremely efficient residential buildings may only use 5,000 BTUs/ft^2 or 2 kWh/ft^2 annually for all uses, while very inefficient buildings may use 100,000 BTUs/ft^2 or 40 kWh/ft^2 annually.

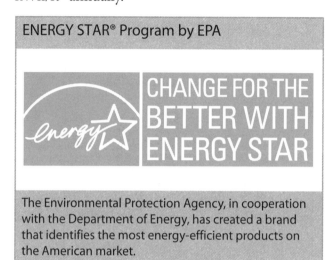

ENERGY STAR® Program by EPA

The Environmental Protection Agency, in cooperation with the Department of Energy, has created a brand that identifies the most energy-efficient products on the American market.

Before proceeding with any inspection of the building, the auditor should examine the building's energy costs and compute one of these three factors. This will give the auditor a preliminary idea of the opportunity for energy conservation measures.

See "Calculating Loads With Computer Programs" on page 75.

For example, if a home has an HHI of 5, the auditor expects to find a well-insulated home with a good air barrier and an efficient heating system. Opportunities for conservation are probably limited. An HHI of 20, however indicates an inefficient home with a very large opportunity for energy conservation.

A multifamily building using 80,000 BTUs/ft^2 is probably an excellent candidate for energy-efficiency improvements. Energy intensity of 25,000 BTUs/ft^2 indicates a very energy-efficient multifamily building.

See "Energy Indexes for Buildings (Total Energy)" on page 26 for values of these factors and what they indicate about a building. See "Analyzing Annual Energy Costs" on page 277.

Home Energy Rating Systems

Home energy rating systems (HERS) are standardized methods of rating a home's energy efficiency. The purpose of HERS are to provide consumers with information to compare homes, which they are considering purchasing, and to qualify consumers for energy-efficient mortgages. HERS programs are typically run by state rater organizations, in collaboration with Realtors, builders, appraisers, consumer groups, environmental groups, and the secondary mortgage market. The largest U.S. rating organization is the Residential Energy Services Network (RESNET).

See "Energy-Efficiency Organizations" on page 306.

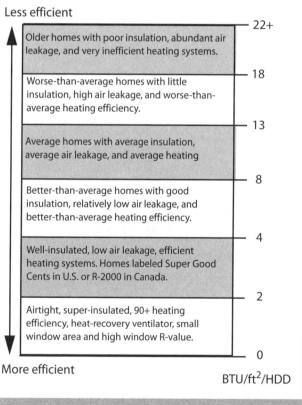

Home Heating Index

The Home Heating Index, measured in annual BTUs per square foot per heating degree day, is a common way of comparing homes heated by fossil fuel. Electrically heated homes and multifamily buildings have a different scale $^1/_3$ to $^2/_3$ smaller than the one shown.

HERS Rating with Other Energy Indexes

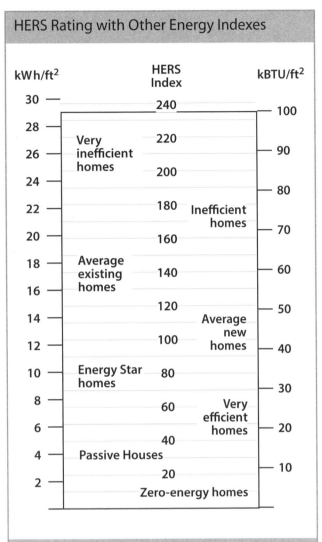

The HERS index is common way of rating the energy-efficiency of homes. This chart compares the HERS index with two other energy indexes: thousands of annual BTUS per square foot and annual kilowatt-hours per square foot.

Energy Indexes for Buildings (Total Energy)

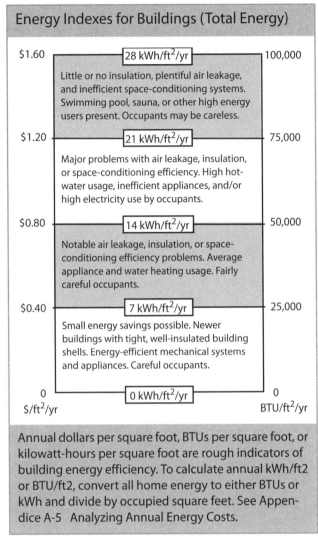

Annual dollars per square foot, BTUs per square foot, or kilowatt-hours per square foot are rough indicators of building energy efficiency. To calculate annual kWh/ft2 or BTU/ft2, convert all home energy to either BTUs or kWh and divide by occupied square feet. See Appendice A-5   Analyzing Annual Energy Costs.

The home energy rater gathers data about the home and enters into a home-rating computer program. This rating program compares the rated home with a reference home and assigns the home a point score depending on its relative efficiency. The reference home, built to the International Energy Conservation Code (IECC), represents a rating of 100 and a zero-energy home represents a rating of 0. A rating of 85 or lower can earn the home the ENERGY STAR label or a tax credit.

Along with the rating report, the home owner receives a list of cost-effective options for improving the home's energy rating. The cost of improvements can often be included in a mortgage and will pay off in long term energy and comfort benefits.

Cost-Effectiveness of Energy Retrofits

Cost-effectiveness describes how quickly an energy retrofit returns its initial investment. Several common ratios are used to measure cost-effectiveness. The simplest ratio is dividing the initial cost by the annual savings to find the number of years—payback period—a retrofit takes to pay its initial cost back in savings. Dividing the annual savings by the initial cost (giving the inverse of the first ratio) is the annual return expressed as a percent. For example, if a retrofit costs $1000 and saves $100 per year, its payback period is 10 years and its annual return is 10%.

Life-cycle costing is a more sophisticated way to measure cost-effectiveness. The theory of life-cycle costing is that, when contemplating any action, one should compare the *life-cycle cost* of taking the action with the life-cycle cost of not taking the action. If the life-cycle cost of acting is less than the cost of inaction, then one should act.

For example, an existing heating system will use $1200 per year over the next 25 years, costing $30,000 if no action—retrofit or replacement—is taken. A new heating system costing $5000 will use only $600 per year or $15,000 over 25 years. The new system's initial cost of $5000 plus its fuel costs of $15,000 equals $20,000. Replacing the heating system is cheaper than not replacing it, so it's prudent to replace it.

Some government and utility programs require using a *savings-to-investment ratio (SIR)*, sometimes called a *benefit/cost ratio (BCR)*. These are ratios of the life-cycle savings divided by the initial investment. In the above example, take the life-cycle savings ($30,000 – $20,000 = $10,000) divided by the initial cost of $5000 to arrive at an SIR of 2. An SIR of 2 means that the retrofit will pay for itself twice during its life-cycle.

Actual calculations of SIR or BCR are usually performed by computers, because they are quite complex. These calculations adjust future savings for energy cost escalation, inflation, and for the banking principle that future monetary savings are less valuable than current cash.

See "Calculating Building Heat Loads" on page 68.

This chapter discusses the physical principles essential for understanding energy flows in residential buildings. Building energy efficiency can't be applied like a recipe or building code because too many variables are involved. Energy specialists need energy principles to understand unusual problems and to cut through the confusion of competing energy-saving claims. Understand the principles underlying comfort, heat flow, and electricity use, and you'll make good decisions about which energy-conserving measures to apply.

Buildings use energy for temperature control, lighting, hot water, appliances, and entertainment. Energy use can be excessive because of heat leakage through building shells, inefficient heating and cooling systems, or lack of awareness of efficient operating principles. Waste can be associated with lights, appliances, and other energy-using household devices because of obsolete design or careless operation.

What is Energy?

Energy is a measurable quantity of heat, work, or light. *Potential energy* is stored energy, like a cord of wood. *Kinetic energy* is transitional energy, like a flame.

More than 99% of the energy we use comes from the sun. The only other significant source is nuclear material in the earth. Plants build their tissues with sunlight, and the composition of all fossil fuels is ancient plant and animal tissue. We burn fossil fuels to produce heat and work energy.

We measure energy many ways: therms of natural gas, kilowatt-hours of electricity, barrels of oil, gallons of propane, and pounds of steam are all common measurements of energy. Although energy measurement takes many forms, all types of energy are equivalent.

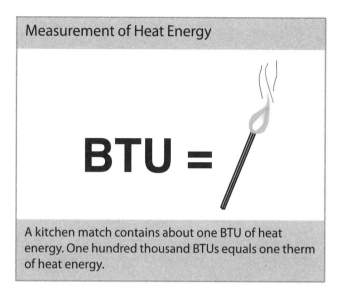

Measurement of Heat Energy

BTU =

A kitchen match contains about one BTU of heat energy. One hundred thousand BTUs equals one therm of heat energy.

The energy from last summer's sunshine is chemically locked in the produce we buy at the grocery store. That chemical energy in food is burned in our bodies to provide the kinetic energy and heat required to keep the human machine functioning. Solar energy from the age of the dinosaurs, stored for eons as chemical energy in deposits of coal and oil, provides energy for our modern world.

Laws of Thermodynamics

Two laws of the science of thermodynamics govern the behavior of heat in our universe. These laws were first described in the nineteenth century and helped to spawn the industrial revolution. Remember that no device, system, or idea can violate these laws. Attempts have been made but no exceptions have ever been demonstrated.

The first law of thermodynamics says that energy is neither created nor destroyed. Energy merely moves from place to place and changes form. The potential energy of gasoline becomes the automobile's movement, the engine's heat, and tires' friction on the road.

The second law of thermodynamics says that heat moves from high temperature regions to low temperature regions — never the reverse (without additional energy from an external source).

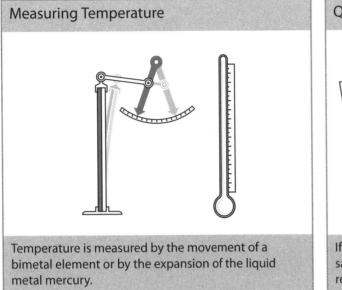

Measuring Temperature

Temperature is measured by the movement of a bimetal element or by the expansion of the liquid metal mercury.

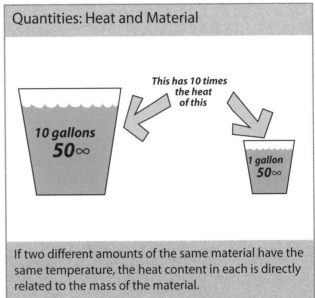

Quantities: Heat and Material

This has 10 times the heat of this

10 gallons 50∞

1 gallon 50∞

If two different amounts of the same material have the same temperature, the heat content in each is directly related to the mass of the material.

Temperature and Heat

Temperature is a measure of how fast the molecules in a substance are moving or vibrating. Temperature is the average kinetic energy or motion of molecules. Molecules in a solid are stationary, but they vibrate faster and faster as heat is added, raising the temperature.

Heat flows because of a difference in temperature between two places. Heat is measured in *British thermal units (BTU)*, which is the amount of heat required to raise a pound of water's temperature 1°F. A BTU is approximately the amount of heat released by burning one wooden kitchen match. The number of BTUs of heat that a pound of any material absorbs or releases for each degree of temperature change is called its *specific heat*. It is measured in BTUs per pound per degree Fahrenheit (BTU/lb./°F). Water has a specific heat of 1 BTU/lb./°F. It takes only 0.2 BTU to raise a pound of aluminum 1°F, so aluminum has a specific heat of 0.2 BTU/lb./°F. If we add one BTU to a pound of aluminum, it will get 5°F warmer.

The temperature of a given weight of material tells us how much energy that material contains, which is called *enthalpy*.

Sensible and Latent Heat

The relationship between water's temperature and its heat content is predictable—add a BTU to a pound of water, and by definition, it gets one Fahrenheit degree warmer. Add 150 BTUs to a pound of 50°F water, and its temperature increases 150°F to the temperature of 200°F. This *sensible* relationship ends at 212°F — water's boiling point. With continued heating, the pound of water remains at 212°F, while it absorbs 970 BTUs during its complete evaporation into steam — six times the heat it absorbed going from 50°F to 212°F.

This unexpected or hidden heat, which is released or absorbed as a substance changes form, is called *latent heat*. Our pound of liquid water vaporized when we added 970 BTUs, which is called the *latent heat of evaporation* for water. If we could catch all the steam and recondense it, the 970 BTUs would be released again. This is the principle of steam heating.

Boiling and Freezing Points

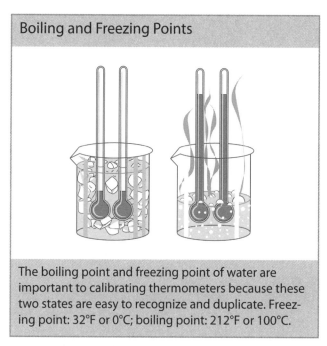

The boiling point and freezing point of water are important to calibrating thermometers because these two states are easy to recognize and duplicate. Freezing point: 32°F or 0°C; boiling point: 212°F or 100°C.

Latent Heat

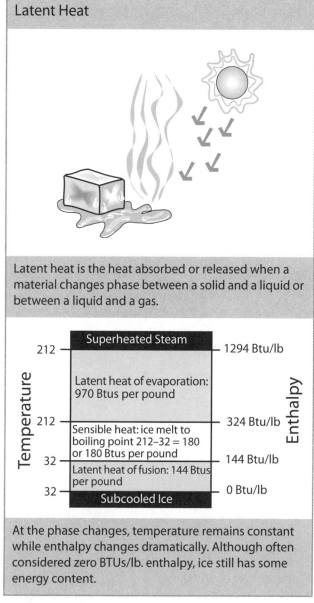

Latent heat is the heat absorbed or released when a material changes phase between a solid and a liquid or between a liquid and a gas.

At the phase changes, temperature remains constant while enthalpy changes dramatically. Although often considered zero BTUs/lb. enthalpy, ice still has some energy content.

Our pound of water would go through a similar metamorphosis if we were to cool it: the water would lose 1°F for every BTU removed until reaching its freezing point, 32°F. We would then have to remove 144 BTUs — water's *latent heat of fusion* — to turn the pound of water into a block of ice. Conversely, it would take 144 BTUs of heat to melt the pound of ice again.

Steam-heating systems, air conditioners, and refrigerators use latent heat to carry energy from one place to another. In steam heating systems, water is vaporized at a boiler and condensed back to a liquid in radiators. In an air conditioner, a special fluid called a refrigerant vaporizes at the evaporator, absorbing heat from inside the home in the process. The hot gas is then piped outdoors to a condenser, where it *condenses* back to a liquid, releasing its latent heat into the outdoor air.

Heat and Work

The American system of measurement has many ways of describing energy — the BTU for heat and the foot-pound for work being two of the most common. If you lift a one-pound weight one foot off the floor, you have done one *foot-pound* of work.

To prove that heat and work are equivalent, a British physicist, James Joule, used mechanical energy (or work) to stir water. He found that for every 778 foot-pounds of work he performed stirring one pound of water, the pound of water absorbed 1 BTU. Joule determined this by measuring temperature change of stirred water in an insulated tank. Now we know that 778 foot-pounds is equivalent to 1 BTU. This was an essential piece of knowledge for the industrial revolution.

The *joule,* an international energy unit, describes both work and heat. A million BTUs (MMBTU) approximately equals a gigajoule (billion joules).

Work Equals Heat

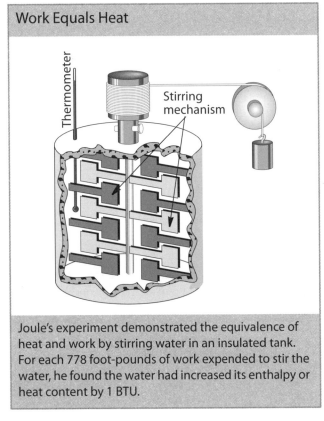

Thermometer

Stirring mechanism

Joule's experiment demonstrated the equivalence of heat and work by stirring water in an insulated tank. For each 778 foot-pounds of work expended to stir the water, he found the water had increased its enthalpy or heat content by 1 BTU.

Power and Energy Units

Power Unit	Energy Unit
BTU/hour (BTUH)	BTU
watt (joule/second)	watt-hour (3600* joules)
kilowatt (1kilojoule/second)	kilowatt-hour (3.6 megajoules)
foot-pound/minute	foot-pounds

* A factor of 3600 is obtained by converting seconds into hours. 60 min. X 60 sec.

Energy Versus Power

The differences between energy and power are fundamental, although the two are often confused. At the beginning of this chapter, we defined *energy* as a measurable quantity of heat, work, or light. *Power* is energy divided by time. Power is the rate work is done or heat is released.

Measurements of energy include foot-pounds of work, BTUs of heat, and kilowatt-hours of electricity.

The 100,000-BTUs/hour figure on the nameplate of your furnace is its power rating — its ability to deliver heat to the house when needed. Its power rating is the same in the summer, when it is idle, as in winter, when it's running. The winter operating hours determine how much fuel is converted to heat and how much the occupants pay the utility company.

One horsepower is 33,000 foot-pounds per minute, and it's a rather antiquated American unit for measuring mechanical power. Electrical power is measured in watts and kilowatts. A watt is actually a joule per second, so, like all power measurements, it is energy divided by time.

To get the quantity of energy produced or consumed, multiply power by the time the energy system is operating. If a 100,000-BTU/hour furnace runs for 10 hours, it converts 1 million BTUs of the fuel's potential energy to heat. If a 1500 watt heater runs for 10 hours, 15,000 watt-hours or 15 kilowatt-hours of electricity is consumed.

If a wood cutter cuts a cord of wood per day (power rating), and works for seven days, then he cuts seven cords of wood (energy). Converting the woodcutter's week of work into BTUs, we would multiply seven cords by 20 million BTUs (the heat content of one cord of hardwood) to get a total of 140 million BTUs of energy collected.

If a wood stove burned a cord in 200 hours of operation, its power would be approximately 100,000 BTUs per hour (20 million BTUs ÷ 200 hours = 100,000 BTUs/hour).

See "Conversion Factors" on page 274.

Pressure Versus Flow

Fluids flow because pressure pushes them along an open path allowing their flow. Both the pressure and a path are necessary for flow. Water, air, heat, and electricity follow similar laws as they flow from place to place — each in a unique way.

Pressure builds because of a difference in some measurable condition between two areas, which are sometimes labeled positive and negative to denote a pressure difference. Heat moves from place to place because of a difference in temperature (°F). Electricity moves because of a difference in electrical energy (volts). The wind blows because of differences in air pressure (pascals, inches of mercury). Water flows downhill because of a difference in altitude (feet). Water vapor flows because of a difference in concentration in water vapor molecules between two areas (pounds of water vapor per pound of dry air).

If a pressure and a path exist, fluids flow from the high-pressure region to the low-pressure region. If the pressure continues, the flow continues. If the pressure equalizes, the flow stops. For example, wind moves air from a high pressure region to a low pressure region, until the pressure difference between the two regions has equalized.

Where there is a pressure difference but no path, there's no flow. A large pressure difference exists between the air inside and outside your car tires, but, hopefully, there is no flow because there are no paths — holes in the tires. If a light switch is turned off, the switch creates a break in the path, interrupting electricity's flow, even though there is voltage — electrical pressure — in the circuit.

The substance connecting two regions may be: a *conductor,* where the medium can flow rapidly; a *resistor,* where the medium flows slowly; or a *barrier,* which stops flow or slows it down to a negligible rate. Glass, for instance, is a heat and light conductor, an electrical resistor, and an air and vapor barrier.

See "Air Pressure and Flow" on page 79 and "Ohm's Law" on page 43 for practical examples.

Energy Transformation and Heat Flow

Energy is neither created nor destroyed. Energy merely flows from place to place and changes form. While it is more accurate to say that energy is transformed or converted to another form, it's more common to say that energy is used or consumed.

Energy Transformation

Potential energy is energy locked in a stable state that can be used for work or heat. Our woodcutter's seven cords of wood remains potential energy until they are burned in a wood stove. Your body converts chemical energy from food to heat and motion. A large snowbank melts to become a million pounds of water flowing through a dam's turbine.

Burning wood or water flowing through the turbine represent kinetic energy. When gasoline explodes in an engine's cylinder, its potential energy becomes the kinetic energy of the rotating crankshaft.

Energy Transport

It is usually more convenient to convert potential energy to kinetic energy at a central location like a power station or boiler room. This confines the heavy machinery, mess, and danger of energy conversion to appropriately designed facilities.

Energy transport is the intentional movement of energy from one place to another. The fuel pump delivers gas to the carburetor, so the engine can burn the fuel. The furnace fan delivers hot air through ducts to the heat registers in the home. Steam pressure moves latent heat from a steam boiler through pipes to radiators. Generators at the power plant push electricity down the wires to your home.

Potential and Kinetic Energy

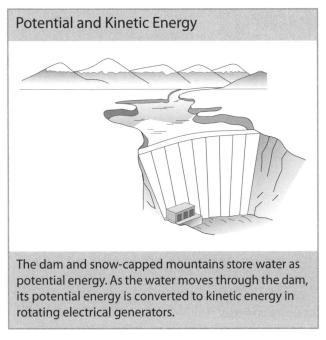

The dam and snow-capped mountains store water as potential energy. As the water moves through the dam, its potential energy is converted to kinetic energy in rotating electrical generators.

Temperature Difference

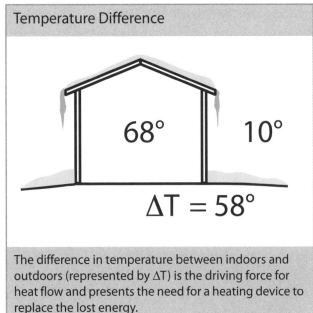

The difference in temperature between indoors and outdoors (represented by ΔT) is the driving force for heat flow and presents the need for a heating device to replace the lost energy.

Electricity is the easiest form of energy to move. It flows easily through copper or aluminum wires over long distances.

Mechanical energy is the most difficult type of energy to move. Rotating shafts and belts can move the mechanical energy only a short distance, while a significant part of the energy is dissipated through friction.

Some of the heating energy flowing through pipes and ducts is lost by conduction, convection, and radiation from heated pipes and ducts to their surroundings and also by air, steam, or water escaping from their conduits.

See "Forced-Air Systems" on page 161, "Hot-Water and Steam-Heating Systems" on page 165, and "Electric Circuits and Devices" on page 43.

Types of Heat Flow

Heat travels from areas of high temperature to areas of lower temperature in three ways: *conduction, convection,* and *radiation*.

Conduction is the way heat flows in solids. Heat flows through a solid by the vibrations of its stationary molecules spreading through the material.

Convection is the way heat flows in fluids where the molecules can move around, as in water and air. Winds and ocean currents transmit heat from warm areas to cooler areas around the globe by convection.

Radiation is the way heat flows in a line of sight between bodies of different temperatures. Heat radiation occurs between all objects that can "see" each other through space or through a gas, like air.

Conduction — Conduction is the most familiar and predictable type of heat flow. Heat conducts through solid objects and between objects touching one another. When you grab a hot frying pan, you get burned because the pan's heat conducts into your hand. As an object becomes warmer, the molecules vibrate, bump, and rub against each other more vigorously, passing heat through the material. This flow of heat is always from higher temperature to lower temperature.

The *K-value* or conductance measures the rate of heat conduction through a one-square-foot slab of any material one-inch thick. Metals like aluminum have high K-values, while K-values for insulators like plastic foam are low. The *R-value* is just a measured K-value of a specific product or material.

See "Heat Transmission" on page 59, "Calculating Building Heat Loads" on page 68, "Thermal Transmittance (U-factor)" on page 126 and "Materials/Building Assembly R-Values" on page 278.

Convection — Convection is heat transferred by a moving fluid like air or water. Convection happens when a part of the fluid moves because of temperature and density differences in the fluid. *Density* measures how many pounds a cubic foot of fluid weighs. Warmer fluid segments with lower density tend to rise, while denser, cooler fluid segments fall.

As heat is added to one part of a fluid, the molecules there race around faster, colliding more often and driving each other further apart. The greater spacing caused by the collisions reduces the density of the heated mass of fluid. The hotter fluid rises, and the cooler, denser fluid descends. The old cliche, "heat rises," is actually incorrect because heat moves in all directions. The truth is, a fluid's hottest molecules rise to the top.

Most convection, which is relevant to residential energy, occurs between a surface and a fluid — between your skin and a cool night breeze, for instance. Hot combustion gases convect against the metal surfaces of a furnace, transferring heat to the metal. Blow on your coffee to cool it, and you are using forced convection.

See "Air Movement" on page 210 for information about convective cooling.

Convection of Fluids

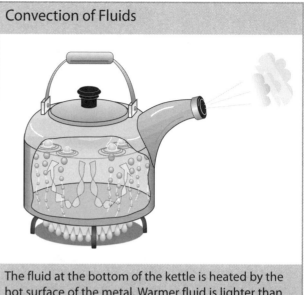

The fluid at the bottom of the kettle is heated by the hot surface of the metal. Warmer fluid is lighter than cooler fluid. The cooler fluid falls and the warmer fluid rises. This is what people mean when they say, "Heat rises." The current caused by this movement is called natural convection.

Radiation — Radiant heat flies through space from one object to another. The sun's radiant heat on your face or a cold window pane sucking radiant heat from the back of your neck are two examples of how you feel radiant heat. Objects, within a line of sight of one another, exchange heat radiation continuously. In this exchange, there is a net heat flow from the high-temperature object to the low-temperature object as dictated by the second law of thermodynamics. The high temperature object gets cooler and the low-temperature object gets warmer as a result of the radiant-heat exchange.

There are two types of thermal radiation important to the study of residential energy efficiency. The first is *solar energy*. The second is *infrared radiation* from objects on earth, emitted as different wavelengths depending on the emitter's temperature. Radiation is actually a continuous spectrum, but we divide types of radiation into solar and infrared to simplify our discussions of these two radiation types because they are important and different from one another.

Electromagnetic Spectrum

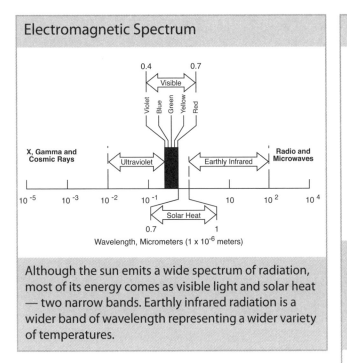

Although the sun emits a wide spectrum of radiation, most of its energy comes as visible light and solar heat — two narrow bands. Earthly infrared radiation is a wider band of wavelength representing a wider variety of temperatures.

The Sun's Changing Path Across the Sky

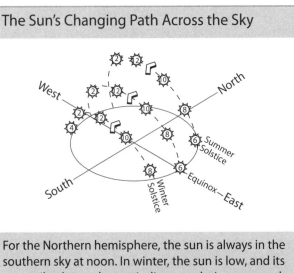

For the Northern hemisphere, the sun is always in the southern sky at noon. In winter, the sun is low, and its rays strike the earth at an indirect angle. In summer, the sun rises higher, its rays strike the earth at a more direct angle, and it stays in the sky longer each day, which accounts for summer's warm weather.

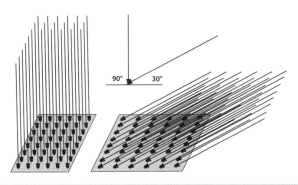

Summer solar radiation strikes the earth at nearly a 90° angle. Winter solar radiation comes from a lower angle; the same solar rays are spread across more surface area, and they travel a greater distance through the atmosphere.

The *electromagnetic spectrum* is a graphic way of describing the types of waves that radiate through our universe. The electromagnetic spectrum runs from short-wavelength x-rays, gamma rays, and cosmic rays, to long-wavelength radio waves and microwaves. Solar energy is a narrow band of this spectrum because of the sun's specific temperature — around 10,000°F. The earth's infrared radiation occupies a wider band on the radiation spectrum relating to the wide temperature variation of the objects in our environment — commonly 0°F to 2000°F.

About 49% of the sun's energy comes to earth as solar heat, 46% comes as visible light, and the remaining 5% is ultraviolet radiation. The earth's ozone layer filters most of the ultraviolet (UV) radiation, which is fortunate, since life on earth wouldn't survive constant bombardment by unfiltered UV rays. The atmosphere absorbs 10% to 20% of incoming solar radiation. Approximately 35% to 40% of the solar radiation is reflected by the earth. The remaining 40% to 55% is absorbed by the earth.

The sun's rays are at their maximum density on a surface at a 90° angle (also called right angle or normal). As the incidence angle varies from normal, solar radiation density decreases. When the sun is directly overhead, its rays are more intense because they travel through less of the earth's heat-absorbing atmosphere. When the sun is lower in the sky, the rays are less intense because they travel farther through the earth's atmosphere.

Greenhouse Effect

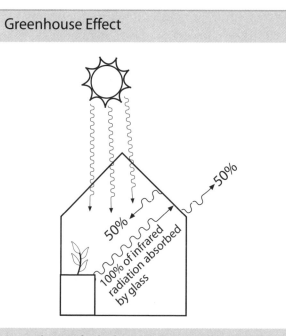

50%

50%

100% of infrared radiation absorbed by glass

Around 87% of solar heat is transmitted by the glass in this greenhouse. The heat is absorbed by objects inside the greenhouse. The objects re-radiate the heat as infrared radiation, which is nearly 100% absorbed by the glass. 50% of that absorbed heat is re-radiated outdoors and 50% is re-radiated indoors. Heat is therefore concentrated in the greenhouse, and its temperature rises as a result of the solar transmission.

Behavior of Radiant Energy

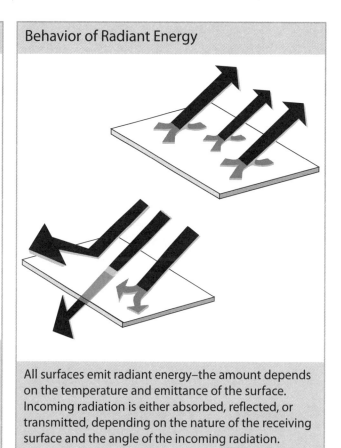

All surfaces emit radiant energy–the amount depends on the temperature and emittance of the surface. Incoming radiation is either absorbed, reflected, or transmitted, depending on the nature of the receiving surface and the angle of the incoming radiation.

The amount of infrared radiation emitted by an object depends on its temperature and its surface characteristics. Warmer objects emit radiant heat more rapidly than cooler ones. Most common objects emit infrared radiation readily. The exceptions are objects with metallized surfaces. The numerical rating of *emittance* is based on a theoretically perfect emitter having an emittance of 1, or 100%. Most common objects have emittances of 85% to 95%. Metallized surfaces like aluminum foil and galvanized steel have emittances of 5% to 20%.

When solar or infrared heat rays strikes an object, the rays are absorbed, reflected, and transmitted, depending on specific properties of that object. These properties are called *absorbance*, *reflectance*, and *transmittance*. Since all radiant heat striking an object is either absorbed, reflected, or transmitted, the values for these properties added together equal 1 or 100%.

Bright white and polished metal objects reflect 80% to 98% of incoming solar energy. Other objects absorb 40% to 95% of incoming solar radiation depending on their color — darker colors absorbing a greater percentage than lighter colors. Glass has special qualities, absorbing or reflecting only 10% to 20% of incident solar radiation and transmitting around 80% to 90% of incident solar radiation.

Most common materials — even glass — absorb almost all incoming infrared heat from earthly objects. The exceptions are polished metal surfaces that reflect most infrared radiation. Polished aluminum, steel, and certain metal alloys of tin, silver, and nickel are the only common substances that reflect both solar and infrared radiation.

See "Conservation Measures for Roofs" on page 207 for information on practical applications.

Glass' solar transmittance and infrared absorptance explain how glass traps heat inside a greenhouse, causing the *greenhouse effect.* Solar heat passes through a greenhouse window and strikes objects inside, warming them. The warm objects in the greenhouse emit infrared heat, which the glass absorbs. Part of that absorbed heat escapes outside, and part radiates and convects back inside, reheating the greenhouse.

Metallized glass coatings called low-e (low emissivity) decrease the glass' emittance. Low-e glass has a greater thermal resistance than un-coated glass because of this low emittance. Metallized coatings also reduce the glass' solar transmittance by reflecting some solar radiation.

See "Solar and Optical Characteristics" on page 127 for more information on glass coatings, and "Heat Gain" on page 203.

Energy, Comfort, Climate

The outdoor climate has the most influence on human comfort of any common factor. The temperature, relative humidity, solar radiation, precipitation, and wind affect the immediate comfort of people outside. The conditions outdoors determine what *space-conditioning* needs to be done to maintain indoor comfort.

We expect more thermal comfort in our homes and offices today than in the past. Individual preferences vary widely, but most people prefer an indoor air temperature of between 65°F and 85°F year-round. The heating and cooling necessary to maintain these temperatures requires between 30% and 70% of an average home's annual energy consumption.

We feel comfortable when we are in a state of thermal equilibrium with our environment without having to sweat or shiver. In thermal equilibrium, the human body is losing as much heat to its surroundings as it is gaining from metabolism.

Air temperature is usually the primary factor determining comfort, while the temperature of walls, ceilings, floors, and furnishings, called *radiant temperature,* is also very important. Together these two temperatures create a composite effect that determines comfort in both summer and winter. A high winter radiant temperature can counteract the comfort effects of low air temperature and vice versa.

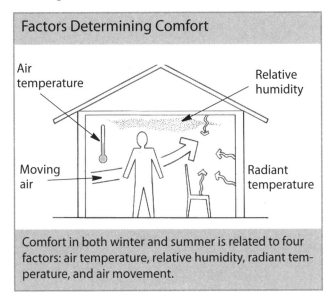

Factors Determining Comfort

Air temperature

Relative humidity

Moving air

Radiant temperature

Comfort in both winter and summer is related to four factors: air temperature, relative humidity, radiant temperature, and air movement.

Temperature

Air temperature is the most noticeable characteristic of climate and the most important factor in determining heating energy use. Outdoor temperature is always changing according to the season, the weather, and the time of day. Heating engineers use a unit of measurement called a *heating degree-day (HDD)* to describe how long the temperature is below 65°F during each day, month, or year. *Cooling degree-days* measure the air temperature differences between the outdoors and 78°F over the hot summer season. The temperatures, from which the degree-day difference is measured, are called the *balance points.*

The *heating balance point* is the outdoor temperature where no indoor heating is needed — usually assumed to be 65°F when the assumed thermostat setting is 70°F. A very well-insulated home may need no heat until the outdoor temperature reaches 50°F, so we'd say that its balance point is 50°F.

The local weather bureau computes the number of heating degree-days daily by figuring how long the average outdoor temperature was below 65°F. If the high was 30°F and the low was 0°F, then the average temperature for that day is 15°F. Subtract that 15°F from the 65°F heating balance point, and you get a 50° temperature difference over one day or 50 heating degree-days.

Heating degree-days are directly related to heating costs. It requires roughly twice as much fuel to heat a home in Duluth, Minnesota, with 9724 heating degree days annually compared to an identical home in St. Louis, Missouri, with 4758 annual heating degree-days.

See "Climatic Data for U.S. Cities" on page 282.

Cooling degree-days measure the intensity of the summer climate. To find cooling degree days, calculate how long the average temperature was above the *cooling balance point* of 78°F by totaling up the daily degree-day values. Cooling degree-days are less reliable as a predictor of summer cooling costs than heating degree-days are for winter heating costs, because amount of shade and relative humidity are often more important than the outdoor air temperature in determining comfort.

See "Calculating Building Heat Loads" on page 68.

Humidity and Moving Air

The air temperature and amount of water vapor in the air determine how much heat the air contains. The higher the humidity at a given temperature, the more heat the air holds. *Relative humidity* (rh) measures how saturated the air is with a percentage of water vapor. Completely saturated air has 100% rh.

Relative humidity is a very important summer comfort factor, since it determines how rapidly sweat can evaporate from the skin. Also, humid air contains more heat than drier air, but this fact exercises less influence on comfort than humidity's sweat suppression. Humid air may feel better to your throat and lungs indoors during winter, but there is little or no heating-energy advantage to higher relative humidity because heat flow depends on temperature difference.

Warmer air can hold more moisture than cooler air. For example, if outside air at 91°F and 50% rh cools to 70°F, the relative humidity rises to 100%. This cooled air contains exactly the same amount of water vapor, but at 91°F, the air is only 50% saturated, while at 70°F, it is 100% saturated. Saturated 91°F air (100% rh) holds twice as much water vapor as the 70°F air at saturation.

The outdoor relative humidity depends on rainfall, nearness to bodies of water, cloudiness, windiness, and other environmental factors. Indoor humidity is governed by the temperature and humidity of outdoor air, the amount of moisture generated within the home's shell, and the rate at which fresh air passes through the home.

When humid air moves near a cool object, tiny beads of water called *condensation* begin to form on its surface (or frost on a freezing-cold surface). Such condensation is undesirable because it fosters the growth of microbes and insects.

Moving air is integral for summer comfort; rapidly moving air increases bodily heat losses through convection and sweat evaporation. Air circulation also is important in winter to avoid air stagnation and large room-temperature variations. However, air currents can reduce comfort in winter if not properly managed.

Keeping indoor relative humidity at less than 60% during the summer promotes comfort, and will prevent condensation on cooler surfaces of an air-conditioned home. Indoor humidity should be less than 40% during cold weather to prevent condensation on cold windows and other surfaces.

See "Water Vapor and Humidity" on page 41 for more information.

Moisture Flow

Moisture flow through buildings is essential knowledge for the energy specialist. This section explains the way water and water vapor move through a building and its materials.

> To learn about moisture and health, see "Moisture Management" on page 245.

Characteristics of H_2O

A molecule of water contains two relatively small hydrogen atoms and one relatively large oxygen atom composing the compound with the chemical name H_2O. Water is the only common substance that we encounter in all three of the states of matter: solid, liquid, and gas.

Unlike many other substances, the solid state (ice) is less dense than the liquid. Liquid water expands when it freezes. If the liquid freezes while it is in or near a building material, the movement of the expanding ice can damage the building material.

A water molecule is like a magnet because it has two oppositely charged poles. Liquid water molecules clump together with their positive and negative poles facing one another.

Individual water vapor molecules, floating around in the air, are about one-third of the size of the other air molecules: nitrogen and oxygen. A very small water droplet (fog) is about 3500 times the diameter of a water molecule. A material, like Tyvek and Gortex, can block both liquid water and air, while letting water vapor through. These special materials have pores big enough to pass water vapor but small enough to block air molecules and the smallest water droplets. A material, like polyethylene or aluminum foil, that blocks water vapor also blocks air and liquid water because of this size consideration.

Moisture and Materials

We classify materials as either porous or non-porous to water and water vapor. Porous materials include wood products, insulation, and masonry materials. Non-porous materials, which are impervious to moisture, include glass, plastic, steel, and aluminum.

Adsorption is when porous materials attract and store individual water molecules on the surfaces of their pores. The water-vapor molecules cling to walls of the pores. In drier conditions, the pores *desorb* the water vapor, clinging to their surfaces, and the water vapor exits the material. Many materials such as wood or brick expand and contract with the adsorption and desorption of water vapor.

If the porous material continues adsorbing water vapor, the pores eventually run out of surface area to hold the vapor molecules on the surface of the pores. Then the water molecules start to clump into a liquid, filling the pores with liquid water.

Moisture Movement through Buildings

Moisture enters buildings and moves through them as both liquid water and water vapor. This movement happens in four ways.

♦ *Liquid flow.* Driven by gravity, or pressure differences, water flows into a building's holes and cracks. Roof leaks and plumbing leaks can deposit large amounts of water in a home.

♦ *Capillary seepage.* Liquid water creates a suction of its own as it moves through tiny spaces within and between building materials. This capillary suction draws water seepage from the ground. Seepage also redistributes water from leaks, spills, and condensation.

♦ *Air movement.* Air movement carries water vapor into and out of the building and its cavities. Air pressure difference is the driving force for this air movement, and holes in the building shell are the leakage paths. If the air reaches saturation (also called the dew point), condensation will occur.

◆ *Vapor diffusion.* Water vapor will move through solid objects depending on their permeance and the vapor pressure.

Water Vapor and Humidity

Water vapor is lighter than air and the water vapor molecule is smaller than air's other molecules — nitrogen and oxygen. Therefore, water vapor can rise faster and squeeze through smaller microscopic spaces than air. When water vapor moves through a solid material, this is called vapor diffusion.

Materials vary in their permeability to water vapor. Porous materials like brick and insulation transmit water vapor relatively rapidly and are said to have a high permeability. Plywood and drywall have a medium permeability. House wrap is a specially designed material that repels water while letting water vapor through because of house wrap's high permeability. Metals and plastic films, often called *vapor barriers*, slow vapor diffusion to a trickle.

A force called vapor pressure drives vapor diffusion. *Vapor pressure* is created by a difference in the amount of water vapor in two bodies of air, which are separated by some barrier, like a wall. The amount of water vapor in the air — called *absolute humidity* or *humidity ratio* — is expressed in pounds of water vapor per pound of dry air. Vapor pressure is the difference in absolute humidity between two air masses. The greater the vapor pressure, the faster water vapor flows through building materials separating the two air masses.

Relative humidity (rh) — the percentage of the maximum moisture that air at a given temperature can hold — is 100% when the air is saturated with moisture. Add more moisture to saturated air, and moisture condenses on cool objects. Relative humidity is 50% when the air at a particular temperature is only half saturated with water vapor. The moisture content of building materials is directly related to the relative humidity of the air surrounding them.

Converting Energy for Home Use

In all homes, energy is converted from one form to another — electricity to light, gas to heated water — within its walls to provide occupants comfort, water heating, refrigeration, lighting, entertainment, and a variety of other services.

Combustion Heating

Most homes in the United States are heated by combustion heating systems. When the carbon and hydrogen atoms in fuel molecules mix with oxygen and a flame, the chemical chain reaction we call burning begins. Heat is liberated in the chemical process, and we use this heat for space and water heating.

The heat from the flame and hot gases heats a metal structure, called a heat exchanger, which then heats air or water. The flame heats the heat exchanger first and foremost by radiation and also by convection of its combustion gases. Pipes or ducts carry the heated air or water to the building's rooms. The transfer of chemical energy into heat at the flame is usually more than 99% efficient. However the farther the heat travels away from the flame, into the heat exchanger and through the distribution system, the more heat is lost. These progressive heat losses make most central heating systems less than 70% efficient at converting the fuel's chemical energy to useful heat for the home.

See "Combustion Heating Basics" on page 142.

Heat Transfer from Combustion

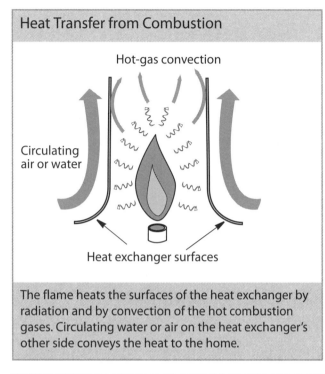

Hot-gas convection

Circulating air or water

Heat exchanger surfaces

The flame heats the surfaces of the heat exchanger by radiation and by convection of the hot combustion gases. Circulating water or air on the heat exchanger's other side conveys the heat to the home.

Combustion of Propane

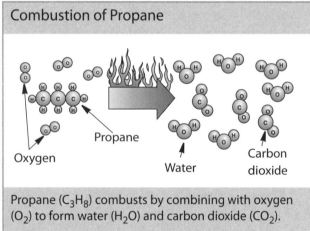

Oxygen

Propane

Water

Carbon dioxide

Propane (C_3H_8) combusts by combining with oxygen (O_2) to form water (H_2O) and carbon dioxide (CO_2).

Electric Resistance Heating

Electric resistance heating changes electricity, usually generated by heat, back into heat. The electric current passes through resistive wires, bars, or plates. Electric heaters are often located in rooms and perform their heating through natural convection and radiation. Electric furnaces blow air through their electric resistance coils. Electric water heaters and heating boilers have their electric resistance bar surrounded by water, so they heat by conduction and convection.

See "Electric Heat" on page 180.

Lighting

Electricity is converted into light in residential buildings in *incandescent* or *fluorescent* lights. In an incandescent light bulb, a tiny metal wire called a filament glows white hot when electric current passes through it. Only 10% of the electricity is converted into light, with the other 90% becoming heat. Fluorescent lamps produce light by passing electric current through a metallic gas. The flow of electricity through the gas excites special chemicals called phosphors, causing them to glow or "fluoresce." The glowing phosphors coat the inside of the fluorescent tube. Fluorescent lamps convert 80% of the electricity they use into light. Using fluorescent lights instead of incandescent lights can reduce the amount of electricity used for lighting by about 75%.

For more information, see Chapter 7 Lighting and Appliances.

The Refrigeration Cycle

Refrigerators, air conditioners, and heat pumps move heat from one location to another using latent heat. One location is heated and one location is cooled. When liquid *refrigerant* vaporizes in the *evaporator* of an air conditioner, it absorbs heat from the metal in the evaporator coil. The evaporator coil then becomes cold and removes heat from the warm air being blown through the coil. The vaporized refrigerant carries the heat it collected from the indoor air to the *compressor*, where the refrigerant vapor is compressed and sent to the condenser. In the *condenser* the refrigerant condenses back to a liquid, releasing its latent heat of vaporization and heating the condenser coil. The condenser coil has a higher temperature than the air moving through it, so the heat flows from the coil to the air.

The liquid refrigerant collects in the condenser and flows toward the evaporator, pushed by the compressor's pressure. The *expansion device*, which is like a spray nozzle, sprays liquid refrigerant into the evaporator, where it evaporates once again. The evaporating refrigerant removes heat from the evaporator coil, and the cycle repeats.

See "Checking Refrigerant Charge" on page 221 for more detail on the refrigeration cycle.

The Refrigeration Cycle

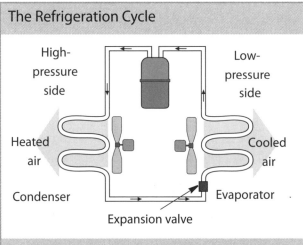

High-pressure side

Low-pressure side

Heated air

Cooled air

Condenser

Evaporator

Expansion valve

Refrigerant evaporates in the evaporator, absorbing heat from the metal tubes, fins, and passing air. The compressor compresses the refrigerant, preparing it to condense within the condenser. The refrigerant's latent heat is then transferred to the condenser's tubes and fins and then to the passing air.

Electric Circuits and Devices

Electrical principles are presented next because electricity is so important to home energy use. Electricity is the most refined and versatile form of energy. It can be converted into light, heat, or motion. Electricity heats homes, spins motors, lights lamps, cooks, and entertains. Electric circuits providing heat, light, or motion are called *power circuits*. Electricity also regulates most energy-using devices — furnaces, water heaters, and major appliances — using *control circuits*.

Ohm's Law

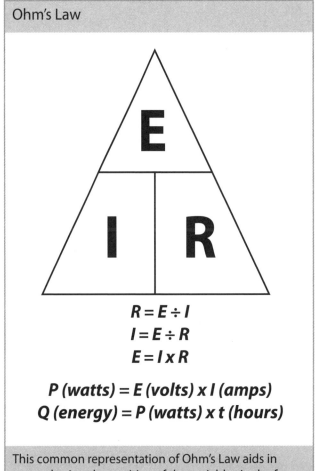

$$R = E \div I$$
$$I = E \div R$$
$$E = I \times R$$

$$P \ (watts) = E \ (volts) \times I \ (amps)$$
$$Q \ (energy) = P \ (watts) \times t \ (hours)$$

This common representation of Ohm's Law aids in remembering the position of the variables in the formula. E is voltage in volts. I is current in amps. R is resistance in ohms.

An electrical generator pushes electrons through a metal wire, imparting them with electrical energy. Whenever an abundance of electrical energy exists in one area along with a relative lack of electrical energy in another, *voltage* (also called *potential difference*) exists between the two areas. Electricity flows from electrically charged areas to electrically neutral areas. The earth is electrically neutral and is used for the neutral part of circuits.

Most electrical generators are turned by rotating machines called turbines. A turbine is turned by pressurized steam, flowing water, or wind. Heat for the steam turbine comes from the combustion of oil, gas, coal, or thermonuclear reaction.

Electrical Symbols

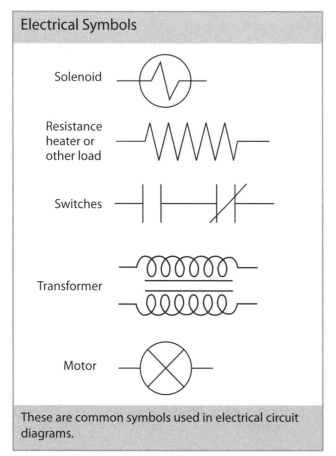

Solenoid

Resistance heater or other load

Switches

Transformer

Motor

These are common symbols used in electrical circuit diagrams.

An electric *circuit* consists of three essential parts: a source of electricity; a *path* for the electricity to flow; and a *load*, a device that uses electricity. Most circuits also have a *switch* to start and stop the flow of electricity. The switch creates an air gap in the hot wire of the circuit. We say that a switch is *open* if it is creating an air gap and stopping electricity, and *closed* if it is connecting the circuit.

Electrical Principles

The flow of electricity is described by a well-known formula called Ohm's Law —
E (voltage) = I (current) x R (resistance). E stands for *electromotive force*, but is better known as voltage. *Voltage*, expressed in volts, measures the electrical pressure. *Amperes*, or amps, measures current — the flow of electrons. And resistance describes the circuit's opposition to current in units called *ohms*.

Current in amps multiplied by voltage in volts equals the power of the circuit in watts. And watts multiplied by time, in hours, equals watt-hours of energy. This simple relationship between current, voltage, power, and energy is true for electric-resistance devices like heaters and incandescent lights. However, actual energy consumption for motors, transformers, and other devices with coils is less than amperage times voltage because of an effect known as reactance, which is beyond the scope of this discussion.

Series Versus Parallel Circuits

Series circuits form a single looping path from the source to the load and back to the source. The electrical current is the same in all parts of the circuit. Series circuits control heating systems and simple appliances.

Several switches placed in series allow any of these switches to interrupt electrical current to the load. Therefore, a series control circuit can decide that both safety and necessity are present before connecting the load. Both the safety switch and control switch must be closed for electricity to flow to the load.

Parallel circuits form ladder rungs between the hot and neutral wires. In home wiring, each rung is a light, outlet, or appliance. In parallel circuits, voltage is the same on all rungs.

Several switches placed in parallel circuits allow any of these switches to connect a load. Heating and cooling systems often use parallel switches to start the blower — one switch for heating and one for cooling.

Control Circuits

Control circuits are often low-voltage circuits using transformers to step down the voltage. This lower voltage is safer for remote controls and requires smaller and less expensive switches, wiring, and control components. Newer appliances have electronic controls that use even less power than traditional low-voltage control circuits.

A control circuit employs a *controller*, like a thermostat, with a *sensing device*, like a bimetal spring or thermistor to control electric power to a *final control element*, like a gas valve, oil burner, fan, or pump. Controllers and sensing devices may be the traditional electromechanical or the newer electronic types.

Transformers and Power Supplies

A *transformer* is a device that transforms or changes voltage from one circuit to another. Power companies use high voltage to transport electricity over long distances to reduce line losses, and then step voltage down with transformers to make it safe for local customers.

Step-down transformers within the home reduce voltage from around 115 volts to 24 volts for controlling heating and cooling systems. This lower voltage is safer and more convenient for installing the thermostat without having to run sheathed cable. Dedicated 24-volt controls provide more precise control of energy systems than their 115-volt counterparts.

Electronic controls allow even more precise control than low-voltage electromechanical controls. An electronic power supply acts like a transformer to reduce voltages to levels required by the electronic sensing devices and microprocessors. A microprocessor is an electronic brain that can make decisions about control based on a number of inputs.

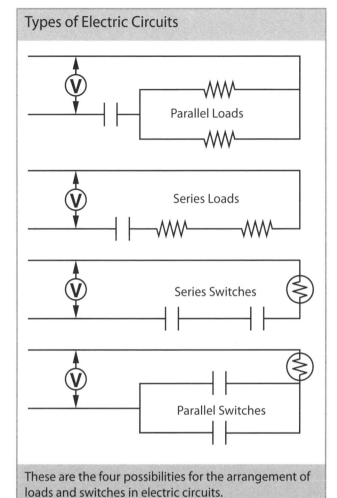

Types of Electric Circuits

Parallel Loads

Series Loads

Series Switches

Parallel Switches

These are the four possibilities for the arrangement of loads and switches in electric circuits.

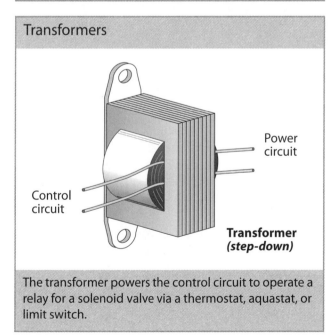

Transformers

Power circuit

Control circuit

Transformer (step-down)

The transformer powers the control circuit to operate a relay for a solenoid valve via a thermostat, aquastat, or limit switch.

Solenoids

A wire coiled around an iron bar will magnetize it, causing it to move when electricity flows through the coil. This principle is called *solenoid action* and is used to open and close solenoid valves and switches called *relays* and *contactors*. An example of a solenoid valve is the automatic gas valve on a gas furnace. Relays are powered by the control circuit. Relays connect and disconnect loads like solenoids and small motors in the power circuit. Larger motors and electric heating elements require sturdier automatic switches called contactors.

Types of Solenoids

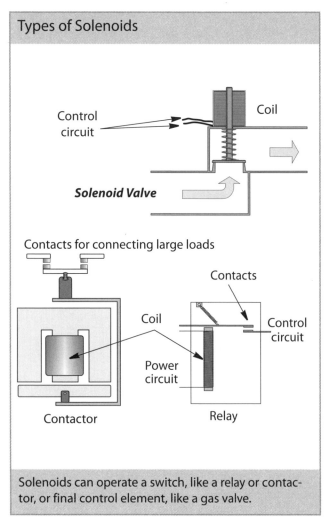

Solenoids can operate a switch, like a relay or contactor, or final control element, like a gas valve.

Temperature-sensitive Elements

Bimetal elements or bulb-and-bellows elements move electrical contacts or a valve stem in response to temperature changes. The most common devices using temperature-sensitive elements are thermostats and *limits*. Limits are safety switches that interrupt power if temperatures get too high.

Bimetal elements are temperature-sensitive metal coils and strips. A thermostat uses a bimetal element to turn the heating system on and off. The bimetal element is two thin metal pieces with different rates of expansion bonded together. It bends, rotates, or snaps inside out as the temperature changes. This motion is used to move a switch's contacts or a final control element.

Bulb-and-bellows controls use the variation in volume of a liquid or gas to move electrical contacts or a final control element.

Electromechanical Heat Sensor

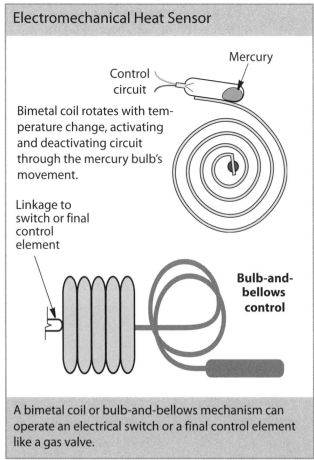

A bimetal coil or bulb-and-bellows mechanism can operate an electrical switch or a final control element like a gas valve.

Simple Heating Control Circuit

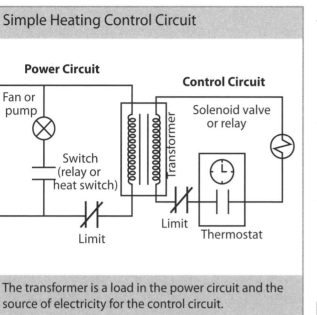

The transformer is a load in the power circuit and the source of electricity for the control circuit.

Variable Resistors

Variable resistance elements are a part of many electromechanical and electronic control systems. When electricity flows through an electric resistance wire, the electricity is converted to heat. This principle is used by tiny electric resistance heaters that are part of various control devices. Thermostats and electric furnace controls have small resistance heaters combined with their bimetal operators that serve as timers.

Copper wire coiled on a bobbin is also used to sense temperature because the wire's resistance varies significantly with temperature. Variable resistors, called *potentiometers*, are used to tune electronic circuits. Variable electronic resistors are discussed in the next section.

See "Heating Comfort Controls" on page 158 and "Electric Furnaces" on page 180.

Electronic Sensing and Control Devices

Electronic sensors and control devices are part of many sophisticated modern control systems. The most common electronic sensors found in residential control systems are *thermistors* and

photoresistors. Thermistors sense changes in temperature and photoresistors sense changes in light level. A small sensing current runs from an electronic power supply to a *transistor* through a thermistor, photoresistor, or other electronic sensor, which serves as an automatic switch to activate or deactivate the transistor. The transistor works like a relay to start a burner, compressor, fan, or pump.

A microprocessor can store information entered by the user or collected from sensors for deciding how to operate the system. Electronic control systems are used on many modern heating systems, multifamily lighting and domestic hot water systems, sprinkling systems, and security systems.

Electronic Control Components

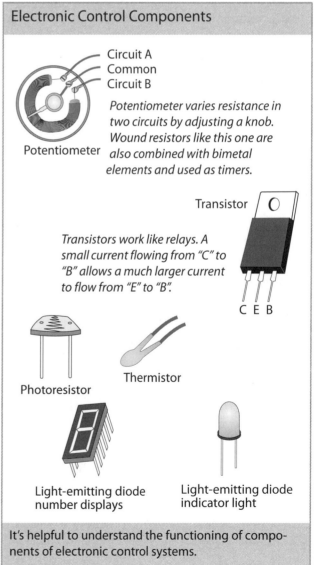

It's helpful to understand the functioning of components of electronic control systems.

Home Electrical Wiring

Electrical circuits in homes are mainly power circuits. Power circuits carry 115 volt or 230 volt electricity to an electric device such as a light, fan, pump, or heater. Home power circuits also supply electricity to *duplex receptacles*, which provide power to portable electric devices, such as room heaters and appliances.

Home electrical systems consist of parallel circuits originating in a *main service panel box*. Each of the branch circuits is wired in parallel with the others. The outlets, lights, heaters, and appliances sharing a branch circuit are also in parallel, using the same voltage.

Service Equipment

The 230-volt home electrical system consists of *service wires*; an *electric meter*; *feeder wires*; one or two *main switches*; a *main service panel box* with *circuit breakers* or *fuses*; and the wires, receptacles, and fixtures in the home.

The main service wires come through the ground or overhead from the utility company's transformer. These three wires, two hot wires and a neutral wire, attach to the utility side of the electric meter. Attached to the house side of the electric meter are the feeder wires. The feeder wires are two hot wires (red and black), a neutral wire (white), and an equipment grounding wire (green or bare). The neutral wire and grounding wire are attached together at the meter and attached to a copper grounding rod driven into the earth outside the home. The feeder wires are either part of a cable or are carried in a metal *conduit* (pipe).

The feeder wires run from the meter and main switch into the home's service panel box. The black and red feeder wires are connected to *bus bars*, which hold the breakers or fuses in the panel box. A bus bar is a large electrical terminal where many wires may be connected. The white feeder wire is the neutral and is connected to the neutral bus bar, which is electrically insulated from the panel box. The bare feeder wire is the grounding wire and is connected to the grounding bus bar, where all the ground wires from the branch circuits are also attached.

Branch and Appliance Circuits

Branch circuits are systems of wire, outlets, and built-in fixtures for lighting, heating, and other purposes. *Appliance circuits* are circuits serving a single appliance like a furnace, air conditioner, electric range, or electric dryer.

The breakers or fuses protect the wire in branch circuits from carrying too much electrical current. When a breaker trips or a fuse blows, the cause of the circuit overload should be found and remedied. If a breaker on a circuit fails, or if the fuse blows, it should be replaced with another having the proper amp rating to match the wire used in the home (15 amps for older home circuits and 20 amps for newer home branch circuits).

Energy auditors should check fuses and breakers before insulating to insure no oversized circuit protectors exist in the panel box. Oversized fuses or breakers will allow excessive amperage to flow, possibly heating the wires. Insulation could make a bad problem worse if the overheated wires are surrounded by the newly installed insulation.

A short circuit is an accidental circuit with no intentional load. Short circuits in appliances are particularly dangerous in the kitchen and bathroom because of the presence of water in those areas. In newer homes, circuits in the kitchen, bathroom, and garage are protected by special breakers known as *ground fault circuit interrupters (GFCI)*. These GFCIs will trip if they detect electricity flowing in the grounding wires. Electricity won't flow in the grounding wires unless there is a short circuit.

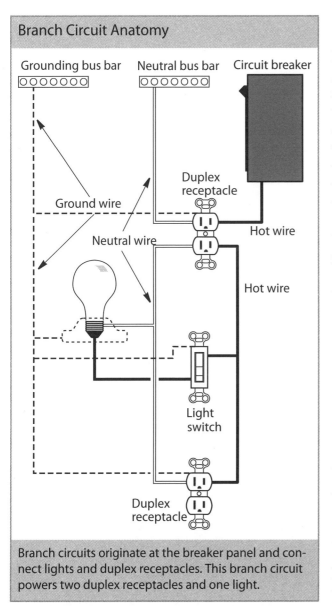

Branch Circuit Anatomy

Grounding bus bar   Neutral bus bar   Circuit breaker

Ground wire

Duplex receptacle

Neutral wire

Hot wire

Hot wire

Light switch

Duplex receptacle

Branch circuits originate at the breaker panel and connect lights and duplex receptacles. This branch circuit powers two duplex receptacles and one light.

Grounding

Home electrical systems use the earth or the ground in two ways. The first is to ground the neutral feeder wire. The earth is electrically neutral and provides a kind of vacuum that draws electricity from the hot wires toward the earth through the home's electrical devices. The neutral wire is also grounded by the electric utility at the transformer, generator, and other locations in the transmission system.

Equipment used in electrical systems also is grounded. The *equipment grounding* wire is the bare wire connected to: each green grounding terminal of a receptacle; each metal electrical box (including the main panel box); and the metal cabinets of fixtures and appliances. The grounding bus bar in the breaker box is electrically connected to all the branch circuits. This network of equipment grounding connections gives stray electricity an easy and safe path to flow into the ground rather than flowing through some unlucky person in the event of a short circuit.

A bare copper wire also connects the metal piping and sometimes the metal ducts to the grounding bus bar. The home's piping system usually runs into the ground and helps establish a conductive attachment to the ground. However, the main reason for bonding pipes and ducts to a ground is to lead stray current away in the event that a hot wire shorts to a pipe or wire.

It's very important that all hot wires be connected to breakers or fuses, and that neutral wires be connected to the neutral bus bar in the panel box. Sometimes the neutral bus is accidentally connected to a hot wire somewhere in the system. This can happen at an outlet or light, if the hot and neutral wires are reversed. When the wires are reversed at a receptacle, the white wire is connected to the brass-colored terminal and the black wire is connected to the silver-colored terminal of the outlet. This reversal is dangerous, and it can be detected using a *circuit tester*, a plug-in device with lights indicating correct or incorrect wiring.

Home Electrical System

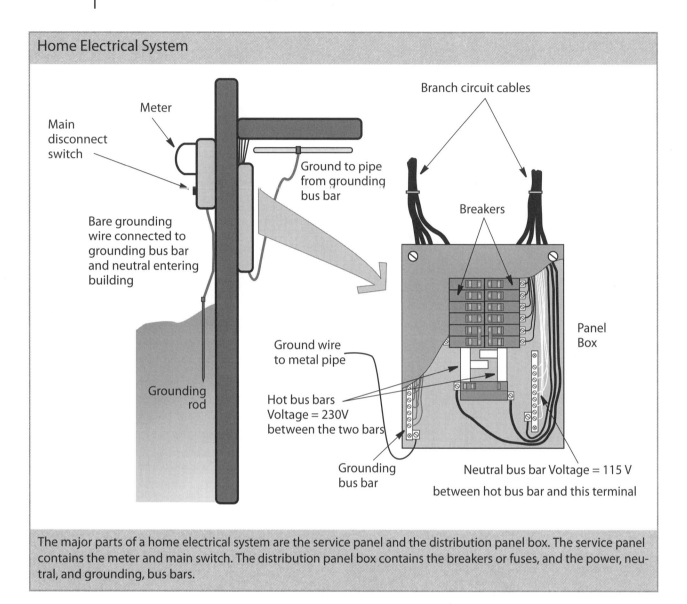

Meter

Main disconnect switch

Branch circuit cables

Ground to pipe from grounding bus bar

Breakers

Bare grounding wire connected to grounding bus bar and neutral entering building

Grounding rod

Ground wire to metal pipe

Hot bus bars Voltage = 230V between the two bars

Panel Box

Grounding bus bar

Neutral bus bar Voltage = 115 V

between hot bus bar and this terminal

The major parts of a home electrical system are the service panel and the distribution panel box. The service panel contains the meter and main switch. The distribution panel box contains the breakers or fuses, and the power, neutral, and grounding, bus bars.

This chapter explains building construction, building-shell heat flows, building inspection and diagnosis, and calculations of heat loss and gain. The chapter's goals are to link physics with building construction in order to give you a better understanding of energy flows through the building shell.

An ideal building maximizes heat retention during the winter and minimizes heat gains during the summer to reduce heating and cooling energy consumption. The best way to achieve energy efficiency in a new building is by energy-efficient design, planning, and construction. In existing buildings, technicians perform modifications — called weatherization — to reduce heat loss and heat gain.

Making decisions about a building's weatherization is the job of an energy auditor. Energy auditors take measurements, estimate costs, develop energy-savings projections, and perform physical inspections of buildings to decide which retrofits to recommend.

See "An Energy Audit's Purpose" on page 20.

For large residential buildings, the auditors may be architects and engineers. For homes, a trained energy auditor (who may even perform part of the weatherization work) makes decisions about weatherization projects.

Heat loss and gain through the building shell are the largest energy demands on residential buildings. To maintain comfort, heating and cooling systems supply or remove heat at a rate roughly equaling heat's flow rate through the building shell.

The amount of heating energy needed by the home over a heating season is the sum of heat transmission losses through the floor, exterior walls, and ceiling, added to the air leakage, minus

solar radiation gain and internal heat production. Cooling energy needs are determined by solar radiation, internal heat, air leakage, and heat transmission. Total heating energy and total cooling energy needed by a building also includes the inefficiencies of the heating and cooling systems.

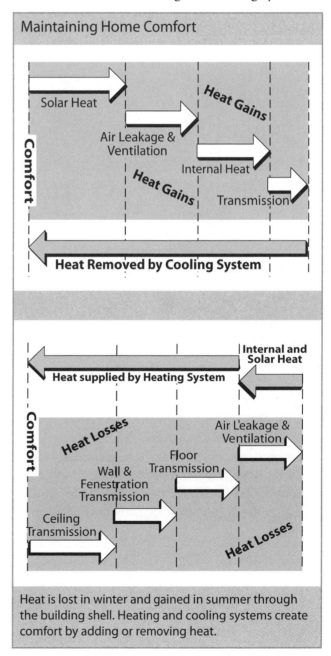

Heat is lost in winter and gained in summer through the building shell. Heating and cooling systems create comfort by adding or removing heat.

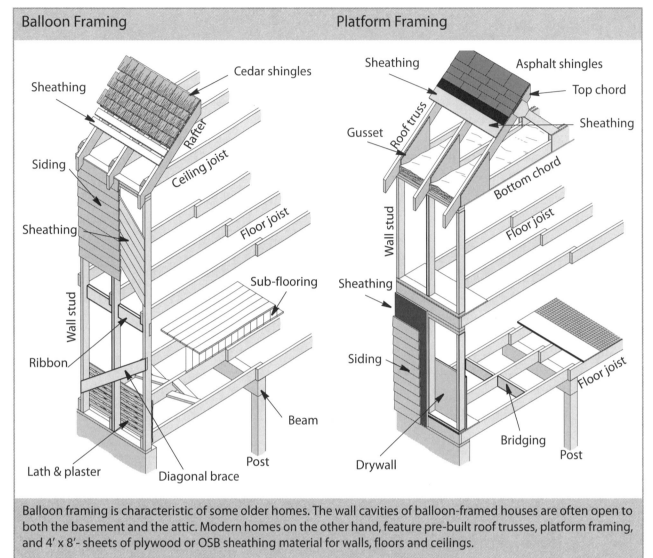

Balloon framing is characteristic of some older homes. The wall cavities of balloon-framed houses are often open to both the basement and the attic. Modern homes on the other hand, feature pre-built roof trusses, platform framing, and 4' x 8'- sheets of plywood or OSB sheathing material for walls, floors and ceilings.

Energy-efficient buildings have a *thermal boundary,* which is a line or plane defined by insulation and an air barrier. The air barrier is any interior or exterior sheeting material that resists airflow through it. An effective air barrier is nearly airtight. In hot climates, energy-efficient buildings block solar radiation with exterior shade (from trees), reflective exterior surfaces, and window shading.

Building Construction

Buildings have construction flaws that waste energy, reduce comfort, and encourage building deterioration. Knowledge about construction characteristics helps you locate and correct these flaws.

Building materials have different thermal conductivities. Metals such as aluminum and steel conduct heat rapidly, while insulating materials such as mineral fiber and plastic foam conduct heat slowly. The thermal conductance of wood, masonry, and plastic are between these extremes.

The simplest buildings are just large six-sided rectangular boxes. The building shell includes its foundation, bottom floor, exterior walls, and roof assembly. These components generally have at least two layers with a cavity between. For example, a wall has interior sheeting and exterior siding; the roof assembly has a ceiling inside and a roof outside.

The building shell's seams at edges, corners, and around openings are the obvious thermal weak points, containing heat-conductive structural members and leaky joints between building materials.

Penetrations through insulation and air barriers occur where mechanical and electrical components pass through the building shell. These are often major flaws in the building shell.

Protrusions and indentations to the building's shell create seams, thermal bridges, and areas where the insulation and air barrier aren't continuous. Protrusions include bay windows, dormers, and porches. Indentations include recessed entrances, porches, and windows. These building-shell irregularities promote air leakage between indoors and outdoors and convection within building cavities.

Structural Design

Building structures are classified as planer or skeletal design, depending on whether they are supported by columns and beams or by panels. Many buildings combine these two structural styles.

Planer construction is usually simpler (such as masonry or framed walls) with familiar interior and exterior surfaces. Wood-frame structures have many joints between their different components, making airtightness an important design and construction issue. Insulation is installed between the framing and sometimes attached over the framing to reduce conduction through these structural components. Masonry structures, when they are insulated, have surface-applied insulation. See "Home Types and Average Energy Costs" on page 13.

Skeletal construction often contains deeper floor and ceiling cavities and more vertical shafts than planer construction. The steel columns and beams of a skeletal steel framework are hidden behind non-structural walls and suspended ceilings. Less-conductive building components called thermal breaks are used to separate metal, concrete, and glass from each other. A thermal break prevents direct linkage between indoors and outdoors through these very conductive materials.

Foundations support the building with masonry walls, piers, or slabs. They transfer this weight to the ground and also tie the building to the ground for seismic and wind resistance. Masonry materials are preferred for foundations because they are heavy and they resist rot and corrosion.

Foundations should be surrounded by dry ground. However, in real life, they frequently encounter ground moisture or runoff from surrounding roofs or adjacent land. Consider foundation moisture problems when planning weatherization projects.

Single-family Home Construction

Many wood-frame homes, built before 1940, used *balloon-frame construction*, which features wall studs that may be two stories high. These tall studs usually have no top or bottom plates. Floor joists and ceiling joists are attached to the studs and supported by ribbons. The stud cavities are often open to both the basement and attic.

Modern wood-frame homes are generally of *platform-frame construction*. Each floor, framed with structural lumber and sheathed with plywood or particle board, serves as a platform for framing the exterior walls. The top plate of the first floor's exterior wall becomes the platform for framing the second floor and walls.

Some homes may have elements of both styles of framing. For example, newer balloon-framed homes may have a bottom plate that sits on the first floor. A platform-framed split-level home may have a balloon-framed interior wall in the center of the home.

More modern homes use plywood or composite board to sheath exterior walls, roof, and floor. Drywall usually covers the interior surfaces. Siding includes a wide variety of materials such as: wood, brick, composite wood material, vinyl, steel, and aluminum. Some modern homes use steel studs, which require insulated sheathing to prevent severe thermal bridging.

Older homes used $3/4$-to-1 $1/4$-inch-thick lumber as roof and wall sheathing and sub-flooring. Lath and plaster usually covered interior wall and ceiling framing. Slate, cedar, and tile were widely used as roof shingles, although most have been replaced with asphalt or fiberglass shingles. Siding materials included stucco, brick, asbestos shingle, and wood. You can expect to find multiple layers of sheathing on some interior and exterior surfaces of older homes, because workers installed one layer of roofing, siding, or interior sheathing over another through the decades.

The exterior walls of some homes are made completely of masonry materials: block, brick, concrete, or stone. Masonry materials have low R-values, but the effect of their mass may slow heat transmission significantly in warmer climates.

See "Mass Factors for 6-inch Concrete Walls Insulated Interior or Exterior for Six Locations" on page 280.

Single-family: points of weakness — A home's energy weaknesses are usually concentrated around irregularities in its building shell. A building's protrusions and indentations, with their increased seams and surface area, are particular problems at the following locations:

♦ Porches.

♦ Roof overhangs.

♦ Shafts containing chimneys and pipes.

♦ Protruding or indented windows and doorways.

♦ Crawl spaces and basements connecting the home to outdoors.

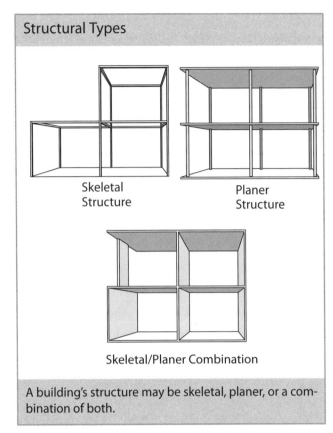

Structural Types

Skeletal Structure

Planer Structure

Skeletal/Planer Combination

A building's structure may be skeletal, planer, or a combination of both.

Outdoor and indoor air can mingle in cavities of a building's shell — especially where the shell is penetrated or discontinuous. This reduces the effectiveness of insulation. Here are some areas to watch for:

♦ Wall cavities partially or completely devoid of insulation.

♦ Suspended ceilings between floors.

♦ Attics and roof cavities.

♦ Concentrations of plumbing pipes near bathrooms and kitchens.

♦ Concentrations of wires near the service panel box.

♦ Building cavities used as ducts.

♦ Interconnecting spaces between floor, wall, and ceiling cavities.

See "Single-family Structural Leakage Sites" on page 93.

Multifamily Building Construction

Multifamily buildings employ a wide variety of construction methods. Smaller multifamily buildings are similar to homes using masonry and wood frame construction. Multistory residential buildings usually have nearly flat, trussed roofs with built-up asphalt roofing, metal roofing, or synthetic rubber roofing over wood, concrete, or steel roof decks.

Concrete and steel are the main structural materials in many larger multifamily buildings. Steel skeletons are common for high rises. Floors are often reinforced concrete poured over corrugated metal decking. The walls may be non-structural curtains of lightweight steel and aluminum frames, glass, and metal sheeting.

Some multifamily structures are built with concrete columns and reinforced concrete floors. Some concrete floors have integral concrete beams that form large T-shaped floor sections.

Larger residential buildings, such as high-rises, have less exterior surface area per square foot of floor area than homes, making heat transmission through the shell relatively less important than in smaller buildings. High-rises also have relatively higher internal heat gains from people, lights, appliances, and other heat sources. Internal heat helps warm the building in winter, but adds to the cooling load in summer. In fact, cooling may dominate the high-rise's energy costs — even in spring and fall. Most of this accumulating heat is internal heat, solar heat, and air leakage.

Airtightness and solar reflectance are very important to minimizing multifamily shell-related energy consumption. Weather-tightness and airtightness are important for preventing building deterioration. Protecting the very heat-conductive steel framework from condensation in both the heating and cooling seasons is also vitally important for durability.

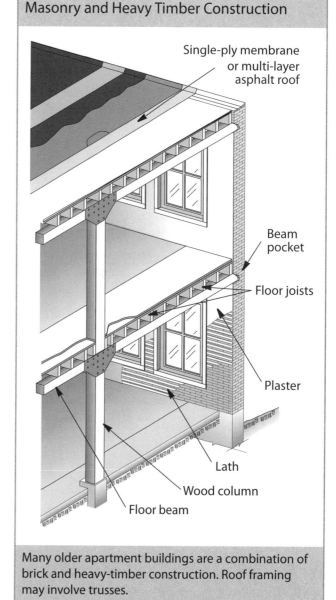

Masonry and Heavy Timber Construction

Single-ply membrane or multi-layer asphalt roof

Beam pocket

Floor joists

Plaster

Lath

Wood column

Floor beam

Many older apartment buildings are a combination of brick and heavy-timber construction. Roof framing may involve trusses.

Multifamily: points of weakness — Irregularities on the exteriors of multifamily buildings are potential sources for infiltrating and exfiltrating air. The following protrusions, indentations, and penetrations are weaknesses:

♦ Thermal bridging from steel and aluminum components.

♦ Protruding or recessed balconies, eaves, windows, and canopies.

♦ Roof protrusions and penetrations, such as rooftop elevator shacks and air handlers.

Concrete and Steel Construction

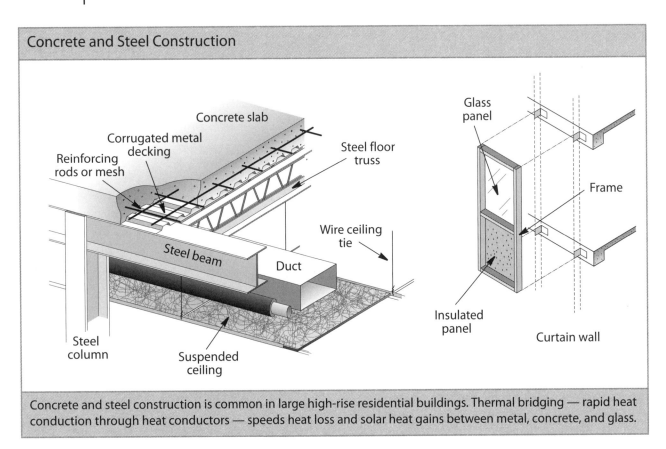

Concrete and steel construction is common in large high-rise residential buildings. Thermal bridging — rapid heat conduction through heat conductors — speeds heat loss and solar heat gains between metal, concrete, and glass.

- Air intake and exhaust vents for heating, cooling, and ventilation systems.

A multifamily building's horizontal cavities and vertical shafts are conduits for air leakage and mixing of indoor and outdoor air. These include:

- Suspended ceilings.
- Supply ducts in floor and ceiling cavities.
- Building cavities used as return ducts.
- Elevator shafts.
- Ventilation shafts.
- Plumbing shafts.
- Chimneys.
- Stairwells.

See "Multifamily Buildings — Air Leakage" on page 97.

Mobile Home Construction

About 6% of the homes in the U.S. are mobile homes. A mobile home is a factory-built wood-framed building, attached to a steel trailer or chassis. Workers assemble components such as the roof, floor, or walls separately and fasten them together later on the assembly line.

The wood-frame floor assembly fastens to a steel trailer. Water lines, waste lines, ducts, insulation, and the underbelly (the protective covering underneath the floor) all attach to the floor before workers bolt the floor to the trailer.

Workers install the floor covering, furnace, and major plumbing fixtures before they attach the walls to the floor. Exterior walls are pre-assembled, with interior paneling or drywall attached to the wall framing. Then a crane places the wall assemblies on the floor.

Workers build the roof assembly, including ceiling and roof trusses separately. Later, they place the roof on top of the walls and fasten it in place.

After the roof and walls are wired and insulated, workers install roofing and siding, then windows and doors. Finally, the interior trim work is completed, and the home is transported to its site.

Mobile homes are built in various sizes by more than 100 manufacturers nationwide. Single-wide homes once dominated the market, but now double-wides are more popular. Most currently manufactured mobile homes are at least 14 or 16 feet wide. Older mobile homes are 10 to 14 feet wide. Using 12-to-16–foot-wide sections, double-wide and triple-wide homes reach total widths of 24 to 48 feet. Standard lengths for mobile home sections range from 40 to 80 feet.

Mobile homes: points of weakness — The following list details where air leaks and insulation flaws are most commonly found in mobile homes:

♦ Joints and holes in forced-air distribution systems.

♦ Torn or missing belly paper.

♦ Joints between the halves of double-section homes; around the perimeter of each section — floor, walls, and ceiling.

♦ Plumbing penetrations in: interior walls, external water heater closets, under bathtubs, behind washing machines, and under sinks.

♦ Joints between the main structure and building additions.

Mobile Home Construction Characteristics

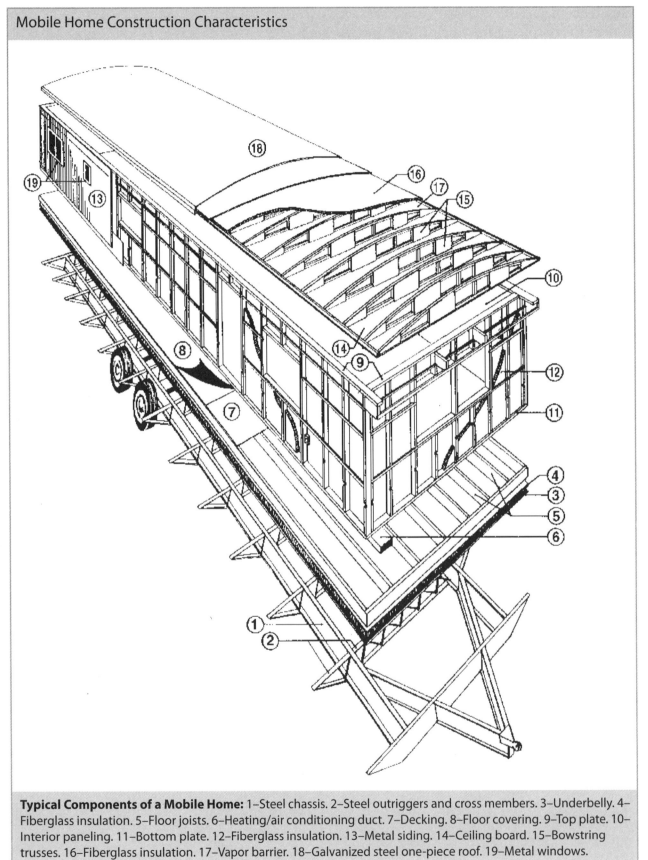

Typical Components of a Mobile Home: 1–Steel chassis. 2–Steel outriggers and cross members. 3–Underbelly. 4–Fiberglass insulation. 5–Floor joists. 6–Heating/air conditioning duct. 7–Decking. 8–Floor covering. 9–Top plate. 10–Interior paneling. 11–Bottom plate. 12–Fiberglass insulation. 13–Metal siding. 14–Ceiling board. 15–Bowstring trusses. 16–Fiberglass insulation. 17–Vapor barrier. 18–Galvanized steel one-piece roof. 19–Metal windows.

Building-Shell Heat Flow

Heat flows through the building shell by three mechanisms: heat transmission, air leakage, and solar radiation. Transmission and air leakage occur through four independent pathways: floors and foundations; walls; roofs and ceilings; and *fenestration* — windows and doors. Solar radiation occurs through all of these but the foundation and floor.

Heat transmission through the building shell depends on two factors: thermal resistance and surface area. Air leakage in cubic feet of air per minute (CFM) depends on the surface area of the shell's holes and the pressure differences between indoors and outdoors. Solar radiation depends on the climate, season, and the building's solar exposure.

Windows are a special concern because of low thermal resistance, high solar transmittance, and significant surface area. Although they may be a comfort problem, doors have less energy loss compared to windows because of their smaller surface area.

During winter, heat flows because of the indoor-outdoor temperature difference. During summer the main heat-driving force is solar radiation.

Effect of Insulation

Radiation · Convection · No Insulation · **Indoors** *(warm)* · **Outdoors** *(cold)* · Conduction · Insulation

The uninsulated wall transmits heat through its air space by convection and radiation. In the insulated wall, heat must conduct through the tiny air pockets trapped by the insulation — a slower process.

Heat Transmission

Heat transmission is driven by the temperature difference between indoors and outdoors. A building's thermal resistance determines how much heat transmits through the shell.

When we say that insulation resists heat transmission, we mean it resists conduction, convection, and radiation heat flow through a building component. In the case of an uninsulated wall cavity, convection and radiation dominate heat transmission through the wall's empty cavity. Insulation, installed in that wall cavity, forces the heat to conduct from fiber to fiber and through the insulation's tiny air pockets — a slower heat-transmission process than convection and radiation.

See "Insulation Characteristics" on page 105.

Conductivity of building materials — A material's thermal conductivity describes how much heat in BTUs flows through a 1-inch-thick by 1-foot-square slab of that material each hour, when there is a 1-degree-Fahrenheit temperature difference between the slab's two surfaces. Thermal conductivity, denoted by the letter k, allows us to compare how well common building materials conduct heat.

Aluminum is the most conductive common building material: Its thermal conductivity is more than four times greater than steel, 900 times greater than wood, and 7,800 times greater than air. One square foot of steel, the next most conductive building material, conducts as much heat as 50 square feet of concrete, 200 square feet of wood, or 1200 square feet of glass wool, assuming all are the same thickness.

When very conductive materials are touching one another, heat flows rapidly through the building shell because even a small contact area can transfer heat rapidly. This phenomenon is called *thermal bridging*. Thermal bridging causes cold interior surfaces (such as aluminum window frames) during winter, and hot interior surfaces (such as west-facing masonry walls) during summer. Using less-conductive gaskets, called *thermal breaks*, between conductive materials such as glass and steel reduces this rapid heat flow.

Building-shell components, such as walls and roof assemblies, contain a variety of materials in their cross-sections. Depending on the location within a wall or roof, insulation or structural framing might be encountered. In a wood-framed wall, about 20% of the wall's surface area is solid wood and 80% is insulated stud space. The wall's average thermal resistance is an area-weighted average of these two different cross-sections.

Thermal Conductivity: Building Materials

Material	Thermal Conductivity (k) BTU-in/hr•ft•°F
Aluminum	1400
Steel	310
Glass	7.8
Concrete	5.8
Brick	4.3
Wood	1.6
Rubber	1.4
Glass wool	0.26
Air	0.18

Thermal Conductivity: k–value

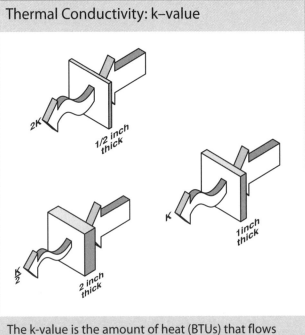

The k-value is the amount of heat (BTUs) that flows each hour through a 1-square-foot slab of material 1 inch thick, with a 1°F temperature difference between the slab's two sides. Heat-conduction rate depends on the material's thickness as shown here.

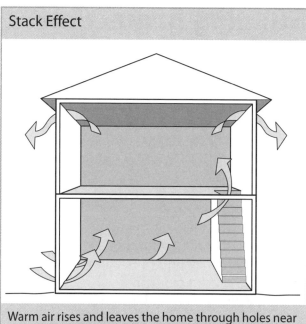

Stack Effect

Warm air rises and leaves the home through holes near the ceiling. Cold air enters near the floor to replace it.

Air Leakage

Air leaks into and out of buildings through penetrations in the building shell's interior and exterior skins. Although you'll find obvious air leaks around windows and doors, large hidden penetrations often dominate air leakage. Air leaks are either direct, penetrating all the way through the shell at one location, or indirect, entering at one location and exiting at another.

On continuous areas of the shell, an effective air barrier should border and touch the insulation. Without an effective air barrier, migrating air can move through the insulation, convect heat from the insulation's surface, or carry heat around the insulation. The leakage rate for building materials is measured in CFM per square foot of surface area or CFM per linear foot for joints between materials.

Existing buildings usually have several partial air barriers, rather than one single component designed as an airtight air barrier. For example, a home's wall has interior paneling, insulation, exterior sheathing, and siding — all of which resist airflow but don't stop it. Any airtight and continuous building component — exterior sheeting, interior sheeting, air-barrier building paper — can be an effective air barrier if installed in an airtight manner.

Irregularities in the building's exterior shell — such as protrusions and penetrations — promote air leakage and may harbor a concentration of joints between building materials. These areas create insulation and air-sealing problems even for builders who understand the desirability of continuity at the thermal boundary.

See Chapter 3 Air Leakage.

Fenestration

Windows give natural light and views to rooms and are necessary for the resident's mental health. However, windows are often a built-in thermal flaw. The best new windows have R-values up to R-20, but most windows remain between R-1 and R-3. Windows are often the major source of solar heat gain during summer. Window glass transmits from 20% to 84% of the sun's heat depending on whether it is clear glass, low-e glass, reflective glass, or heat-absorbing glass. The building's window surface area, R-value, and solar transmittance determine the comfort and energy-efficiency of windows.

Windows affect comfort more directly than other building components because of their low thermal resistance and high solar transmittance. During winter, windows cool sensitive human body parts directly by radiation. Cold window glass cools air near its surface, causing this air to move downward, creating cool convection currents. Air leakage through windows adds to the feeling that windows are a major energy problem. In summer, a window's solar heat warms the room's furniture, flooring, and other surfaces, driving radiant and ambient temperatures up, causing discomfort, and consuming electricity for air conditioning.

Many people assume window air leakage is a major energy and comfort problem, but in fact, most of the discomfort comes from windows' low radiant temperature and convection currents created by their high heat transmittance. Many buildings have poor air quality due to their relative airtightness and lack of mechanical ventilation. Windows allow some incidental air leakage, which provides minimum ventilation to rooms with windows. To satisfy residents' need for fresh air, some new windows are manufactured with adjustable openings designed to admit ventilating air continuously.

Doors have a small surface area compared to other building components, making them relatively less important. Comfort, rather than overall energy loss, is generally the motive for weatherizing doors. Leakage around door frames causes discomfort, depending on a door's location, but a door's heat loss is comparatively small.

See Chapter 5 Windows and Doors.

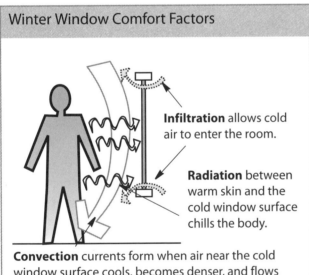

Winter Window Comfort Factors

Infiltration allows cold air to enter the room.

Radiation between warm skin and the cold window surface chills the body.

Convection currents form when air near the cold window surface cools, becomes denser, and flows downward, creating a continuous flow pattern.

Windows create three wintertime comfort problems.

Building Inspection and Diagnosis

Before you propose energy retrofits, a trained energy auditor should inspect and diagnose the building. The energy auditor must consider all major issues relating to energy conservation, health and safety, and building durability.

The inspection and analysis may include diagnostic equipment such as blower doors, infrared scanners, and heating-efficiency testers. This evaluation often incorporates utility-bill analysis and energy-savings predictions. Calculations determine the size of heating and cooling equipment, if replacement is a retrofit option.

See "Finding Air Leaks" on page 86 for more information on actually locating air leaks.

Defining the Thermal Boundary

A thermal boundary should surround the conditioned space. Insulation and an air barrier are located at this thermal boundary. The conditioned space includes the building's heated or cooled areas. Heat transmission through the shell depends on the insulation's thermal resistance and the shell's surface area. Air leakage depends on building pressures and hole sizes — two factors determining the CFM-airflow between the building and outdoors.

Many buildings' total enclosed space is conditioned space, while other buildings contain areas that are neither heated nor cooled. These unconditioned spaces include attics, crawl spaces, and attached garages. Some places, such as furnace and boiler rooms, are warmed by waste heat. These are called unintentionally conditioned spaces. Unintentionally conditioned spaces and unconditioned spaces — also known as intermediate zones or buffer zones — are located between conditioned spaces and outdoors, slowing the building's heat flow.

Thermal Boundary Decisions

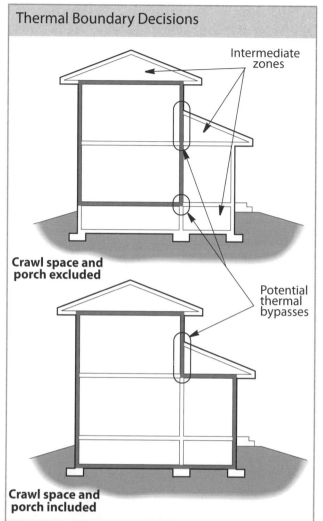

Crawl space and porch excluded

Crawl space and porch included

The energy auditor and technicians choose thermal boundaries when they decide where to insulate. Those decisions are based on how the home's spaces are used and on practical considerations like access and cost of materials.

Story-and-a-Half Home

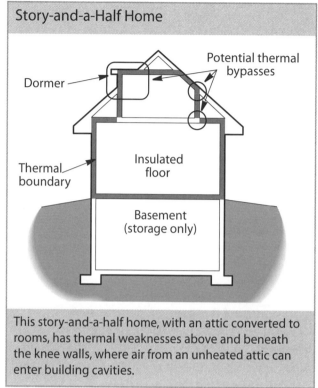

This story-and-a-half home, with an attic converted to rooms, has thermal weaknesses above and beneath the knee walls, where air from an unheated attic can enter building cavities.

♦ The shell's existing insulation location and R-value.

♦ The effectiveness of existing air barriers.

♦ Incorporating potential areas of future use within the thermal boundary.

Energy auditors inspect the continuity of the air barrier and insulation. They develop a strategy for adding insulation and for sealing air leaks in the chosen air barrier, be it the building's interior surface, its exterior surface, or some other potential air barrier.

The air barrier and the insulation should be very close together. Air flowing against, around, or through the insulation is one of the most common energy wasters. Convecting air carries heat from one surface to another across air spaces. Airflow carrying heat across the thermal boundary and around the insulation is called a thermal bypass. When wind-driven air flows through the insulation, reducing its thermal resistance, this is called wind washing.

Defining the conditioned space includes evaluating the air barrier and insulation at the thermal boundary. The building may not have insulation or an air barrier totally surrounding the conditioned space. In that case, the energy audit should consider the cost-effectiveness of completing the air barrier and insulation, to surround the building entirely. A thermal boundary may surround only conditioned spaces, or it may include unconditioned spaces also. Factors involved in selecting the thermal boundary's location include:

Though they may be outside the building's conditioned space, central forced-air furnaces, central air conditioners, and ducts are connected to the conditioned space. The cabinets of furnaces or air conditioners and the entire surface area of ducts outside the conditioned space must be considered to be inside the thermal boundary because the building's indoor air circulates inside the ducts. This is why ducts and furnace cabinets, located in unconditioned spaces, should be air-sealed and insulated.

See "Where to Insulate" on page 116, "Air Leakage Through Construction Materials" on page 77, and "Simple Air-leakage Diagnostic Methods" on page 87.

Unoccupied basements and crawl spaces

— The specific example of unoccupied basements and crawl spaces illustrates the decision-making complexities facing an energy auditor. No general rule applies when you consider whether to include a home's unoccupied basement or crawl space within the thermal boundary by retrofit insulation and air-sealing. This decision depends on climate, ground dampness, and the presence of ducts and pipes within the space, among other factors.

The most important practical consideration affecting this decision is the ease and cost of air sealing and insulating the floor versus air sealing and insulating foundation walls. For example, installing floor insulation can be a miserable job in a shallow crawl space; foundation insulation can be expensive when the foundation is built of rubble stone. Another important factor is that either the floor or the foundation may already be a good air barrier. If so, install the insulation at the most airtight location to reduce the effort needed for air sealing.

Energy auditors should consider potential energy-savings, moisture issues, and practical concerns when deciding whether to place the basement or crawl space inside or outside the thermal boundary.

Colder climates favor insulating the floor between the house and the crawl space (putting the crawl space outside the thermal boundary) because the cold ground causes greater heat loss through the floor compared to warmer climates.

Warmer climates favor including these partially subterranean areas within the thermal boundary. Heat loss through the floor in warmer climates is less compared to colder climates. The floor's heat loss to the cooler ground may aid in cooling the home during hot weather.

In a warm climate, it may not be cost-effective to insulate the floor or foundation walls. However, the energy auditor may decide to isolate a crawl space and the ground underneath it to mitigate existing moisture problems. This retrofit would include sealing the vents and installing an airtight ground-moisture barrier.

See "Basement and Crawl Space Insulation" on page 120.

Arguments favoring inclusion of unused basements and crawl spaces within the thermal boundary include these.

◆ Possible future occupancy of a basement.

◆ Waste heat from the furnace and water heater reduces heat loss through the floor above.

◆ Floor insulation can be difficult to install.

◆ The possibility of pipes freezing in cold climates if insulation and air sealing measures are installed between the house and basement.

Arguments favoring exclusion of unused basements and crawl spaces include these.

◆ Waste heat should be reduced at its source by insulating ducts, water heaters, pipes, and so on.

◆ Lacking heat sources, the basement or crawl space stays between ground temperature and outdoor temperature, which is usually above freezing.

- The floor is sometimes easier to air seal than the foundation because you can seal it from above or underneath or both.

- Floor insulation is inexpensive and often easy to install.

- In dry temperate or cold climates, comfort increases with floor insulation.

- Installing heating cable on pipes is often cheaper than heating an unused space to keep pipes thawed.

Consider the following specific examples.

House A's floor, over an unused basement in a cold dry climate, is easily accessible for insulation and air sealing. The ducts are fairly airtight, but uninsulated. The floor above the basement is a fairly good air barrier, but the foundation is leaky and difficult to insulate. A tight floor and leaky foundation walls favors air-sealing and insulating ducts, air-sealing and insulating the floor, blowing insulation into the walls of the basement's stairway, and installing electric heating cable on pipes close to the foundation's perimeter in very cold climates. The basement is placed outside the home's thermal boundary by these retrofits.

House B, located in a milder climate, has a pump and pressure tank in its crawl space. The ground under the house is covered by a moisture barrier, and the house has no moisture problems. Ducts are fairly leaky and lack insulation, but they would be difficult to insulate and air-seal. This situation favors sealing the crawl space vents and then insulating and air sealing the foundation walls and rim joist, thus including the crawl space within the home's thermal boundary.

As with any energy improvements, basement and crawl-space retrofits must compete with other energy improvements for available funds based on cost-effectiveness and practical feasibility. Insulating foundation walls or the first floor may not be cost-effective in the warmer U.S. climates.

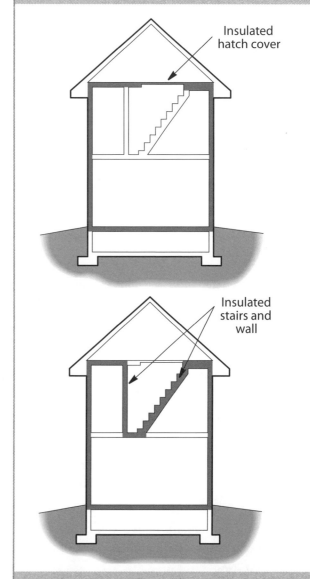

Thermal Boundary Choices for Attic Stairs

Insulated hatch cover

Insulated stairs and wall

An insulated cover is the simplest way to define the thermal boundary around attic stairs. The alternative is to insulate and air-seal the stairs and surrounding walls. Stairs into an unconditioned basement present the same choice.

Visual Inspection

One way to learn about a building's construction is to inspect it thoroughly, including looking into floor, wall, and ceiling cavities. Experienced auditors know how buildings are constructed by having audited other buildings of the same type.

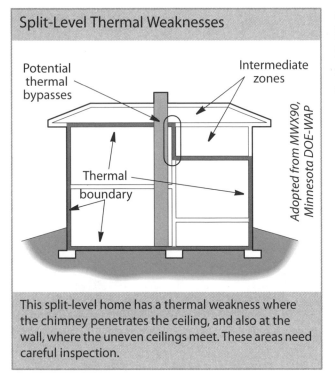

Split-Level Thermal Weaknesses

Potential thermal bypasses

Intermediate zones

Thermal boundary

Adopted from MWX90, Minnesota DOE-WAP

This split-level home has a thermal weakness where the chimney penetrates the ceiling, and also at the wall, where the uneven ceilings meet. These areas need careful inspection.

A thorough outdoor inspection may answer the following questions:

♦ What vertical shafts come through the roof (if visible from the ground)?

♦ Do the walls have protrusions or indentations, such as porches, bay windows, or cantilevered floors that break the continuity of the air barrier and insulation?

♦ Are there major seams between the building component elements? Are they deteriorated?

♦ Was the building built at one time, or in several parts? Is there an attached or built-in garage?

♦ Is the exterior shell airtight or leaky?

Answers to those questions help determine remedies for the building shell's energy and maintenance flaws.

Your interior inspection should identify the building's conditioned, unconditioned, and unintentionally conditioned areas. Determine insulation levels of the walls, floors, and roofs. Inspect the air barrier and insulation surrounding the conditioned space and notice voids, edge gaps, or

other flaws. Interior inspection involves checking basements, crawl spaces, attics, and other less visible areas for major air leakage sites. When inspecting the building visually from its interior, answer the following questions:

♦ What areas are used and unused?

♦ Where is the existing thermal boundary?

♦ What penetrations break wall, floor, and ceiling continuity?

♦ What indentations and shafts are intruding into the conditioned space from outdoors or from unconditioned spaces?

♦ What structures protrude from the building shell and are they currently conditioned or unconditioned?

♦ Are the insulation and air barrier continuous at the perimeter of the protrusions and indentations?

♦ What are the current and potential health and safety concerns?

See "Finding Air Leaks" on page 86.

Building Diagnostic Procedures

Visually inspecting all of a building's potential flaws can be difficult and time-consuming. A more practical, swift, and accurate way to diagnose building shell problems involves three diagnostic procedures: blower-door testing, infrared scanning, and duct-blower testing.

Since a large percentage of heat flow occurs at the building's thermal weak points, finding their locations is essential. Rather than seeking out each possible flaw and applying a prescriptive treatment, you can test and diagnose the problems and treat them in order of priority. Diagnostic equipment can reduce the time needed to find the important flaws in the insulation and air barrier.

In the 1970s, scientists and technicians began using blower doors and tracer-gas analysis to measure and locate air leaks. *Blower doors* are pressure-testing devices for the air barrier of a home. Infrared scanners allow the energy specialist to view heat flow through the building's thermal flaws.

Ducts, because they are full of indoor air, should be inside the thermal boundary. Tests on homes with ducted forced-air distribution systems generally indicate more air leaks than homes without ducts. Testing shows that ducted forced-air systems, when switched on, increased air leakage up to five times more than when those same systems were not operating. Special duct testing devices — called *duct blowers* — are often necessary to diagnose and correct duct air leakage.

Blower-door testing is a practical and effective technique for estimating air leakage in homes. The blower door consists of a panel with a built-in fan that fits an open doorway. The fan pressurizes the home to a standard pressure. Gauges then measure the air leakage.

Blower-door testing helps energy professionals determine airtightness and decide if air-sealing work is necessary. If the building needs air-tightening, a blower door also helps locate specific areas in the home that allow air leakage. See "Blower-Door Testing" on page 82.

Duct Leakage Comparisons

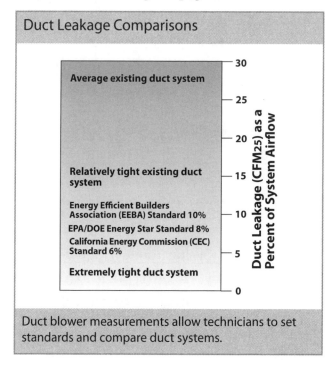

Duct blower measurements allow technicians to set standards and compare duct systems.

Blower-Door Testing

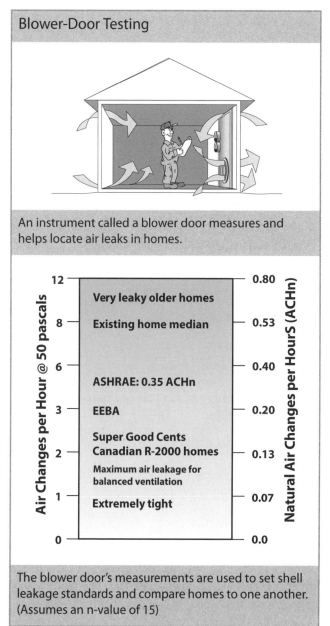

An instrument called a blower door measures and helps locate air leaks in homes.

The blower door's measurements are used to set shell leakage standards and compare homes to one another. (Assumes an n-value of 15)

Duct blowers are actually small blower doors connected to the duct system. Duct blowers measure the severity of duct leakage and help locate leaks. See "Duct-testing Strategies" on page 91.

Infrared scanners are optical viewers or cameras that reveal temperature differences. (Standard cameras reveal differences in light brightness.) Using infrared scanners, energy auditors can detect heat transmission and air leakage. Finding hidden air leaks is possible using the blower door and infrared scanner together. See "Infrared Scanners" on page 89.

Calculating Building Heat Loads

In a building, there are three primary modes of heat transfer to consider when calculating space-conditioning loads: heat transmission, air exchange, and solar radiation. These losses and gains are collectively referred to as heating and cooling loads. The purpose of calculating these loads is to size heating and cooling equipment and to determine annual heating and cooling energy consumption.

Consider the following factors when calculating a building's heating and cooling loads.

◆ Heat transmission through walls, floors, ceilings, windows and doors

◆ Air leakage and ventilation

◆ Solar radiation through glass

◆ Solar radiation falling on roofs and walls

◆ Buffering effect of heat stored in building components (mass)

◆ Internal heat gains

◆ External and internal moisture (latent) loads

◆ Local climate

◆ Indoor temperature

Computer-based energy modeling programs greatly simplify load calculations. However, users of these programs should have a basic understanding of underlying concepts in order to achieve accurate results.

Utility- and government-sponsored conservation programs often require computer-based energy modeling since this standardizes the evaluation process and may help to maximize the energy saved per dollar invested.

Heat transmission — The amount of heat that flows through a building assembly such as a wall depends on the indoor-outdoor temperature difference, the exposed surface area, and the thermal resistance or R-value of the materials that make up the assembly.

Wall U-factor and R-value Calculations

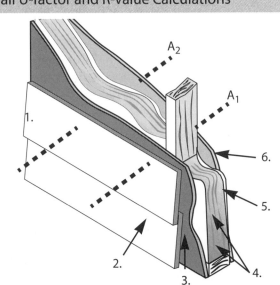

Numbered Wall Component	R (A₁) Framing	R (A₂) Insul.
1. Outside Air Film	0.17	0.17
2. Lapped Wood Siding	0.81	0.81
3. OSB Sheathing ($^1/_2$")	0.62	0.62
4. Framing or Insulation	*4.38	13.0
5. Gypsum Wall Board ($^1/_2$")	0.45	0.45
6. Inside Air Film	0.68	0.68
Total R	7.11	15.7
U-factor	0.141	0.0637
Percentage of total wall area	0.25	0.75

* R-value of 3.5-inch wood stud

Calculation: Area-Weighted Average U-Factor

$$U = (A_1 \times U_1) + (A_2 \times U_2)$$

$$U = (0.25 \times 0.141) + (0.75 \times 0.0637)$$

$$U = 0.0830$$

Calculation of R-value from Average U-factor

$$R = 1/U = 1/0.0830 = R\text{-}12.0$$

U-factors for the framed (A₁) and insulated wall (A₂) areas are blended by an area-weighted average. The inverse of this averaged U-factor is the average R-value.

Building assemblies usually contain layers of materials. You can calculate the thermal resistance of the structure by adding the R-values. For example, if you install R-4 insulated sheathing on an R-15 wall, the total R-value for the wall becomes R-19.

See "Materials/Building Assembly R-Values" on page 278.

The figure and table shown on page 68 demonstrate how to calculate the effective R-value for a wall, where studs and plates interrupt the insulation. In this example, the framing lumber occupies 25% of the wall while the insulation occupies 75%. This ratio is called the framing factor. Most energy modeling programs calculate area-weighted R-values and require the user to enter the R-value of the insulation and, in some cases, the R-value of the framing.

By convention, the thermal performance for windows, skylights, and glass doors is specified in terms of thermal transmittance, or U-factor, which is the inverse of the R-value. The U-factor is measured in BTUs per hour per degree Fahrenheit (°F) per square foot. A material with a thermal resistance of R-1 has a U-factor of 1, an R-2 material has a U-factor of 0.50, an R-4 material has a U-factor of 0.25, and so on.

Once you know the R-value (or U-factor) of a component, you can easily calculate its heat transmission (q) by multiplying the component's transmittance (U), exposed surface area in square feet (A), and temperature difference in °F (ΔT) together.

$$q \text{ (BTUH)} = U \times A \times \Delta T$$

The exposed surface area of a wall, ceiling or floor is typically measured to the outside edge of the framing. The surface area of windows and doors is typically based on rough opening dimensions. The ΔT is the difference between the indoor and outdoor design temperatures, described later in this section.

Air exchange — You must account for air leakage and ventilation when calculating heating and cooling loads. The impact of air exchange on heating and cooling loads depends on the temperature difference between the outdoor and indoor air and the rate of air exchange into and out of the building.

For every cubic foot of air that enters a building, a cubic foot escapes. The energy that heated or cooled the escaping air is lost when it leaves the building. You can limit ventilation or reclaim the escaping air's energy through a heat-recovery ventilator or an energy-recovery ventilator, to minimize the energy cost of ventilation.

See "ASHRAE Ventilation Standard" on page 251.

Air leakage is difficult to quantify without using a blower door. Air leakage is either expressed in cubic feet per minute (CFM) or air changes per hour (ACH), also known as the air exchange rate. CFM can be converted to ACH and vice versa if the volume of the space is known:

$$ACH = (CFM \times 60) \div Volume \text{ (cu.ft.)}$$

$$CFM = (ACH \times Volume \text{ cu. ft.}) \div 60$$

Each cubic foot of air that enters the home requires 0.018 BTU to change its temperature by 1°F. If you know the airflow rate (CFM) and how many degrees (°F) the outdoor air needs to change, you can estimate the amount of heat to be added or removed from the incoming air.

$$q \text{ (BTUH)} = CFM \times 0.018 \times \Delta T \times 60$$

Solar radiation — When solar radiation passes through a window or glass door, it heats the building. Solar heat gain reduces a building's heating load during the winter and increases the cooling load during the summer. The amount of solar gain depends on orientation, reflectivity, shading, and glass properties.

You must account for solar gain when calculating the annual heating and cooling loads. Solar gain is usually ignored when calculating the heating design load for equipment sizing since peak heating loads occur at night and during months when available solar energy is small. The exception is highly insulated buildings that are designed to be solar heated. Cooling equipment must always be sized to handle solar gain since peak solar gain coincides with peak cooling loads.

Solar heat gain calculations are complex and best performed by software programs. Solar heat gains through windows are the most important. The software user provides data for each window: the orientation, *Solar Heat Gain Coefficient* (from the window's energy label), and a *shading coefficient*. Most programs calculate the effect of overhang shading based on user inputs that define the geometry of the overhang.

Other Load Factors

There are some other factors to consider when calculating heating and cooling loads. The mass of building components, heat gains from things inside the building, and latent heat in moisture all contribute to the building's heating and cooling load.

Thermal mass — A building absorbs and releases heat in cycles as the outdoor temperature changes. Mass can have a significant buffering effect on heating and cooling loads, especially for buildings with masonry slabs or high-mass walls. Passive solar homes are optimized to maximize solar gain and heat storage during the winter and minimize solar gain during the summer.

The effects of thermal mass are typically ignored when calculating design loads for equipment sizing since the equipment must be able to handle peak loads during periods of prolonged cold or hot weather when a building's mass can become fully depleted or fully saturated.

In hot sunny climates, thermal mass and solar gain can greatly reduce the heating load. Likewise in cool climates, thermal mass can reduce or even eliminate the need for air conditioning. Unfortunately, established load calculation procedures don't account for the effect of thermal mass.

Internal heat loads — People, lights, and appliances all generate sensible heat. These internal loads are usually ignored when sizing heating equipment, but they must be included when sizing cooling equipment. Each occupant is assumed to generate 230 BTUH. Appliance, equipment, and lighting loads can be estimated based on their power ratings and frequency of use. Load calculation procedures include tables with typical internal load profiles.

Moisture loads — Air conditioners remove both sensible and latent heat from buildings. An air conditioner's latent load results from water vapor condensation on the evaporator coil. Air leakage is a major source of moisture in buildings, which depends on the air-leakage rate and the humidity of the outside air. Internal moisture generated by people, bathrooms, cooking, laundry, and plants add further to the latent load. The amount of moisture that an air conditioner removes depends on its latent capacity and the amount of moisture in the air. The energy required to condense this moisture must be included in the cooling-load calculations.

Calculating Heating Load or Input Rating

Transmission Heating Load

Transmittance		Area		Temperature difference		Transmissive Load
$U \; \frac{BTUs}{ft^2 \cdot hr \cdot °F}$	X	$A \; ft^2$	X	$\Delta T \; °F$	=	$q \; \frac{BTUs}{hr}$
0.083	X	7000	X	79	=	$45,899 \; \frac{BTUs}{hr}$

Air Exchange Heating Load

Air's heat capacity		Air flow rate		Temperature difference		
$\frac{BTUs}{ft^3 \cdot °F}$	X	$F \; \frac{ft^3}{hr.}$	X	$\Delta T \; °F$	=	$q \; \frac{BTUs}{hr}$
0.018	X	4500	X	79	=	$6399 \; \frac{BTUs}{hr}$

This simplified heat load (q) calculation assumes that a home in Madison, Wisconsin has a surface area of 7000 square feet, an average R-value of 12 (U=0.083), air leakage of 4500 cubic feet per hour (0.50 air change per hour). Madison's design temperature is -9°F, 79°F temperature difference (ΔT) from the 70° desired indoor temperature. Real heat load calculations employ separate calculations for walls, windows, ceilings, and floors with their different U-factors.

Calculating Heater Output and Input

$$q_{(transmis.)} + q_{(air)} = \text{Output Rating}$$

$$45,899 \; \tfrac{BTUs}{hr} + 6399 \; \tfrac{BTUs}{hr} = 52,298 \; \tfrac{BTUs}{hr}$$

$$\frac{\text{Output Rating}}{\text{Heating Efficiency}} = \text{Input Rating}$$

$$\frac{52,298 \; \frac{BTUs}{hr}}{.80} = 65,373 \; \tfrac{BTUs}{hr}$$

The difference between input and output is the heat wasted up the chimney and through the heater's cabinet. The heater's input rating is usually increased by 10% or more as a safety factor to insure customer satisfaction during the coldest weather.

Heating and Cooling Design Loads

When working with heating and cooling loads, don't confuse *design* loads with *seasonal* or *annual* loads. The design load, expressed in BTUH (BTUs per hour), is the predicted *rate* at which heat must be added or removed from a building at near-peak conditions, while the seasonal or annual load, expressed in MMBTU (millions of BTUs), is the amount of heat added or removed over the course of a season or a year.

Heating and cooling design loads provide a basis for sizing space conditioning equipment. Complete procedures for calculating heating and cooling loads are found in the ASHRAE *Handbook of Fundamentals* as well as *Manual J*, published by ACCA. ASHRAE is the American Society of Heating, Refrigerating, and Air Conditioning Engineers and ACCA is the Air Conditioning Contractors of America.

Ideally, equipment capacity should closely match a building's load at the design conditions. Design conditions include outdoor temperature, solar radiation, wind, indoor temperature, and relative humidity. Note that design conditions aren't the same as worst-case conditions. You don't need to size equipment based on worst-case climate extremes, and it isn't advisable.

ASHRAE maintains a climatic database for over 1,500 locations in the United States and Canada, last updated in 2009. This database includes statistical temperatures and other weather data. The 99th and 1st percentile temperatures are commonly used for sizing heating and cooling equipment.

The outdoor design temperatures for Baltimore are 17°F and 91°F. Over a period of decades in Baltimore, the temperature was at or below 17° for one percent of the hours, while exceeding 91° for one percent of the hours.

ACCA and ENERGY STAR have adopted the 99%–1% outside design temperatures. This means that space-conditioning (heating and cooling) systems are designed to operate continuously at these two design temperatures. Due to the buffering effect of a building's mass, the indoor temperature is unlikely to deviate more than a couple of degrees from the thermostat setpoint when design temperatures are exceeded (low or high).

Indoor design temperatures for new homes are typically 70°F for heating and 75°F for cooling. In existing homes, consider the occupants' temperature preferences instead of these default temperatures. Indoor humidity is assumed to be 50% in most climate zones. Cooling system sizing is affected by both the sensible (dry bulb) and latent (wet bulb) design temperatures, while the heating system is only affected by the dry bulb temperature.

For definitions of wet-bulb and dry-bulb temperatures, see "Glossary" on page 257.

Benefits of right-sizing — Contractors and homeowners both should understand the importance of proper sizing, especially for air conditioners. Oversized HVAC equipment has the following disadvantages.

♦ Oversized equipment costs more and requires larger electrical circuits.

♦ Oversized compressors have a shorter life expectancy due to short cycling.

♦ Excess capacity results in comfort issues due to larger temperature variations.

♦ Oversized air conditioners remove less moisture, an issue in humid climates.

♦ Excess capacity compromises indoor air quality (less run time = less filtration).

♦ Excess cooling capacity increases potential for structural damage from moisture.

♦ Oversized equipment costs more to operate due to inefficient short cycling.

See "Sizing and Selecting Air Conditioners" on page 215.

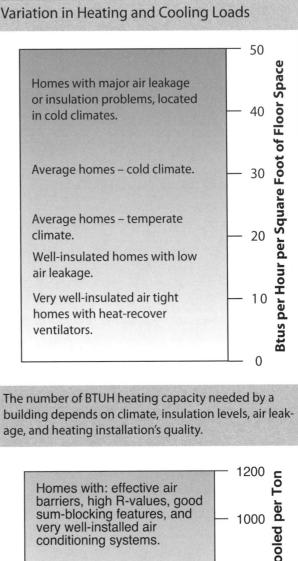

Variation in Heating and Cooling Loads

Homes with major air leakage or insulation problems, located in cold climates.

Average homes – cold climate.

Average homes – temperate climate.

Well-insulated homes with low air leakage.

Very well-insulated air tight homes with heat-recover ventilators.

Btus per Hour per Square Foot of Floor Space

The number of BTUH heating capacity needed by a building depends on climate, insulation levels, air leakage, and heating installation's quality.

Homes with: effective air barriers, high R-values, good sum-blocking features, and very well-installed air conditioning systems.

Homes with: average airtightness, R-values, shade, and reasonably well-installed air conditioning sytstems.

Homes with: air leakage or insulation problems, little shade, and poorly installed air-conditioning systems.

Computer rooms, sun rooms and other areas with high solar or internal loads.

Square Feet of Floor Space Cooled per Ton

The number of square feet of floor space that can be cooled by a ton of air-conditioning capacity depends on climate, shade, insulation levels, internal heat gains and air leakage.

Heating and cooling equipment efficiency —
Heating and cooling system efficiency is the output capacity divided by the equipment's instantaneous energy consumption (input). Efficiency losses include both energy waste and energy conversion losses, which are reflected in the equipment's rated output capacity. Therefore, equipment efficiency isn't necessary for the load calculation procedure. Rather, efficiency ratings play an important role in equipment selection.

See "Types of Efficiency" on page 148 and "Air-conditioner Efficiency" on page 214.

Heating and cooling distribution losses —
Duct efficiency losses include both heat transmission and air leakage. Heat transmission through the duct walls depends on the temperature difference, surface area, insulation R-value, and the amount of air flowing through the duct.

For practical reasons, duct-efficiency losses are considered part of the building load. ASHRAE establishes procedures and equations for estimating duct efficiency losses, which then become part of the building load.

Duct air leakage is difficult to estimate without measurement using a duct blower. The impact of duct leakage depends on the amount of leakage and where the leaks are located. Leakage on the return side can increase or decrease the load, depending on the ambient temperature and humidity of the air entering the return ducts. Leakage on the supply side, when located outside the thermal boundary, always increases the load since the heating or cooling system must condition more air to make up for the conditioned air that escapes.

See "Duct Air Leakage" on page 89.

Air-handler cabinets also transmit heat and leak air. These heat losses and heat gains don't figure into equipment efficiency ratings because the cabinet is assumed to be located inside the thermal boundary. When an air handler is located outside the thermal boundary, you should include cabinet heat flows for the load calculations.

Penetrations for refrigerant lines and condensation drains are often serious air leaks. When you conduct a duct leakage test, the cabinet is part of the tested duct system so any leaks are included in your duct-leakage measurement.

Whenever possible, mechanical equipment and duct systems should be located inside the thermal boundary. Efficiency losses associated with interior ducts are generally ignored when calculating heating and cooling loads. However, these losses affect the performance of the air distribution system and should ideally be reduced by air sealing and insulation.

Annual heating and cooling loads —
The primary purpose of calculating annual heating and cooling loads is to predict savings from energy-efficiency improvements. Calculating these annual loads before and after an improvement estimates the savings provided by that improvement.

The heat loss (Q) in BTUs over any time period (usually a season or a year) can be calculated by multiplying the total heat transmittance (U), area in square feet (A), temperature difference in °F (ΔT), and time period in hours (t). This formula is as follows:

$$Q\ (BTU) = U \times A \times \Delta T \times t$$

Degree-days combine ΔT and t in the above formula. Heating degree-days (HDDs) and cooling degree-days (CDDs) are typically based on a balance-point temperature of 65°F. The balance point, also called the base, is the outdoor temperature at which no heating or cooling is required. The degree-day base is typically set lower than the heating and cooling design indoor temperatures due to the effects of solar gain.

Heating degree-days are calculated by subtracting the average daily temperature from the base, while cooling degree-days are calculated by subtracting the base from the average daily temperature. (Ignore negative numbers because no space conditioning is required if degree days are zero or negative.) For example, if the high temperature on a particular day is 45°F and the low temperature is 15°F, then the average temperature is 30°F. In this case, 35 heating degree-days would accumulate for that day. Use the formulas below to calculate HDDs and CDDs.

$$HDDs = 65 - 1/2(T_{high} + T_{low})$$

$$CDDs = 1/2(T_{high} + T_{low}) - 65$$

The annual heating and cooling degree-days are the total degree-day values for an entire year. The average HDDs and CDDs for a location are based on historical climate records. For example, Caribou, Maine, experiences an average of 9767 HDD, while Wilmington, North Carolina, experiences 2347 HDD.

While degree-day calculations provide a rough estimate of annual heating or cooling loads, an energy-modeling program is an essential tool for making accurate and repeatable calculations. When analyzing existing homes, some energy-modeling programs can refine their predictions using historical energy usage from utility bills, which greatly improves accuracy. Some energy modeling programs prioritize suggested energy improvements based on their cost-effectiveness.

Seasonal Heat Load: Effect of Insulation

Transmittance	Area	Heating degree-days	Change days to hours	Annual heat loss
$U \frac{BTUs}{ft^2 \cdot hr \cdot °F}$	$\times A \, ft^2$	$\times \Delta T \frac{HDDs}{year}$	$\times 24 \frac{hrs.}{day}$	$= Q$ Therms or Decatherms per year

Before insulation

0.29	$\times 100$	$\times 5864$	$\times 24$	$= \begin{array}{c} 40.8 \\ 4.08 \end{array}$ Therms or Decatherms per year

After insulation

0.069	$\times 100$	$\times 5864$	$\times 24$	$= \begin{array}{c} 9.71 \\ .971 \end{array}$ Therms or Decatherms per year

Calculation of Savings

$$40.8 \tfrac{Therms}{year} - 9.71 \tfrac{Therms}{year} = 31.1 \tfrac{Therms}{year}$$

$$31.1 \tfrac{Therms}{year} \times 0.805 \tfrac{\$}{Therm} = 25 \tfrac{\$}{year} \quad \text{Savings}$$

Cost of Wall Insulation

$$0.75 \tfrac{\$}{ft^2} \times 100 \, ft^2 = \$75 \quad \text{Cost}$$

Payback and Annual Return

$$\text{Payback} = \frac{Cost}{Savings} = \frac{\$75}{25 \tfrac{\$}{year}} = 3 \text{ years}$$

$$\begin{array}{c} \text{Annual} \\ \text{Return} \end{array} = \frac{Savings}{Cost} = \frac{25 \tfrac{\$}{year}}{\$75} = \frac{33\%}{year}$$

These calculations outline an economic analysis of installing R-11 insulation in an uninsulated wall. We first calculate savings in therms, then convert therms to dollars.

Manual J Computer Calculation of Room Heat Flows and Air-Handler Airflows

Room	Area (ft²)	Heating load (BTUH)	Heating Airflow (cfm)	Cooling load (BTUH)	Cooling Airflow (cfm)
Living room	255	4670	188	4568	221
Dining room	224	4219	195	2271	188
Kitchen	144	3201	91	2456	119
Bedroom 1	158	4410	142	1799	98
Bedroom 2	106	1730	53	771	41
Bedroom 3	99	3941	151	2492	136
Bathroom 1	80	1532	65	1206	78
Bathroom 2	60	771	29	521	39
Totals	**1126**	**24,474**	**914**	**16,084**	**920**

Calculating Loads With Computer Programs

Many energy auditors and HVAC contractors use computer programs to make heat-load calculations easy. The programs perform only as well as the person who enters the data.

Utility and government conservation programs prefer computer programs because they standardize decision-making procedures and help maximize energy savings per dollar invested.

Computer programs designed to calculate heating and cooling load can do one or more of the following.

♦ Calculate heating and cooling loads by room, as in the table above.

♦ Calculate airflow or water flow needed to heat and cool the building at design conditions.

♦ Calculate duct sizes or pipe sizes for the heating and cooling delivery system.

Computer programs designed to calculate seasonal energy loads can do one or more of the following.

♦ Calculate heat loss and heat gain before and after a retrofit to estimate the cost-effectiveness of energy retrofits.

♦ Predict energy usage to compare with actual energy use. This comparison helps evaluate the calculation's accuracy and indicates whether the building has significant hidden problems.

♦ Simulate variable building operations to see how energy consumption changes. These programs are especially useful for analyzing large, complicated buildings.

♦ Manage and keep records of decision-making for weatherization and home-performance jobs.

See "Analyzing Annual Energy Costs" on page 277.

Air leakage in buildings represents from 5% to 40% of the space-conditioning costs. Controlling air leakage is one of the most important functions of weatherization, and often the most difficult.

An air barrier is a building component designed to stop air leakage. The air barrier combined with the insulation defines the thermal boundary.

The main goals of air leakage control are these.

♦ Save energy.

♦ Increase comfort.

♦ Protect insulation's thermal integrity.

♦ Reduce direct cooling or heating of people and building components by outdoor air.

♦ Avoid moisture migration into building cavities.

Air sealing may provide these additional benefits.

♦ Reduce vermin's access to indoors.

♦ Reduce flow of air pollution from external sources.

♦ Reduce rainwater leakage.

♦ Enhance fire safety.

We used to think that existing buildings were relatively airtight, except for seams where building materials joined, especially around windows and doors. In the past, engineers tried to estimate air leakage based on the length and width of cracks between building materials. Estimating crack size wasn't accurate because it neglected major air leaks in hidden locations.

From 1975 to 1985, scientists and technicians developed instruments to evaluate air leakage, including blower doors, infrared scanners, and tracer-gas analysis. With these developments, we now know that the building's hidden air leaks are usually more important than seams between building materials. As a result, technicians found new ways of finding and sealing these hidden air leakage pathways.

Air Leakage Through Construction Materials

Material	$CFM_{50}/100\ ft^2$
$^5/_8$" oriented-strand board	0.09
$^1/_2$" drywall	0.26
4-mil air barrier paper	0.26
$^1/_8$" hardboard	0.37
1" EPS (dense)	1.5
(materials below not considered air barriers)	
15# perforated asphalt felt	5.3
Standard concrete block	7.9
1" EPS (light)	170
$^5/_8$" tongue & groove boards	300
6" fiberglass batt	490
3" vermiculite	930
1.5" spray-on cellulose	1160

These values represent the approximate air leakage through each square foot of material during a 50-pascal blower-door test.

Based on: "Air Permeance of Building Materials" research report by Canada Mortgage Housing Corporation. Units converted from all-metric by the author.

In the 1990s, Canadian building scientists measured the air permeability of various building materials and joints. They also measured durability of air barriers in very high winds.

Most homes and small multifamily buildings are ventilated by natural air leakage, and this fact informs decisions about whether to seal air leaks and how airtight to make a home. Scientists, engineers, and technicians continue to debate whether air leakage is an acceptable strategy to ventilate homes.

Some recent state building codes now require strong and effective air barriers and mechanical ventilation systems. Canadian builders, architects, and engineers have understood the need for air and vapor barriers for years because of their cold climate and the moisture problems that result from ineffective air and vapor barriers.

This chapter discusses the principles of air leakage, diagnosis of air leaks, construction flaws that allow air leakage, and methods and materials for sealing air leaks.

Air-Sealing Principles

Air leakage from one zone to another requires a hole between the zones and pressure to push air through that hole. The airflow rate through a hole or group of holes depends on two factors: the cross-sectional area of the holes and the difference in pressure (ΔP). Air leaking in is called infiltration, and air leaking out is called exfiltration.

Natural airflows are usually small and variable — too difficult to measure. A blower door's pressure and airflow, however, are steady and measurable. Measuring pressure and airflow with a blower door allows you to estimate the size of holes.

Direct air leakage occurs at windows, doors, and other concentrations of seams, where air leaks directly through the shell. Indirect air leakage enters the building shell in one location, flows through building cavities, and emerges at a different location.

Many indirect air leaks are found in intermediate zones like attics and crawl spaces. One seldom-recognized air-leakage source is airflow through building materials themselves. Concrete block, brick, perforated felt, and most insulation materials have relatively high air permeability and aren't considered air barriers.

Manometer Readings

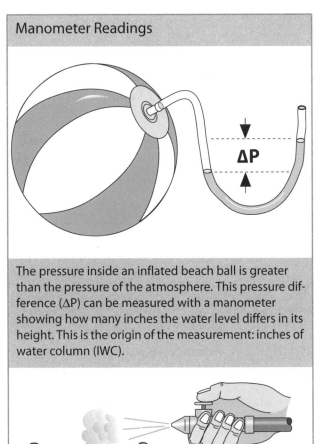

The pressure inside an inflated beach ball is greater than the pressure of the atmosphere. This pressure difference (ΔP) can be measured with a manometer showing how many inches the water level differs in its height. This is the origin of the measurement: inches of water column (IWC).

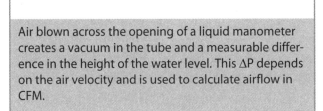

Air blown across the opening of a liquid manometer creates a vacuum in the tube and a measurable difference in the height of the water level. This ΔP depends on the air velocity and is used to calculate airflow in CFM.

Pressures driving natural air leakage come from wind, exhaust fans, furnace blowers, chimneys, and the stack effect. The stack effect (also called chimney effect) is caused by density differences between warm and cool air masses.

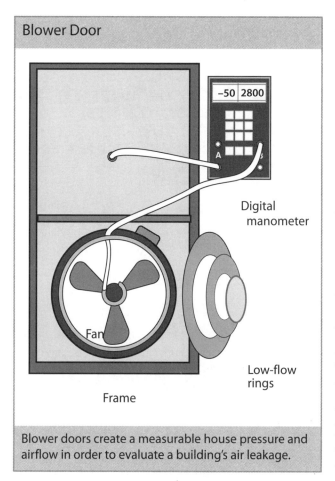

Blower Door

-50 2800

Digital
manometer

Fan

Low-flow
rings

Frame

Blower doors create a measurable house pressure and airflow in order to evaluate a building's air leakage.

Chimneys and exhaust fans (including clothes dryers) remove air from the home, creating a slight vacuum, often called depressurization. The wind, furnace blower, and stack effect tend to pressurize some areas of the home and depressurize others.

Beyond air leakage, air can also move around inside building cavities, increasing the rate of heat transmission. Air convects inside building cavities, carrying heat from one surface to another. Air can wash over the insulation's surface, convecting heat away. Or air can convect through an insulation material, reducing its thermal resistance.

Ideally, an effective air barrier surrounds the home on all sides, adjacent to its insulation. An effective air barrier prevents most air leakage and convection. However, most American homes have flawed air barriers that can be significantly improved by diagnosis and air sealing.

Air Pressure and Flow

Air pressure, airflow, and the size of air leaks are directly related to each other. A pressure difference on opposite sides of a hole causes an increase in airflow through the hole. Bigger holes pass more air at the same pressure than smaller ones.

Pressure and airflow can be measured by instruments called manometers. Manometers come in three common types: a transparent tube filled with water; a round gauge with a needle indicating the pressure or flow amount; or a digital manometer, giving a digital readout of pressure.

The air inside an inflated beach ball is denser than the atmosphere outside. Measure this pressure difference by attaching a manometer to the beach ball's valve. The lighter atmosphere presses on one side of the liquid, and the denser beach ball air presses on the other. The distance that the beach ball's denser air moves the water column off level — measured in inches — is a unit of air pressure.

The small air pressure differences caused by wind, blower doors, furnace fans, and chimneys are measured in inches of water column (abbreviated IWC) in the American measurement system. The more common metric unit for small air pressures is the pascal — 249 pascals equal 1.0 IWC.

When talking about pressure differences between two areas, we say that the zone having denser air is pressurized, or is the high-pressure area. The zone with less dense air is depressurized, is under vacuum, or is the low-pressure area.

Another type of manometer is a round gauge with an arc-shaped scale for measuring either pressure (in pascals) or airflow cubic feet per minute (CFM). This gauge has a high pressure tap and a low pressure tap. If the gauge is physically located in the low pressure area — as with typical blower-door testing — its low pressure tap is open to that area (indoors), and a hose is used to expose its high pressure tap to the high pressure area (outdoors).

The digital manometer measures pressure by way of sensors, called pressure transducers. Digital manometers give their readings on a digital screen, and some can measure both house pressure and flow simultaneously.

Airflow is then measured by connecting the manometer's low pressure tap to a hose held parallel to the airflow stream. Air flowing perpendicular to the opening at the hose's end creates vacuum within the hose. This vacuum's strength is directly related to the airflow rate. Manometers convert the pressure they sense to airflow by an airflow scale on the gauge face or by an electronic calculator in the digital manometer.

Pressures Driving Air Leakage

Air flowing inside or outside a building creates pressures that affect the building. Buildings aren't equal with respect to their air pressures. Because of differences in pressure, one single-family home may have two to four times the air leakage of another home with the same air leaks. Homes with forced-air distribution systems, fireplaces, and large kitchen exhaust fans have larger pressures than homes without these features. Homes on hilltops in high-wind areas may have twice the air leakage of homes in less windy regions.

This section describes how a building's height, its chimneys, exhaust fans, and furnace blowers, along with the wind, affect its air pressures.

Stack-effect pressure — Cooler air is denser than warmer air, and this density difference creates a pressure that causes air to move. The air inside a home tends to stratify in layers due to density differences. During the heating season, hot air rises to the top and cooler air falls to the bottom. If the home has leaks, warm air leaves through higher openings, and cool air enters through lower openings. This pattern of air leakage is called the stack effect because it resembles airflow in a chimney. During the cooling season the stack effect can reverse causing infiltration higher in the building and exfiltration in the lower.

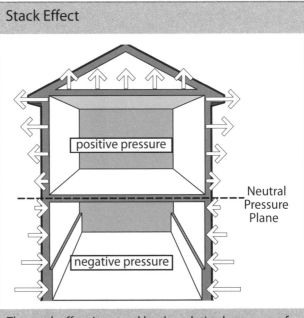

Stack Effect

The stack effect is caused by the relative buoyancy of warmer air. Warmer air's upward force exerts an outward pressure. Airflow, through holes in the home's top, creates suction at lower levels, pulling air in. Arrows indicate the direction and intensity of air pressure.

A building's natural pressure difference with the outdoors varies depending on location. Somewhere near the building's midpoint of height is a boundary region, called the neutral pressure plane, which separates the building's negative and positive pressure zones. A hole near the neutral pressure plane allows little or no leakage because there is no indoor/outdoor pressure difference there.

The pressures created by stack effect are greatest at the highest and lowest points in the building. Therefore, a hole in a basement or attic will allow more air infiltration than an equal-sized hole near the neutral pressure plane.

Wind pressure — Wind blowing against a wall creates an area of high pressure, driving outdoor air into the windward side of the home. The wind's force is enhanced or hindered by building and landscaping features that act as dams — porch roofs, overhangs, inside building corners, fences, or vegetation.

Wind Pressure

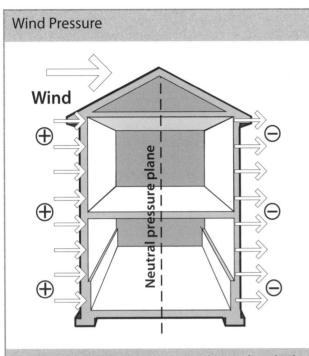

Wind creates a positive pressure on the windward side of the home and negative pressures on leeward side with reference to the home's interior. Wind pressures push and pull air through holes in the building shell.

Chimney and Exhaust Pressure

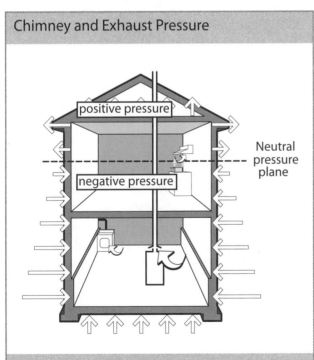

The chimney, clothes dryer, and kitchen exhaust fan exhaust air from the home, putting most of the home's volume under negative pressure.

The wind creates a vacuum at wall and roof surfaces parallel to its flow. The leeward side, facing away from the wind, is usually either neutral or depressurized.

The wind's speed is greater the higher from the ground you measure. As building height increases, wind's force against the building increases. Wind speed is affected by trees, fences, neighboring buildings, and hills that block or divert wind. Wind speed varies widely between geographic regions and even within local areas. Strong wind gusts can damage air barriers and permanently increase air-leakage rates.

Chimney and exhaust pressures — Chimneys, exhaust fans, and clothes dryers create a slight vacuum indoors because they exhaust air out of the building. They also move the neutral pressure plane up because more of the building's interior space is under negative pressure. A fan that forces air into the home moves the neutral pressure plane down, putting more of the home under positive pressure.

Replacement air, for air exiting exhaust devices, is called make-up air for exhaust fans or combustion air for combustion appliances. Make-up air and combustion air enter through air leaks, intentional openings, or ducts. Make-up air or combustion air may even come down a chimney if negative pressures become too great — a dangerous situation called backdrafting.

Duct pressure — The furnace blower circulates air through the furnace and its supply and return ducts. Supply registers blow air into a room, pressurizing nearby areas of the room. Return registers suck air out of rooms, depressurizing areas near these registers.

If the ducts are leaking, or return air is restricted, rooms may have high positive or negative pressures. These pressures are often large enough to double or triple the building shell's air leakage, compared to air leakage when the furnace blower is off.

Blower-Door Testing

The blower-door apparatus includes these components.

♦ A frame and flexible panel to plug an open doorway.

♦ A variable speed fan to create pressure and airflow.

♦ A manometer for measuring the pressure difference between the home and outdoors — called house pressure.

♦ Hoses for attaching the manometer to outdoors and to the fan.

Blower-door testing is the most practical way to predict energy savings from air-sealing methods. Measuring air leakage allows technicians to evaluate existing ventilation levels and apply economic limits to air sealing. Economic air-sealing limits prevent technicians from spending too much time and material sealing small, elusive air leaks.

Compare blower-door operation with inflating a leaky beach ball. Inflating a beach ball doesn't require much air if the ball has no leaks. But if there are a couple of pin holes, then you must continually supply a tiny but steady stream of air to keep the ball fully inflated. If there are a few raisin-sized holes or hundreds of pinholes, you must blow into the ball continuously and vigorously to keep it fully inflated. The total size of all the holes and the pressure difference between the ball and the air outside determine the rate at which you need to blow air to keep the ball inflated.

Like your lungs inflating the beach ball, the blower door pressurizes the home by blowing air in or depressurizes it by sucking air out. Depressurization, which creates a vacuum indoors, is the most common procedure because air comes in through air leaks, allowing you to feel and locate the leaks.

The combined area of the building's holes and the pressure difference between indoors and outdoors determine how much air volume the blower door blows. This airflow is measured in CFM. The standard yardstick for measuring a home's air leakage is the airflow through a blower door at 50 pascals of house pressure — abbreviated CFM_{50}.

Preparation and Set-up

Blower-door testing involves: preparing the home for the test, setting up the blower door in a doorway, connecting its gauges, turning on the blower door, and reading the pressure and airflow rate from gauges.

Preparing the home includes these steps.

♦ Closing primary windows and storm windows.

♦ Opening all interior doors.

♦ Disabling heaters and water heaters by turning down their thermostats.

♦ Covering ashes in wood stoves and fireplaces with damp newspaper to prevent the ashes from being sucked into the home.

♦ Shutting fireplace dampers, fireplace glass doors, wood-stove dampers, and wood-stove air intakes.

The blower-door operator slowly brings up the house pressure to 50 pascals using the fan's variable speed control. The operator inspects the home's interior during the test's first moments to ensure that dust is not being pulled in through a fireplace, wood stove, or other dirty area. With the house pressure at exactly 50 pascals, the operator notes the CFM_{50} from the airflow gauge or digital display.

Blower-Door Testing

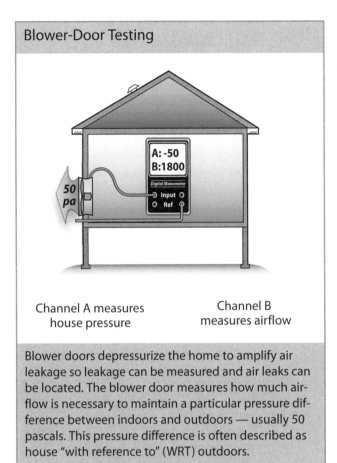

Channel A measures house pressure

Channel B measures airflow

Blower doors depressurize the home to amplify air leakage so leakage can be measured and air leaks can be located. The blower door measures how much airflow is necessary to maintain a particular pressure difference between indoors and outdoors — usually 50 pascals. This pressure difference is often described as house "with reference to" (WRT) outdoors.

Blower-door Measurements

There are several common factors used to quantify air leakage with the blower door:

1. The 50-Pascal Airflow Rate — A blower-door reading, expressed in cubic feet per minute (CFM_{50}), is the actual flow rate measured at 50 Pascals of house pressure. CFM_{50} is the simplest and most direct measurement of the airtightness of a building.
2. The 50-Pascal Air Change Rate (ACH_{50}) — A blower-door reading, expressed in air changes per hour at 50 Pascals, is calculated by multiplying the CFM_{50} by 60 min/hour and then dividing by the house volume in cubic feet.
3. Natural Air Change Rate (ACH_n) — Natural air change is expressed in air changes per hour. The 50-pascal air change (ACH_{50}) rate, modified by numerical factors (reflecting wind speed, shielding of the building by external elements, and the building's height and

size), gives a rough estimate of the natural air change rate.

4. Approximate Leakage Area — Different calculation procedures are used to estimate the surface area of air leaks. The simplest of these is approximate leakage area, a rough estimate of the surface area, in square inches, of all the building's air leaks combined into a single hole. Many technicians divide CFM_{50} by 10 to reach an acceptable estimate of leakage area.

Appendix A-1 Energy Related Formulas lists more formulas related to air leakage.

Ventilation and Air Leakage

Either air leakage or a whole-building ventilation system must provide acceptable indoor air quality. The American Society of Heating, Refrigerating, and Air Conditioning Engineers (ASHRAE) sets total ventilation requirements (TVRs) to ensure acceptable indoor air quality in homes.

The older ASHRAE Standard 62-1989 allowed for air leakage as a primary ventilation strategy. The current ASHRAE Standard 62.2-2013 doesn't consider air leakage as a legitimate ventilation strategy. ASHRAE Standard 62.2-2013 specifies ventilation fan sizes according to floor area and number of bedrooms. However, the standard allows an infiltration credit to reduce the TVR for leaky homes that are blower-door tested.

See "ASHRAE Ventilation Standard" on page 251.

There are three basic strategies for reducing air leakage while providing adequate ventilation.

1. Seal the home to the point where air leakage ventilates the home adequately under the infiltration-credit provisions of ASHRAE 62.2-2013.
2. Seal the home as tight as possible and install a whole-building ventilation system using exhaust or supply ventilation (ASHRAE 62.2-2013).
3. Seal the home very airtight, during a major home-performance retrofit and install a heat-

recovery ventilator (HRV) or energy-recovery ventilator (ERV) (ASHRAE 62.2-2013).

The first option allows air leakage to ventilate if the ASHRAE 62.2-2013 infiltration credit shows enough air leakage. The last two options comply with the ASHRAE Standard 62.2-2013 requirement for mechanical whole-building ventilation in most homes. The third option recognizes that HRVs and ERVs work best in very airtight homes.

Many residential buildings have indoor air pollution caused by combustion heating, tobacco smoking, moisture problems, and other environmental pollutants. Reducing air leakage without first reducing indoor pollution or installing a whole-building ventilation system is unwise.

See "Indoor Pollutants" on page 241.

Air-sealing Economic Limits

The following guidelines are rough rules-of-thumb for decision-making about how much labor and material to devote to air sealing.

Applying a dollar spending limit for obtaining reducing air leakage is one way to establish an economic limit for air-sealing. For example, if the air-sealing budget is $350, and the cost for air-sealing labor and materials is $35 per 100 CFM_{50}, then the air-leakage reduction limit is 1000 CFM_{50}.

The home's initial air leakage measurement can also help determine the air-sealing economic limit. The leakier the home is, the more you can spend to seal air leaks cost-effectively. Homes with more than 6000 CFM_{50} may merit days of labor and hundreds of dollars in materials. Homes in the 2500-to-4000-CFM_{50} range merit less resources. Homes with less than 1000 CFM_{50} are difficult to improve.

Appendix A-12 Air-Sealing Economic Limits, provides a method for establishing air-sealing economic limits, depending on your local fuel cost and climate. See also "Blower-Door Testing" on page 67 for another comparison of house types and air leakage.

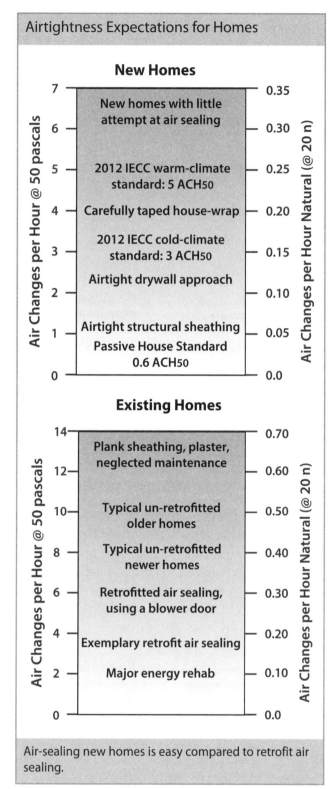

Airtightness Expectations for Homes

New Homes

(Air Changes per Hour @ 50 pascals / Air Changes per Hour Natural (@ 20 n))

- New homes with little attempt at air sealing
- 2012 IECC warm-climate standard: 5 ACH50
- Carefully taped house-wrap
- 2012 IECC cold-climate standard: 3 ACH50
- Airtight drywall approach
- Airtight structural sheathing
- Passive House Standard 0.6 ACH50

Existing Homes

(Air Changes per Hour @ 50 pascals / Air Changes per Hour Natural (@ 20 n))

- Plank sheathing, plaster, neglected maintenance
- Typical un-retrofitted older homes
- Typical un-retrofitted newer homes
- Retrofitted air sealing, using a blower door
- Exemplary retrofit air sealing
- Major energy rehab

Air-sealing new homes is easy compared to retrofit air sealing.

House-pressure Limits

In existing homes, limiting indoor negative and positive pressure is important for safety, health, durability, comfort, and energy efficiency. Exhaust air from chimneys, exhaust fans, and clothes dryers creates a slight vacuum in the house, especially near these devices. Acting alone or in combination, these exhaust devices can depressurize the zone containing the combustion appliance, causing backdrafting or flame roll-out. Backdrafting is a threat primarily to combustion appliances that have their combustion chambers open to indoors, and which also have naturally drafting chimneys. The depressurization limit for a combustion zone is often set at –3 to –5 pascals with reference to outdoors.

More severe negative pressures in the –6 to –10 range may cause flame roll-out (a fire that burns outside the appliance) in open-combustion appliances such as standard furnaces and water heaters. Flame roll-out is a common cause of house fires.

Negative pressures in the home can also pull sewer gases, moisture, and soil gases (including pesticide residues and radon) into the home. Positive or negative pressures can move moisture-laden air through holes in the building shell, where moisture may condense on cold surfaces within building cavities. Building experts have observed pressure-derived moisture problems at only ±1 pascal.

To reduce depressurization, technicians provide combustion-air inlets and make-up air to exhaust fans. Passive make-up air or combustion-air openings may be ineffective unless they are large enough. In rare cases, fan-powered combustion and make-up air are required for safe combustion. The safest option is to isolate the combustion zone through careful air-sealing and supply combustion air from outdoors.

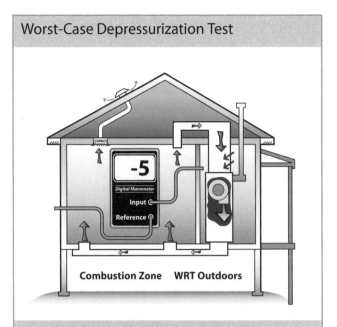

Worst-Case Depressurization Test

-5
Digital Manometer
Input
Reference

Combustion Zone   WRT Outdoors

Technicians create a worst-case condition for the naturally drafting chimney by activating the furnace, exhaust fans, and a clothes dryer at the same time. If the pressure difference between the combustion appliance zone (CAZ) and outdoors is more negative than 3 pascals, action is taken to mitigate the negative pressure.

Sealing duct air leaks and improving ducted air circulation are effective ways of relieving common house pressures caused by leaky ducts or unbalanced airflow between supply and return ducts. Pressure differences between rooms with closed interior doors should generally be less than 3 pascals.

See "Airflow and Performance in Central Air Conditioners" on page 217 and "Duct Airflow Problems" on page 165.

Wind can cause positive pressure or excessive negative pressure in naturally drafting chimneys. Wind is a major driving force for air leakage because it directly affects house pressure. Windbreaks of trees and shrubs can save up to 30% of heating cost. Diverting warm winds away from air-conditioned homes can save cooling energy.

The chart in Appendix A-13 Air Leakage at Various House Pressures, describes the relationship between house pressure and air leakage.

Finding Air Leaks

Energy specialists inspect many buildings where the architect and builder failed to plan and install an effective air barrier. Any gaps or holes in the building's exterior floor, walls, or ceiling contribute to air leakage. Years of wear, weather, remodeling, and other modifications create additional air leaks.

When a home is depressurized by a blower door, even small leaks around doors and windows become obvious. However, most buildings have less obvious but more important air leaks — larger, hidden, or under a greater pressure — located in attics and basements.

Leaks are often located in places where you don't expect them to be. Technicians have developed diagnostic procedures to avoid guesswork, unnecessary air sealing, and needless crawling into dark and dirty places.

To control air leakage, it's important for a home to have a continuous air barrier that separates the indoor air from the outdoor air. You can use a blower door to find discontinuity between building components like floors and walls or walls and ceilings.

Another secret to effective air sealing is knowing the relative leakiness of building materials and building assemblies. Oriented-strand board (OSB) or drywall, installed carefully and glued to the frame during construction, can be extremely airtight. Polyethylene vapor barrier and house wrap can also be very airtight if sealed at all seams and protected from wind during construction. Segmented building assemblies like lap siding or wood shingles over plank sheathing are very leaky. Concrete block, brick, stone, and tongue-and-groove paneling are also quite permeable to airflow.

See "Thermal Boundary Decisions" on page 63 for examples of locating the thermal boundary. See "Air Leakage Through Construction Materials" on page 77.

Air-Leakage Sites

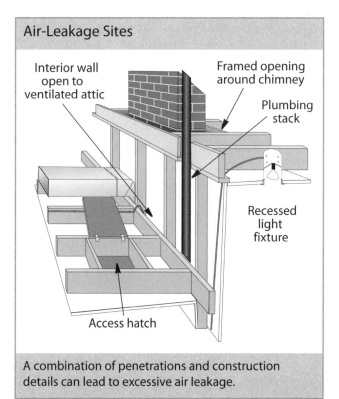

Interior wall open to ventilated attic

Framed opening around chimney

Plumbing stack

Recessed light fixture

Access hatch

A combination of penetrations and construction details can lead to excessive air leakage.

Testing Air Barriers

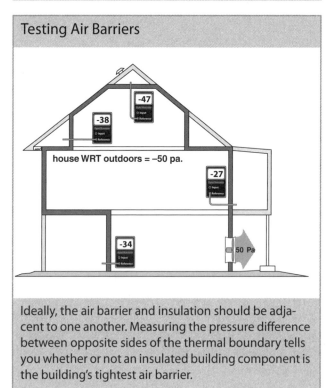

-47

-38

house WRT outdoors = –50 pa.

-27

-34

50 Pa

Ideally, the air barrier and insulation should be adjacent to one another. Measuring the pressure difference between opposite sides of the thermal boundary tells you whether or not an insulated building component is the building's tightest air barrier.

Ideally, ducts should be installed inside the thermal boundary, making duct leakage is a minor problem. However, more often ducts are located in an intermediate zone, where duct air leakage wastes energy and causes house-pressure problems within the living space. Technicians use a variety of special procedures to locate air leaks in ducts using a blower door, duct blower, or pressure pan.

Simple Air-leakage Diagnostic Methods

The diagnostic procedures described here are helpful in finding the primary air barrier and sealing its high-priority air leaks. Big leaks and leaks at the building's high and low points (which experience high pressure) have the highest air-sealing priority.

Use your hand to sense air leaks inside the building during a blower-door depressurization. Smoke from a smoke generator can identify leaks when you're working from an attic or crawl space because the smoke moves into air leaks. A smoke generator is a plastic or glass chemical-smoke container.

You can also pressurize the building, instead of depressurizing it, and then observe the attic floor from the attic. Look for signs of air blowing through the ceiling and into the attic (such as small dust clouds or wavering cobwebs). Smoke works very well during blower-door pressurization because you can see the smoke leaving the conditioned zone through leaks.

Technicians sometimes use interior doors to test parts of a home's air barrier. Three common methods, used during a blower-door test, can give you a rough idea of which areas of the building are leaky and which are tight.

1. Compare rooms to one another by closing the door to a 1-inch-wide opening and feeling how much air is coming from each room.
2. Close interior doors one by one and measure the pressure difference between the home's main body and that room. The greater the manometer's negative reading during depressurization, the more leakage through that room.

3. Open and close doors to rooms and intermediate zones, noting the effect on blower-door airflow (CFM_{50}).

Measuring pressure differences across interior doors allows you to quantify that leakage very roughly. If the room has no pressure difference across its door during depressurization, then little leakage is occurring through that room to the outdoors. If the pressure difference is –30 pascals, then that bedroom seems to be partially connected to the outdoors (which is –50 pascals).

Using the third technique, close the doors to two bedrooms, one after the other, and note the reduction of airflow through the blower door. If closing one bedroom door reduced the airflow 400 CFM_{50}, and then closing the second reduced the flow 150 CFM_{50}, you know that the air barrier in the first bedroom has more air leakage than the air barrier in the second bedroom.

Opening basement doors, crawl space hatches, or attic hatches can give an indication of whether the floors or ceilings (between living spaces and these intermediate zones) are effective air barriers. If the blower door shows little airflow difference between an open or closed basement door, then the foundation wall, not the floor, is the primary air barrier. This comparison helps determine how much time and material to spend air sealing a particular air barrier.

For example: To test the airtightness of a home's ceiling, depressurize the building to 50 pascals, and then insert a manometer hose through a small hole in the ceiling so that the hose's tip reaches above the insulation. Below are three possible pressure readings, with a probable explanation for each.

◆ 50 pascals: The attic has the same pressure as the indoor/outdoor pressure difference, indicating the ceiling is the tightest air barrier, the attic is well-connected to the outdoors, and the roof isn't acting as an air barrier at all.

- 25 pascals: The ceiling is a partial air barrier, and the roof is a partial air barrier; they are equally airtight or leaky.

- 5 pascals: The home is almost completely connected to the attic. The roof is the tightest air barrier, and the ceiling is a leaky secondary air barrier.

The attic is usually considered outside the conditioned space, but a 5-pascal pressure difference across the ceiling disproves that assumption. Air leaks are hiding somewhere in that ceiling. Of course, the attic could be considered a conditioned zone if it contains a furnace and air conditioner, or if the roof is airtight and insulated.

Technicians may employ a similar procedure to test the airtightness of the floor, foundation, or walls — drilling holes, inserting the manometer tube, then reading the manometer — if this information is needed to prioritize air sealing. You measure the largest pressure difference across the tightest air barrier. A 50-pascal pressure difference indicates that the air barrier being tested is very airtight compared to any alternative air barrier. A 25-pascal pressure difference means the two air barriers are equally airtight.

Technicians prefer to seal one air barrier — the one where existing or proposed insulation is located. Knowing which of two possible air barriers is tightest may not provide enough information for optimal decision-making. Determining the amount of air leakage (CFM_{50}) through the primary air barrier helps determine the amount of effort to spend to seal that air barrier. Technicians sometimes use advanced diagnostic techniques that involve opening a hole of a known size in one of the two air barriers. That opening may be an attic hatch, crawl space hatch, basement door, door to an attached garage, or the existing attic vents.

Using the surface area of these openings, their effect on interzone pressure difference, and the opening's effect on blower-door airflow, technicians can calculate how many CFM_{50} are leaking through a section of the air barrier. That airflow

value guides the technician in determining how much effort is merited to seal the air barrier. The calculation techniques, related to these methods, are beyond this book's scope.

Tracer-gas Testing

Tracer-gas testing is primarily a research technique, but researchers sometimes use it to troubleshoot air leakage or indoor air quality in large multifamily buildings. Tracer-gas testing is somewhat more accurate for predicting natural air change rate because tracer-gas testing occurs under natural conditions, unlike blower-door testing, which occurs under pressurized conditions.

Tracer-gas testing involves releasing a harmless gas — sulphur hexafluoride, carbon dioxide, or perfluorocarbon — into the building and then measuring how much the tracer gas is diluted by infiltrating outdoor air after a period of time.

Technicians either release the tracer gas all at once or install a constant-gas emitter. The all-at-once release can be into a single apartment or into a common air handler to be distributed more widely. Samples are taken at regular intervals for several hours. The samples are sent to a lab where a sophisticated gas analyzer measures the concentration of tracer gas in each sample.

A constant-emitter-tracer-gas test uses a constant emitter and receivers placed at various locations within the living space. The receiver is a container of material that absorbs tracer gas at a predictable rate, depending on the gas' concentration in surrounding air. The receivers are sent to a lab for analysis.

Tracer-gas analysis is far less practical than blower-door testing because it requires more time and expensive laboratory equipment. Tracer-gas testing only makes sense for scientific research, or for expensive or health-threatening problems in large buildings.

Infrared Scanners

Infrared scanners let you observe temperature differences visually. Mirrors, cooled by liquid nitrogen, liquid argon, or electricity help form the visual image. Manufacturers have reduced the cost of infrared scanners in the last few years. Energy auditors, inspectors, and technicians save time because the scanners quickly pinpoint thermal flaws in the building shell.

Buildings are usually inspected with infrared scanners from indoors because solar heat can interfere with outdoor inspections. When there's a considerable temperature difference (at least 30°F) between indoors and outdoors, the scanner shows the temperature difference of thermal weak points as colder (in winter) or warmer (in summer) compared to their surroundings.

Infrared scanners used with blower doors are a quick and effective way to inspect a building's air barrier. Cold winter air, pulled in by the blower door during winter testing, cools surfaces along the airflow path. This cold airflow makes surfaces bordering the airflow appear darkly streaked in the scanner. It's common practice to view interior surfaces, without the blower door running to locate thermal bridges, and also with the blower door running to observe air leaks.

Duct Air Leakage

Studies from throughout North America indicate that duct leakage typically wastes 10% to 30% of the heating or cooling energy purchased by the homeowner.

When ducts are located in conditioned areas, duct leakage may cause minor inefficiency and indoor temperature variations, but it isn't a major energy problem. Duct sealing yields the biggest savings when the ducts are located in an intermediate zone where duct leaks exchange air freely with outdoor air. This air exchange between ducts and

outdoor air wastes energy in two ways. First, conditioned air is lost, and second, outdoor air enters and needs to be conditioned.

Duct air leakage also pressurizes or depressurizes the home, providing a driving force for air leakage through the building shell. Operation of a leaky forced-air system increases home air leakage an average of two to five times.

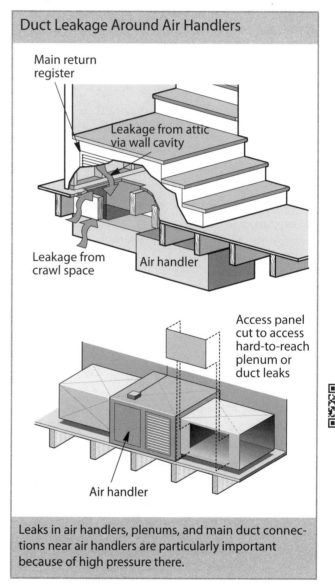

Duct Leakage Around Air Handlers

Main return register

Leakage from attic via wall cavity

Leakage from crawl space

Air handler

Access panel cut to access hard-to-reach plenum or duct leaks

Air handler

Leaks in air handlers, plenums, and main duct connections near air handlers are particularly important because of high pressure there.

Leaky supply ducts are one of the most severe energy problems commonly found in homes because the leaking supply air is 20°F to 70°F warmer than indoor air in winter and 15°F to 25°F cooler in summer. Furnaces and packaged air conditioners located on rooftops, the ground outdoors, crawl spaces, and attics are often major air-leakage sites.

Since the sheet metal, fiberglass duct board, and insulated plastic flex ducts composing supply duct systems are all effective air barriers, air leakage only occurs at joints, seams, and ruptures. Metal ducts with no sealant are often the leakiest. Fiberglass ducts and flex ducts are often installed improperly or deteriorate with age, leading to significant supply-duct leakage.

Some of the worst duct air leaks occur in the air handler and at joints between the air handler and the main supply and return air ducts, which are called plenums. The plenums are sheet-metal boxes that connect to the top, bottom, or side of the air handling unit. Plenums serve as the main outlet and inlet to the air handler. Some return plenums use plywood or fiberglass duct-board boxes. These boxes frequently leak while being exposed to the duct system's highest pressures.

Mechanical contractors often use wall, floor, and ceiling cavities as return ducts. These cavities usually have serious air leaks. If a building cavity, used as a return duct, is somehow connected to the outdoors or an intermediate zone, then a significant percentage of return air may come from outdoors.

Sealing duct leaks near combustion furnaces is very important for the safety of the residents. A large return-air leak near the furnace can suck flue gases down the chimney into the living space — a very dangerous condition. The same depressurization can draw moisture or soil gases into the home.

> See "Dirt on the blower's fan blades greatly reduces airflow over the heat exchanger. Cleaning the fan blades thoroughly is important because leftover dirt can leave the fan wheel out of balance." on page 163 for more information.

Floor and Wall Cavities as Ducts

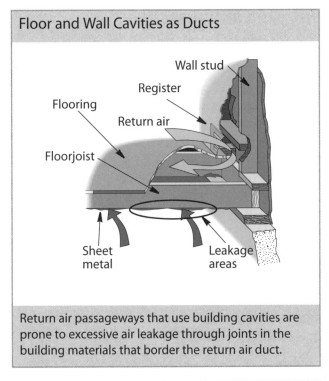

Return air passageways that use building cavities are prone to excessive air leakage through joints in the building materials that border the return air duct.

Sealing Flexduct

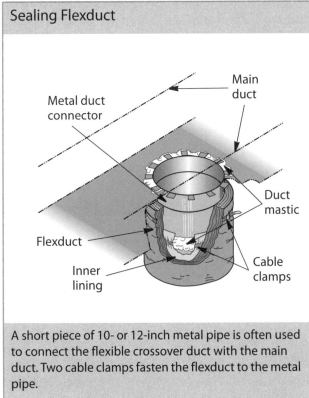

A short piece of 10- or 12-inch metal pipe is often used to connect the flexible crossover duct with the main duct. Two cable clamps fasten the flexduct to the metal pipe.

Duct-testing Strategies

One of the simplest ways to detect duct leakage is to feel with your hand for air leaking out of supply ducts while the furnace blower is on. Use a smoke generator to detect return duct leaks pulling smoke in. A trouble light, flashlight, and mirror help visually pinpoint leaks inside ducts.

The blower door is a more sophisticated tool for finding duct leaks. Air flowing from registers during a blower-door test indicates air leakage from outdoors through the ducts. With the building depressurized, use your hand or a smoke generator to detect air leakage at registers.

A gasketed pan connected to a manometer, called a pressure pan, is used to temporarily block registers and measure the blower-door-induced duct pressure at the register. With the blower depressurizing the home to 50 pascals, technicians block registers one at a time and measure the pressure created by air leaking into the duct system. Technicians normally find pressures ranging from 1 to 30 pascals. The size of pressure measurements at registers indicates the severity of air leaks or nearness to the pressure pan. Registers of newly installed ducts should read less than 0.5 pascals and existing duct registers should read less than 1 pascal after being sealed. The pressure-pan method speeds up the process of finding and sealing duct leaks. Pinpointing the precise duct leakage location still requires visual or tactile duct inspection.

An accurate way to measure duct leakage is with a duct blower, a device that resembles a blower door. The duct blower connects to the air handler or a large return air register. The duct blower pressurizes the ducts after you block all the registers. Measuring the air flowing through the duct blower's fan housing gives an accurate measurement of duct air leakage. Duct leakage measured by this method can be occurring from inside or outside the thermal boundary.

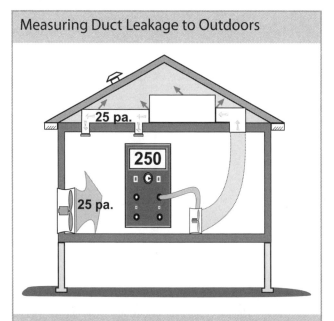

Measuring Duct Leakage to Outdoors

The house and its ducts are both pressurized to 25 pascals. When there is no pressure difference between the house and ducts, there should be no airflow between them. All the airflow going through the duct blower (250 CFM_{25}) is going outdoors. The same manometer measures both airflow and pressure differences, as required in this test.

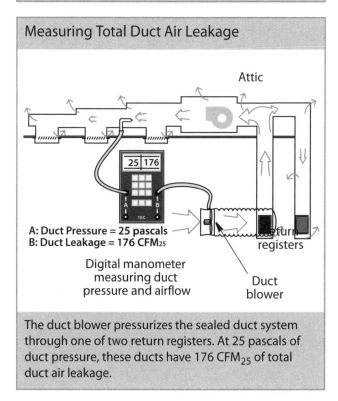

Measuring Total Duct Air Leakage

A: Duct Pressure = 25 pascals
B: Duct Leakage = 176 CFM_{25}

Digital manometer measuring duct pressure and airflow

Duct blower

Attic

return registers

The duct blower pressurizes the sealed duct system through one of two return registers. At 25 pascals of duct pressure, these ducts have 176 CFM_{25} of total duct air leakage.

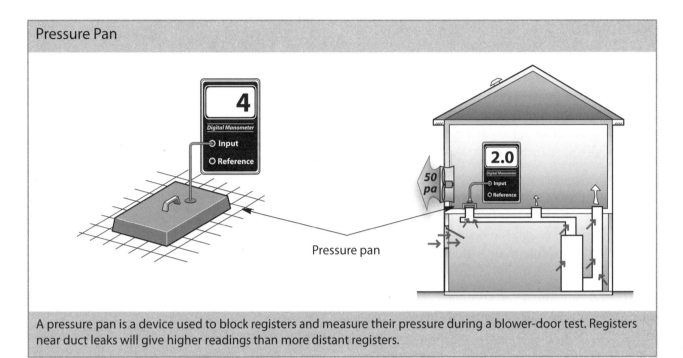

Pressure Pan

A pressure pan is a device used to block registers and measure their pressure during a blower-door test. Registers near duct leaks will give higher readings than more distant registers.

Whether the ducts are inside or outside the thermal boundary affects air-sealing priorities. Ducts outside the thermal boundary are most important to seal. The airtightness of any air barrier outside the ducts — foundation walls, roof, garage doors — will affect their leakage. A tight space, like an unvented crawl space, inhibits duct leakage. A leaky space, like an attached garage with leaky garage doors, encourages duct leakage.

To measure how much duct air leaks outdoors, technicians pressurize the home with a blower door, while pressurizing the ducts with a duct blower — usually 25 pascals positive pressure each. The airflow indicated by the duct blower's manometer represents duct leakage to the outdoors, which is directly related to the possible energy savings from duct air sealing.

Leakage ranges from less than 50 CFM_{25} for a fairly tight residential duct system, to more than 500 CFM_{25} for a very leaky duct system. The higher the leakage, the better opportunity for energy savings.

See "Duct Airflow Problems" on page 165 and "Airflow and Performance in Central Air Conditioners" on page 217 for information on measuring ducted airflow.

Construction Flaws and Air Leakage

The ideal building, from a thermal viewpoint, is a simple 6-sided box. This ideal building has no protrusions or indentations. The insulation and air barrier, located adjacent to each other, form a thermal boundary that completely surrounds the conditioned space. Shafts and horizontal building cavities are air-sealed. They don't connect to one another, nor do they connect the indoors to the outdoors.

Few buildings have these ideal characteristics. Most builders, architects, and the general public don't yet understand the benefits of a continuous air barrier at the building's thermal boundary. The building professionals who do understand air barriers use one of these construction details as the air barrier.

♦ Exterior sheathing installed vertically— supported and sealed at seams and at the perimeter of building assemblies.

♦ An interior vapor retarder or exterior water-resistive barrier that doubles as the air barrier.

♦ Drywall applied with gaskets around the perimeters of assemblies and openings indoors.

The construction flaws outlined in this section aren't in themselves a problem. They add complexity to a building's shell, but they can be air-sealed during construction. However, since builders frequently fail to seal these potential thermal flaws during construction, energy specialists attempt to seal them during building weatherization.

See "Building Construction" on page 52.

Single-family Structural Leakage Sites

Homes and small multifamily buildings have typical air-barrier flaws caused by common construction practices. Effective retrofit air-sealing targets the building's big leaks first. Air leaks are sealed at the surfaces, seams, and edges of the building cavities surrounding the conditioned space. Air leaks totally hidden inside cavities are sometimes sealed by installing densely packed fibrous insulation.

See "Single-family Home Construction" on page 53 and "Air-sealing Strategy" on page 99.

Dropped ceilings — Dropped ceilings create invisible horizontal cavities that give convection and air leakage a way to move heat around the insulation. Dropped ceilings in older homes frequently hide falling plaster and often are directly connected to the attic. The suspended ceiling's fiberboard is no air barrier and it has plenty of seams.

Soffited ceilings (narrow sections of dropped ceiling) above bathtubs, cabinets, and stairways often connect directly to unconditioned attics or unconditioned floor cavities above them. Even if the cavity created by the dropped ceiling is airtight, convecting air from the unconditioned attic moves in and out, increasing heat transfer. If the interior surface of the cavity is leaky, indoor air

leaks into interior partition walls, exterior walls, attics, or floor cavities. Outdoor air, if it is able to flow through adjacent cavities, mixes with indoor air through leaks in the dropped ceiling's interior surfaces.

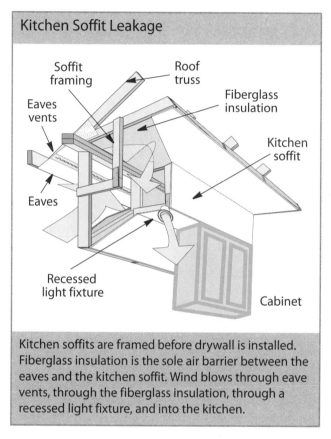

Kitchen Soffit Leakage

Kitchen soffits are framed before drywall is installed. Fiberglass insulation is the sole air barrier between the eaves and the kitchen soffit. Wind blows through eave vents, through the fiberglass insulation, through a recessed light fixture, and into the kitchen.

Cathedral Ceiling with Recessed Light

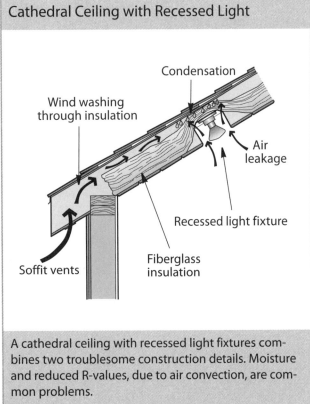

A cathedral ceiling with recessed light fixtures combines two troublesome construction details. Moisture and reduced R-values, due to air convection, are common problems.

Floor-Wall Junction

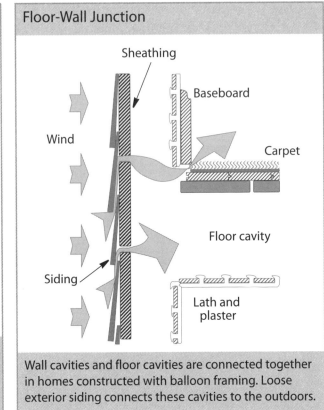

Wall cavities and floor cavities are connected together in homes constructed with balloon framing. Loose exterior siding connects these cavities to the outdoors.

Cathedral ceilings — It is difficult to avoid creating thermal flaws during original construction of cathedral ceilings, and these ceilings are difficult to fix later. Cathedral ceilings are thermally weak at their eaves because of wind washing and air intrusion into fiberglass-batt insulation's porous edges (usually terminating above the exterior wall's top plate). Infrared scanning usually shows the interior wall/ceiling junction as an obvious thermal weakness.

Indoor air leaks into the cathedral ceiling through cracks in tongue-and-groove wood ceilings, around recessed light fixtures, and through joints at beams or interior partitions. Condensation, cause by humid indoor air or outdoor air, can dampen insulation and other building materials. Ventilation to remove this moisture in many cathedral ceilings is absent or ineffective, especially if the roof has no continuous ridge vent. Scissor trusses, which are discussed in the next chapter, are an effective way to avoid these problems during original construction.

Wall cavities — Balloon framing, illustrated in the previous chapter, creates an air convection raceway around the conditioned space. Even if the shell has an effective air barrier, this convection speeds heat transfer. Most balloon-framed walls don't have bottom and top plates (although some do). Exterior or interior walls may be open to the unconditioned basement or attic.

If the balloon-framing techniques extend to outdoor porches and bay windows, air leakage may be the home's dominant energy problem. The porches and bay windows may connect the continuous balloon-framed floor, wall, and ceiling cavities directly to the outdoors through porch lights or any abundance of exterior joints.

Either balloon-framed or platform-framed walls may be open — bare of interior or exterior sheeting — behind bathtubs, behind porch roofs, and behind interior soffits. The missing air barrier provides outdoor or indoor air entry to wall cavities.

The wall's junctions to the ceiling, roof, and floor are also major air-leakage sites in most buildings, even new ones.

Floor cavities connected to outdoors —

Overhanging floors, which jut out past the supporting wall below — designed to add floor space to a second floor or to provide framing for a porch roof — may give outdoor air an entryway to the floor cavity. Again, even if the air barrier is effective, convection encourages heat transfer. If the soffit underneath the cantilevered floor is leaky, air leakage connects that floor cavity to outdoors.

The finished attic of a one-and-one-half-story home is a common case of a floor cavity connected to the outdoors. The wedge-shaped section of attic behind the second-story knee-walls is usually ventilated, or is at least fairly leaky. And the floor-joist space underneath the kneewalls is usually not sealed. These rectangular holes total dozens of square feet of opening into the floor cavity that should be inside a tight air barrier rather than connected to outdoors. Outdoor air convects through the cavity, speeding heat flow. Outdoor air also leaks indoors if the floor cavity leaks into conditioned spaces.

Roofs joining walls —
Areas where roofs join walls are a particularly tricky section of a building's thermal boundary. Porch roofs, in particular, can create a connection between indoors and outdoors through joints in the porch's ceiling or cracks around its roof perimeter. The porch's roof cavity may connect directly to the second story's floor cavity or exterior wall cavities.

Porch roof protrusion, formed by overhanging floor joists, can allow a leaky porch ceiling or soffit to feed outdoor air into the second floor's cavity. Another possibility is that the porch roof rafters were nailed to the second story wall studs before sheathing was applied. This practice connects the second floor cavity and its exterior wall to that porch roof cavity. A third possibility is that the porch was constructed after sheathing was

applied, but before siding. In this case, there is sheathing behind the porch roof. However, cracks between the sheathing planks can amount to large air leakage into wall and floor cavities.

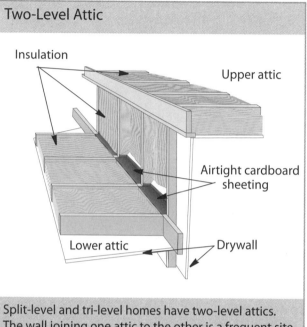

Two-Level Attic

Insulation

Upper attic

Airtight cardboard sheeting

Lower attic

Drywall

Split-level and tri-level homes have two-level attics. The wall joining one attic to the other is a frequent site of air leakage from the attics down into the wall cavity. Here, cardboard sheeting blocks the opening from the attics into the wall cavity.

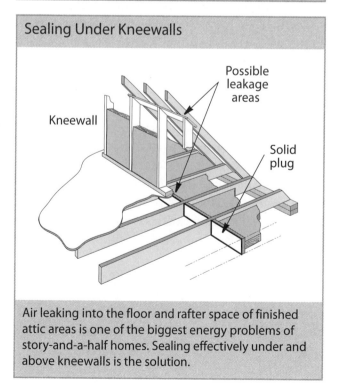

Sealing Under Kneewalls

Possible leakage areas

Kneewall

Solid plug

Air leaking into the floor and rafter space of finished attic areas is one of the biggest energy problems of story-and-a-half homes. Sealing effectively under and above kneewalls is the solution.

Porch Roof Air Leakage

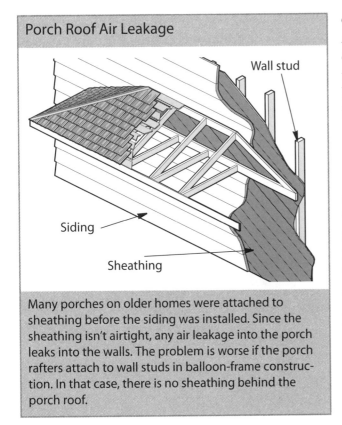

Wall stud

Siding

Sheathing

Many porches on older homes were attached to sheathing before the siding was installed. Since the sheathing isn't airtight, any air leakage into the porch leaks into the walls. The problem is worse if the porch rafters attach to wall studs in balloon-frame construction. In that case, there is no sheathing behind the porch roof.

Plumbing penetrations — You can follow air leakage pathways in many homes by following plumbing. The bathroom, in particular, creates air leakage through tubs sitting against unsheathed wall studs, gaping holes in the floor underneath bathtubs, and plumbing walls with large holes in their top and bottom plates.

The main vertical drain pipe (called the soil stack) is often enclosed in a wall or in its own framed enclosure, which transports air between the basement and attic through leaks at penetrations in the floor and ceiling. Suspended ceilings are sometimes installed to hide horizontal piping. Here again is the familiar problem of horizontal and vertical building cavities connected together, and possibly also connected to outdoors.

Attic and basement stairways — A stairway is a rectangular hole in one floor leading to another floor. On either side of the stairs are walls. Stairways leading to areas considered outside the conditioned space offer two choices for air sealing and insulation. Stairs to the attic are

often considered part of the conditioned space. An insulated and weather-stripped hatch cover or door can be installed at the top of the stairs. Or, the stairway's walls and the stairs themselves can be air sealed and insulated, isolating them from the conditioned space around them.

See "Thermal Boundary Choices for Attic Stairs" on page 65.

Recessed light fixtures — Recessed light fixtures are often a direct leak through the air barrier. These fixtures, when they contain incandescent bulbs, must be ventilated by holes in their enclosure to purge heat from the fixture.

Installed in soffits, cathedral ceilings, and suspended ceilings, recessed light fixtures connect the conditioned space to attics or roof cavities. Not only do they exchange air between conditioned spaces and building cavities, recessed light fixtures also allow warm, moist indoor air to reach cold roof decking, causing condensation.

One remedy is to replace the fixture with an airtight recessed fixture. Another remedy is to build an airtight drywall or sheet-metal box around the recessed fixture.

Chimneys — Chimneys are designed to move lots of air. Many older homes, especially large ones, have multiple fireplaces and chimneys. Any fireplace chimney can be a massive air leak if it has a leaky damper or an open one, or if the chimney has no damper. Unused central heating chimneys can also exhaust conditioned air from the home. Chimneys, especially masonry chimneys built on the home's exterior wall, can backdraft continuously providing make-up air to a depressurized home.

Inflatable pillow-like bags or flexible foam plugs are effective for sealing fireplace chimneys. The tops of unused chimneys should have airtight metal caps to prevent water from eventually damaging the home.

Airflow Through Concrete Block

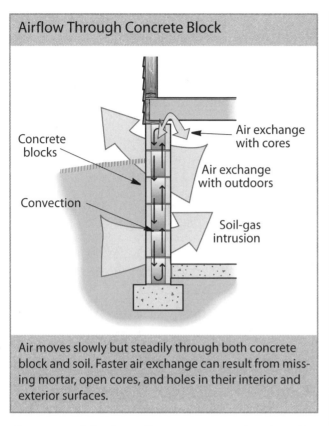

Air moves slowly but steadily through both concrete block and soil. Faster air exchange can result from missing mortar, open cores, and holes in their interior and exterior surfaces.

Air Leakage in High-Rise Residence

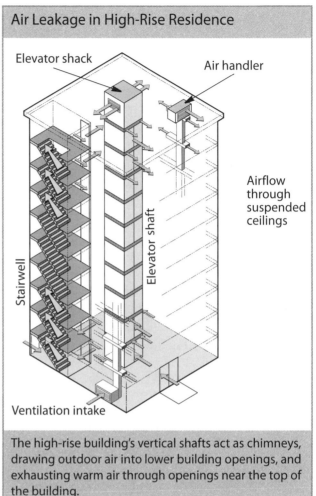

The high-rise building's vertical shafts act as chimneys, drawing outdoor air into lower building openings, and exhausting warm air through openings near the top of the building.

Concrete-block walls — Concrete-block walls are not themselves air barriers. Concrete blocks transmit air at a rate approximately 5 times greater than the Canadian standard for an air barrier. New buildings should use air-barrier systems designed to seal concrete-block walls. Since soil isn't an air barrier either, the block wall can transmit soil gases to the home.

If the cores of the blocks are open at the wall's top, the concrete block wall is a mixing chamber for outdoor and indoor air. The cores of concrete blocks should be filled with insulation. If not, air travels unimpeded throughout the wall's area, since the mortar doesn't seal spaces inside the block. Convection within the cores also speeds heat transfer through the wall.

Multifamily Buildings — Air Leakage

Multifamily buildings, like single-family buildings, vary widely in their air leakage. However, multifamily buildings tend to be tighter because they have less exterior surface area per living unit. The building exterior is often quite weather-tight to resist rain and wind, which become stronger forces at higher elevations above the ground.

Vertical shafts and horizontal cavities circulate air within them and frequently have leaks to the outdoors. The multifamily building has greater pressures than the single-family building. This greater pressure leads to greater airflow, which wastes energy, redistributes conditioned air, and affects the indoor environment throughout the building. For example, higher floors may use less heating energy because of the migration of heated air from lower floors. Pressure and airflow can overpower forced-air heating, cooling, and ventilation systems, creating energy, comfort, and indoor air quality problems.

Air seals for multifamily buildings should be structurally strong in order to resist large pressures. Stack effect and wind can send gusts howling through vertical shafts that blow lightweight patches right out of their holes.

Air-sealing materials installed between floors and through shafts of large multifamily buildings should be fire-resistant. Fire-resistant air seals prevent vertical shafts and horizontal cavities from becoming an air source or portal for a spreading fire. Among the fire-resistant materials used are non-combustible caulk, fire-resistant foam, drywall, mortar, and metal sheeting.

See "Multifamily Building Construction" on page 55.

Vertical shafts — Most larger buildings have a variety of vertical shafts for elevators, stairs, pipes, wires, and steel columns. Vertical shafts also include dumbwaiters, laundry chutes, garbage chutes, ventilation shafts, and incinerator shafts. Openings between indoor spaces and these shafts cause major air leakage. Openings at the shafts' bottoms and tops establish drafts that pull air into the shafts from penetrations linked with the building interior.

Most of these shafts should be considered as outside the conditioned space, with the obvious exceptions of interior open stairways. Many formerly open stairways have been retrofitted with fire walls and doors to prevent a fire from spreading rapidly through an open stairway.

Ceiling and floor cavities — Horizontal cavities in multifamily buildings are often several feet deep, giving air convection and intruding outdoor air a large conduit. If floor and ceiling cavities contain outdoor air, the air can enter the condi-

tioned spaces through ceiling seams, recessed light fixtures, plumbing penetrations, and other openings in ceilings and floors.

Sometimes the floor cavities are directly connected to the outdoors through seams in protruding areas like balconies, bay windows, or overhangs. The same cavities may be used for return air to large air handlers that heat, cool, and ventilate the building.

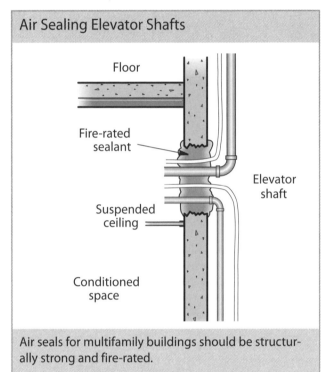

Air Sealing Elevator Shafts

Floor

Fire-rated sealant

Elevator shaft

Suspended ceiling

Conditioned space

Air seals for multifamily buildings should be structurally strong and fire-rated.

Ventilation systems — During the early part of the 20th century, many building designers and health experts believed that a building couldn't have too much ventilation. Older buildings may have natural ventilation systems or power ventilators that include shafts from the basement through the building, terminating on the roof.

The most common type of shaft links the kitchens and/or bathrooms with the outdoors. These shafts may provide minimal to excessive ventilation. Tracer-gas testing and other diagnostic methods may be necessary to discover the adequacy of existing ventilation systems.

See "ASHRAE Ventilation Standard" on page 251.

Air-Sealing Methods and Materials

The reason for presenting information about construction details in this chapter and the previous chapter is that the size, shape, and location of air leaks in buildings are determined by a building's design, its materials, and their installation. The choice of air-sealing methods and materials depends on the following.

♦ The air leak's size, shape, location, and the location's visibility to occupants.

♦ The air-sealing material's compatibility with existing materials.

♦ The pressure difference the patch or sealant has to resist.

Seal the biggest leaks first. Plug major leaks around plumbing, wiring, flues, and joints in the building sections. Joints in supply ducts are very cost-effective to seal. The most effective methods seal large air leaks at the building's surfaces and inside its cavities with permanent airtight patches. Holes in attics, under floors, and above suspended ceilings are usually accessible, but getting to them requires some tolerance for discomfort.

Air-sealing Strategy

Some technicians believe that sealing all visible cracks in the building's interior and exterior will stop air leakage. Of course, there's hope that every tube of caulk and every piece of weatherstrip will tighten a building. However, often there are so many parallel airflow paths that caulking and weatherstripping hardly matter. The building's hidden air leaks matter more than obvious cracks and small holes. The bigger leaks are found around penetrations and collections of seams where the building shell changes direction.

In climates with cold winters, it's preferable to seal air leaks from indoors, establishing the air barrier at the interior surfaces of exterior walls and ceil-

ings. Interior wallboard and plaster are good air barriers. Air inside the home is more humid during the heating season, so moisture tends to travel from indoors to outdoors. An air barrier at the interior surface of exterior walls and ceilings prevents warm, moist air from migrating into the attic and wall cavities. In warm, humid climates where central air-conditioning is used, the air barrier is more useful on the building's exterior surface.

Wood-frame walls are often leaky, but they're almost impossible to seal effectively with caulking or other materials. When a home is retrofitted with densely packed fibrous insulation, large air leakage reductions often occur, even when technicians were unsuccessful at air sealing by other methods. Densely packed insulation's fibers plug air leaks while the insulation is being blown. The blown insulation fills the cavities and stops them from being air-leakage conduits. Densely packed insulation can also plug floor cavities, porch roofs, and other inaccessible building cavities.

Sealing duct air leakage can be extremely tricky, especially in multistory buildings. Often the ducts are hidden behind walls and ceilings — inaccessible except by demolishing interior finish. In these cases, air-sealing specialists concentrate on sealing the building materials around the ducts, including them completely within the building's thermal boundary, to reclaim lost energy.

Air sealing and renovation — Energy specialists should urge homeowners, contractors, and building managers to focus on air sealing whenever they renovate. Air sealing can be highly effective when it is a planned part of renovation because technicians can use more destructive methods to access air leaks. For example, technicians can drill through the interior wall surfaces for blowing walls and through flooring to insulate a rim joist area between floors. Also, renovators can patch, repaint, and install new flooring in an airtight manner during the planned renovation.

Installing high-density wall insulation can be timed with siding replacement. Siding replacement is also a terrific opportunity to install vapor-permeable air barrier under the new siding.

Repainting presents an opportunity to caulk all cracks in wall and ceiling surfaces for airtightness and visual appeal. Recarpeting presents the opportunity to seal the floor-wall junction — which is a large air leak.

See Chapter 4 Insulation.

Air-sealing Materials and Application

A large selection of air-sealing materials is available. In general, air sealing aids in fire containment — delaying a fire from spreading between rooms or buildings. In fact, there are specific air-sealing code requirements for fire-rated assemblies. The most common types of air-sealing materials and their applications are discussed here.

Rigid panels — These materials are stronger and more damage-resistant than flexible sheeting. Rigid panels also are used to cover surface penetrations leading to hidden areas. The building codes prefer rigid panels for air sealing chases and other vertical cavities, and require rigid panels for this use in new buildings as fire stops.

Rigid materials are the best for sealing large air leaks permanently. The rigid patch resists pressure and mechanical damage better than flexible materials. Rigid patching materials include plywood, OSB, and drywall. If workers may need future access, fasten the panel with screws and a gasket or non-adhesive caulk.

Film or flexible sheeting — Polyethylene film and cross-linked polyethylene paper (Tyvek® etc.), are the most common types of flexible air barriers. These materials vary in thickness from .003 to .010 of an inch. Common polyethylene film is also a vapor barrier. Cross-linked woven polyethylene isn't a vapor barrier. It is designed as a breathable weather and air barrier that lets water vapor pass through it.

Films are the easiest air-sealing materials to cut and fasten, but they can tear or pull away from fasteners when exposed to high pressures from wind.

Hand stuffing — Technicians stuff foam rubber and fiberglass insulation into voids to reduce air movement through the void. Stuffing and filling materials are used in cracks, crevices, and cavities whose interior surfaces can't be sealed due to lack of access and too many seams. By filling the cavity's whole void, the technician retards leakage through penetrations and airflow through the cavity. Fibrous insulation and lightweight foam rubber isn't an air barrier and must be packed densely enough to provide significant resistance to air movement. Enclosing fibrous insulation in a plastic bag can provide a much more effective air barrier than the insulation by itself.

Blown insulation — Cellulose and fiberglass loose-fill insulation are good airflow resisters for inaccessible building cavities that are air-leakage pathways. Technicians can seal areas where they can't even crawl or reach by using fill tubes to blow tightly packed insulation into cavities, but this is a last resort.

See "Blown Cellulose" on page 111.

Dense-Pack Insulation to Resist Airflow

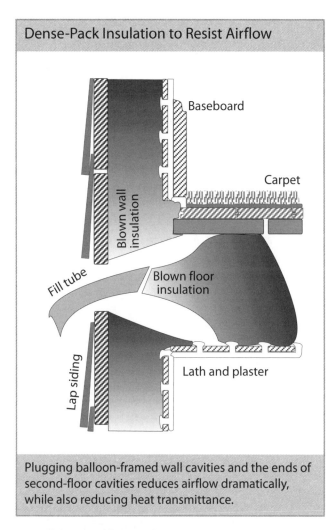

Baseboard

Carpet

Blown wall insulation

Fill tube

Blown floor insulation

Lap siding

Lath and plaster

Plugging balloon-framed wall cavities and the ends of second-floor cavities reduces airflow dramatically, while also reducing heat transmittance.

Caulking and mastic — Applied as fairly stiff liquids, these sealants fill and seal smaller and more consistent joints between building materials. Selecting a caulk involves recognition of the substrate materials (the materials bordering the joint), the gap size, weather exposure, and joint movement.

Caulking and mastic can seal narrow consistent cracks that remain relatively stationary. For sealing joints in metal, glass, and plastic — materials that move significantly with temperature — the sealant must be flexible and have good adhesion. Many glass installations use gaskets, rather than caulking because the gasket accommodates more movement while maintaining a seal.

Common caulks, like acrylic latex, siliconized acrylic latex, and butyl, are adequate for gaps less than $3/8$ inch between wood and other common building materials. Caulk works well indoors when sealing for air leakage and painting.

Joints bordering masonry, steel, and aluminum require more flexible, more durable, and more expensive caulking. Silicone and polyurethane offer superior weatherability, adhesion, and flexibility compared to less expensive caulks. When in doubt about selection, especially when replacing failed caulk, use a high-performance caulk like polyurethane or silicone. Polyurethane can be painted, but silicone can't.

Some of the largest and most predictable air leakage reductions, achievable by a sealant, come from sealing supply and return ducts. Latex duct sealant is the best material for sealing ducts. A reinforcing fiber tape (used also for patching plaster and drywall) prevents the duct sealant from cracking at the joint. Pure silicone caulking also is acceptable for sealing ducts and is easier to remove, should the air handler need replacement, for example.

Caulks are sold in a wide variety of formulations. Read the specifications carefully, especially when choosing a caulk for joints bordered by different substrates.

Sealing Ducts with Mastic

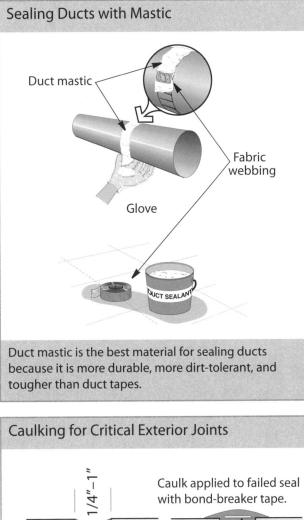

Duct mastic

Fabric webbing

Glove

Duct mastic is the best material for sealing ducts because it is more durable, more dirt-tolerant, and tougher than duct tapes.

Caulking for Critical Exterior Joints

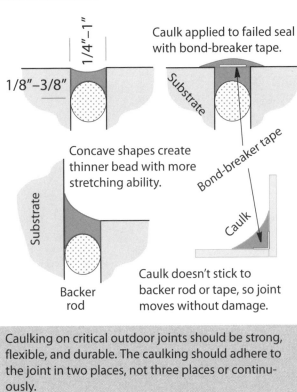

1/4"–1"

1/8"–3/8"

Caulk applied to failed seal with bond-breaker tape.

Substrate

Concave shapes create thinner bead with more stretching ability.

Bond-breaker tape

Substrate

Caulk

Backer rod

Caulk doesn't stick to backer rod or tape, so joint moves without damage.

Caulking on critical outdoor joints should be strong, flexible, and durable. The caulking should adhere to the joint in two places, not three places or continuously.

Installing caulk — Preparation and installation are just as important as selecting the right caulk. Exterior joints, designed to seal out air and water, must tolerate moisture, ultraviolet light, joint movement, and air pressure. These joints require careful preparation, including cleaning, priming, packing, and tooling.

Porous substrates like wood and masonry usually need scraping, wire-brushing, and dusting. Nonporous materials, like aluminum and steel, usually require cleaning with a solvent. Use rubbing alcohol and water for common dirt and methyl ethyl ketone or toluene for oil and grease. Priming both sides of the gap is sometimes necessary, depending on the substrate and caulking formulation.

Backing, in the form of either polyethylene-foam rod or bond-breaker tape, is advised to prevent three-sided adhesion. Three-sided adhesion may tear the caulking bead, backing, or substrate during joint movement. Tooling the caulking with a rounded spatula creates an hour-glass shape and slender profile that optimizes the bead's stretching ability.

Liquid foam — Liquid high-density polyurethane foam fills large and variable-sized cracks very effectively. This one-part high-density foam, which comes in expanding or non-expanding varieties, is superior to caulk for filling large cracks with varying width and depth. The cracks should be at least $1/4$ inch in width. This one-part foam sticks mercilessly to skin and fabrics, so wear gloves and long sleeves.

Expanding polyurethane foam also comes in a two-part formulation that sprays onto a surface rather than squirting into a crack. Two-part foam has good adhesion and structural strength; it is an ideal sealant for rough-duty perforated surfaces and irregular cracks because the foam bridges over irregularities and seals the entire surface. Low-density polyurethane foam is sprayed or injected as an air sealer although it is not as strong or as airtight as the high-density polyurethane foams (one-part and two-part).

Gaskets — A gasket is a flexible material, designed to seal a gap between two less flexible materials. Gaskets seal joints between metal and glass in window systems and serve as thermal breaks between conductive building materials. Other gaskets are designed to seal between building materials in the construction of an air barrier.

Tapes — Tapes can be effective air-sealing materials when used exactly as the manufacturer specifies. Contractor's tape is a versatile product that can seal a variety of materials. Air-barrier tape is made by the manufacturers of air-barrier paper to seal the paper at its seams. Tapes are more prone to failure than other types of air-sealing materials because their thin adhesives are prone to drying and failure from material movement.

Tapes often fail to permanently seal ducts because they may have been applied to dusty surfaces, or because their adhesives heat-dried and failed. High-quality foil tapes are available that adequately seal new metal ducts and duct board. However, even the highest quality tapes will fail from air pressure or gravity pull.

Adhesives — Adhesives are used to adhere films, thin panels, gaskets, and tape. Thin adhesives, like those used on duct tape and plastic self-adhering weatherstrip, require very clean and very smooth surfaces to adhere. Adhesives applied in thicker layers are appropriate for most rougher or textured building surfaces. Common adhesive bonds to a variety of materials. Specialized adhesives are formulated for specific purposes like gluing foam insulation to concrete.

Some caulks and sealants have sufficient adhesion to be used as adhesives. These include polyurethane foam and caulk, duct mastic, and siliconized acrylic-latex caulk.

Safety concerns — Consult the Material Safety Data Sheet (MSDS) to review the health hazards of caulk, foam, and adhesives. Use ventilation and wear an organic-vapor respirator when you install caulk, foam, or adhesive indoors.

Heat transmission is the average home's leading cause of winter heat loss. Most single-family homes lose two to three times as much energy through transmission as through air leakage. Insulation slows heat transmission through the building's floor, walls, and the ceiling or roof.

Insulation performs these thermal functions.

♦ Conserves energy by slowing heat transmission.

♦ Enhances comfort by reducing temperature variations within the conditioned space.

♦ Reduces the size of heating and cooling equipment needed by a building in direct proportion to R-value.

♦ Prevents wintertime condensation by preventing low interior surface temperatures.

Insulation may also offer these secondary benefits.

♦ Adds structural strength.

♦ Reduces noise and vibration.

♦ Impedes air leakage and water vapor transmission.

♦ Improves the building's fire resistance.

This chapter tells how insulation works, describes insulation types, and discusses other important issues relating to insulation.

Insulation Characteristics

Insulation is installed in building cavities or attached to the building shell's interior or exterior surfaces.

Insulation slows heat transmission in two important ways.

Density of Insulation Versus R-Value

Insulation's density affects its R-value, depending on the material.

1. By forcing the heat to conduct through minute connections among fibers or foam bubbles, or through a gas. Gases are generally poor heat conductors.
2. By reducing heat radiation and air convection within cavities where insulation is installed.

Insulating materials aren't as continuous or dense as other building material that are heat conductors. Insulation harbors millions of tiny air pockets within their fibers or bubbles (in plastic foam insulation). Heat transmission proceeds slowly through insulation, having to cross this myriad of slow-conducting air pockets.

Whole-Wall R-Values from Full-Scale Tests

Wall Type	W-W R
Standard 2-by-4	9.7
2-by-6 perfect installation	12.8
2-by-6 poor installation	11.0
Steel frame wall C-stud	5.6
Steel stud wall w/EPS sheathing	10.5
Structural 6-inch EPS-insulated panel	21.6
Stucco-covered straw bale	16–28
Lightweight concrete block	10–30
Insulating concrete form	26–44

These values are calculated using data from full-scale wall thermal-resistance tests performed at Oak Ridge National Laboratory. W-W R or whole-wall R-value measures R-value of the entire wall section, including framing material. The first four examples here are stud walls insulated with fiberglass batts. The last two examples include the thermal mass factor.

Insulation Thermal Performance factors

Insulation's ability to resist heat flow is measured by its R-value. "R" stands for thermal resistance. The R-value in any building assembly, created by a combination of insulation and other building materials, is affected by the following factors:

♦ Thermal bridging or thermal shorts in the assembly.

♦ Type and density of the insulation.

♦ Air leakage and convection from voids, gaps, or low insulation density.

♦ Water's presence within the assembly.

♦ Mass of the insulated assembly.

Two types of wall R-values are referenced in this book: clear-wall R and whole-wall R. Clear-wall R is the average R of the cavity between framing members. Whole-wall R is the average R-value of the wall including framing materials. See "Materials/Building Assembly R-Values" on page 278.

Steel-Stud Walls

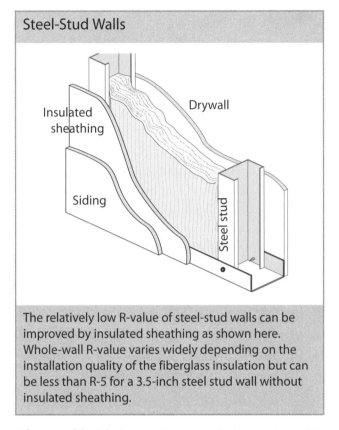

The relatively low R-value of steel-stud walls can be improved by insulated sheathing as shown here. Whole-wall R-value varies widely depending on the installation quality of the fiberglass insulation but can be less than R-5 for a 3.5-inch steel stud wall without insulated sheathing.

Thermal bridging — Thermal bridging is rapid heat transfer through thermally conductive building materials like wood, steel, and aluminum. Strategies for reducing thermal bridging include minimizing framing materials and applying insulated sheathing to building surfaces as a thermal break.

Steel framing is a challenge to insulate adequately, especially in cold climates. Steel framed assemblies have a low whole-wall R-value. Without insulated sheathing, the steel studs can cause condensation in cavities and wetting of surrounding building materials.

See "Approximate R-Values of Wall Assemblies from Guarded Hot Box Testing" on page 280.

Insulation type and density — Some common insulating materials have an ideal density, where the R-value per inch is at its maximum. Compressing fiberglass and mineral wool to a specific density increases R-values per inch; after that optimal density, compressing the insulation decreases R-value per inch. For instance, mineral wool has a maximum R-value of R-3.6 per inch at about 4 pounds per cubic foot (lb/ft^3). At lower densities, mineral wool's R-value per inch is less (R-2.7 at 1 lb/ft^3), and at greater densities is also less (R-3.2 at 6 lb/ft^3).

Fiberglass reaches its highest R-value per inch of about R-4.2 at about 3.2 lb/ft^3. Cellulose has a maximum R-value per inch of about R-3.9 at between 1 and 2 lb/ft^3.

Convection and air leakage — Air convection within insulated building cavities increases heat transmission. Air convects heat off one surface and transports the heat to the adjacent surface — between drywall and the facing of batt insulation, for example. Convecting air can also find its way through channels around the insulation's edge gaps — between batts and framing lumber, for example. Edge gaps of only 4% of the insulated surface area can produce up to a 30% loss in effective R-value for R-19 ceiling insulation.

If air from inside or outside the building leaks into an insulated cavity, the effectiveness of the insulation is further reduced. This reduction typically varies from 15–50%. Air can even flow through fibrous insulating materials such as loosely installed fiberglass. Insulation's installed density is an important issue, especially in cold climates.

Wind also affects insulation performance. Wind convects heat away from the surfaces of a building. If voids and edge gaps exist, wind can push outdoor air through building cavities around the insulation or push air through insulation. These effects increase heat transmission.

Moisture condensation — Absorbed water decreases the R-value of insulation. Water fills the insulation's air spaces and conducts heat far better than air. Water and ice also damage insulation. Wet insulation corrodes metals and supplies water to insects and microorganisms that rot organic building materials.

Insulation R-Values per Inch

Insulation Type	R/inch
Fiberglass batts, blown, board	2.6–4.2
Cellulose blown	3.2–3.6
Mineral wool batts, blown, board	2.6–4.4
Vermiculite or perlite	2.1–2.4
Expanded polystyrene (white)	3.6–4.4
Extruded polystyrene (blue/pink)	5.0
Polyisocyanurate board	5.6–7.6

R-values vary by insulation type, density, and the quality of installation.

Air leakage is the most potent moisture-carrying mechanism, which causes condensation in building cavities. Vapor diffusion is water vapor traveling through permeable materials like drywall and masonry. Low-R building materials combined with water-absorbent building materials create the largest potential moisture problems.

Thermal mass effect — The mass of building components, particularly walls, affects the heat flow through them. Especially in sunny climates with large temperature swings, massive building assemblies absorb energy surpluses from both the indoors and outdoors, slowing heat transmission.

The thermal mass factor is a multiplier to the calculated R-value, which estimates a higher R-value that accounts for the thermal mass effect. This thermal-mass factor varies, depending on the calculated R-value of the massive wall. The higher the massive wall's R-value, the greater the mass factor. The mass factor varies from around 1 to 2.6, according to tests performed at Oak Ridge National Laboratory on full-scale massive walls.

Walls insulated on the exterior perform better than walls insulated on the interior. Walls insulated on the exterior have mass factors as high as 2.6, while walls insulated on the interior have mass factors only as high as 1.5. The mass factors vary according to calculated R-value and climate. Of the six cities simulated in the testing, Phoenix benefited most from mass factors, and Minneapolis benefited least. In general, hot climates benefit more than cold climates from the mass effect.

See "Mass Factors for 6-inch Concrete Walls Insulated Interior or Exterior for Six Locations" on page 280.

Insulation Types

Insulation materials are mineral or organic materials that trap gases in small spaces. Gases conduct heat slower than solids or liquids. Mineral insulations include: mineral and glass fibers, vermiculite, and perlite. Organic insulating materials include plastic foams and cellulose.

See "Insulation Characteristics" on page 296.

Insulation comes in various product types: flexible materials, such as batts and blankets; rigid materials, such as foamboard and fiberboard; sprayed-on materials, such as polyurethane; and loose-fill insulation, such as cellulose. Batts are narrow blankets sized to fit between wall studs, floor joists, and ceiling joists.

Loose-fill insulation has particular importance to energy retrofits because of its ability to fill spaces inside closed cavities, such as walls. Sprayed insulations are often used to retrofit masonry walls, especially those with irregular surfaces.

Insulation board is popular for retrofit projects where it attaches to framing or building surfaces. Most often, this insulation board is covered by new interior or exterior finish materials, such as siding, roofing, or drywall.

Fiberglass is the most popular insulating material. Fiberglass is manufactured in batts, blankets, loose fill, and rigid boards. Cellulose insulation is also popular for residential buildings; it is manufactured as a loose-fill insulation from wood fiber or recycled paper. Plastic foam insulation is manufactured in 4-by-8-foot sheets in thicknesses from $1/4$ inch to 4 inches.

It's important to know each insulation material's temperature, toxicity, fire, and moisture characteristics. High temperatures and sunlight damage foam insulation. Fiberglass irritates skin and lungs. Cellulose absorbs water in humid conditions. Kraft paper batt facing is flammable. And foam insulation produces toxic smoke when burned.

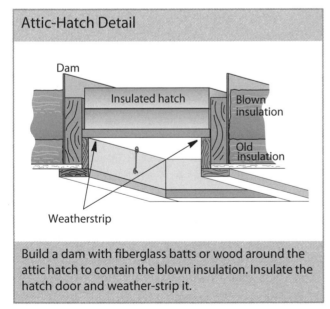

Attic-Hatch Detail

Build a dam with fiberglass batts or wood around the attic hatch to contain the blown insulation. Insulate the hatch door and weather-strip it.

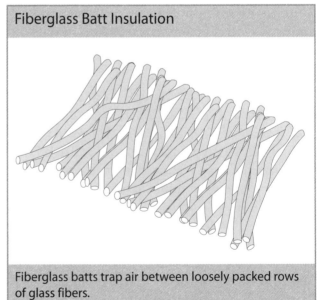

Fiberglass Batt Insulation

Fiberglass batts trap air between loosely packed rows of glass fibers.

Rim-Joist and Foundation Insulation

Foam board rim insulation sealed with liquid foam or caulk is superior to fiberglass alone because fiberglass allows convection currents and airborne moisture to pass through it.

Vinyl-faced blanket

Ground-moisture barrier

Fiberglass blankets work well to insulate dry crawl spaces if they are well-installed. Ground-moisture barriers protect insulation from moisture.

Installing Fiberglass Batts in Walls

Electrical cable compresses the batt creating an air pocket that reduces the wall's thermal resistance.

This batt was split and pulled apart to fit around the electrical cable. Fitting batts tightly on top and bottom and eliminating air pockets allows the batt to achieve its full potential R-value.

Fiberglass and Mineral Wool

Fiberglass and mineral wool are common insulations made from melting glass, rock, and slag and drawing the molten material into fibers. The fibers themselves are installed as loose-fill insulation in open cavities like attics. Or the fibers are bound together in batts, blankets, and boards by organic resins.

Fiberglass batts and blankets are the most common and widely available American insulation products. Mineral wool has a small U.S. market, but it is common in Canada and Europe.

Batts are most commonly installed in building cavities during construction. Batts fit between framing members that are spaced on 16-inch or 24-inch centers. As a retrofit, workers install batts in ceilings and floors. Blankets have a variety of special uses, such as metal-building insulation, duct and tank insulation, and sound insulation. Blankets are available in rolls 3 to 6 feet wide.

Batts and blankets are composed of glass fibers, held together by an adhesive binder. A facing of kraft paper, foil-kraft paper, or vinyl is often attached during manufacturing to facilitate fastening and as an air and moisture barrier. Fiberglass itself is noncombustible. Its binder is combustible, and common facings are combustible or even flammable. Fiberglass and mineral wool absorb very little water and are not organic.

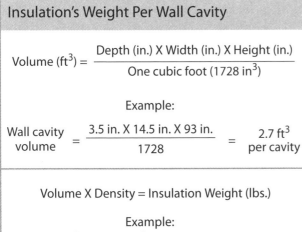

Insulation's Weight Per Wall Cavity

$$\text{Volume (ft}^3) = \frac{\text{Depth (in.) X Width (in.) X Height (in.)}}{\text{One cubic foot (1728 in}^3)}$$

Example:

$$\text{Wall cavity volume} = \frac{3.5 \text{ in. X } 14.5 \text{ in. X } 93 \text{ in.}}{1728} = 2.7 \text{ ft}^3 \text{ per cavity}$$

Volume X Density = Insulation Weight (lbs.)

Example:
2.7 ft^3 X 3.5 lbs./ft^3 = 9.5 lbs. of insulation

A full 8' wall cavity with studs 16" on center is approximately 2.7 ft^3 in volume. Cellulose should pack to 3.5 pounds per cubic foot density. Therefore, each stud cavity should contain at least 9.5 pounds of insulation.

The main advantages of fiberglass batts are low cost and availability. The R-value of fiberglass is around R-3 per inch at a density of 0.65 lb/ft^3, and R-4.3 per inch at 3.2 lb/ft^3. Batts have a lower R-value per inch than the short-fiber fiberglass loose-fill insulation because of the batt's binder, its longer fibers, and parallel fiber orientation.

Newer medium-density batts have twice the density of standard batts, and high-density batts have three times the standard density. The medium-density batts have R-3.8 per inch, and high-density batts have R-4.3 per inch. The medium-density batts achieve an R-21 at 5.5 inches thick. The high-density batts achieve an R-15 at 3.5 inches thick and R-23 at 5.5 inches thick.

The thermal performance of batts depends on proper installation. To attain maximum R-value, a batt should be in continuous contact with all the surrounding cavity surfaces where it is installed. Workers should cut batts exactly to length because if they are too long they bunch up, and if too short the spaces at top and bottom promote convection.

Rigid fibrous insulation — Rigid fiberglass or mineral wool board are used for insulating masonry, steel, and wood building components. These products are rare in American residential construction because of their high cost. Rigid fibrous board insulation excels at draining water through itself and away, making it appropriate for foundation insulation and marine applications. Rigid fibrous board insulation is also used where high operating temperatures are required, such as solar collectors or heating devices.

Blown fiberglass and mineral wool —

Blown fiberglass is manufactured in two types: chopped-up batt waste and virgin short fibers. The batt waste has longer fibers and binder, so its R-value per inch is lower than the virgin fibers, which are thinner and shorter. The shorter thinner fibers create smaller and more numerous air spaces.

Fiberglass for blowing is packed in compressed 24-to-40-pound bales. The compressed fiberglass requires a blowing machine with an agitator that tears the compressed fiberglass up into small pieces that travel fluidly through the blower hose without plugging up.

It's easy to over-fluff fiberglass in attics, leading to low densities and excessive air-permeability. Cellulose insulation is superior to fiberglass at resisting convection as attic insulation because it blows at a higher density. However, a good blowing machine can achieve an adequate density for blown fiberglass. Such a blowing machine possesses the power to tear the fiberglass bale into small pieces and to then move it in a continuous mass through the blower hose. Fiberglass in attics should be at least 0.70 lb/ft^3 density. At that attic density, expect 3 to 6 percent settling.

Blown fiberglass generally gives better R-values in closed cavities than fiberglass batts or cellulose. The density of blown fiberglass insulation should be greater than 1 lb/ft^3 in closed floor and ceiling cavities. Fiberglass blown into walls should be greater than 2.0 lb/ft^3.

To test the density of blown insulation, calculate the volume for a small area of cavity. Multiply the desired density times the volume to get the number of pounds of insulation that should blow into that area. The insulation's bag weight should be listed on its label, so you can compare the number of pounds you're installing to the weight you calculated for the test area.

Blown fiberglass is the best type of blown insulation for weaker kinds of closed cavities, such as the roofs and walls of metal-skinned mobile homes. Blown fiberglass installs inside roof and floor cavities at a lower density than cellulose blowing insulation. This lower density means that blown fiberglass puts less pressure on the ceiling, wall or underbelly, reducing the possibility of damage.

Blown mineral wool is denser than fiberglass and less likely to have low density and cold-weather air circulation within it. Mineral wool no longer has a significant share of the American insulation market.

See "Insulation Characteristics" on page 296 and "Materials/Building Assembly R-Values" on page 278.

Blown Cellulose

Blown cellulose is usually ground-up newspapers or wood waste, treated with fire retardants. This insulation blows quickly and easily, achieving a high density in walls when installed with a fill-tube. Cellulose usually contains a lot of small fibers that tend to pack into cracks and crevices of closed building cavities, retarding airflow through these cavities. This characteristic of cellulose is used extensively for air sealing older homes.

Attic insulation should achieve a density of 1.2 to 1.6 lb/ft^3. At this range of attic insulation density, expect at least 15% settling. Wall insulation should be 3.5 to 4.0 lb/ft^3 to avoid settling. Cellulose has a maximum R-value per inch of around R-4 at a density between 1 and 2 lb/ft^3. The R-value per inch falls off to about R-3.3 at 4.0 lb/ft^3 density.

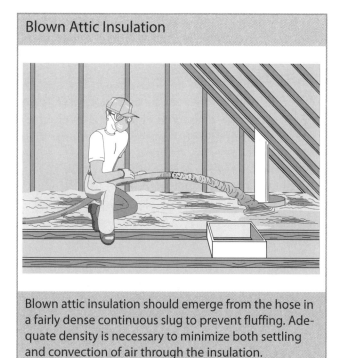

Blown Attic Insulation

Blown attic insulation should emerge from the hose in a fairly dense continuous slug to prevent fluffing. Adequate density is necessary to minimize both settling and convection of air through the insulation.

The major disadvantage of cellulose is that it absorbs much more water than fiberglass or mineral wool. In fact, cellulose can absorb up to 130% of its weight in water if subjected to constantly high relative humidity (rh) — over 90% rh. This high water absorption becomes a problem if water leaks from the outdoors because cellulose wicks water into itself and stores it. Water absorption is also a problem in coastal climates having consistently high rh.

Furthermore, water can carry fire retardants out of the cellulose. The solution of water and fire retardant reduces fire resistance and corrodes metal building materials. If insulation must touch bare metal building materials, use cellulose treated with a noncorrosive fire retardant.

Vermiculite and Perlite

Vermiculite and perlite are made by heating rock pellets until they pop, like popcorn. These light-weight pellets are gray or brown and $^3/_{16}$ inch or less in diameter.

Vermiculite and perlite are usually poured in place. Vermiculite and perlite are not likely to leave voids by damming up inside walls like blown fibrous insulations. Vermiculite and perlite work well in vertical cavities with rough surfaces and ledges that might dam blown insulation — concrete block cores, for example.

Vermiculite and perlite are sometimes mixed with cement and aggregate to produce a lightweight and less heat-conductive mortar or concrete.

Vermiculite and perlite are commonly found as attic insulation in homes built before 1950. They have R-values per inch of R-2.4 or less, and they are relatively expensive. For these reasons, they are not widely used.

Vermiculite may contain asbestos, which can be proven or disproven by a common laboratory test. Workers must not disturb asbestos unless they are licensed to handle asbestos.

Plastic Foam Panels

Rigid insulation panels have a wide variety of applications. Polyurethane and polystyrene panels (usually 4-by-8 feet) serve as interior and exterior sheathing for residential and commercial construction. Their rigidity sometimes lends structural strength to building assemblies, particularly when combined with wood sheathing. For example, polystyrene sandwiched between plywood or composite wood sheathing is used for structural wall and roof systems in energy-efficient new homes. Polyurethane installed inside doors adds to their rigidity.

Foam insulation sheathing reduces thermal bridging through structural elements like wood and steel studs, where the foam serves as a thermal break. These 4-by-8-foot panels also have many retrofit insulation uses. Foam insulation panels should be considered whenever a building undergoes interior or exterior renovation — when replacing siding for example.

When installed above the ground, plastic foam insulation must be covered with a material that resists ultraviolet radiation, mechanical damage, and moisture. Protective coverings include a variety of plastic, metal, and masonry.

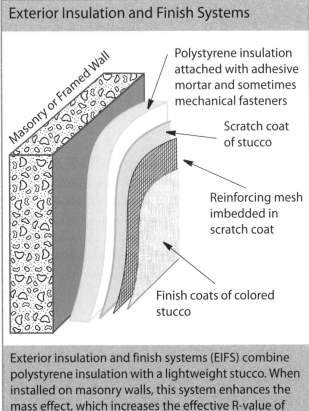

Exterior Insulation and Finish Systems

Masonry or Framed Wall

Polystyrene insulation attached with adhesive mortar and sometimes mechanical fasteners

Scratch coat of stucco

Reinforcing mesh imbedded in scratch coat

Finish coats of colored stucco

Exterior insulation and finish systems (EIFS) combine polystyrene insulation with a lightweight stucco. When installed on masonry walls, this system enhances the mass effect, which increases the effective R-value of the wall by a factor of 1.2 to 2.6, depending on climate.

When used to insulate roofs from the attic or crawl-space walls in the crawl space, foam panels may require covering by an *ignition barrier*. This ignition barrier may be wood paneling, fibrous insulation, drywall, or galvanized steel. When used on the interior of a building, facing the living space, foam panels must be covered by a thermal barrier of half-inch drywall.

Foam insulation panels are commonly used for exterior building insulation. Technicians nail urethane panels to roof assemblies and cover them with rubber membranes or other roofing materials. Plastic foam insulation is available in a variety of thicknesses with plywood, drywall, or other materials bonded to it. These products can be particularly useful in retrofitting masonry buildings.

Expanded polystyrene — Expanded polystyrene (EPS) is used to insulate roofs, walls, foundations, exterior doors, and garage doors. EPS is manufactured in many small factories throughout North America by expanding polystyrene granules in a mold. EPS comes in densities of 1.0, 1.5, and 2.0 pounds per cubic foot with R-values varying from R-3.2 to R-4.7 per inch, with higher density producing higher R-value.

Masonry coatings are also available that adhere to polystyrene insulation after it is attached to the exterior walls of a building. These stucco-like coatings, known as exterior insulation and finish systems (EIFS), are usually applied in multiple layers and contain acrylic adhesive. A fiber screening, applied with the first coat, reinforces this latex stucco. This type of exterior insulation is one of the few practical options for exterior insulation of solid masonry walls. Exterior insulation avoids disturbing the building's interior. Exterior insulation is comparatively expensive and must be carefully detailed to avoid water intrusion and mechanical damage.

Extruded polystyrene — Only a few manufacturers make extruded polystyrene (like putting cookies through a cookie press). Extruded polystyrene (XPS) is more expensive than expanded polystyrene (EPS). Extruded polystyrene has good strength, an R-value of about R-5 per inch, and excellent moisture resistance due to its smooth water-resistant surface. These qualities make XPS a good choice for underground foundation insulation.

Polyisocyanurate — Polyisocyanurate gives excellent service when space limitations are a consideration, because of its superior R-value per inch of thickness (R-6 to R-7 per inch). Polyisocyanurate is usually faced with aluminum foil or a fibrous paper, to protect its fragile surface. If one or both of its surfaces face an air space, the foil could serve as a radiant barrier, although this type of installation isn't common. Polyisocyanurate's R-value deteriorates slightly over time as its chlorofluorocarbon intercellular gas escapes and is replaced by air.

Foam Insulation: Sprayed and Injected

There are several types of foam insulation formulated for spraying and/or injecting into closed cavities. The most common types are high-density and low-density polyurethane, which are sprayed in place. During installation, polyurethane resin combines with a blowing agent, such as hydrochlorofluorocarbon gas (HCFC) or carbon dioxide (CO_2), which causes the resin to expand into a foam, encapsulating millions of tiny gas cavities.

High-density polyurethane — High-density sprayed polyurethane insulation has excellent adhesion, structural strength, air-sealing capacity, and thermal resistance. HCFC gas is the reason for polyurethane's superior R-value of R-6.0 to R-7.0 per inch. High-density polyurethane foam is sprayed on roofs, masonry, metal buildings, industrial tanks, and many manufactured products. High-density foam's initially high R-value per inch becomes less over time as air replaces the hydrocarbon gas.

Low-density polyurethane — Low-density polyurethane foam can be either sprayed or injected. Low-density polyurethane is water soluble and assumes a dry density of 0.5 to 1.0 lb/ft^3. Its R-value is between 3.7 to 4.7 per inch. Low-density urethane foam uses alternative blowing agents to HCFCs, including carbon dioxide.

Air Krete® — Air Krete® is a proprietary foam, composed of expanded Portland cement and sand. Air Krete is the only non-combustible foam in common usage.

Tripolymer — Tripolymer is a proprietary, low-expansion injectable foam installed at around 1.2 pcf at an R-value of 5.1 per inch. The material has very low flammability and smoke generation during a fire. It is widely used to insulate hollow masonry walls. It is water soluble and can be injected through a fill tube.

Urea-formaldehyde — Urea-formaldehyde was injected into walls in the 1970s and early 1980s but was discredited because of its shrinkage and formaldehyde emissions. Urea-formaldehyde is no longer available.

Facings and Barriers

This section discusses barriers and facings that work with insulation materials. The most important types of barriers are water-resistive barriers, air barriers, vapor barriers, and fire barriers.

Various facings get fastened to insulating materials during manufacturing. Fiberglass batt or blanket insulation is available with a variety of facings. Some common insulation facings are: kraft paper, aluminum foil, aluminum foil/kraft paper laminate, and white vinyl sheeting.

Facings protect the insulation's surface, provide an air barrier and/or vapor barrier, facilitate fastening, and help to hold the insulation together. All of the common facings attached to fiberglass batts are air barriers and most are vapor barriers. However, their effectiveness as an air barrier depends on nearly flawless installation. Besides being an air and vapor barrier, aluminum foil is also a radiant barrier, retarding radiant heat flow when it faces an air gap.

Most facings are combustible except aluminum foil. Kraft paper by itself or attached to other materials, such as aluminum foil or polyethylene, is flammable — meaning it burns if you light it with a match. Tar paper and some vinyl facings are also flammable.

Water-Resistive Barriers

Water-resistive barriers (WRB) stop rain water from traveling through the cladding or siding into the sheathing behind it. Early water-resistive barriers included kraft paper treated with asphalt or wax. Modern water-resistive barriers include perforated asphalt felt and woven polyolefin paper (Tyvek® and other brand names). The asphalt felt is perforated to allow water vapor out of the wall cavity. The polyolefin is perforated or has openings large enough for water vapor molecules and small enough to block liquid water and air within its weave.

Woven polyolefin house wrap, installed on the exterior of new homes, acts as a water resistive barrier. The house wrap stops rain water while letting water vapor escape from the wall assembly. House wrap may also serve as an air barrier when sealed carefully at seams. To be effective as a air barrier, the house wrap must be protected from sun and wind damage during construction. This protection includes careful fastening, seam-sealing, and timely siding application to cover the house wrap before the sun and wind damage it.

Drainage planes and rain screens — The water-resistive barrier may border very narrow space ($<1/8$ inch), called a drainage plane, where water can drain to the bottom of the wall and out. When there is a substantial, planned space between the exterior cladding and the water resistive barrier, this assembly is called a rain screen. The rain screen has a screened opening at its bottom for drainage called a weep screen.

When the rain screen is open to the outdoor pressures at the top and bottom of the wall, it is called a pressure-equalized rain screen, which reduces the pressure of wind-driven rain across the wall assembly.

Good masons install masonry wall cladding such as brick veneer, stucco, and stone veneer with pressure-equalized rain screens. The space between the sheathing and cladding should be sufficient to drain the wall allowing for mortar deposition into the space.

Air Barriers

Air barriers stop moisture-laden air from entering building cavities. Air barriers reduce both air leakage and air convection in building assemblies.

Air barriers also reduce wind-driven air intrusion around and through insulation. This air intrusion reduces the insulation's R-value when it happens.

An increasing number of energy-efficient new buildings use interior drywall or the exterior sheathing as their air barrier. Drywall and wood sheathing materials like plywood and oriented strand board are very good air barriers. Structural materials are preferable to house wrap as air barriers, because although house wrap is airtight, house wrap isn't easy to seal and isn't structurally strong. Plywood, OSB, and drywall are easier to seal effectively and strong enough to resist large wind gusts without damage.

In existing buildings, you can consider any airtight interior or exterior surface as an air barrier. Plaster and stucco are good air barriers because they are continuous and airtight. Carefully installed drywall is an air barrier. Walls in existing homes become acceptable air barriers when carefully sealed. Retrofitting an existing building requires caulk or foam around windows, doors, electric switches and receptacles, the floor/wall junction, and the wall-ceiling junction. However, the airtightness of a retrofit job that seals all the above areas is never as good as a new home designed with an air barrier and tested before the builders install the finish materials.

> See "Air Leakage Through Construction Materials" on page 77 for more information on airflow through building materials. See "Air-Sealing Methods and Materials" on page 99 for more information about creating air barriers.

Vapor Retarders and Vapor Barriers

A vapor retarder is a material that resists vapor diffusion through the building shell. A vapor barrier is a very effective vapor retarder, or a Class I vapor retarder.

During cold winter weather, large indoor-outdoor temperature differences lead to very high vapor pressure between cold, dry outdoor air, and warm, moist indoor air. The most common application of vapor barriers is on the interior surfaces of exterior walls in cold-climate buildings to prevent condensation in building assemblies.

The vapor pressure moves water vapor from outdoors toward indoors during humid summer weather while an air-conditioner is cooling and drying indoor air. Builders sometimes install vapor barriers on exterior walls in hot humid climates. Foil-faced foam sheathing works well for this purpose.

Vapor retarders are semi-permeable to water vapor and include: plywood, EPS, XPS, fiber-faced polyisocyanurate, and OSB.

Classes of Vapor Retarders

Vapor Retarder	Perms
Class I vapor retarder (vapor barrier)	<0.1
Class II vapor retarder	0.1–1.0
Class III vapor retarder	1.0–10
1 perm = 1 grain per square foot per hour per inch of Mercury pressure.	

Polyethylene sheeting and aluminum foil are the most common vapor barriers. Oil-base primers and vapor-barrier paints are vapor barriers. Insulation facings, which qualify as vapor barriers, include aluminum foil, coated kraft paper, and the vinyl used for metal building insulation and water-heater wrap.

Vapor barriers aren't necessary or even desirable in all buildings or in all climates because they can trap moisture. Buildings that are either heated or air conditioned for most of the year typically remain drier without vapor barriers. Consider the following vapor-retarder advice.

♦ Avoid using a vapor barrier unless you need one.

♦ Avoid installing vapor barriers on both sides of building assemblies.

♦ Avoid installing vapor barriers, including vinyl wall coverings, on the interior of air-conditioned buildings.

◆ Ventilate buildings according to ASHRAE standards to control humidity.

See "Air and moisture barriers" on page 248 and "Radiant barriers" on page 208.

Fire Barriers

The building codes are very focused about preventing the spread of fire within and between buildings. Fire barrier is a term with a specific meaning in the building code: A building assembly that has been tested and certified to withstand and contain a fire for a particular time period.

A thermal barrier is a material or assembly that protects the materials behind it from reaching a temperature of 250°F during a fire. One-half-inch drywall is the most commonly used thermal barrier and is rated for 15 minutes of protection. Fiberglass-faced drywall is a 1-hour thermal barrier.

An ignition barrier is a material used with foam insulation to prevent the foam from igniting. The code specifies a number of materials that can serve as ignition barriers including drywall, plywood, fibrous insulation, galvanized steel, and intumescent paint.

A fire partition is a fire barrier that prevents the spread of fire between rooms on one level of a building. A firewall is a structural fire barrier between buildings that is designed to remain standing during and after a fire. No building renovation or energy retrofit should damage or penetrate a firewall or fire partition.

Retrofitting Insulation

The biggest challenge to installing retrofit insulation is gaining access to the building cavities. Insulators gain access to building cavities by drilling holes or by removing building materials. These activities can create dust, which is a respiratory hazard for workers and customers. Insula-tors must follow DOE and EPA rules about protecting workers and customers from dust and particularly lead dust.

Like many industries where the work can be dirty, hot, and unpleasant, insulation companies often have problems with employee turnover, motivation and training. These human challenges can affect installation quality, which is essential to the insulation's performance. For this reason, it's important that energy specialists who specify, supervise, and install insulation be familiar with insulation principles, characteristics, and correct installation techniques.

Where to Insulate

Choices of where to insulate depend on existing insulation, retrofit insulation cost, the air barrier's location (if present), access, and a number of site-specific, practical considerations.

People often wonder whether it's more important to insulate the walls or the ceiling. The answer depends on the existing R-value in each area: the lowest R-value choice is favored if there isn't money budgeted for both. Cost is also a major factor. If installing insulation in the ceiling costs $0.75 per square foot and wall insulation costs $1.50 per square foot, then this cost difference must be factored in with the pre-retrofit and post-retrofit R-values to calculate which retrofit is most cost-effective.

See "Defining the Thermal Boundary" on page 62, "Heat Transmission" on page 59, and "Calculating Heating Load or Input Rating" on page 71.

Where to Install Insulation

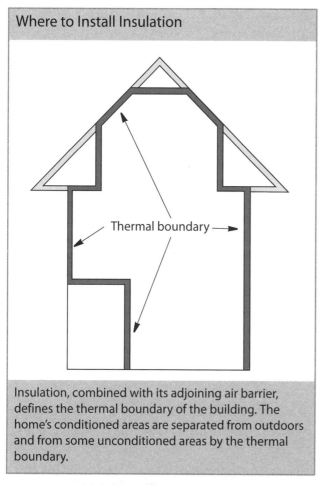

Insulation, combined with its adjoining air barrier, defines the thermal boundary of the building. The home's conditioned areas are separated from outdoors and from some unconditioned areas by the thermal boundary.

Baffles at Eaves

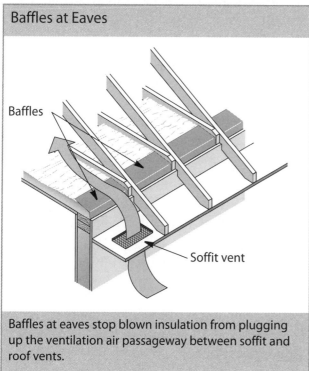

Baffles at eaves stop blown insulation from plugging up the ventilation air passageway between soffit and roof vents.

Fill Tubes for Blowing Fibrous Insulation

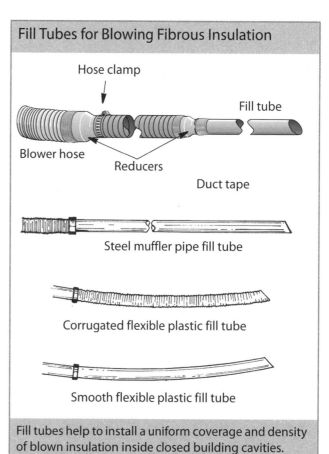

Fill tubes help to install a uniform coverage and density of blown insulation inside closed building cavities.

Blowing Loose-fill Insulation

Insulation blowing machines break up the bundled insulation and capture the insulation in a sealed chamber at the bottom of the machine's hopper. Air pressure, created by a compressor or blower, blows the insulation out of this chamber and through the hose.

There are two common types of insulation blowing machines: electric-powered and gasoline-engine-powered. Most professional insulation companies use gas-powered machines, which blow insulation more quickly and hold more bags in their hoppers compared to electric-powered machines.

Smaller electric machines can also do a good job of blowing insulation. Blowing fiberglass challenges some smaller electric machines, however, and blowing can be very slow if the machine isn't designed for blowing fiberglass, or if the machine is in poor repair.

Blowing Dense-Packed Insulation into Walls

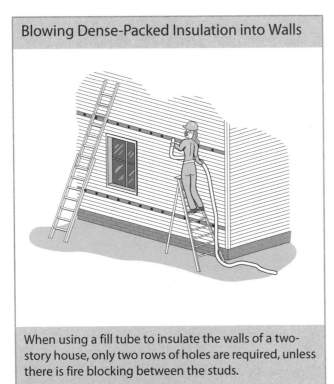

When using a fill tube to insulate the walls of a two-story house, only two rows of holes are required, unless there is fire blocking between the studs.

Insulation Settling in Walls

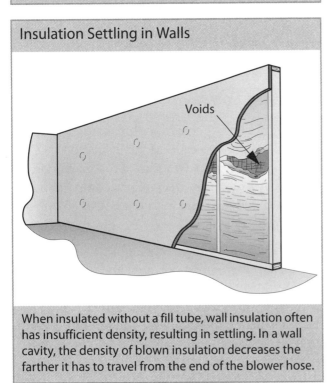

Voids

When insulated without a fill tube, wall insulation often has insufficient density, resulting in settling. In a wall cavity, the density of blown insulation decreases the farther it has to travel from the end of the blower hose.

Controls on the blowing machine adjust the air pressure and insulation delivery rate. The operator varies air pressure and delivery rate depending on whether workers are insulating an open or closed cavity. If blowing into an open attic, the material delivery rate should be high to install insulation at close to its settled density and to avoid fluffing the insulation. In closed cavities, the machine's delivery rate and pressure should fill the cavity quickly and steadily without bulging interior or exterior surfaces and without clogging the hose.

Hoses and fittings are important to efficient insulation blowing. Connections between blower hoses, connections, and fill tubes should be as airtight as possible to avoid weakening the pressure needed to blow the insulation.

Filling closed building cavities involves reducing the diameter of the hose from 3 or 4 inches down to $1^1/_2$ or 2 inches. It's wise to make these hose reductions gradually. Use metal or rubber reducers to reduce the hose's diameter an inch at a time to avoid plugging the hose. Use the biggest tube diameter that fits comfortably into the cavity. Common diameters are $1^1/_2$, 2, and $2^1/_2$ inches.

In closed cavities (walls, floors, ceilings closed on both sides), blown insulation won't reliably travel more than 18 inches. If you assume the insulation will travel farther, you may create voids and low-density insulation. A fill-tube, inserted into the farthest corners of the cavity, fills the cavity evenly and completely.

A flexible fill tube is considerably more rigid than standard blower hose. The rigidity allows the technician to push the fill tube 6 feet or more into a closed cavity without bending or crimping. But the tube is still flexible enough to bend around corners and snake past obstacles.

Use rigid fill tubes for filling roofs and floor cavities, which are inaccessible from indoors. Metal electrical conduit, copper drain pipe, steel muffler pipe, or polyvinylchloride (PVC) pipe all work well. Technicians prefer 2-inch and sometimes $2^1/_2$-inch diameters for the rigid fill tube. You can stiffen standard blower hose by taping a piece of PVC pipe or electrical conduit to the flexible hose. This trick sometimes eliminates the need for a separate fill tube.

Insulation blowing safety — Remember that blowing insulation creates dust that can irritate or damage lungs. Always wear a respirator when you are blowing insulation. Installers should protect skin with gloves, long sleeves, and coveralls, and protect eyes with goggles or safety glasses.

Static electricity sometimes builds up in fill tubes and shocks installers. Fill tubes made of PVC pipe are most likely to shock. Fill tubes made of lightweight electrical conduit, muffler pipe, and copper drain pipe are more static-free than PVC.

Grounding the blower hose or spraying small amounts of water into the hopper of the blowing machine reduces static electricity.

Sprayed and Injected Insulation

Sprayed insulation is a logical choice for insulating rough surfaces or for places where insulation batts or boards are difficult to fasten. Sprayed insulations are often applied to wall cavities of new homes before the interior finish. Injected insulation is squirted into closed building cavities through holes. When properly installed, sprayed and injected insulation prevents convection in walls, and seals out air better than batts or loose fill.

Sprayed and injected foam insulation —

Sprayed and injected foam insulation requires special equipment and training. Liquid foam is difficult to install and requires careful mixing, equipment maintenance, and installer training. Successful foam installation is temperature sensitive. Installers can create large bubbles that lead to poor performance when the sprayed mixture is imperfect or they spray the foam in too thick a layer.

Polyurethane is available in a variety of formulations that install at 0.5 to 3.0 pounds per cubic foot density. Installers spray all densities of polyurethane, but they only inject the lower densities (<1 lb/cf). Installers inject low-density polyurethane foam through multiple holes in each cavity using a nozzle that penetrates the wall.

Installers inject Tripolymer foam and Air-Krete® foam into wall cavities with a fill tube, which the installers clean during installation with water or compressed air.

Some liquid foam formulations release toxic gases. Consult the product's material safety data sheet (MSDS) for instructions about personal protective equipment before installing foam.

See "Foam Insulation: Sprayed and Injected" on page 113.

Sprayed cellulose and fiberglass — Installers spray cellulose and fiberglass insulation using an insulation blower, equipped with a water pump, hose, and spray nozzle. The fibrous insulation travels through a blower hose and meets a sprayed water-glue mixture that dampens the insulation and propels it toward its intended target. The water-glue mixture binds the loose fill cellulose or fiberglass insulation together and adheres it to the surface.

Installers spray fiberglass and cellulose on metal buildings and masonry walls in dry locations. Sprayed cellulose and fiberglass offer good fire resistance and noise reduction. However, sprayed cellulose and fiberglass are porous to airflow.

The dried sprayed insulation has a fragile surface, so it shouldn't be installed in places where it may be bumped or abraded. In humid locations, fibrous sprayed insulation — particularly cellulose — may absorb large quantities of water, reducing thermal resistance and weakening the insulation's adhesion.

Installers spray fibrous insulation into wall cavities in new homes. To avoid dampness and moisture problems in wall cavities, the builder allows the sprayed fiberglass or cellulose adequate time and plentiful ventilation for drying before covering it.

A proprietary variation of sprayed fibrous insulation is the blow-in batt system, or BIBS, which uses less water during installation. Installers blow the BIBS fiberglass insulation into open wall cavities, where a stretched net is stapled to the wall studs and holds the insulation in place.

Basement and Crawl Space Insulation

Before installing foundation insulation, make sure the foundation is well-drained and dry. If necessary, improve the drainage. Always install a plastic ground-moisture barrier on dirt crawl-space floors. Basement insulation can create moisture problems or worsen existing ones. If stubborn moisture problems exist, don't insulate the basement or crawl space.

See "Preventing Moisture Problems" on page 248 for more information.

There may be a substantial difference in energy savings between insulating the inside or the outside of a basement or crawl space. Exterior insulation creates a greater thermal mass factor than interior insulation. Exterior insulation also keeps the masonry wall warmer, preventing moisture condensation and possible freezing within the wall. Basement or crawl space insulation is cost-effective in cold climates but may not be cost-effective in warm climates, because the ground is often cooler than indoor air during the summer. Buildings in warm climates may actually lose heat to the basement or crawl space, saving air-conditioning costs.

Exterior insulation — Exterior insulation is usually the more expensive method because of the special coverings and flashing details necessary to protect foam insulation from ultraviolet light, moisture, mechanical damage, and insects. Excavation is expensive too, especially in cold climates where installing the insulation 2 to 8 feet below grade is recommended. Installers glue the foam insulation to the exterior surface or hold it to the foundation wall with the backfilled dirt or gravel. During installation, foundation waterproofing should be inspected and improved if

necessary. Exterior foam foundation insulation must be carefully designed in regions where termites and carpenter ants are a problem.

Interior insulation — Interior foundation insulation is easier to install and may be more cost-effective in cold climates than exterior insulation because of its lower cost. Interior insulation prevents the home's escaping heat from heating the foundation wall, possibly allowing frozen soil to exert more pressure on the foundation. Therefore, interior insulation should be avoided when the soil near the foundation is prone to frost heaving.

Two methods of interior foundation insulation are common. A fiberglass-batt insulated stud wall is the most common. However, specialty foam board, with fastening strips embedded in its surface, is quicker and more effective than building a stud wall. The insulation's fastening strips are wood, usually $3/4$-inch thick, and are embedded in a matching groove, so that the strip is flush with the surface of the foam insulation. The foam insulation is installed using a foam-compatible adhesive and mechanical fasteners. The vertical wood strips aid in fastening the insulation to the masonry foundation wall, using gunpowder-driven masonry nails or special masonry screws that require no anchors. Their 16- or 24-inch spacing accommodates drywall that fastens to these strips with 1-inch screws.

Crawl space walls in absolutely dry locations can be insulated on their interior surface with fiberglass batts or blankets attached to the sill plate. Blankets 4 or 5 feet wide are superior to narrower batts because there are fewer seams in the finished installation. The rim joist space on top of the sill plate is insulated separately using batts that fit snugly between the rim joists. This practice risks moisture problems. Building inspectors may require termite inspection area at the building's sill plate.

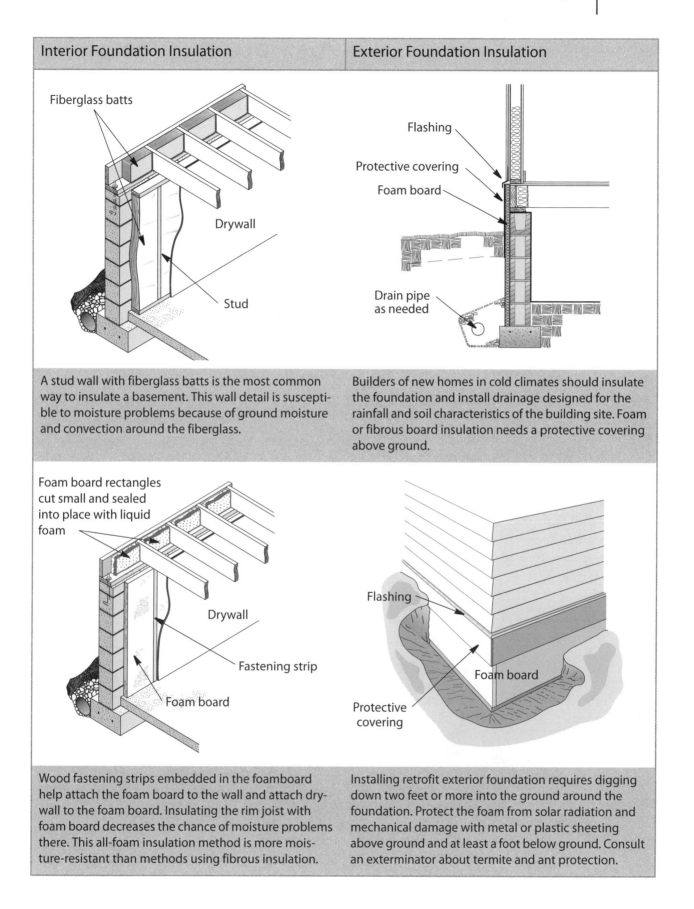

Interior Foundation Insulation

Fiberglass batts

Drywall

Stud

A stud wall with fiberglass batts is the most common way to insulate a basement. This wall detail is susceptible to moisture problems because of ground moisture and convection around the fiberglass.

Foam board rectangles cut small and sealed into place with liquid foam

Drywall

Fastening strip

Foam board

Wood fastening strips embedded in the foamboard help attach the foam board to the wall and attach drywall to the foam board. Insulating the rim joist with foam board decreases the chance of moisture problems there. This all-foam insulation method is more moisture-resistant than methods using fibrous insulation.

Exterior Foundation Insulation

Flashing

Protective covering

Foam board

Drain pipe as needed

Builders of new homes in cold climates should insulate the foundation and install drainage designed for the rainfall and soil characteristics of the building site. Foam or fibrous board insulation needs a protective covering above ground.

Flashing

Foam board

Protective covering

Installing retrofit exterior foundation requires digging down two feet or more into the ground around the foundation. Protect the foam from solar radiation and mechanical damage with metal or plastic sheeting above ground and at least a foot below ground. Consult an exterminator about termite and ant protection.

Floor Insulation

Floor insulation is installed under the lowest floor where the crawl space or basement isn't heated. Like basement and crawl space insulation, floor insulation is cold-climate energy measure.

Fiberglass batts — R-19 or greater — are used for floor insulation. Unfaced batts are best for avoiding moisture problems in the insulation because they don't have a vapor barrier to trap moisture coming either from the ground or from the indoors.

The unfaced batts are held in place with lath, stapled twine, or wire insulation supports. Careful installers install the batts so they touch the underside of the floor. A gap between the insulation and the floor allows air convection to decrease the insulation's thermal performance, so avoid that.

Batts with perforated facing surrounding the fiberglass prevents most release of fibers and protects the batt from minor mechanical damage. This type of batt is ideal for unheated basements that are used for storage or work areas.

In cold climates, floor insulation is often less expensive and more effective than foundation insulation when the crawl space or basement isn't heated or cooled. Trained installers air-seal the floor before they insulate it.

Insulation in New Construction

Builders use many innovative products and methods for integrating high thermal resistance into new homes and multifamily buildings. Improved framing techniques substantially improve the overall thermal resistance of modern wood-framed buildings. Structural insulated panels and high-R, high-mass walls minimize heating and cooling energy, using different materials and skills. These less common techniques produce buildings that are very airtight and require mechanical ventilation for acceptable indoor-air quality.

Improved Framing

Framing wood or steel has a low thermal resistance compared to insulation. Minimizing framing lumber allows insulation to occupy a greater percentage of a building shell's surface area and volume.

The simplest improved framing methods include these features.

♦ Framing 24 inches on center rather than 16 inches on center.

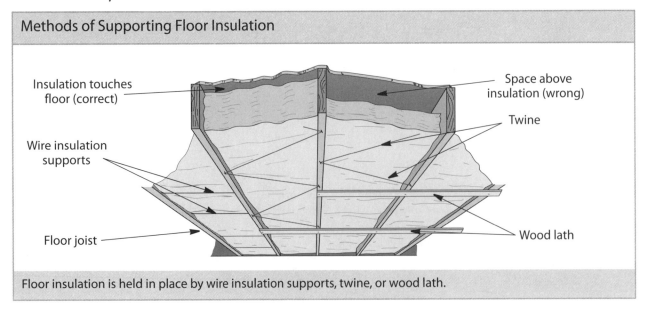

Methods of Supporting Floor Insulation

Insulation touches floor (correct)

Space above insulation (wrong)

Twine

Wire insulation supports

Floor joist

Wood lath

Floor insulation is held in place by wire insulation supports, twine, or wood lath.

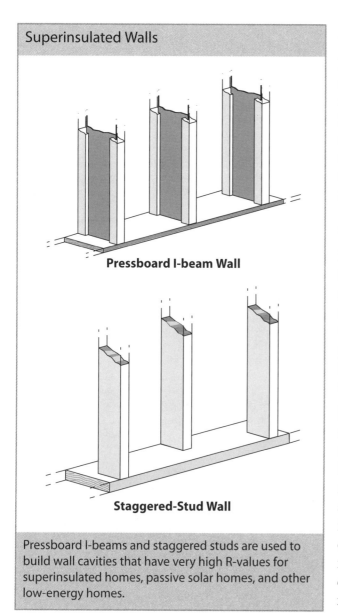

Superinsulated Walls

Pressboard I-beam Wall

Staggered-Stud Wall

Pressboard I-beams and staggered studs are used to build wall cavities that have very high R-values for superinsulated homes, passive solar homes, and other low-energy homes.

Structural Insulated Panels (SIPS)

Interlocking foam-filled building panels have created some very energy-efficient homes by eliminating most thermal bridging and air convection in the walls and ceilings. Wall and roof panels are available in thicknesses of 4-inch, 6-inch, 8-inch, and 12-inch. Structural insulated panels require special skills, techniques, and tools not common to other construction methods.

High-mass Wall Systems

High-mass wall systems have good thermal resistance and very little thermal bridging, air leakage, or convection. Insulated concrete forms have revolutionized insulation for concrete foundation walls and above-grade concrete walls. Many proprietary insulated concrete forms are available. Insulated concrete forms have thermal mass factors ranging from 1.2 to 2.0.

Lightweight concrete blocks with insulated cores are becoming more common as builders understand the mass effect. Insulation for cores includes vermiculite, polystyrene beads, Tripolymer foam, Air Krete, and foam inserts. Aerated, autoclaved concrete blocks show particular promise for high-R, high-mass walls and can have effective R-values as high as R-17 in some climates. Other lightweight concrete blocks use sawdust, polystyrene beads, and other insulating materials as part of their aggregate.

Tilt-up concrete-wall construction is also a viable option in some regions. Builders pour concrete in a horizontal slab on top of insulating material and then tilt the wall up into place. Some tilt-up walls employ modular foam insulation systems designed specifically for tilt-up construction.

See "Mass Factors for 6-inch Concrete Walls Insulated Interior or Exterior for Six Locations" on page 280 for more information on effective R-values of high-mass walls.

♦ Using more insulation and less framing in corners, interior wall intersections, and headers.

♦ Using insulated sheathing under siding.

Superinsulation framing techniques create deeper insulation layers. The most common of these framing techniques uses staggered studs or specialized composite framing members.

Raised-heel trusses allow installers to blow the full depth of attic insulation out above the exterior-wall plate. Scissor trusses frame sloped ceilings without the thermal-resistance and moisture problems common to the narrower cavities.

Energy-Efficient Trusses for New Homes

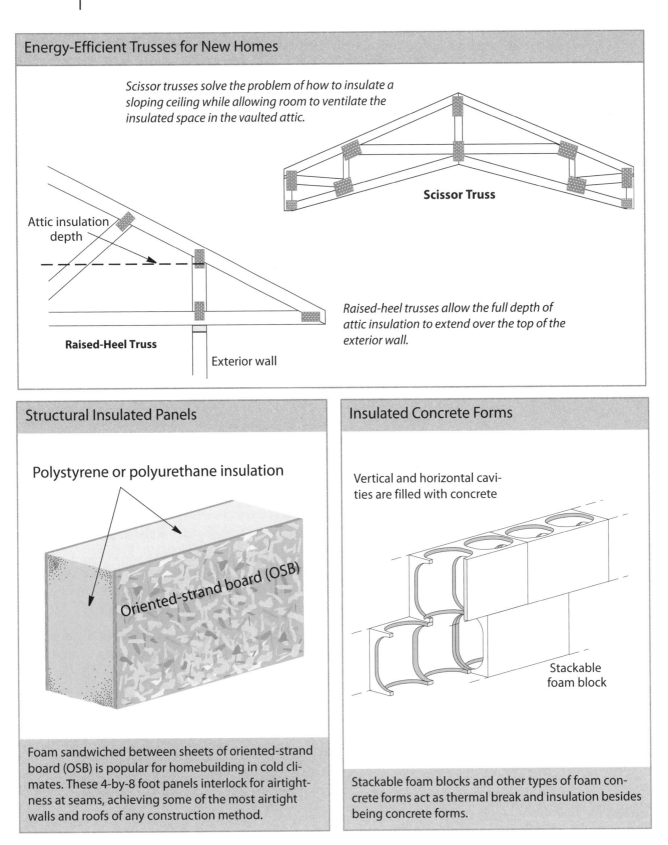

Scissor trusses solve the problem of how to insulate a sloping ceiling while allowing room to ventilate the insulated space in the vaulted attic.

Scissor Truss

Attic insulation depth

Raised-heel trusses allow the full depth of attic insulation to extend over the top of the exterior wall.

Raised-Heel Truss

Exterior wall

Structural Insulated Panels

Polystyrene or polyurethane insulation

Oriented-strand board (OSB)

Foam sandwiched between sheets of oriented-strand board (OSB) is popular for homebuilding in cold climates. These 4-by-8 foot panels interlock for airtightness at seams, achieving some of the most airtight walls and roofs of any construction method.

Insulated Concrete Forms

Vertical and horizontal cavities are filled with concrete

Stackable foam block

Stackable foam blocks and other types of foam concrete forms act as thermal break and insulation besides being concrete forms.

Windows are a significant source of transmission heat loss in cold climates and a significant source of solar heat gain in temperate or hot climates. Windows exist to provide natural light, ventilation, and a view to the outdoors. These functions make windows a formidable energy problem. The difficulty is limiting heat loss and gain while preserving natural light and view.

Window energy conservation measures may be expensive too; retrofit or replacement window costs commonly range from $5 to $50 per square foot of window area. Any window upgrade for energy efficiency must be designed to significantly reduce thermal transmittance, reduce solar transmittance, or reduce both. Air leakage reduction is usually a secondary benefit producing only small energy savings, unless the window has large visible air leaks.

Doors generally have a thermal transmittance higher than walls, but lower than windows. Their surface area is small and replacement cost is high, so door replacement is not usually considered a cost-effective energy conservation measure. However, doors can be a significant air leakage problem due to faulty operation or poor air seals.

This chapter outlines the most important energy characteristics of windows and doors, identifies concerns unique to older windows when improving energy performance, and defines the challenging terminology associated with window ratings. Windows and doors are also referred to as *fenestration*.

For a discussion of comfort and windows, see "Fenestration" on page 61.

Window Characteristics

Windows are composed of the following parts:

♦ Glass Assembly — One or more glass panes with spacers and gaskets, if needed.

♦ Sash — Frames the glass assembly. Sashes are either movable for ventilation, or fixed.

♦ Frame — Surrounds the sash and is the window part attached to the building.

♦ Rough Opening — Structural framing around the window to which the window frame is attached.

Energy Characteristics of Typical Window Glass Options

Glazing Assembly	U-factor	R-value	SHGC	VT
Single glass	1.1	0.9	0.87	0.90
Standard insulated glass	0.50	2.0	0.76	0.81
High-SHGC, low-e insulated glass	0.30	3.3	0.74	0.76
Medium-SHGC, low-e insulated glass	0.26	3.8	0.58	0.78
Low-SHGC, low-e insulated glass	0.29	3.4	0.35	0.65
Triple glazed 2 low-e insulated coatings	0.12	8.3	0.50	0.65

Understanding state-of-the-art window features is difficult because heat flow through windows is complicated, and the terminology is unnecessarily complex. Conduction, convection, and radiation are all important window heat-flow mechanisms. The high conductivity of glass is tolerated because of its other useful and unusual qualities, including the fact that glass absorbs most infrared radiation while transmitting most solar radiation.

Thermal transmittance (U-factor) and solar heat gain are the most important energy considerations for windows. The window's air leakage, optical characteristics, frame material, and type of glass assembly also enter into window selection.

Radiation, convection, and infiltration from windows reduce indoor comfort. Radiation is more complex with windows than with other building components.

Window Research, Testing, and Rating

Four organizations serve as gate keepers for information about window thermal and structural characteristics. Their roles are briefly explained here to facilitate further information gathering.

National Fenestration Rating Council (NFRC): A public/private collaborative agency created to establish standardized window testing and rating. The Council simulates window performance with computers, then verifies that simulation with laboratory testing. NFRC labels are applied to windows made by member manufacturers listing thermal transmittance (U-factor), solar transmittance, visible transmittance, and air leakage. Condensation resistance is also being listed on some window models.

American Society of Heating, Refrigerating and Air Conditioning Engineers (ASHRAE): A professional society providing the theoretical framework for calculating heat flows through windows. ASHRAE's Handbook of the Fundamentals is the most common technical reference about window heat flows.

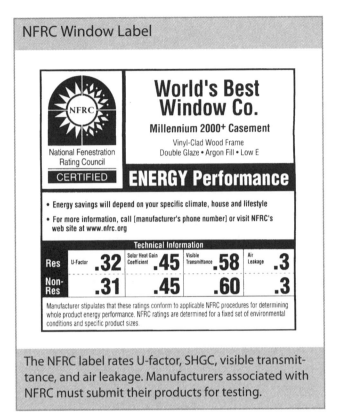

NFRC Window Label

The NFRC label rates U-factor, SHGC, visible transmittance, and air leakage. Manufacturers associated with NFRC must submit their products for testing.

Lawrence Berkeley Laboratory (LBL): North America's most authoritative and prolific window research facility. LBL excels at computer simulation of window heat flows. LBL researches and develops new window technologies and distributes information about windows.

American Society for Testing and Materials (ASTM): Develops testing methodology for all types of building systems. Testing methods are specified by building codes and rating organizations like the NFRC. Windows are tested under ASTM standards for air leakage, water leakage, and structural strength.

Thermal Transmittance (U-factor)

The window industry describes and rates its products by U-factor or thermal transmittance. The U-factor includes heat transfer by conduction, convection, and radiation through the window assembly.

The U-factor is the reciprocal or inverse of R-value (U=1/R). U-factor is measured in units of BTUs per square foot per hour per degree Fahrenheit. As U-factor decreases, heat flow decreases. Lower U-factors are more energy-conserving than higher U-factors.

The U-factors of windows are rated using an area-weighted average of different sections of the window that have distinctly different U-factors: the frame, the edge of the glass area (a 2.5-inch band), and the central area of the glass.

Solar and Optical Characteristics

Solar heat gain shares importance with thermal transmittance as a primary window energy characteristic. Solar heat gain through windows can account for up to 40% of the total heat removed by an air conditioner. There are three common factors used to measure solar heat gain, and you are likely to encounter any of them. Each of these factors is a ratio and has no unit of measurement. Therefore, each factor may be expressed as a decimal number between 0 and 1.0 or as a percentage.

Solar Heat Gain Coefficient (SHGC): The ratio of solar heat passing through the glass to solar heat falling on the glass at a 90° angle. Includes radiant heat transmitted, and also the solar heat absorbed and re-radiated indoors. Single pane glass has a SHGC of 0.87.

Shading Coefficient (SC): Compares the solar transmittance of a glass assembly—with its interior and exterior shading devices—to that of single-pane glass, which has a shading coefficient of one. The shading coefficient is always less than one and approximately 1.15 times greater than the SHGC of the glass assembly being considered.

Generally, buildings in hot, sunny climates should employ window glass with SHGC of less than 0.50. South-facing windows used for passive solar heating need a SHGC of 0.70 or more.

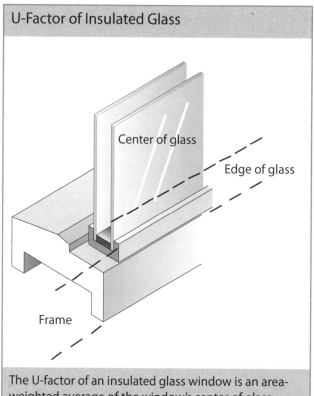

U-Factor of Insulated Glass

Center of glass

Edge of glass

Frame

The U-factor of an insulated glass window is an area-weighted average of the window's center of glass, edge of glass, and window frame.

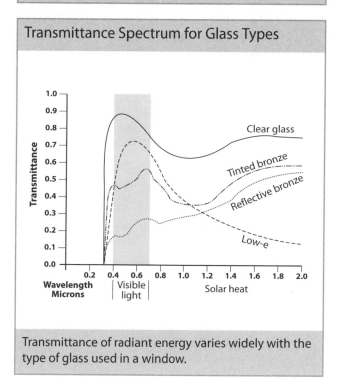

Transmittance Spectrum for Glass Types

Clear glass

Tinted bronze

Reflective bronze

Low-e

Transmittance

Wavelength Microns — Visible light — Solar heat

Transmittance of radiant energy varies widely with the type of glass used in a window.

Heat Gain Through Insulated Glass

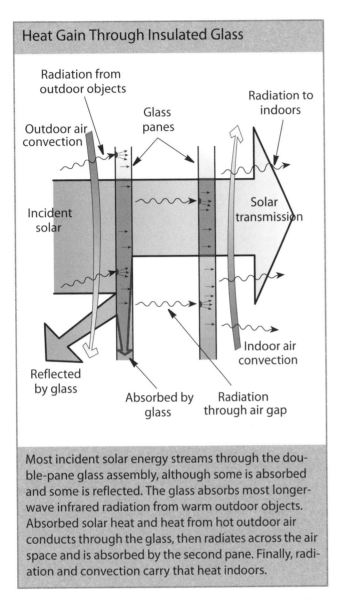

Most incident solar energy streams through the double-pane glass assembly, although some is absorbed and some is reflected. The glass absorbs most longer-wave infrared radiation from warm outdoor objects. Absorbed solar heat and heat from hot outdoor air conducts through the glass, then radiates across the air space and is absorbed by the second pane. Finally, radiation and convection carry that heat indoors.

Visible transmittance (VT): Measures how much visible light is admitted by the window glass. Visible transmittance is important because one of the window's main functions is to admit visible light. Reflective coatings and tints—some of which cut visible transmittance to 30%—aren't acceptable in many residential applications. A window's ultraviolet-blocking ability is important to consumers concerned about the destructive effect of ultraviolet radiation on furnishings.

Each glass type has a solar transmission chart showing the transmission percentage of solar heat and visible light. These transmission charts can be used as a guide for comparison shopping when selecting a window's optical characteristics.

See "Radiation" on page 35 for a better understanding of radiation.

Air Leakage

Window air leakage is usually a less important energy consideration than thermal transmittance during the heating season or solar heat gain during the cooling season. Exceptions to this generalization include old windows that are falling apart from neglect, or windows that are poorly installed and have significant air leakage around frame edges.

Windows and doors are less an air leakage problem than most people believe. Most existing buildings have hidden air leaks in the floor, ceiling, and wall cavities that overshadow the leaks around windows and doors. In fact, sometimes you can tightly seal all the window and door openings with duct tape and plastic without noticing a significant change in leakiness as measured by the blower door. In contrast, sealing the supply and return registers of a warm air heating system or insulating walls with dense-pack cellulose will often reduce air leakage by 15% to 30% in older homes.

Residential windows are leak-tested at a pressure roughly equaling a 25 mile-per-hour (m.p.h.) wind under controlled laboratory conditions. This test is known as ASTM E283. The test results are expressed in cubic feet per minute (CFM) of air leakage for each linear foot of crack between the sash and frame of the window. New windows vary from 0.1 CFM/linear foot (lf) to 0.5 CFM/lf. This is a very airtight range of numbers. Window air leakage is often dominated not by frame/sash cracks, but by installation flaws between the window frame and rough opening.

The NFRC air-leakage rating lists CFM-per-square-foot of window surface area. This ranges from about 1.0 all the way down to 0.06. Window air leakage varies according to the window vent's operation. Casement and awning windows have compression weatherstripping, which is more effective than the felt weatherstripping of sliding windows. Therefore, casement and awning windows have lower air leakage rates than sliding windows.

Window air leakage may help to maintain good indoor air quality in relatively airtight buildings. In fact, some manufacturers make windows with adjustable vents designed to remain permanently open.

Resistance to Condensation

Water condensation on glass leads to the deterioration of the window and the opening surrounding the window. Condensation is one of the most common consumer complaints about windows. Condensation is mainly a winter problem, which gets worse as the outdoor temperature drops. The NFRC now has a window rating of condensation resistance with a scale of 1 to 100.

Mitigating condensation problems requires raising the thermal resistance of the window's interior surface or reducing the home's relative humidity, and may require both. Consumers sometimes think that condensation is leaking from the outdoors or is caused by the window's age. When the new windows they buy to fix the problem also sweat, consumers are often disappointed.

The energy specialist should know how much thermal resistance needs to increase and/or how much relative humidity needs to decrease in order to solve a window condensation problem. The chart shown here plots the outdoor temperature and relative humidity where condensation will happen for window R-values from R-1 to R-4 (U = 1.0 to 0.25).

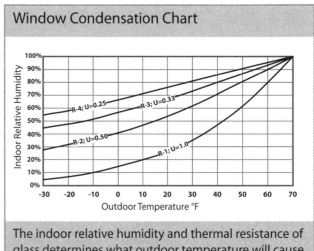

Window Condensation Chart

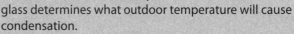

The indoor relative humidity and thermal resistance of glass determines what outdoor temperature will cause condensation.

Low-e Insulated Glass Unit (IGU)

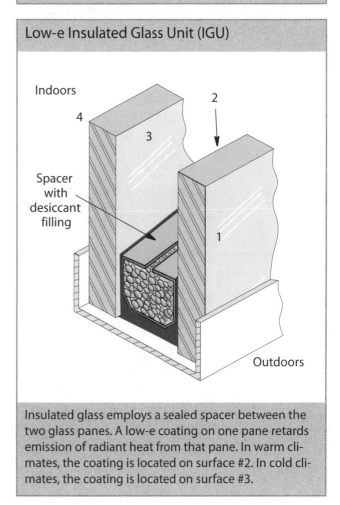

Insulated glass employs a sealed spacer between the two glass panes. A low-e coating on one pane retards emission of radiant heat from that pane. In warm climates, the coating is located on surface #2. In cold climates, the coating is located on surface #3.

Window Structure

Frame and sash materials are important for thermal performance, maintenance, and life-span. Wood frames have good thermal performance and life-span, but maintenance is an ongoing chore. Metal frames have excellent life-span and freedom from maintenance, but poor thermal performance. Vinyl frames have excellent thermal performance and freedom from maintenance. However, with the many manufacturers making vinyl windows, their formulation and resistance to heat and ultraviolet radiation differs widely.

Sash Operation and Frame Type

Windows have two types of sash: fixed sash and movable sash. Movable sashes either slide within their frames or open inwardly or outwardly on hinges. Vertical sliding windows include double-hung windows, where both sashes move, and single-hung, where only the bottom sash moves. Horizontal sliders usually feature only one sliding sash with one fixed sash. Sliding windows are usually less expensive than hinged windows.

Horizontally hinged windows are called hopper or awning windows. Vertically hinged windows are called casement windows. Hinged windows generally offer better ventilation and seal more tightly than sliding windows. Casement windows can be planned to project outward to catch wind, enhancing natural ventilation.

Aluminum-frame windows have been thermally improved by splitting their frames in half and then joining them back together with an insulating gasket called a thermal break. However, aluminum remains the most conductive frame and is prone to condensation problems in winter months.

Wood-frame window manufacturers have improved exterior maintenance by covering the frame's exterior with metal cladding. Metal clad wood windows are popular for custom new homes.

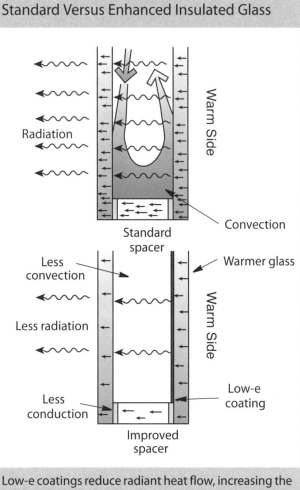

Standard Versus Enhanced Insulated Glass

Radiation
Warm Side
Convection
Standard spacer

Less convection
Warmer glass
Less radiation
Warm Side
Less conduction
Low-e coating
Improved spacer

Low-e coatings reduce radiant heat flow, increasing the temperature of the warm-side glass pane. This temperature increase reduces conduction through the glass. Improved spacers reduce conduction heat flow. Heavier gases like argon reduce convection between the glass panes.

New fiberglass-frame windows are energy efficient, strong, and low-maintenance. Fiberglass is stronger than vinyl and expands and contracts less with temperature change than aluminum or vinyl. Fiberglass comes with baked-on finishes or can be painted. Some window frames combine fiberglass with a wood interior frame. The best fiberglass windows have foam-insulated frames and sashes.

Vinyl-frame windows are the best-selling window type. Low cost and freedom from maintenance are key features accounting for vinyl windows' popularity. Vinyl windows are made by many manufacturers and vary in the quality of their vinyl formulation and assembly. Expectations of life span vary because of differences in stability and ultraviolet resistance.

Glass Characteristics and Assemblies

Energy-efficient windows use three strategies to improve the R-value of glass: multiple panes, gas fillings, and special coatings. The very best windows combine two or more of these strategies.

A wide variety of window glass assemblies is available, featuring from one to four glazing layers. Some advanced windows use flexible plastic inner glazings. The glass or plastic glazing often have a low-e coating on one side to retard the radiant heat flow. Low-e coatings are also designed to regulate solar heat gain. Low-e glass is available in high solar transmittance, medium, and low solar transmittance for use in various climates. It is now common for window customers to specify different low-e specifications for walls facing different cardinal directions.

Low-e coatings are used on only one surface of one glass pane in the standard double-pane or insulated glass window. The coating faces the air space between the panes on either the inner or the outer pane to protect the coating from damage. For heating-dominated climates, the coating is on the inner pane. In cooling-dominated climates, the coating is on the outer pane. This is because the low-e coating works best as an emittance retarder. The glass absorbs radiant heat, then the low-e coating resists the heat's reradiation.

The low-e coatings come in two varieties: soft coats and hard coats. The soft coats, made of silver, are the most effective at reflecting heat, but they are fragile and must be enclosed in a double-pane window assembly shortly after the glass is manufactured. The hard coats (of tin-oxide) reflect less heat than the soft coats. But the hard coats are more resistant to mechanical damage.

The pyrolytic, or heat-treated hard coat low-e glass is sometimes used in single-glass storm windows. The low-e surface is more difficult to clean than a standard glass surface. Therefore it's best to install the low-e surface toward a relatively airtight air space.

Gases like carbon dioxide and argon, which have a higher R-value than air, fill the space between panes in some high-tech windows. Carbon dioxide and argon weigh more than air. The greater weight of these gases reduces convection between the glass panes, compared with air.

Insulated glass manufacturers now use improved edge spacers for assembling the insulated glass units. The conventional spacers are made of aluminum, which conducts heat very rapidly. New spacers, made from dense foam plastic or plastic-steel composite materials, reduce the heat loss through the edge of the insulated glass.

Options for Window and Door Improvements

Window treatments including: repairs, retrofits, weatherstripping, storm windows, and window coverings should be considered before a deciding to replace windows. Window upgrades may be a sensitive issue for older structures in the following circumstances.

♦ Home has a traditional appearance

♦ Home is designated as a historic landmark

♦ Home is located a within zoned historic district

Window improvement, of any kind, is of interest to property owners, lenders, Realtors, appraisers, regulating agencies, non-profit organizations, insurance companies, the window replacement industry, and the preservation trades. These entities may be interested in more than thermal performance and ventilation. Cost benefits, durability, egress, lead-based paint mitigation, privacy, noise control, dust control, ultraviolet light control, personal comfort, water leakage, environmental issues, and historic sensitivity also receive a lot of attention.

Many property owners just have very strong opinions about what happens with their windows. Not many other building components evoke the discussion and interest that windows do.

These issues around windows seem to be amplified by the number of window openings, the frequency in which property owners operate their windows, and the windows' prominence as architectural features. For all these reasons, window energy performance improvements must be balanced with other concerns.

Window Repairs and Weatherstripping

Repairing windows (and doors), perhaps even restoring them to near original condition, is a growing specialty in the preservation trades. Weatherstripping and wood repair technology have greatly advanced over decades. There are a wide range of new materials and skill levels required to apply the materials. Entire books and web sites are now dedicated to window repair and restoration. Energy professionals who evaluate traditional homes should understand the basics of this growing field.

Because this topic of windows is so complex, explaining all the options and procedures available to stabilize and weatherstrip windows is beyond the scope of this book. Energy auditors should know that window repair and renovation are possible in most cases, and that decisions to replace rather than repair should depend on wisely reasoned choices.

For some understanding of the wide selection of weatherstrips available, general guidance follows:

Silicone products are far more durable than vinyl products, and they remain flexible at much lower temperatures. For amusement on your day off, put a rubberized vinyl product in your freezer and see what happens.

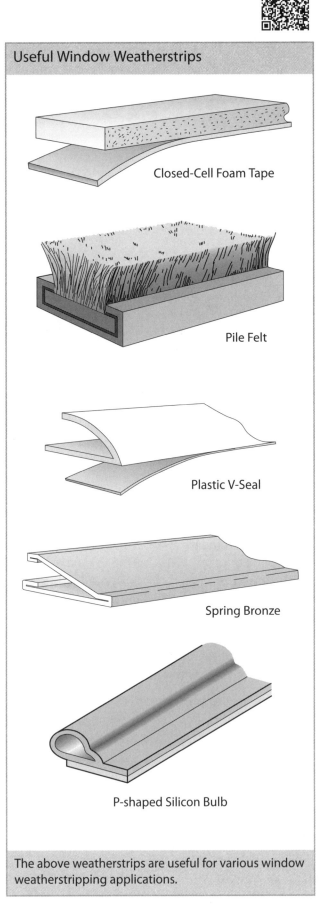

Useful Window Weatherstrips

Closed-Cell Foam Tape

Pile Felt

Plastic V-Seal

Spring Bronze

P-shaped Silicon Bulb

The above weatherstrips are useful for various window weatherstripping applications.

Vinyl or polypropylene V-shaped leaf seals, particularly those available from chain-store construction suppliers, tend to be very thin-gauge and are prone to buckling in many applications. Seek vendors that offer a thicker-gauge product.

Self-adhesive weatherstrip that adheres to a surface without fasteners requires immaculate surface preparation, but still may tend to peel off after a season or two.

Pile type weatherstrips are effective within tight tolerances, but they may wear past those tolerances over time. Foam weatherstrips are inexpensive, locally available, and relatively easy to apply; but they tend to degrade quickly from weather and sun exposure.

The preferred, and most durable weatherstrip mounting method for silicone and polypropylene weatherstrips is within a kerf, cut by a router with a slotting bit. This type of product is relatively inexpensive, conforms well to irregular surfaces (especially silicone), and can be mounted unobtrusively. However the kerf-installed weatherstrips are not generally available locally, and installing them requires skill and time.

Spring bronze and zinc products, available in a variety of shapes and sizes, are traditional and are very durable, if installed correctly. Spring-metal strips are also among the most expensive of all weatherstripping options. Spring metal also may not seal as well against irregular surfaces as silicone products.

Weatherstrips, overall, may be installed in various combinations and locations to achieve optimal energy performance and sash operation. No one product or mounting location is sure to work on all windows.

Selecting New Windows

There are a variety of energy selection criteria for new windows, depending on climate and the building owner's maintenance and specification requirements.

Window selection criteria depend on a number of factors including: climate coldness (in heating degree days [HDD]), its sunniness (both winter and summer), the window's orientation, and the light, ventilation, and heat it's expected to provide.

U-factor is the most important criterion for cold climates. Don't replace windows in northern climates without making a significant reduction in U-factor. U-factors for windows range from 1 to about 0.18. A U-factor of 0.35 is often given as a maximum for cold climates, but lower is better to minimize heat transmission and window condensation.

In the warmest U.S. climates, windows should have window shading coefficients of less than 0.25, a figure that includes exterior and interior shading devices. An SHGC of 0.4 or less for the window glass would be a good start toward achieving the 0.25 shading coefficient.

Low-e double-pane glass returns its investment in all but the very hottest U.S. climates. The exterior pane's interior surface is the best place for the low-e coating for cooling-dominated climates. In heating-dominated climates, the low-e coating should be on the exterior surface of the interior pane.

Buildings in cold climates should have a U-factor of less than 0.35. If solar heating from south-facing glass is part of a building's heating strategy, select glass with at least 0.7 SHGC, which requires insulated glass with a high-transmittance low-e coating. West-facing glass and east-facing glass should have a SGHC of less than 0.30 in hot climates when a building is air conditioned.

Installing Block-Frame and Fastening-Fin Windows

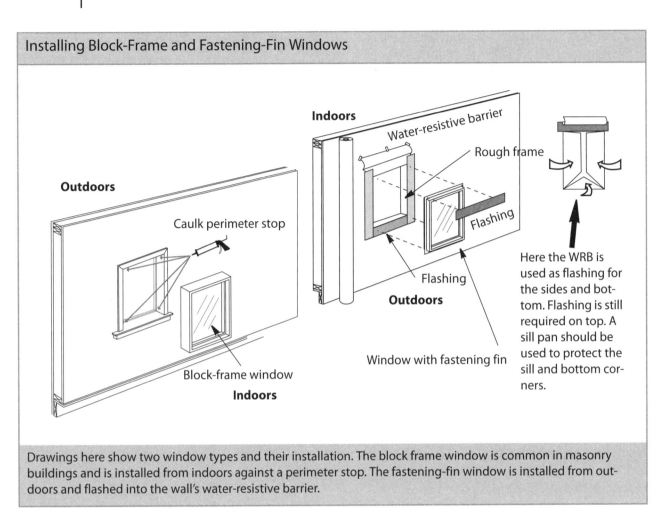

Outdoors

Caulk perimeter stop

Block-frame window

Indoors

Indoors

Water-resistive barrier

Rough frame

Flashing

Flashing

Outdoors

Window with fastening fin

Here the WRB is used as flashing for the sides and bottom. Flashing is still required on top. A sill pan should be used to protect the sill and bottom corners.

Drawings here show two window types and their installation. The block frame window is common in masonry buildings and is installed from indoors against a perimeter stop. The fastening-fin window is installed from outdoors and flashed into the wall's water-resistive barrier.

Window Replacement

Replacing windows generally has a long payback period, or a small return on investment. However, if a building is well insulated and the heating and air conditioning system is efficient, window replacement may be the logical next step to making the building more energy efficient.

The most important consideration for window replacement is sizing the windows correctly. This may involve removing casing or drilling holes in the window frame to locate the rough opening's boundaries. The installer gives the window supplier either the rough opening size or the window-frame size, depending on the method of installation.

Installation options — There are three common options for installing new windows:

1. Installing the custom-sized window inside the existing window frame. This is often done when replacing double-hung windows with vinyl or aluminum windows.
2. Installing a custom-sized window in the existing rough opening. Most window replacements use this option.
3. Installing a standard-sized window in a re-sized rough opening is the most expensive option, because it may involve installing a new header (beam) above the new window opening, as well as disturbing siding and interior finish.

Installing a new window in the old window frame is the cheapest but often the least satisfactory option. If the window is worn out, its frame is probably fairly worn too. Using the old window frame, while cheaper, should only be used when the existing frame has a beautiful interior finish and an exterior finish that will hold paint.

Using the existing rough opening gives a much more original-looking appearance than using the old window frame and facilitates better air sealing. Installing the new window in the existing rough opening requires considerably more labor than installing the new window in the existing window frame but considerably less than building a new rough opening. Resizing the rough opening, especially enlarging it, approximately doubles the labor cost over using the existing rough opening.

Rough openings are typically $1^1/_2$ to 2 inches larger than the window frame. Since air leakage around new window sashes is quite low, leakage around the frame should be low too. Many window installers use non-expanding one-part polyurethane foam for filling the gap between window frame and rough opening. In some cases, expanding foam can warp a window or door frame.

Durability issues — The modern approach to window replacement is to provide a low-maintenance window exterior. Vinyl, metal, or fiberglass qualify as low-maintenance materials.

Replacing the window often involves repairing water damage to the siding or interior finish around the rough opening. Protecting the new window from moisture damage outdoors involves flashing the window's top with metal flashing that goes under the siding and over the window casing. The remainder of the window perimeter should be sealed with caulking chosen according to the materials bordering the joint.

See "Caulking and mastic" on page 101.

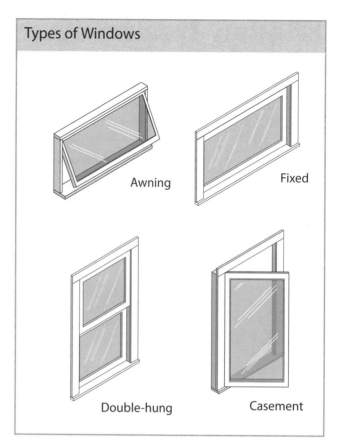

Types of Windows

Awning

Fixed

Double-hung

Casement

Exemplary window replacement — Energy specialists should encourage customers to consider replacing both windows and siding to facilitate the installation of insulated sheathing under the new siding. Thermal bridging in wall assemblies is one of the main challenges to making existing frame buildings more comfortable and energy efficient. Windows have large areas of thermal bridging surrounding their perimeters—typically 4 to 12 inches from the window frame. Replacing the old thermally inefficient windows, therefore, solves only part of the thermal-resistance problem.

Another reason to replace windows and siding at the same time is to facilitate the integration of window flashing with the wall's water-resistive barrier. Many replacement windows are installed inadequately, creating water and air leaks. Properly integrating new window flashing with the home's existing water-resistive barrier without removing the siding can be difficult.

Window Treatments

A variety of treatments are used to enhance the winter and summer thermal performance of windows. Window treatments for cold weather are generally different than window treatments for hot weather. Cold weather window treatments reduce the window's U-factor and include storm windows and window insulation. Hot weather improvements reduce solar heat gain and include sun screens, awnings, window films, interior shades and blinds, and shutters.

See "Shading Windows" on page 205 for an extensive discussion of window shading.

Exterior Storm Windows

Exterior storm windows are the primary window's first defense against the weather. They are important to preserving old buildings and their windows.

If the exterior storm window is too airtight, the storm can trap moist air from indoors and contribute to fogging and icing of the exterior window. The fogging or icing can be reduced or eliminated by tightening the primary window.

Exterior storm windows appear very similar to one another making it difficult to categorize these windows by quality. The following is a list of features which are important in selecting an exterior metal storm window:

♦ Frame should be sturdy—sashes should not have a tendency to fall apart or deform during installation.

♦ The gasket that seals the glass should surround the edge of the glass and not just wedge the glass into place on the sides of the sash.

♦ Interlock at the meeting rail should be tightly sealed.

♦ The frame should have weep holes on the bottom to let water out of the window assembly.

♦ The window should fit well; installation work should be good quality.

♦ Sashes should be removable from indoors.

♦ Plastic parts should be confined to those parts that need to slide against the aluminum. Other parts should be metal.

Exterior storm windows with plastic frames and sashes are available, but not yet popular. Plastic must have the ability to withstand the extremes of temperature and ultraviolet sunlight.

Wood-framed storm/screen combination units are increasingly popular with period home enthusiasts. Well-designed and constructed wooden storm windows still require occasional painting, but have the advantage of blending well with the architecture.

Interior Storm Windows

Interior storm windows are designed with an effective perimeter air seal to prevent the warm, moist, indoor air from depositing condensation on the cool primary window during the winter.

Many interior storm windows have flexible or rigid plastic glazing that gives them a slightly higher R-value than glass interior storms.

It's important to look closely at the frames, sashes, and seals of the interior storm window assembly to estimate how long the window will last. Be skeptical about magnetic tape and other components that depend on adhesives as their sole means of attachment to the existing window frame.

Installing an inexpensive metal primary window at the interior side of the exterior primary window is a popular treatment for creating double glazing in hotels and apartment buildings. Mobile homes also use the strategy of having a secondary operable window inside the exterior primary window.

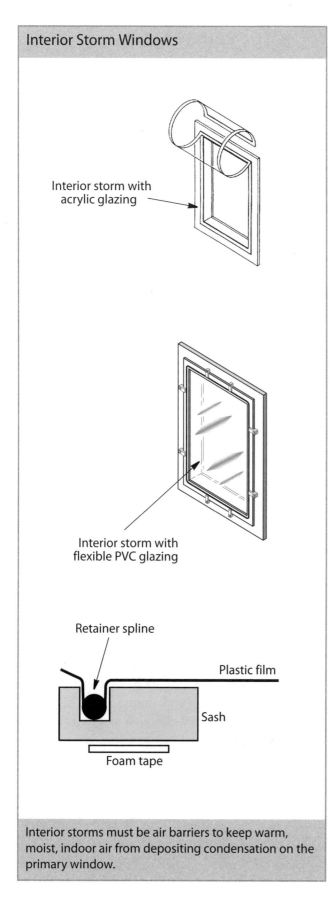

Interior Storm Windows

Interior storm with acrylic glazing

Interior storm with flexible PVC glazing

Retainer spline

Plastic film

Sash

Foam tape

Interior storms must be air barriers to keep warm, moist, indoor air from depositing condensation on the primary window.

Double Window System

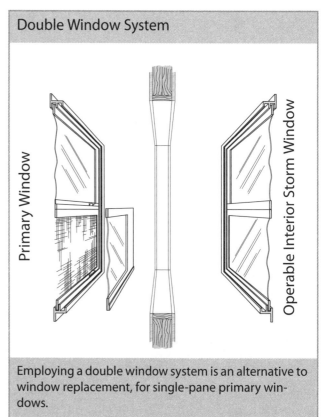

Primary Window

Operable Interior Storm Window

Employing a double window system is an alternative to window replacement, for single-pane primary windows.

Insulating Shades and Draperies

Insulating shades and draperies are very effective for insulating windows and improving comfort indoors. They are expensive and require many years to return the investment, but they cost considerably less per square foot than a new window. Insulation for the building shell and storm windows should take priority over insulating window coverings.

If your home is well-insulated and the windows present a comfort problem in cold weather, window insulation will improve your comfort and save energy. The shades, draperies, or shutters are more effective if they are airtight, because they create a dead air space between themselves and the glass, and because the airtight seal prevents warm, moist indoor air from depositing condensation on the glass.

Doors

Besides being a home's barrier against the weather, exterior doors let people and their possessions enter and leave. They must keep intruders out. Doors are used for ventilation and cooling during warm weather. Like windows, doors have energy problems relating to their function as portals.

Replacing a door just for the energy benefit would be at the low end of the energy-conservation measures list because the door's surface area is small, and its replacement cost is high. When replacing an exterior door for any reason, it pays to consider its thermal features.

Door Components

Almost all doors in buildings have similar components. The door frame, like a window frame, houses the door and attaches it to the building. Hinges mount the door to its frame and allow it to swing. The door closes against its door stop. The threshold, at the door frame's bottom, helps seal out air and dust. The lockset, consisting of door knobs and a latching system, latches the door in a closed position. The latch inserts into a strike plate, attached to the door frame.

Door Types

Solid wood doors are still the most common exterior door type for residential buildings. Solid-core wood doors are made of high-quality lumber or are particle board cores dressed with thin wood veneers. Solid-core wood doors have an R-value of around 2.5 (U=0.40). Wood panel doors, with decorative recessed areas, have a slightly lower R-value of around 1.75 (U=0.57).

In the old days, carpenters would install a door frame and then hang the door. Today, exterior doors are sold as pre-hung units with the frame, stop, hinges, threshold, and door packaged together ready to install into the rough opening.

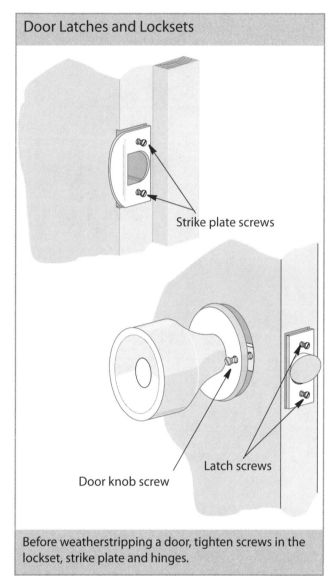

Door Latches and Locksets

Strike plate screws

Latch screws

Door knob screw

Before weatherstripping a door, tighten screws in the lockset, strike plate and hinges.

Most modern residential doors are insulated with polyurethane or polyisocyanurate foam insulation. The insulation core is surrounded by a wood frame and sheeted with a steel or fiberglass veneer. Insulated panel doors have R-values of between R-5 and R-7 (U=0.20 to U=0.14). These new doors usually have effective magnetic or foam weatherstrips.

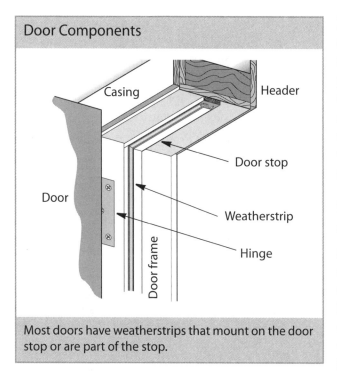

Door Components

Casing

Header

Door stop

Door

Weatherstrip

Door frame

Hinge

Most doors have weatherstrips that mount on the door stop or are part of the stop.

Door Repairs and Weatherstripping

Doors share many of the modification concerns of windows, so apply similar care and judgment. Exterior doors provide both egress and ventilation, while requiring security features such as locking knobsets and deadbolts. Aside from potential historical significance, main entry doors are focal points because they are the building's public gateway.

From an energy performance point of view, energy auditors recognize that entry doors usually sustain much more use and abuse than windows. Entry doors may go out of adjustment and lose an optimal seal for a number of reasons.

♦ Use and abuse

♦ Large size and weight

♦ Knobsets and locks exchanged a number of times over years

♦ Moisture content of the wood in the door

Make necessary adjustments to the door for proper clearances and full operation before installing weatherstrip.

Many doors need some adjustment before weatherstrip is installed. Some doors are warped and technicians either move the nailed door stop or plane the integral door stop to meet the irregular curving door surface. Check the weatherstrip, door, and door jamb to make sure they are all compatible before recommending or installing weatherstrip. Make sure that the hinges, knobset, and strike plates are tight.

Weatherstrip Selection and Installation —

Take great care in selecting door weatherstrips and thresholds. Sharp metal edges may scratch clothing or bare arms, and high thresholds may create a tripping hazard. The weatherstrip should be readily replaceable, since it tends to suffer damage, especially on the strike side. Ideally, weatherstrip should be continuous and only interrupted by the door-frame corners and to bypass the hinges and strike plates as necessary. The more continuous the strip, the more effective the seal.

Check for gaps where weatherstrip abuts the threshold. In addition to air leakage, water and dust tend to leak at these locations.

Bump-up surface mounted weatherstrip is relatively inexpensive to purchase and easy to install, but there should be a space between the door knobset enough to clear a person's knuckles. Bump-up weatherstrip also requires creating screw or nail holes, and surface mounting is more visually intrusive, which may be an issue on historic properties.

Vinyl-covered foam products are relatively inexpensive, easily replaced, and readily purchased through most lumber and hardware suppliers. They may be surface mounted, or more commonly found inserted into pre-cut slots on pre-hung doors.

Spring bronze weatherstrips are a common and more traditional solution to door sealing. However, the product is more expensive, the seal is not continuous, and it is prone to going out of adjustment and/or becoming an injury hazard over time. Spring bronze products also cover the door hinges, making hinge adjustment or replacement more difficult.

Silicone bulb, fitted into a frame kerf at the stop, is a durable and unobtrusive weatherstrip that also conforms easily to irregular surfaces, bends around arcs, and creates a continuous seal. A disadvantage is that a special router and careful handling are required to cut the kerf.

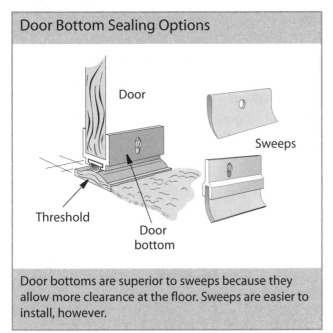

Door Bottom Sealing Options

Door bottoms are superior to sweeps because they allow more clearance at the floor. Sweeps are easier to install, however.

To seal the gap at the bottom of the door, a variety of thresholds, door bottoms, and sweeps are available. Door bottoms and sweeps attach to the bottom of the door and seal the door to the threshold.

Vinyl door bottoms and sweeps, even rubberized ones, suffer more wear than jamb weatherstrips because they are routinely flexed to extremes, even when stiff in cold weather. Certain plastic products with improved temperature performance are better than vinyl, but none perform better than silicone. Plastic weatherseals should not be mounted to the threshold where people tread on them. Proper adjustment of sweep clearance over the threshold is also critical for durability. Metal weatherseals usually don't endure well in this location.

Lastly, the door bottom sealing assembly should divert any water draining from the face of the door to a sloping portion of the sill—and so channel water away from the building. This is usually done with a drip edge applied to the door exterior, which may or may not be integrated with the door bottom or sweep.

Storm Doors

Storm doors reduce air infiltration and increase the R-value of wood doors from the R-1.75 to R-2.5 range to the R-2.7 to R-3.3 range, depending on whether the storm door is made of wood or metal. Storm doors improve the comfort of the area around the doorway. However, the cost per square foot for a storm door is high, and the payback period is comparatively long.

Storm doors can offer outstanding cooling benefits by creating a large screened opening to aid in ventilation.

A building's heating system provides heat at roughly the same rate as heat is being lost at the design temperatures if it is correctly sized. *Output* is the heater's heat-production rate. The *heating load* is the building's heat loss rate. A heater's output should be larger than the building's heating load, except in the very severest weather conditions, so the heater cycles on and off to satisfy the load for most of the heating season.

The word *heater*, as used here, means a furnace, boiler, or space heater, and *heating system* means the heater and its distribution system. A *circulator* is a blower or pump for moving the heating fluid — air, water, or steam.

There are two types of heaters: room heaters and central heaters. Room heaters deliver all their heat into one area — generally a single room. Central heaters convert fossil fuel or electricity to heat in a central location and employ ducts or pipes to distribute the heat.

Typical Annual Heating Energy Use

Region & Fuel	Single Family	Multi-family	Mobile Home
Northern U.S.			
Electric (kWh)	*9k–14k	4k–9k	6k–8k
Gas (MMBTU)	80–115	60–70	60–70
Oil (MMBTU)	80–115	55–65	55–65
Southern U.S.			
Electric (kWh)	*4k–6k	2k–4k	1K–5k
Gas (MMBTU)	35–80	20–35	25–40
Oil (MMBTU)	45–90	20–60	20–60

* k=1000. From Lawrence Berkeley Laboratory and Energy Information Administration. (1997)

Combustion fuels like gas, oil, and wood convert their potential energy to heat at *delivered efficiency* ranging from 35% to 95%. Delivered efficiency is the heating system's useful heat output divided by the energy input into the heating system. Efficiency is an important concept with combustion heating and there are several types of efficiency discussed in this chapter. The general formula for calculating efficiency is the following.

$$\text{Efficiency} = \frac{\text{Output}}{\text{Input}}$$

Electric resistance heat is considered 100% efficient. Heat pumps are a special type of electric heat that move heat from outdoors to indoors during the heating season and from indoors to outdoors during the cooling season. Heat pumps are generally more than 100% efficient because they can move more than a kilowatt-hour of heat for each kilowatt-hour of electricity they use. However, generating electricity from coal or oil wastes about 70% of the fuel's potential energy. Therefore, electricity is an expensive way to heat.

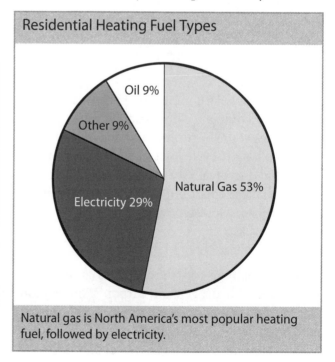

Residential Heating Fuel Types

Natural gas is North America's most popular heating fuel, followed by electricity.

Combustion Heating Basics

This section introduces the principles and components of gas, propane, and oil heaters. Gas and propane heaters are almost identical and are referred to here as gas heaters. Oil heaters are significantly different from gas and propane heaters.

In gas and oil heaters, burners mix fuel with air for burning in a combustion chamber. The *heat exchanger*, surrounding the combustion chamber, transfers heat from the flame and combustion gases to the heating fluid — air, water, or steam. Combustion gases leave the combustion chamber through the heat exchanger's flue(s), which connects to a chimney.

A *flue* is a passageway for venting combustion gases: a flue may be a space between the heat exchanger's sections or a tube within the heat exchanger. Chimneys are made of metal, masonry, or other noncombustible material. The chimney's inner passageway is often also called a flue.

The efficiency of a combustion heater depends on losses to incomplete combustion, chimney losses, heat losses at the beginning and end of the burner cycle (called off-cycle losses), and losses from the pipes and ducts (called distribution losses). Room heaters have no distribution losses, so they are more efficient than central-heating units.

The Combustion Process

Combustion fuels are hydrocarbons — molecules composed of hydrogen and carbon. Combustion is rapid oxidation; oxygen combines with the carbon and hydrogen. Carbon dioxide (CO_2) and water vapor are the main products of this heat-liberating chemical reaction. The flame's heat radiates to surrounding metal and rides on the combustion gases convecting against the heat exchanger's metal surfaces. Some of the flame's heat escapes up the chimney.

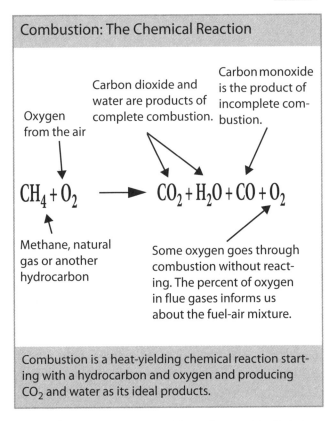

Combustion: The Chemical Reaction

Oxygen from the air

Carbon dioxide and water are products of complete combustion.

Carbon monoxide is the product of incomplete combustion.

$$CH_4 + O_2 \longrightarrow CO_2 + H_2O + CO + O_2$$

Methane, natural gas or another hydrocarbon

Some oxygen goes through combustion without reacting. The percent of oxygen in flue gases informs us about the fuel-air mixture.

Combustion is a heat-yielding chemical reaction starting with a hydrocarbon and oxygen and producing CO_2 and water as its ideal products.

Air is about 21% oxygen. The other 79% of air is nitrogen, most of which travels through the combustion process unreacted. The combustion gases in the chimney contain unreacted oxygen in addition to the unreacted nitrogen. These unreacted gases absorb heat from combustion and carry the heat up the chimney. Unreacted oxygen, measured in the combustion gases, is a sign of *excess air*, which is inversely proportional to efficiency. See "Combustion Heating" on page 41 for more on principles of combustion.

Open versus sealed combustion — The terms open-combustion and sealed-combustion describe whether or not the combustion chamber, heat exchanger, flues, and chimney are open to the surrounding air.

The majority of combustion heaters in homes are open combustion. These heaters draw combustion air from the surrounding room. Older open-combustion heaters also draw indoor air into their chimneys through a dilution device — either a *draft diverter* (gas) or *barometric draft control* (oil). The air that these devices allow into the chimney is called *dilution air*.

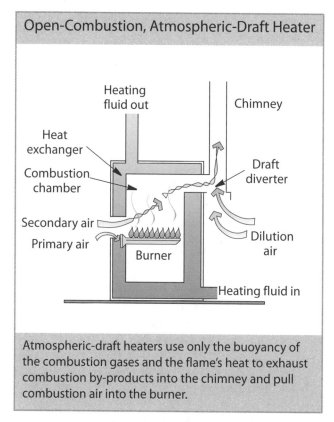

Open-Combustion, Atmospheric-Draft Heater

Heating fluid out

Chimney

Heat exchanger

Combustion chamber

Draft diverter

Secondary air

Primary air

Dilution air

Burner

Heating fluid in

Atmospheric-draft heaters use only the buoyancy of the combustion gases and the flame's heat to exhaust combustion by-products into the chimney and pull combustion air into the burner.

A draft diverter is an opening between the heat exchanger's flues and the chimney. The draft diverter is designed to moderate excessive updrafts and divert downdrafts that might interfere with the burner or extinguish the pilot. A barometric draft control performs the same function except that it regulates dilution air to maintain a consistent chimney draft.

Sealed-combustion heaters are safer and often more efficient than open-combustion heaters. Sealed-combustion heaters have no openings from the home into their heat exchangers or chimneys. Instead, a sealed tube, sometimes combined with the chimney, brings combustion air in from the outdoors.

Burners

The burner's job is to mix the fuel and air and to burn this mixture. The three common burner types are atmospheric burners, inshot burners,

and power burners. Atmospheric burners are the most common type of gas burner. Gas pressure propels gas through a gas orifice into a venturi tube where the gas mixes with *primary air* admitted by an air shutter. A pilot light, hot-surface igniter, or sparking electrode ignites the mixture. *Secondary air* in the combustion chamber around the flame provides oxygen for the fuel's nearly complete combustion.

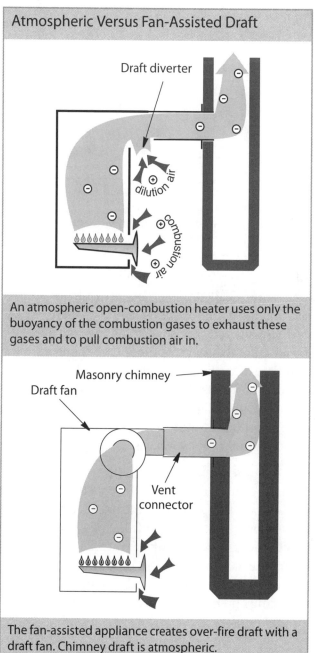

Atmospheric Versus Fan-Assisted Draft

Draft diverter

dilution air

combustion air

An atmospheric open-combustion heater uses only the buoyancy of the combustion gases to exhaust these gases and to pull combustion air in.

Masonry chimney

Draft fan

Vent connector

The fan-assisted appliance creates over-fire draft with a draft fan. Chimney draft is atmospheric.

Power Burner

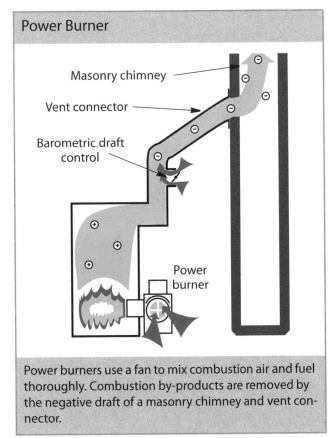

Power burners use a fan to mix combustion air and fuel thoroughly. Combustion by-products are removed by the negative draft of a masonry chimney and vent connector.

Atmospheric Gas Burner

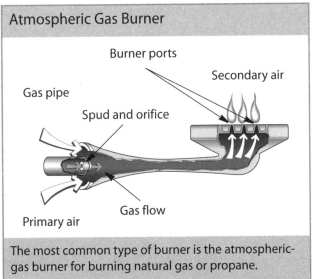

The most common type of burner is the atmospheric-gas burner for burning natural gas or propane.

Many modern furnaces employ an improved burner type called the *inshot burner*. Inshot burners fire into a tube or stamped heat exchanger that is depressurized by a draft-inducing fan. Their flame takes the shape of the heat exchanger. In this type of appliance, the draft-inducing fan pulls the combustion air in and the combustion gases out. This small fan, however, has little or no pressure effect on the atmospheric chimney where it deposits the combustion gases.

Power burners use a blower to pressurize the combustion chamber and move combustion products into the venting system. Electrodes ignite the fuel-air mixture. Shutters on the power burner's blower adjust the fuel-air mixture. The power burner usually deposits its combustion gases into an atmospheric chimney and, like the draft-inducing fan, has little effect on the chimney draft.

The most common type of power burner is the oil-atomizing gun burner. An electric motor on the gun burner runs the blower and an oil pump, delivering the oil at a high pressure. The burner's nozzle sprays the high-pressure oil into the combustion chamber where sparking electrodes ignite the atomized oil.

Power gas burners combine a gas orifice, blower, and electrodes for ignition. Power gas burners are found most commonly in multifamily boilers. Power gas burners occasionally replace inefficient atmospheric burners in older single-family furnaces and boilers.

Draft

Draft is the force that brings combustion air into the combustion chamber and propels the combustion gases out through the venting system. Draft can be separated into two components: *chimney draft* and *over-fire draft*.

Buoyancy of combustion gases results from the difference in density between these gases and cooler air outside the heater and its chimney. The flue-gas temperature, along with the chimney's height and cross-sectional area determine the strength of chimney draft. Heaters, which depend exclusively on buoyancy for both over-fire and chimney draft, are called *atmospheric heaters*.

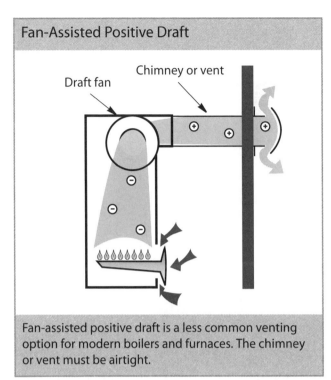

Fan-Assisted Positive Draft

Draft fan

Chimney or vent

Fan-assisted positive draft is a less common venting option for modern boilers and furnaces. The chimney or vent must be airtight.

Many modern furnaces, boilers, and space heaters have *fan-assisted draft*. These fan-assisted-draft heaters have no dilution device. Their draft fan regulates the over-fire draft and creates a steady flow of combustion air and combustion gases. The draft-assisting fan is located at the inlet (*power burner*) or outlet (*draft inducer*) of the heat exchanger. Either way, the appliance usually vents into an atmospheric chimney.

The elimination of the draft diverter and adoption of fan-assisted over-fire draft is largely responsible for an increase in annual fuel utilization efficiency (AFUE) from 65% in atmospheric-draft furnaces to AFUEs above 80% in similar fan-assisted furnaces. Most fan-assisted heaters are vented into vertical chimneys and their draft fans have little or no effect on the atmospheric chimney draft.

When a fan-assisted 80+ AFUE furnace or boiler is vented horizontally, the draft in the stainless-steel vent is positive. The positive-draft vent must be substantially airtight. Sealed-combustion condensing furnaces and boilers vent through plastic pipe because the flue gases are cool and wet. Sealed-combustion condensing furnaces and

boilers require strong draft fans to overcome resistance from both their venting and combustion-air piping.

Power burners use a fan for mixing combustion air with the fuel and injecting the mixture into the combustion chamber. Power burners create a positive over-fire draft, but heaters with power burners (mostly boilers) usually vent into a standard atmospheric chimney.

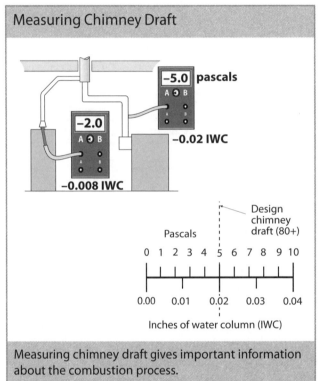

Measuring Chimney Draft

−5.0 **pascals**

−2.0

−0.02 IWC

−0.008 IWC

Pascals

Design chimney draft (80+)

0 1 2 3 4 5 6 7 8 9 10

0.00   0.01   0.02   0.03   0.04

Inches of water column (IWC)

Measuring chimney draft gives important information about the combustion process.

Chimneys, Liners, and Vents

Chimneys vent combustion gases outdoors vertically. Horizontal vents are becoming more common, replacing chimneys in high-efficiency furnaces, boilers, and space heaters. This section discusses chimneys and horizontal vents.

A chimney develops draft because the gases inside the chimney are lighter than air outside the chimney. A heater at the chimney's bottom burns fuel, which creates the column of lighter-than-air gases. The taller the chimney and the hotter its gases (compared with the air outside) the greater the chimney draft.

AGA Venting Categories

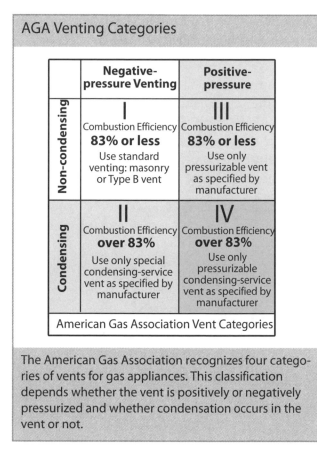

	Negative-pressure Venting	Positive-pressure
Non-condensing	**I** Combustion Efficiency **83% or less** Use standard venting: masonry or Type B vent	**III** Combustion Efficiency **83% or less** Use only pressurizable vent as specified by manufacturer
Condensing	**II** Combustion Efficiency **over 83%** Use only special condensing-service vent as specified by manufacturer	**IV** Combustion Efficiency **over 83%** Use only pressurizable condensing-service vent as specified by manufacturer
American Gas Association Vent Categories		

The American Gas Association recognizes four categories of vents for gas appliances. This classification depends whether the vent is positively or negatively pressurized and whether condensation occurs in the vent or not.

Chimneys are either masonry or factory-built metal. Masonry chimneys should be lined with fire clay although many older masonry chimneys are unlined. Clay tile is the most common liner for a masonry chimney. Masons install clay tile liners during construction with round or square clay pipe. The masons provide a space between the liner and the exterior brick to allow the chimney and the liner to expand and contract at different rates.

Factory-built chimneys, employing two or more concentric metal pipes, are very common for residential chimneys. The air space(s) in the concentric pipe keep combustion gases warm and avoid condensation in the chimney. Double-wall, Type-B vent is widely used as gas-appliance chimney. B-vent consists of an aluminum inner pipe and a galvanized-steel outer pipe. B-vent is also the preferred vent connector for 80+ gas furnaces, as well as the preferred retrofit chimney liner whenever there is space inside a masonry chimney to install B-vent.

Chimneys and Chimney Liners

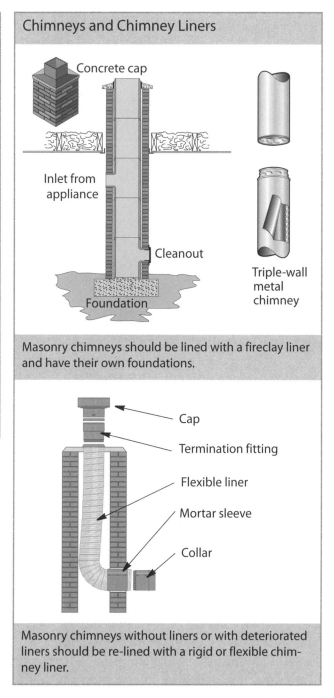

Masonry chimneys should be lined with a fireclay liner and have their own foundations.

Masonry chimneys without liners or with deteriorated liners should be re-lined with a rigid or flexible chimney liner.

Type-L vent is a vent connector for oil and solid-fuel appliances. L-vent consists of a stainless-steel inner pipe and a galvanized-steel outer pipe.

Insulated double-wall chimneys or triple-wall chimneys — called all-fuel chimneys — serve as vertical chimneys for oil and solid-fuel appliances. These chimneys may penetrate combustible building components like floors, ceilings, and roofs with only two inches of clearance.

Power Venter

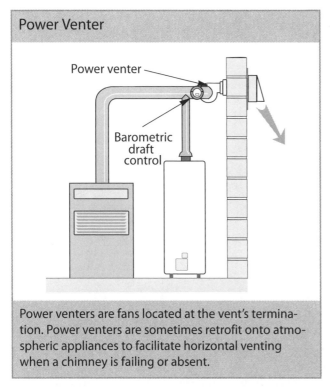

Power venters are fans located at the vent's termination. Power venters are sometimes retrofit onto atmospheric appliances to facilitate horizontal venting when a chimney is failing or absent.

Sealed-Combustion Plastic Venting

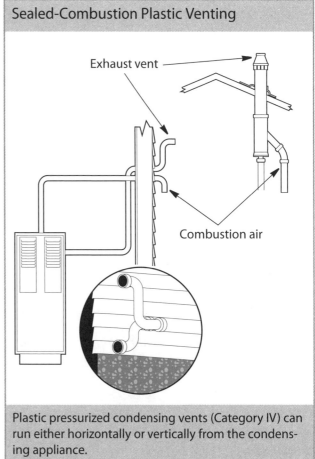

Plastic pressurized condensing vents (Category IV) can run either horizontally or vertically from the condensing appliance.

All-fuel chimneys contain manufactured components from the vent connector to the termination fitting on the roof. Parts include: metal pipe, weight-supporting hardware, insulation shields, roof jacks, and chimney caps. One manufacturer's chimney may be incompatible with another's connecting fittings.

See "Wood Stove Installation" on page 179.

Some space heaters, furnaces, and boilers use factory-built metal chimneys with single stainless steel liners that vent horizontally under positive pressure. Condensing furnaces usually employ horizontal or vertical plastic-pipe chimneys. Stainless-steel and plastic vents powered by fans should become standard for gas and oil appliances in coming years to replace atmospheric chimneys, which aren't very reliable venting systems for today's tighter homes.

The need for chimney liners is often ignored during heating-system replacement. Install a new chimney liner when a replacement heater has a higher firing rate than the old one. For example: when a horizontally vented furnace replaces the chimney-vented one, the water heater now vents alone into the chimney designed for both appliances.

The water heater's oversized chimney now needs a liner. Un-lined chimneys and those deteriorating from acidic combustion gases are retrofitted with stainless-steel, aluminum, or masonry liners. Flexible stainless-steel and aluminum liners are popular because they are easy to install. Stainless steel is more durable and thus preferable to aluminum. The best metal liners are smooth stainless-steel piping. Masonry liners are also an option. Masons pour the liners in place using a variety of proprietary processes.

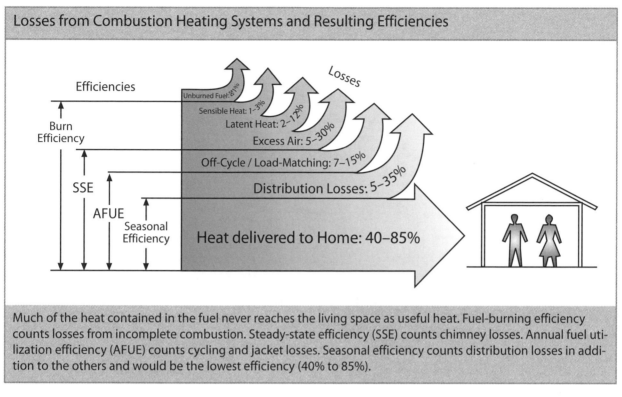

Losses from Combustion Heating Systems and Resulting Efficiencies

Efficiencies

Burn Efficiency

SSE

AFUE

Seasonal Efficiency

Losses

Unburned Fuel: <1%

Sensible Heat: 1–3%

Latent Heat: 2–12%

Excess Air: 5–30%

Off-Cycle / Load-Matching: 7–15%

Distribution Losses: 5–35%

Heat delivered to Home: 40–85%

Much of the heat contained in the fuel never reaches the living space as useful heat. Fuel-burning efficiency counts losses from incomplete combustion. Steady-state efficiency (SSE) counts chimney losses. Annual fuel utilization efficiency (AFUE) counts cycling and jacket losses. Seasonal efficiency counts distribution losses in addition to the others and would be the lowest efficiency (40% to 85%).

Types of Efficiency

Efficiency is an important indicator of heating performance. The fuel buyer pays for the portion of heat wasted in addition to the portion used.

Heating specialists express heating efficiency in four different ways.
1. Fuel burning efficiency.
2. Steady-state efficiency (also called combustion efficiency).
3. Annual fuel utilization efficiency (AFUE).
4. Delivered heating efficiency (also called seasonal efficiency).

The four types of efficiencies to be discussed account for the succession of losses as heat travels from the burner through the heat exchanger and distribution system.

Fuel-burning efficiency is the percentage of the fuel's potential energy converted to heat at the flame. Most modern oil-fired heaters and gas heaters have a fuel-burning efficiency of over 99%.

Steady-state efficiency (SSE) is the percentage of heat captured by heating fluids: air, water, or steam. SSE accounts for fuel-burning losses and chimney losses. The SSE can be measured with CO_2-sensing or oxygen-sensing devices and thermometers.

All combustion furnaces, boilers, and room heaters must leave the factory with an energy guide label listing the AFUE. AFUE is the laboratory-tested efficiency that accounts for: fuel-burning losses, chimney losses, cycling losses, and heat loss through a central heater's cabinet. AFUE does not account for distribution losses through ducts or pipes. The AFUE is the percentage of the potential energy in the fuel that flows into the heating distribution ducts or pipes on a seasonal basis.

Delivered heating efficiency is the most difficult type of heating efficiency to measure because delivered efficiency includes distribution losses. Delivered efficiency is the percentage of the fuel's potential energy that actually heats the living space. With all the ways to lose heat between the flame and the living space, the delivered heating efficiency can be as low as 35%.

Combustion Heating System Energy Loss

The combustion heater liberates chemical energy as heat at its flame. Some of that chemical energy is wasted by incomplete burning. Some of the flame's heat escapes up the chimney. Much of the residual heat remaining after the flame extinguishes is wasted, depending on the efficiency of heat transfer and circulator operation. The distribution system's pipes or ducts lose some of the heat. A central heater's pump or blower uses electrical energy, much of which never contributes heat to conditioned space and so can be considered waste. The following is a more detailed accounting of these losses.

Dilution air — Dilution air is the heated building air used by conventional furnaces and boilers to moderate chimney draft and reduce excess combustion air. There are two common dilution devices that admit dilution air to the chimney: the draft diverter and the barometric draft control. The draft diverter is simply a large opening in the appliance's flue, which allows air into and out of the chimney. The barometric draft control is a damper that allows air in and out of a chimney depending on the pressure in the chimney. The barometric control is widely used with gas and oil power burners and regulates chimney draft, creating more stable and efficient combustion than a draft diverter.

Unfortunately, at least 80 percent of existing gas appliances still have draft diverters rather than barometric draft controls or induced-draft (ID) fans, which regulate combustion gases in high-efficiency furnaces. Most new boilers and water heaters still use draft diverters.

If dilution air is heated building air, the dilution air represents a significant heat loss. Gas furnaces and boilers without draft diverters are above 78%

AFUE, while older models with draft diverters are in the 60% to 70% AFUE range. Therefore, eliminating dilution air is one of the most important advances in heating evolution.

Combustion air — Excess combustion air — more than required to oxidize all the carbon and hydrogen molecules in the fuel — ensures complete combustion and avoids carbon monoxide (CO) production. Excess air also wastes energy. Combustion air provides oxygen to the burning fuel as both primary air or secondary air. Secondary air is the main source of excess air and depends on the air-intake area in front of the burner and the over-fire draft.

Excess combustion air absorbs heat and carries it up the chimney, so the best systems minimize excess air. If it were possible to allow only the exact amount of air absolutely necessary for combustion into the firebox, there would be 0% excess air. Efficient combustion heaters allow 20% excess air, but 100% excess air is not unusual in heaters equipped with draft diverters and having no draft fan. The greater the excess air percentage, the lower the efficiency, and even modern heaters may have high excess air. One failing of modern American heaters is that manufacturers provide no way to adjust the flow of combustion air.

See "Combustion Air Alternatives for Confined Spaces" on page 153.

Cycling losses — The heat required to warm up the furnace or boiler is partially wasted when it cools down. If the heating fluid continues to circulate through the heat exchanger after the burner shuts off, this waste is minimized because the stored heat continues to flow into the building. The amount of cycling losses depends on the following factors.

♦ The number of cycles,

♦ Amount of heat required to warm up the heat exchanger, and

♦ The efficiency of distribution system operating after the burner extinguishes.

Off-cycle losses can be minimized by vent dampers, draft fans, and smaller heat-exchanger passageways that restrict off-cycle airflow through the heat exchanger and venting system. Room heaters have far less off-cycle losses than central heaters because most of the heat stored in the heat exchanger escapes into the room rather than out the vent.

Furnaces and boilers are designed to achieve their maximum efficiency at maximum output and load. When the heating load is less than the heater's output, then the furnace or boiler cycles on and off. Numerous, shorter cycles waste energy through greater off-cycle losses. However, longer cycles may overheat the building, waste energy, and cause discomfort. This is why selecting a furnace's or boiler's output correctly reduces waste caused by both off-cycle losses and overheating. This principle is more important with boilers than with furnaces because of the boiler's heavier heat exchanger and heating fluid.

Distribution losses — Distribution losses typically amount to 5% to 30% of the heat contained in the fuel being burned by a furnace or boiler. Distribution losses are partially reclaimed if the pipes or ducts run through heated spaces. If these distribution losses heat an unconditioned space, heat loss from the conditioned to the unconditioned space is reduced. However, central heating systems are designed to heat rooms through registers, radiators, or baseboard convectors. Usually, distribution losses are at least partially wasted — escaping from unconditioned spaces or overheating conditioned spaces.

Heat escapes the distribution system in two ways.
1. The heating fluid — air, water, or steam — escapes from the ducts or pipes.
2. Convection and radiation carry heat away from pipes and ducts.

Leaks in pipes and ducts are the most severe distribution problems. You can reduce convection and radiation by installing pipe or duct insulation.

If the distribution system is undersized or its circulator is functioning poorly, this reduces heat transfer at the central heater's heat exchanger. More of the flame's heat escapes up the chimney.

Combustion Safety and Efficiency

Combustion heaters are, statistically, among the most dangerous hazards found in residences. Fire and indoor air pollution are the most common problems.

Home-heating systems are more likely to be dangerous than those of multifamily buildings because of stricter multifamily safety standards and the home heater's closer proximity to residents. Room heaters are particularly dangerous, because of their location within the living space.

Ideally, a heating professional performs maintenance and safety checks annually for all oil-fired equipment. Gas furnaces and boilers burn cleaner and have less moving parts than oil, so they need service less often.

Combustion-safety Issues

CO is the greatest indoor pollutant threat from combustion heating. This colorless, odorless gas can sicken or kill the building's occupants. Other gases affecting health include nitrous oxide, water vapor, and sulfur dioxide. These gases can escape into the building's living spaces through cracked heat exchangers, backdrafting, and spillage. Combustion air is essential for safe operation of combustion heaters.

Flame-safeguard controls — Heaters are a major cause of fires. Combustible materials should be kept at a safe distance from hot components of the heater. Electrical components should be inspected for safety at least biannually. A smoke alarm should be located in or near the heater's space.

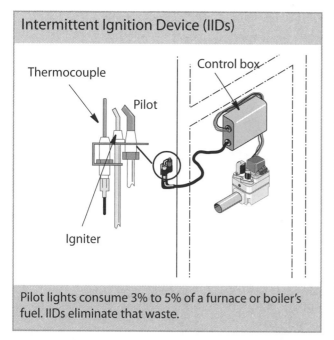

Intermittent Ignition Device (IIDs)

Thermocouple

Control box

Pilot

Igniter

Pilot lights consume 3% to 5% of a furnace or boiler's fuel. IIDs eliminate that waste.

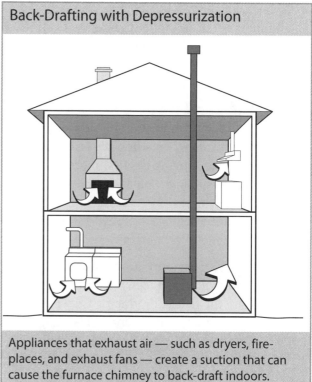

Back-Drafting with Depressurization

Appliances that exhaust air — such as dryers, fireplaces, and exhaust fans — create a suction that can cause the furnace chimney to back-draft indoors.

All combustion heaters should be equipped with a high-limit control to extinguish the burner in the event of overheating. The high-limit control is a bimetal element attached to a switch in the burner's control circuit. The high-limit is tested by disabling the circulator and measuring the fluid temperature (pressure, if fluid is steam) at which the high-limit control extinguishes the burner.

Flame-safety controls protect against fuel delivery to the combustion chamber without ignition. Oil, natural gas, or propane accumulation in the combustion chamber could lead to a fire or explosion. The three most common flame safeguards are the thermocouple, the photocell, and the flame rectifier.

A *thermocouple* is a small electric generator powered by heat from the pilot light of a gas appliance. The thermocouple's electric circuit powers a magnetic valve that remains open as long as electric current is flowing. If the pilot light goes out, the electric current stops, and the spring-loaded valve closes, shutting off the gas.

A *flame rectifier* uses the flame to conduct control current and to change it from AC to DC. Many modern furnaces use flame rectifiers, which both light and sense the flame with a single device.

A *photocell* produces a small electric current from the light emitted by a flame. This current holds the contacts of a relay (magnetic switch) together as long as the photocell senses the flame. If the flame goes out or fails to light initially, the photocell's relay interrupts electricity to the heater's power burner.

Cracked heat exchangers — Cracked heat exchangers are a safety problem specific to combustion furnaces and room heaters. Cracked heat exchangers can allow combustion gases to mix with air from the building. Rust, excessive heat, and weld failure are common causes of cracked heat exchangers. Technicians inspect heat exchangers for cracks visually and by several other techniques including the following.

♦ Observing for flame variation when the blower turns on.

♦ Injecting chemicals or smoke into the combustion chamber and then using detection devices to sense chemicals or smoke in air exiting supply registers.

♦ Shining a bright light into the combustion chamber and looking for light leaks from the building side of the heat exchanger.

♦ Using remote-viewing devices.

Spillage and backdrafting — *Spillage* is a temporary flow of combustion by-products out of the dilution device when a furnace or boiler starts. Weak draft during the first moments after ignition causes spillage. Spillage, if present, usually stops after the chimney warms up. Backdrafting is continuous spillage — a reversal of the chimney's normal direction of flow.

Backdrafting is most common in atmospheric, open-combustion appliances. Severe backdrafting can suffocate the flame, producing CO. The draft diverter or barometric-draft control is designed to let backdrafting flue gases escape from the chimney before they dump down onto the burner.

Backdrafting can be caused by the following.

♦ Suction near the furnace or boiler caused by leaky return ducts, exhaust fans, a clothes dryer, a or fireplace.

♦ Blocked chimney.

♦ Chimney too large or small.

♦ High winds.

Backdrafting may be eliminated by:

♦ Sealing leaky ducts.

♦ Repairing the chimney.

♦ Eliminating depressurization near the chimney.

♦ Providing outdoor combustion air.

♦ Replacing the open-combustion, atmospheric heater with a sealed-combustion or power-draft heater.

See "Duct Air Leakage" on page 89 and "Duct Leakage Comparisons" on page 67.

The safest and most efficient new heaters have fans to vent combustion by-products, and they require little indoor combustion air. These fans reduce the threat of backdrafting.

Chimney draft in atmospheric-draft appliances should be negative 1 to 5 pascals (0.004 to 0.020 inches of water) depending on the outdoor temperature. Colder outdoor temperatures produce higher draft. Measured pressure differences between outdoors and the combustion zone — called depressurization — should not exceed 4 to 5 pascals with exhaust fans and furnace fan running during a worst-case depressurization test. The combustion heater should spill — emit combustion gases from its dilution device — for no longer than one minute under worst-case test conditions.

Combustion Appliance Depressurization Limits

Appliance Type	Max. Depress.
Atmospheric water heater only (Category I, natural draft), open-combustion appliances	–2 pa
Atmospheric water heater (Category I, natural draft) and atmospheric furnace (Category I, natural draft), common-vented, open-combustion appliances	–3 pa
Gas furnace or boiler, Category I or Category I fan-assisted, open-combustion appliances	–5 pa
Oil or gas unit with power burner, low- or high-static pressure burner, open combustion appliances	–5 pa
Wood-burning appliances	–7 pa
Open-combustion furnaces or boilers with fan-powered horizontal venting	–15 pa

Combustion Air Alternatives for Confined Spaces

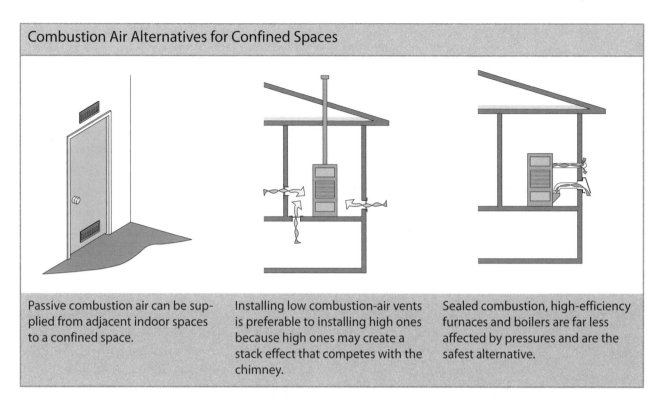

Passive combustion air can be supplied from adjacent indoor spaces to a confined space.	Installing low combustion-air vents is preferable to installing high ones because high ones may create a stack effect that competes with the chimney.	Sealed combustion, high-efficiency furnaces and boilers are far less affected by pressures and are the safest alternative.

Combustion air — Air leakage through the building shell usually provides combustion air. Some codes and code officials require combustion air piped in from outdoors, especially for confined spaces. A confined space is a room containing less than 50 cubic feet of volume for every 1000 BTU per hour of appliance input.

However, if a small mechanical room is connected to adjacent spaces through large air passages like floor-joist spaces, the room may not need additional combustion air despite sheeted walls and a door separating the mechanical room from other indoor spaces. On the other hand, if the home is unusually airtight, even a large mechanical room may be unable to provide adequate combustion air.

A sealed-combustion heating system is always preferable for reliable combustion-air delivery and combustion-gas venting. Passive intake vents from outdoors or neighboring indoor areas are unreliable sources of combustion air, if wind or indoor pressures occur.

The location of a passive combustion air inlet is important. The wind creates a positive-pressure area on the building's windward side and a negative pressure near walls parallel to the wind direction. If the inlet were located in a negative-pressure area, this inlet could suck air out of the building instead of letting air in.

Some codes specify two sources of air to prevent pressure or suction in the mechanical room. With two openings, if one is creating a pressure, the other opening can relieve the pressure. While this approach is better than a single combustion-air source, wind, cold weather, or indoor depressurization can still overwhelm atmospheric chimneys. Combustion-air vents located high in walls or in ceilings may also depressurize the mechanical room by way of the stack effect.

When the combustion-air duct brings outdoor air into a living area, a control mechanism — like a damper — may be necessary to prevent residents from closing the duct permanently because of the drafts it causes. Isolating the central heater in an airtight room and providing this room with outdoor combustion air is preferred over dumping combustion air into living spaces. Connecting the combustion-air duct to the furnace's return ducts solves the comfort problem, but the cold make-up air may cause condensation and corrosion in non-condensing furnaces during cold weather and after thermostat setback. The return air mixed with outdoor air shouldn't enter the furnace at less than 55°F.

Combustion and Dilution Air Requirements

Appliance	Combustion Air (cfm)	Dilution Air (cfm)
Conventional Oil	38	195
Flame-Retention Oil	25	195
High-Efficiency Oil	22	–
Conventional Atmospheric Gas	30	143
Fan-Assisted Gas	26	–
Condensing Gas	17	–
Fireplace (no doors)	100–600	–
Airtight Wood Stove	10–50	–
A.C.S. Hayden, Residential Combustion Appliances: Venting and Indoor Air Quality; and Solid Fuels Encyclopedia		

Combustion and dilution air can create large airflows and result in depressurization of the combustion zone. Depressurization can affect draft and result in carbon-monoxide production. Sometimes providing outdoor combustion air can solve combustion problems. Worst-case draft and depressurization testing can identify the problem as either related to combustion air or not related. Depressurization can also be caused by exhaust fans and furnace blowers, so it makes sense to find the depressurization source before prescribing a solution. Providing combustion air from outdoors may fail to solve a depressurization problem or may make the problem worse.

In tight homes or windy regions, sealed-combustion appliances may be the only reliable venting-and-combustion-air systems. For retrofitting hard-to-vent homes, sealed mechanical rooms with horizontal venting, power venters, and fan-powered combustion air may be necessary.

Flue-gas Testing

Combustion-gas testing is used to estimate steady-state efficiency (SSE). SSE is a good measurement of a heater's potential for improvement, or the cost-effectiveness of replacing the heater.

Heating professionals sample combustion gases as they leave the heat exchanger, before being diluted by the dilution device. They measure SSE with chemical or electronic gas analyzers.

The chemical testers use the predictable change in volume of a liquid chemical as it absorbs carbon dioxide (CO_2) or oxygen (O_2). Entering the percentage of either oxygen or CO_2 with the combustion gas temperature into an equation gives an estimate of SSE.

The electronic analyzers measure the percent of oxygen, using an electronic sensing device whose electric output varies with its exposure to O_2. Electronic analyzers have a built-in calculator that figures SSE automatically.

CO_2 is the product of complete combustion. The higher the percentage of CO_2 the greater the SSE. CO_2 varies between 3% and 13%. Oxygen is an indicator of excess air. The higher the level of O_2, the lower the SSE. Oxygen varies from 3% to 13%. Higher exhaust temperatures predict lower SSE, but the temperature must be compared with oxygen or CO_2 levels to determine SSE. The O_2 level also indicates whether the combustion air is adequate — if the O_2 level is above 4%.

Sealed-Combustion Oil Heating

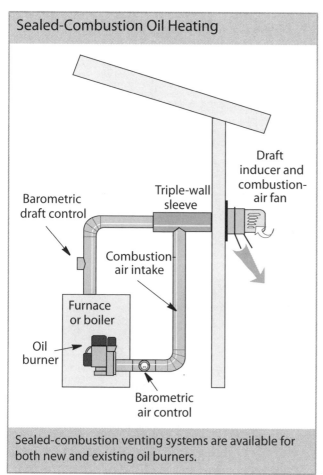

Sealed-combustion venting systems are available for both new and existing oil burners.

Measuring Oil Burner Performance

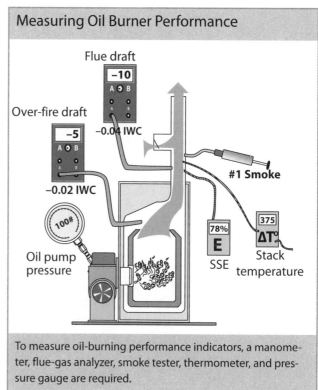

To measure oil-burning performance indicators, a manometer, flue-gas analyzer, smoke tester, thermometer, and pressure gauge are required.

Oil Heating Service

Service technicians should have test equipment and should measure SSE, CO, draft, and all other parameters that are relevant to the seasonal efficiency of a furnace or boiler. A tune-up, performed by a qualified technician, usually saves 5% to 15% of the heating fuel, depending on the heater's existing condition and the technician's skill. Older oil heating units have a maximum SSE of around 80%, which can only be improved significantly by installing a more efficient burner.

Oil safety and efficiency checklist — During the professional service call, the heating technician should test and inspect the oil-heating system for safety and efficiency of combustion by the following actions.

♦ Check the heat exchanger for cracks, corrosion, and soot.

♦ Test the flame sensor.

♦ Perform initial combustion test.

♦ Test for CO and remove the causes, if found.

♦ Clean the oil strainer.

♦ Clean the burner's blower, blast tube, and electrodes.

♦ Replace nozzle, resize it if appropriate.

♦ Replace the oil filter.

♦ Set the gap between electrodes at the correct distance.

♦ Repair oil leaks.

♦ Test oil-pump pressure.

♦ Set heat anticipator to control the circuit current (amps).

♦ Adjust spinner and shutter for minimum smoke.

♦ Adjust barometric damper to .02 IWC over-fire draft.

♦ Perform final combustion test.

Modern oil burners — The most important advance in oil heating has been the flame retention head oil burner (FRHOB). Furnaces and boilers with FRHOBs have steady-state efficiencies of over 80%. Replacing an old oil burner with an FRHOB is usually cost-effective if the existing SSE is less than 75%. Flame-retention-burner motors run at 3450 rpm and older oil burners run at 1725 rpm motor speed. Looking for the nameplate motor speed can help you discriminate between the flame-retention burners and the older models.

When a conventional oil burner is replaced with an FRHOB, the burner orifice may be reduced one size — a procedure called derating — which accounts for: the over-sizing of the original burner, the higher efficiency of the FRHOB, and building shell energy improvements. The smaller nozzle may also save a little fuel.

A derated FRHOB burner pushes less excess air through the combustion chamber. The FRHOB reduces the velocity of flue gases and reduces flue temperature. However, flue temperatures shouldn't fall below 350°F or flue gases could condense, causing corrosion.

Size the burner and nozzle to match the building's heat load, making adjustments for new insulation and air sealing done during weatherization. (With steam heating, size the burner to existing radiation surface area.)

See "Energy-efficient Oil Furnaces and Boilers" on page 175.

The service technician installs a new ceramic combustion chamber, choosing one that fits the size and shape of the burner flame. Or he may change nozzles on the new burner to create a flame that fits an existing combustion chamber. Either way, the flame should fill the combustion chamber without impinging to the point where soot is formed.

Flame-Retention Head-Oil Burner

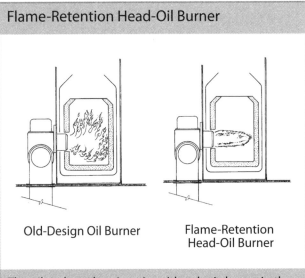

Old-Design Oil Burner | Flame-Retention Head-Oil Burner

The oil and combustion air swirl and mix better in the tight flame pattern, which leads to more complete combustion and better steady-state efficiency.

Oil Combustion Performance Indicator	Non-Flame Retention	Flame Retention
Oxygen (% O_2)	4–9%	4–7%
Stack temperature (°F)	325°–600°	300°–500°
Carbon monoxide (CO) parts per million (ppm)	≤ 100 ppm	≤ 100 ppm
Steady-state efficiency (SSE) (%)	≥ 75%	≥ 80%
Smoke number (1–9)	≤ 2	≤ 1
Excess air (%)	≤ 100%	≤ 25%
Oil pressure pounds per square inch (psi)	≥ 100 psi	≥ 100-150 psi (pmi)*
Over-fire draft (IWC negative)	5 Pa. or .02 IWC	5 Pa. or .02 IWC
Flue draft (IWC negative)	10–25 Pa. or 0.04–0.1 IWC	10–25 Pa. or 0.04–0.1 IWC
* pmi = per manufacturer's instructions		

Gas Heating Professional Service

During the professional service call, the technician should test and inspect the gas heating system for safety and efficiency of combustion by the following actions.

- ◆ Check the combustion chamber for cracks.

- ◆ Test for CO and remove causes, if found.

- ◆ Observe electric control operation and make adjustments to improve efficiency.

- ◆ Inspect thermostat location and the heat anticipator adjustment.

- ◆ Remove dirt, rust, and other debris that may be interfering with the burners. Clean the heat exchanger, if necessary.

- ◆ Adjust air or water temperature to minimum needed for the coldest weather.

- ◆ Test draft and take action to improve draft, if inadequate because of improper venting, obstructed chimney, leaky chimney, or depressurization.

- ◆ Remove blockages and repair leaks in the heating distribution system.

- ◆ Remove dirt, soot, or corrosion from furnace or boiler.

- ◆ Check fuel input and flame characteristics — adjust only if necessary.

Adjusting and maintaining gas burners —

The gas input to a furnace or boiler should be set at the time of installation and should not need adjustment. However, incorrect input is common and can lead to CO production.

The input adjustment screw is located on the automatic gas valve or pressure regulator. The input is measured by timing the gas meter and knowing how many BTUs of potential energy are contained in a cubic foot of the local natural gas. The burner orifices and the burners themselves are designed to operate within a particular range of gas pressure and flow rate.

Performance Indicator	AFUE 60+	AFUE 80+	AFUE 90+
Combustion-zone pressure (Pa)	–4 Pa.	–5 Pa.	–10 Pa.
Carbon monoxide (CO) (ppm)	≤ 100	≤ 100	≤ 100
Stack temperature (°F)	350°–475°	325°–450°	≤ 120°
Temperature rise (°F)	40–70°*	40–70°*	30–70°*
Oxygen (%O_2)	5–10%	4–9%	4–9%
Gas pressure Inches (IWC)	3.2–3.8*	3.2–3.8*	3.2–3.8*
Steady-state efficiency (SSE) (%)	72–78%	78–82%	92–97%
Draft (Pa)	–5	–5	+25–60
* pmi = per manufacturer's instructions			

Modern Automatic Gas Valve

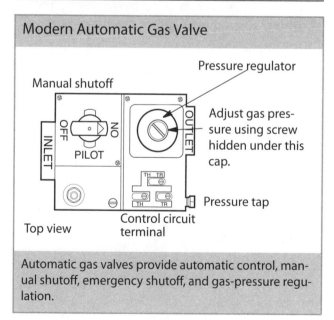

Automatic gas valves provide automatic control, manual shutoff, emergency shutoff, and gas-pressure regulation.

Burners in many combustion heaters have a primary air adjustment. This sliding or rotating cover controls the amount of air that mixes with the gas prior to combustion. Primary air adjustments should be made only if CO is detected; opening the primary air often solves the CO problem.

Dirt or scale on the burner can cause incomplete combustion. Most burners are easily removed for cleaning. Burner flame adjustment usually isn't necessary. Only an experienced service person with the proper testing instruments should adjust the flame.

Vent dampers — A vent damper reduces the heat loss from a furnace or boiler by closing off the chimney when the burner isn't operating. The vent damper prevents heat stored in the furnace or boiler from escaping up the chimney, allowing the circulator to deliver this stored heat to the building.

Vent dampers are cost-effective on large boilers in multifamily buildings, or residential furnaces or boilers located in the living space. Big boilers can lose much of their stored heat to the chimney. Vent dampers minimize this loss. If a furnace or boiler is located within the living space, its draft diverter is constantly sucking heated air up the chimney. Vent dampers minimize this waste.

Electric vent dampers use a solenoid or a small electric motor. A solenoid is a magnetically operated lever that opens the damper when the burner fires and closes it when the burner cycles off. Electric vent dampers — for gas systems with pilot lights — don't close completely. Instead, they leave about 10% of the chimney open to vent the pilot light. Vent dampers for use with oil systems or with gas systems with intermittent ignition devices may have vent dampers that close almost completely.

Thermal vent dampers open the bimetal damper when they sense heat and close the damper when the chimney cools, after the burner goes off. Thermal vent dampers may be dangerous in furnaces or boilers with low draft.

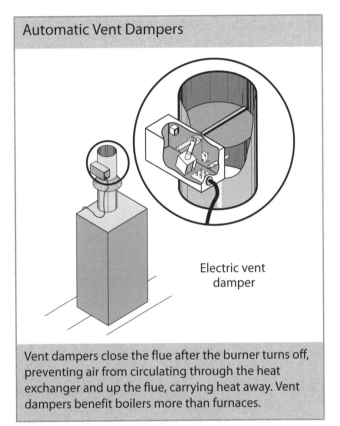

Automatic Vent Dampers

Electric vent damper

Vent dampers close the flue after the burner turns off, preventing air from circulating through the heat exchanger and up the flue, carrying heat away. Vent dampers benefit boilers more than furnaces.

Heating Comfort Controls

The main function of heating controls is to monitor the conditions of and to maintain comfort in the heated space.

Thermostats

Thermostats are automatic switches that respond to changing room temperature. Thermostats turn heating equipment on or off. In residential heating systems, thermostats don't exercise modulating control like a car's gas pedal. The thermostat's operation is like driving your car with your foot to the floor, or off the gas pedal completely. To maintain a fairly steady speed while driving this way, you'd have to fully depress and release the gas pedal frequently. Similarly, the thermostat turns the heater on and off four to eight times per hour to maintain a constant temperature range — usually between 1°F and 2°F of its setpoint.

Thermostats are composed of a temperature-sensitive element and a switch. The temperature-sensitive element is usually a bimetal coil or strip that moves one direction with a temperature drop and the opposite direction with a temperature rise. The bimetal element's movement operates the thermostat's switch. Heat pumps and gas heaters with two-stage gas valves have two-stage thermostats. Two-stage thermostats have two elements and two switches set to activate at two temperatures several degrees apart.

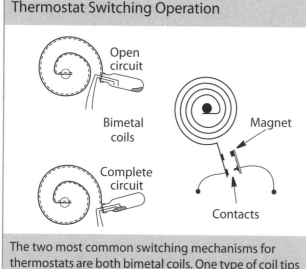

Thermostat Switching Operation

Open circuit

Bimetal coils

Magnet

Complete circuit

Contacts

The two most common switching mechanisms for thermostats are both bimetal coils. One type of coil tips a mercury bulb back and forth to open and close the circuit. The second type makes and breaks contact using the coil's movement with the help of a magnet.

Programmable thermostats — Programmable thermostats combine a clock with a thermostat and can save a significant amount of energy, especially for occupants who leave home during the day. Savings from an 8-hour, 10°F setback ranges from 5% to 15%. Two 8-hour, 10°F setbacks yields 10% to 20% savings. Buildings in milder climates record a greater percentage of savings from night setback than buildings in more severe climates. Setback periods comprise a larger percent of run time in milder climates compared to setback periods in more severe climates.

There are two types of programmable setback thermostats: electromechanical and electronic. The electromechanical models use a mechanical clock and bimetal temperature sensing. Electronic models use electronic temperature sensing and time keeping and are now more common than the electromechanical models.

Programmable thermostats work best on oversized heating systems that can recover from setback quickly.

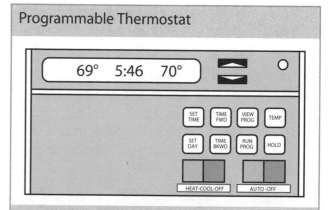

Programmable Thermostat

69°   5:46   70°

SET TIME | TIME FWD | VIEW PROG | TEMP

SET DAY | TIME BKWD | RUN PROG | HOLD

HEAT-COOL-OFF   AUTO-OFF

Programmable thermostats, which allow for two setback periods, work well for occupants with regular schedules, and particularly well for occupants who are gone during the day. Expect savings of 5% to 20% from 5°F to 15°F setbacks.

Non-programmable heat-pump thermostats — Heat pumps are controlled by two-stage thermostats. Two-stage thermostats have two sensors and two switches, which activate the heat pump's two heat sources at two temperature setpoints, which are several degrees apart.

The first stage of the heat pump is the efficient compressor, which moves heat from outdoors efficiently. The second stage of a heat-pump thermostat is the less-efficient auxiliary electric-resistance heat. Most heat-pump thermostats have a light or other indicator that shows when auxiliary heat is on. Residents may also notice that the supply air or baseboard-convector air is warmer when auxiliary heat is activated. For efficiency, the heat pump should run without auxiliary heat for as many hours as possible and at least 80% of the time.

Some heat pumps have a second built-in thermostat that prevents auxiliary heat from activating unless the air temperature or water temperature indicates that the heat source is too cool to recover quickly enough from setback.

Programmable Heat-Pump Thermostats

Heat pumps are less likely to be oversized because larger heat pumps are considerably more expensive than smaller ones. Therefore, heat pumps typically take longer to recover from setback and seldom recover without using auxiliary heat.

Ground-source heat pumps with radiant-floor distribution systems don't function well with a programmable thermostat. The combined lag time for the hydronic heat pump and the radiant floor is too long for a programmable thermostat to save energy or even to control the system effectively.

The following functions, available with some programmable heat-pump thermostats, may offer superior value for home owners who want to optimize heat-pump efficiency.

♦ Allows user to control temperature remotely through a smart phone.

♦ Allows user to control blower speed.

♦ Operates the compressor and multiple stages of auxiliary heat for up to four-stage operation.

♦ Allows user to control cycle length to safeguard the compressor and to enhance efficiency and comfort.

♦ Responds to sensors in the air, ground, or water to minimize auxiliary heat.

♦ Alerts user about auxiliary heat operation.

Zone heating

Zone heating is a practical and effective way to reduce heating costs in homes. Zone heaters are more efficient than central heating systems because zone heaters do not have ducts that lose a portion of the heat a heater produces. In cold climates, the zone heater can supplement the central heating system, providing heat for areas where occupants spend most of their time. A coordinated effort at zone heating can save from 10% to 20% of heating costs. However, the success of zone heating depends on how the residents use the room heaters and the central heating system.

One zone-heating strategy involves controlling the central heat with an automatic thermostat to provide a comfortable temperature throughout the house during the main activity periods. Then the programmable thermostat sets back to a minimum temperature of 55°F to 60°F for the remainder of the time. The bathroom has a radiant panel or heat lamp to provide comfort there. And the residents sleep under electric blankets at night. This zone heating strategy is only effective if the residents understand the idea and cooperate.

Controlling Cycle Length

Adjusting the burner's cycling can save energy and increase comfort if the cycles are too long or too short. Cycle-length adjustment is accomplished with controls that respond to one of the following inputs: the heating fluid's temperature or pressure, the outdoor temperature, or the measured cycle time.

If the cycle is too long, the heater may be overheating the building or producing heat faster than the distribution system can deliver it. Excessively long cycles may produce excessive chimney losses. If the cycle is too long, it makes sense to turn the burner off and on more frequently.

An adjusting lever inside most thermostats adjusts cycle time. This adjustment is called the *heat anticipator*. The heat anticipator's numerical setting should match electric current (in amperes) in the control circuit. But it can be varied slightly to lengthen or shorten burner cycles. The heat anticipator works primarily as a timer.

Aquastats limit cycle length by setting a maximum water temperature in hot-water systems, and pressure controllers limit cycle length in steam systems. More sophisticated controllers, called *reset controllers*, sense outdoor temperature and increase cycle time (steam), or water temperature (hot water) for cold weather, and decrease cycle time or water temperature in milder weather. In hot-water and steam systems, reset controllers avoid overheating in mild weather and under-heating during cold weather. Warm air thermostats can do the same for forced-air systems but are used on very few existing furnaces.

During mild weather, some burners in central heaters cycle on and off without the heat circulating through the distribution system, and heat from this short cycle is wasted. For example, a furnace's burner comes on and turns off before the blower control senses enough heat to turn the blower on. Or, a steam boiler's burner may turn on and off without making steam. Increasing the cycle length or locking out the boiler during mild weather makes sense in these cases.

Circulator Controls

The pumps in hot water systems and the blowers in warm air systems should remain on long enough to deliver most of a burner cycle's heat to the building. In the past, heating specialists have even suggested allowing pumps and blowers to run continuously. However, continuous operation isn't necessary with effective blower and pump controls. The furnace's blower control should start the blower as soon, and turn it off as late, as comfort allows.

Pumps in hot-water systems are controlled in several ways. In many home systems, the pump and burner turn on and off simultaneously, controlled by the thermostat. A better pump control option allows either a thermostat or aquastat to activate the pump independent of the burner. This option allows pumping to continue after the burner shuts off.

Forced-Air Systems

Air, as a heating fluid, has a theoretical efficiency advantage over hot water and steam because air circulates at a lower temperature. Forced-air heating is the most popular residential system because forced air accommodates central cooling and ventilation, using the same air handler and distribution system. Modern energy-efficient furnaces have the highest efficiencies of any combustion heaters.

However, forced-air distribution systems often leak air profusely, spread dust, and lead to overly dry indoor air during the heating season. Forced-air heating systems are also difficult to zone. Zoning means dividing a home or large apartment into zones that are controlled by separate thermostats.

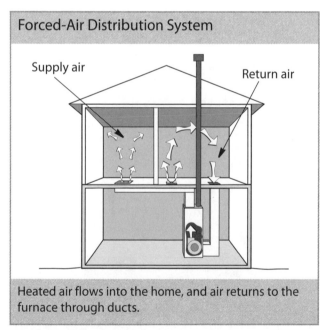

Forced-Air Distribution System

Supply air

Return air

Heated air flows into the home, and air returns to the furnace through ducts.

Separating forced-air systems into zones isn't usually practical or economical, except in large ducted distribution systems. Closing off registers and closing doors in unused rooms usually reduces airflow through the air handler and ducts, thereby reducing the system efficiency.

Zoning forced-air systems can save energy if the duct system is large enough to prevent excessive supply-air temperatures.

The forced-air distribution system consists of furnace or air handler, blower, ducts, filters, registers and grilles.

Forced-air distribution systems waste energy in the following ways:

♦ Air leaks into and out of ducts.

♦ The blower's operating time is too short.

♦ Obstructed airways or blower-speed limit air flow.

♦ Uninsulated ducts installed in unconditioned areas lose excessive heat.

Cumulative savings from the operating and maintenance improvements discussed in the next few sections vary from 5% to 25% of fuel consumption, depending on how much energy the distribution system currently wastes.

Forced-Air Furnace Configurations

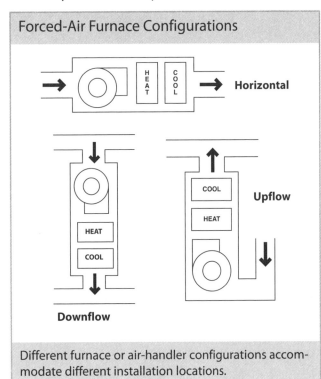

Different furnace or air-handler configurations accommodate different installation locations.

Natural Gas Furnace

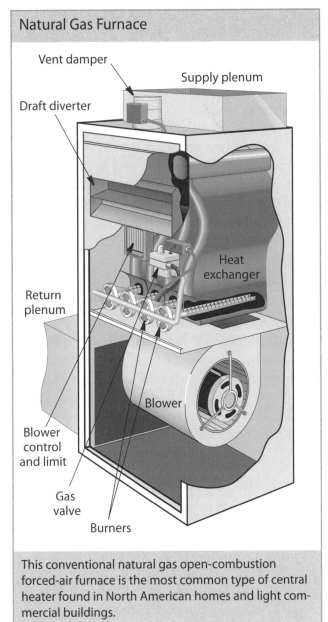

This conventional natural gas open-combustion forced-air furnace is the most common type of central heater found in North American homes and light commercial buildings.

Furnaces — The forced-air furnace is the most common type of central heater for single-family homes and is also common in multifamily buildings and light commercial buildings. Supply and return ducts connect to the furnace cabinet. The blower moves air through the heat exchanger where oil, gas, or electricity heat the air. An air filter in the furnace or return duct keeps the blower and heat exchanger clean.

The thermostat, located in the heated space, controls the burner or heating elements. Another thermostatic control, located inside the furnace, operates the blower. This blower control activates the blower when it senses warm air. A high-limit control, which shares a metal box with the blower control, stops the burner in the event of overheating. Overheating can occur because of duct obstruction, blower failure, or excessive fuel input.

The oldest home furnaces use the buoyancy of heated air to deliver the air from the basement to upper floors. These inefficient gravity furnaces are obsolete, but still survive in a few old homes.

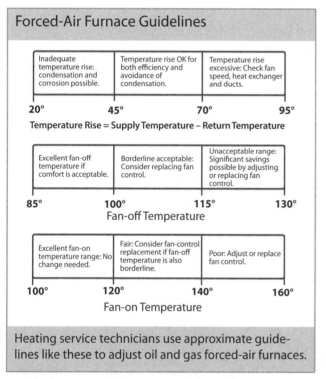

Forced-Air Furnace Guidelines

Inadequate temperature rise: condensation and corrosion possible.	Temperature rise OK for both efficiency and avoidance of condensation.	Temperature rise excessive: Check fan speed, heat exchanger and ducts.

20°   45°   70°   95°

Temperature Rise = Supply Temperature – Return Temperature

Excellent fan-off temperature if comfort is acceptable.	Borderline acceptable: Consider replacing fan control.	Unacceptable range: Significant savings possible by adjusting or replacing fan control.

85°   100°   115°   130°

Fan-off Temperature

Excellent fan-on temperature range: No change needed.	Fair: Consider fan-control replacement if fan-off temperature is also borderline.	Poor: Adjust or replace fan control.

100°   120°   140°   160°

Fan-on Temperature

Heating service technicians use approximate guidelines like these to adjust oil and gas forced-air furnaces.

Blower performance — The blower control turns the fan on when it senses heat in the furnace. It turns the fan off when it senses that the furnace is cool. If the fan control activates the fan too late or shuts it off too early, heat is wasted up the chimney. The blower should run whenever there is useful heat in the furnace to be delivered, as long as it doesn't create a comfort problem in the home. The blower control should be adjusted to turn the blower on at about 110°F to 125°F and off at 90°F to 100°F.

Increasing blower speed can reduce excessively high (over 150°F) delivery temperatures, which are inefficient. Furnace blowers come in two types: belt drive and direct drive. Belt-drive blowers are the older variety and should be checked every year for belt tightness and wear. Belt-drive blowers are adjusted by changing the diameter of their motor's drive pulley — increasing the diameter increases speed. Direct-drive blowers have motors that mount inside their blower wheel. They often have two or more speeds represented by different colored wires. Choosing a higher speed can reduce the furnace air temperature and increase its efficiency.

Dirt on the blower's fan blades greatly reduces airflow over the heat exchanger. Cleaning the fan blades thoroughly is important because leftover dirt can leave the fan wheel out of balance.

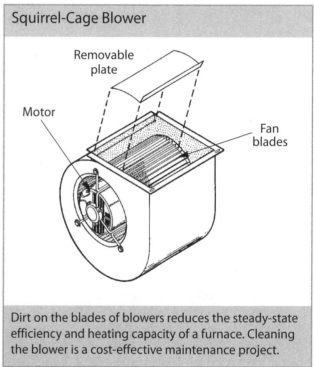

Squirrel-Cage Blower

Removable plate

Motor

Fan blades

Dirt on the blades of blowers reduces the steady-state efficiency and heating capacity of a furnace. Cleaning the blower is a cost-effective maintenance project.

Changing air filters — Air filters prevent dirt from collecting on the fan and heat exchanger of forced-air furnaces. Dirt reduces air movement and efficiency if it builds up on the filters, blower, and heat exchanger. The recommended frequency of filter changes depends on how much dirt travels in the airstream and how long the furnace is running. Filters in some homes may last 6 months before needing replacement or cleaning, while other homes' filters may need to be cleaned or replaced every 2 months. Clean filters also help keep the home clean.

Replacing and Cleaning Filters

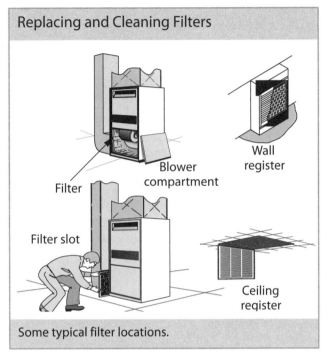

Some typical filter locations.

Duct Sealing and Insulation

Duct sealing is an extremely important and often neglected energy conservation measure. The forced-air supply and return ducts should be an airtight, closed conduit joining the furnace to the building's conditioned spaces. Duct joints should be sealed with duct mastic at all duct joints and seams.

See "Duct Air Leakage" on page 89 for more information on finding and sealing duct leaks.

Fiberglass duct insulation is the most common insulation for ducts. Insulation seams should be sealed with tape. Installers should cut carefully around obstacles to avoid insulation gaps and voids, which are important for a good overall R-value.

Foil-faced or vinyl-faced fiberglass duct insulation fastens to sheet metal ducts by various fastening systems.

♦ Welded or glued-on pins called stuck-ups or stick pins, with self-locking washers.

♦ Twine or wire wrapped around the insulation and duct, then anchored to nearby wood joists.

♦ Plastic ties.

Wrap the insulation all the way around the duct. Tape the seams with a high quality tape, like aluminum foil tape or vinyl tape. The end of each piece of tape should point downward; if it points upward, gravity eventually loosens the adhesive. Metal fasteners hold insulation in place better than tape. Duct insulation, depending entirely on tape to hold it in place, eventually falls off.

Fiberglass duct board and insulated flexduct are duct materials with built-in insulation. They aren't as durable as metal ducts, but are easier to install, so they are common. Duct board and flexduct ducts must have larger cross-sectional area compared to metal ducts, because they are rougher inside and create more air resistance. Duct insulation is sometimes installed inside metal ducts. This interior insulation is called duct liner or liner board. Flexduct, duct board, and liner board deteriorate from age and exposure to moisture.

Duct Insulation

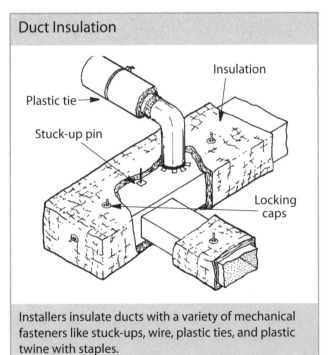

Installers insulate ducts with a variety of mechanical fasteners like stuck-ups, wire, plastic ties, and plastic twine with staples.

Duct Airflow Problems

Heating professionals often find duct systems undersized for the heating output of the furnace. Under-sizing means that the ducts' cross-sectional area is too small and the ducts have too many bends. A high supply-air temperature, or uncomfortable rooms, indicate a duct-sizing or duct-restriction problem. Furniture placement, closed doors, and dirty registers often limit ducted airflow.

A test involving opening the door to a furnace's blower compartment during operation can provide information about duct restriction. If opening the blower-compartment door reduces supply temperature significantly, then improving return air usually improves comfort and boosts efficiency. Improvements to return air include the following.

- Cutting off interior doors to allow air to return from rooms, which have no return register.

- Installing vents in doors or walls, or installing ducts in ceilings to allow air to return from rooms that have no return register.

- Installing a new return duct leading from a hard-to-heat area directly to the furnace cabinet (not to the existing return air ducts).

- Cleaning registers, blowers, and air conditioning coils.

Rooms may be hard to heat because of inadequate supply ducts or registers. Adding another supply duct and register is one option. Increasing the size of the existing supply duct and register is another option.

Hot-Water and Steam-Heating Systems

Hot-water and steam heating are common in many parts of North America. Boilers distribute their heat through a system of pipes and *heat emitters*. The term — *hydronic heating* — means both steam and hot-water heating to some people and to only hot-water heating to other people. We use the term hydronic to refer to water-based heating and cooling systems.

Steam heating is simpler than hot-water heat because it requires no pump. The steam builds pressure in the boiler, expands into pipes, pushing into the heat emitters. After the steam fills the radiators, the steam condenses, transferring its latent heat to the metal radiator. Steam heating is the least efficient heating option because of its high cycling losses and difficulty of achieving precise room-temperature control.

Hot-water heating is easy to zone and offers more energy-efficient control options than steam. However, cooling is difficult to incorporate into small to medium sized steam and hot-water systems. Chillers (water-cooling air conditioners) can use the same hydronic distribution piping; this option only works for large buildings.

Pipe insulation is often cost-effective for steam distribution pipes in most cases and for hot-water distribution pipes, depending on the temperature of the water and the cost of the insulation. Foam pipe sleeves are the most convenient type of pipe insulation for hot-water systems. Steam pipes are insulated with fiberglass, which is resistant to their higher temperature.

See "Pipe Insulation" on page 234.

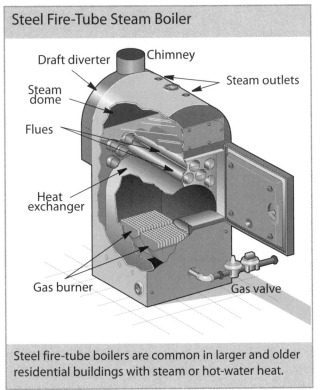

Steel Fire-Tube Steam Boiler

Steel fire-tube boilers are common in larger and older residential buildings with steam or hot-water heat.

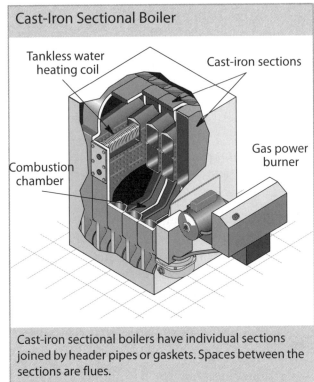

Cast-Iron Sectional Boiler

Cast-iron sectional boilers have individual sections joined by header pipes or gaskets. Spaces between the sections are flues.

Boilers

The three most common types of boilers for single and multifamily buildings are the cast-iron sectional boiler, the copper water-tube boiler, and the steel fire-tube boiler. These boiler designs are used for hot-water and steam heating systems. Hot-water boilers are completely filled with water and don't actually boil their water. Steam boilers have an air space at their water vessel's top, called the steam dome, where steam forms.

High-limit pressure and temperature controls protect boilers from damage by shutting off burners if the boiler gets too hot. Boilers also have another safety control that shuts the burner off if the water level in the boiler falls below a certain line. Local codes often require duplicate high-limit and low-water controls for larger buildings in case one control fails.

Controls also help the boiler optimize its performance and efficiency. Steam boilers often operate at excessive steam pressures, wasting energy. Hot-water boilers often heat water too hot and keep it hot for too long. Heating professionals solve these problems by adjusting automatic controls.

Correctly sizing boilers is important to their efficiency. The more oversized a boiler, the greater its cycling losses and inability to provide adequate heat during the coldest weather. In multifamily buildings, the energy wasted by frequent cycling can be reduced by installing smaller boilers and staging them to match the actual heating load. In an existing multifamily building, owners may install a smaller boiler next to the existing large boiler to heat the building during most of the year when the weather is mild. The older and less-efficient boiler only operates during very cold weather.

Boilers for space heating are sometimes used for water heating as well. See "Water Heating Integrated with Space Conditioning" on page 230.

Hot-water Distribution Systems

Hydronic heating systems combine a boiler or hydronic heat pump with heat emitters, piping, and controls. A pump circulates heat from the boiler or heat pump through the heat emitters. Hydronic systems often include domestic hot-water heating as part of the system.

See "Heat Pumps" on page 182.

The most common heat emitters are standing radiators, baseboard convectors, and fan coils. European-style wall-hung radiators and radiant floors are becoming more common.

An expansion tank allows the water in a hydronic piping system to expand and contract as it's heated and cooled. An air separator and vents expel air from the system to prevent circulation problems and metal corrosion.

Piping and Near-Boiler Devices

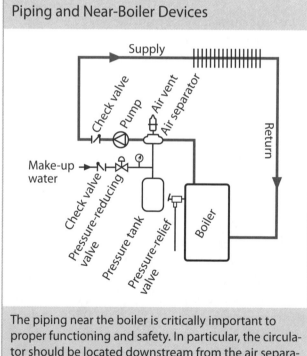

The piping near the boiler is critically important to proper functioning and safety. In particular, the circulator should be located downstream from the air separator and pressure tank.

Piping and distribution — There are three common types of distribution circuitry: series, parallel, and primary-secondary. Series has all the heat emitters in the same loop, which is simple and economical. However the water temperature is lower at the inlet of every successive heat emitter, and this must be factored into design. Parallel is a very common piping method featuring the ability for zoning. A reverse-return parallel piping system equalizes head loss of its parallel circuits to reduce temperature variation in rooms.

Piping systems may be zoned to offer different temperature setpoints and schedules to different parts of a home or multifamily building. One way to zone a hydronic system is with zone valves controlled by thermostats. The other way is with separate circulators for each zone. When the thermostat, located in the zone, calls for heat, the zone valve opens and/or the zone circulator starts. Zone valves have switches inside them that activate circulators and boilers after the valves open.

Modern Zone Control

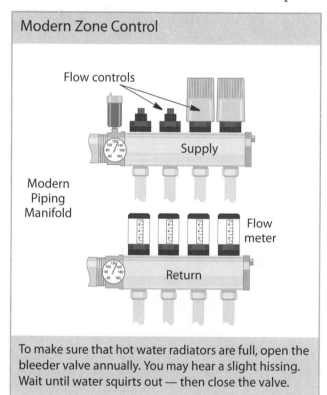

To make sure that hot water radiators are full, open the bleeder valve annually. You may hear a slight hissing. Wait until water squirts out — then close the valve.

The most advanced piping arrangement for using separate circulators is primary-secondary piping. This piping system employs a primary or boiler loop with a number of secondary loops piped through the home's heating zones. The boiler loop has its own circulator, but this loop and circulator doesn't provide water to any heat emitters directly. Each secondary circuit has a circulator that moves warm water to and from the heat emitters.

Piping Strategies: Traditional and Modern

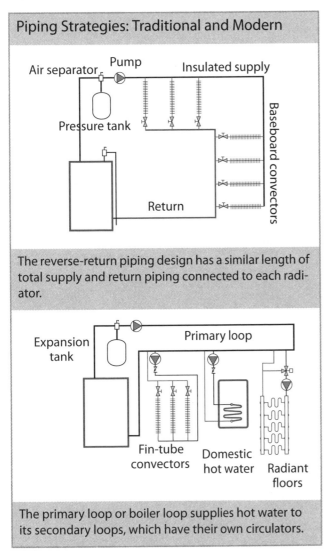

The reverse-return piping design has a similar length of total supply and return piping connected to each radiator.

The primary loop or boiler loop supplies hot water to its secondary loops, which have their own circulators.

The most important benefit of primary-secondary piping is its versatility in providing different water temperatures and flow rates to the different types of heat emitters in the zones, while protecting the boiler from low return-water temperatures that cause flue-gas condensation and corrosion.

Circulators can use considerable electrical energy in larger hydronic systems. Designing the circulator properly and then testing the system for the correct operating pressures minimizes circulator energy. Existing systems with excessive pressure

and operating power can be retrofitted by trimming the pump's impeller on a lathe or ordering a smaller impeller for the pump.

Heat emitters for hydronic systems —

Modern fin-tube convectors are an improvement over old-style hydronic radiators, because the fin-tube convector is longer than a radiator and is installed on the floor where it provides better air convection and air mixing.

Some multifamily buildings use fan-coil units that combine fin-tube piping with a fan to distribute the heat. If they are equipped with drip pans, fan coils can also circulate cooled water during the cooling season. Larger fan coils, called hydronic air handlers, connect to supply and return ducts like a forced-air furnace. Modern hydronic air handlers may contain an A-coil for cooling or a heat-recovery ventilator for whole-building ventilation.

Panel radiators have become popular in recent years for both new and retrofit applications. Panel radiators are made from steel or aluminum panels welded or pressed together into flat sections.

Panel radiators are either designed primarily for radiation or for a combination of radiation and convection. The difference in design between radiators and radiator/convectors is the addition of steel fins mounted vertically to the back of the panel or between two panels.

Radiant floors offer unbeatable comfort, superior energy efficiency, and the ability to use a condensing boiler or hydronic heat pump to its full potential. Radiant floors require relatively low water temperatures that condensing boilers and hydronic heat pumps can provide. Without the radiant floor's low water temperatures, these heat sources can't be as efficient. Radiant tubing can be incorporated into traditional concrete slabs, thin masonry slabs, or all-wood floors.

Common Hydronic Heat Emitters

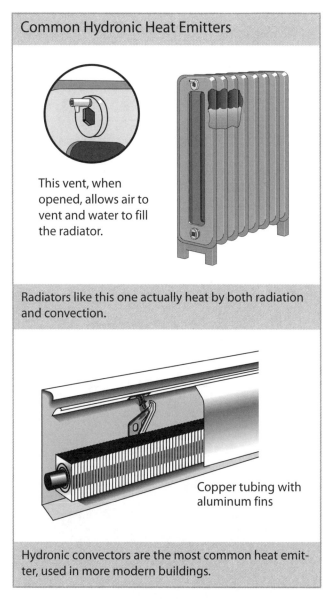

This vent, when opened, allows air to vent and water to fill the radiator.

Radiators like this one actually heat by both radiation and convection.

Copper tubing with aluminum fins

Hydronic convectors are the most common heat emitter, used in more modern buildings.

Controls for hot-water hydronic systems —

The simplest hydronic heating systems have a thermostat controlling a relay that activates both the boiler and circulator. Hot-water boilers also have a control called an aquastat that turns the burner off when the high-limit temperature is reached. The better aquastats have a separate switch that operates the pump after the thermostat turns the burner off to deliver heat stored in the boiler.

Many existing hot-water heating systems circulate or store water hotter than necessary to heat the building. Excessive temperature leads to greater standing losses and overheating the living spaces.

Boilers in single-family homes don't need to store a boiler full of heated water, unless the boiler has a tankless coil for water heating. This situation is sometimes referred to as a hot boiler. If a hot boiler has no tankless coil, a service technician may rewire the controls so that the burner doesn't fire unless the thermostat calls for heat.

The ideal aquastat setting for a boiler would be the lowest setting that gives satisfactory comfort without creating condensation in the boiler or its venting. A range of ideal temperatures between 140°F and 180°F depends on the outdoor temperature. In cold weather, the ideal temperature is higher, and in mild weather it is lower.

Self-adjusting aquastats called reset controllers adjust the water temperature up or down according to the outdoor temperature. Reset controllers are very effective for multifamily buildings where large boilers store many gallons of water. Reset controllers are often combined with cutout controllers that prevent boiler operation when outdoor temperatures rise above 60°F.

Hydronic Air Handler

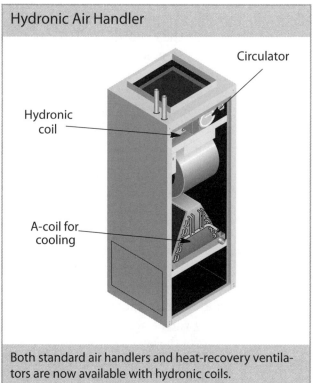

Circulator

Hydronic coil

A-coil for cooling

Both standard air handlers and heat-recovery ventilators are now available with hydronic coils.

Radiant Floors

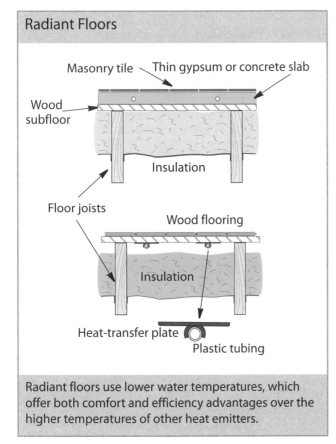

Radiant floors use lower water temperatures, which offer both comfort and efficiency advantages over the higher temperatures of other heat emitters.

Energy Controls: Simple and Complex

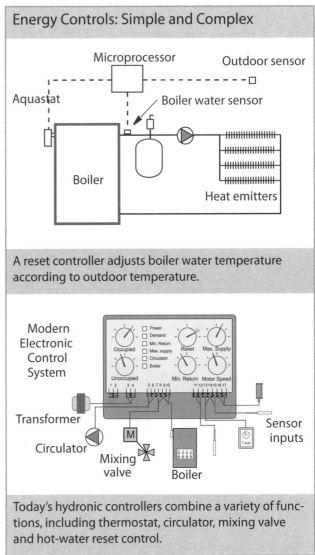

A reset controller adjusts boiler water temperature according to outdoor temperature.

Today's hydronic controllers combine a variety of functions, including thermostat, circulator, mixing valve and hot-water reset control.

Electronic controllers for hydronic systems have improved rapidly in their control capabilities and reliability in the past couple of decades. Their precision and advanced capabilities help to maximize comfort and minimize energy use. Electronic controls can perform more functions and can regulate hydronic systems more precisely than simpler electromechanical controls.

Modern electronic controllers measure temperature, process information, and switch power to the boiler, circulators, zone valves, and mixing valves. Electronic controllers provide digital readouts of system status and give warnings of sensor failure and other system faults. Electronic controllers can: reset boiler water temperature, prevent warm-weather boiler operation, control the position of mixing valves, activate multiple boilers in stages, control the speed of injection pumps, and activate and deactivate heating loads in order of priority.

Thermistors are electronic sensors that measure indoor temperature, outdoor temperature, and water temperature. Thermistors signal the electronic controller to regulate boiler and other components intelligently.

Hydronic heating systems are zoned using several different control strategies. Thermostats control zone valves on systems with a central circulator, or each zone has its own thermostat controlling a dedicated circulator. In advanced systems, zone circulators run constantly at variable speeds, injecting heated water as needed according to the changing demands of the zone. The domestic hot-water system is another zone, heated by the central boiler and equipped with its own circulator and control.

A multi-zone relay center controls the heating zones along with the domestic hot-water circuit. The controls give the domestic hot-water circuit priority whenever residents draw hot water from the tank. The electronic controller can prioritize zone operation to allow a relatively small boiler to heat a relatively large load. Electronic controllers often provide a post-purge control that leaves a circulator on after the heat source turns off to deliver left-over heat into the zones. Electronic controllers can also anticipate large loads and start boilers early to fill the demand.

The multi-zone relay center combines a number of control components into one box, where technicians make connecting all the wiring easy and convenient. Centralized zone controls, mounted on the piping manifolds, makes these controls space-efficient and easy to troubleshoot.

Common problems with hot-water heating systems — Most hydronic systems have iron and steel components that corrode if oxygen sneaks into the system. There are two common ways oxygen gets in.
1. Water escapes through the pressure-relief valve or a leak. The make-up water valve then provides water with dissolved oxygen.
2. The circulator creates too great a suction within the valves and piping. Oxygen from the air is sucked in through vents or small openings in the piping.

A waterlogged pressure tank causes hot-water flow out of the pressure relief valve, wasting energy and bringing new oxygen-bearing water into the system. Technicians either replace the pressure tank or simply recharge it with air.

Air in the hot-water distribution system displaces water in radiators and interferes with circulation. Technicians bleed radiators using special bleed valves and install air eliminators that trap air and vent it out of the system.

A particular threat to boilers is combustion gas condensate that corrodes boilers and chimneys. The most common cause of this condensation is return water temperature to the boiler that is too cool (less than 140°F). Control systems must be designed, installed, and adjusted to avoid this condition.

Steam Distribution Systems

Steam distribution systems consist of a boiler, piping, and radiators or other heat emitters. Other important piping accessories include steam traps, air vents, radiator temperature controls, and condensate tanks, and condensate pumps.

Efficiency-conscious boiler operators set the steam boiler's pressure controller at less than 2 pounds per square inch. Excess steam pressure wastes energy and causes steam systems to malfunction.

Ideally, the boiler cycles off as soon as the radiators are all full of steam to prevent overheating, and a timed-cycle controller varies the cycle length depending on outdoor-temperature signal.

There are two main kinds of steam distribution systems: one-pipe and two-pipe.

One-pipe steam — In one-pipe steam distribution systems, steam expands, filling pipes and radiators using the steam pressure produced by the boiler. Ideally, air leaves the pipes and radiators quickly to allow the steam into the radiators. Air vents expel air from the pipes and radiators to make room for the expanding steam. The air vents close automatically using a bimetal element that senses steam. For air to escape quickly, there must be enough air vents, and the vents must be working. Sometimes scale plugs the vents. Sometimes the main vents aren't large enough, and the air struggles to escape through tiny radiator vents, while steam pressure builds delaying radiator heating.

Gravity-Return Steam Distribution Systems

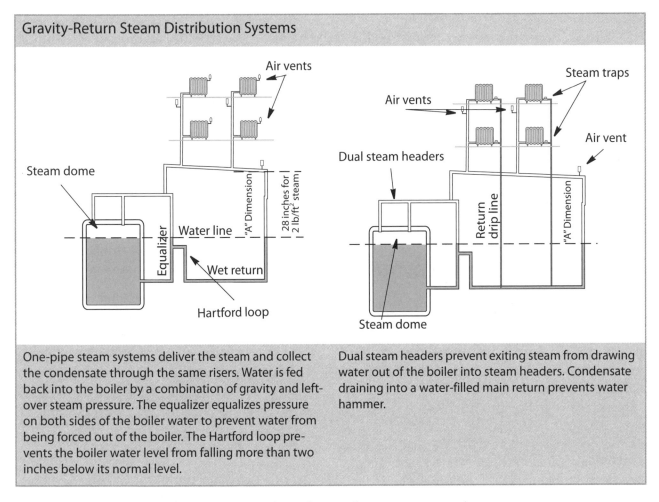

One-pipe steam systems deliver the steam and collect the condensate through the same risers. Water is fed back into the boiler by a combination of gravity and left-over steam pressure. The equalizer equalizes pressure on both sides of the boiler water to prevent water from being forced out of the boiler. The Hartford loop prevents the boiler water level from falling more than two inches below its normal level.

Dual steam headers prevent exiting steam from drawing water out of the boiler into steam headers. Condensate draining into a water-filled main return prevents water hammer.

With one-pipe steam, gravity returns condensed water to the boiler through the same single pipe the steam used to rise up into the radiators. The most common problem with one-pipe steam: parts of the distribution system are blocked by air that can't escape. Condensate flowing down collides with steam coming up, an event called water hammer, when air delays the steam.

When service technicians install large-volume air vents to the ends of main supply pipes, the performance and efficiency of one-pipe systems improves. Replacing undersized or malfunctioning radiator vents allows steam to move more quickly into the radiators.

Thermostatic air vents restrict the flow of air out of the radiator, and thus control the flow of steam into the radiator. Thermostatic air vents can prevent oversized radiators from over-heating rooms.

Whenever water and steam meet, steam pressure hurls the water against pipe joints, causing water hammer. Water hammer can plague steam systems during startup, in cold weather, and when the boiler has been replaced without the proper system-design changes. One-pipe systems also have problems with water hammer, if radiators or pipes rise or fall for some reason. The building settles or pipes sag, for example.

Two-pipe steam — With two-pipe steam distribution systems, steam traps operated by bimetal elements hold the steam in the radiator until it condenses into water. After the steam condenses into water, the trap opens and the water returns to the boiler through the return pipes.

Steam should never return to the boiler room through the return pipes. When the radiator steam traps fail, steam escapes into the boiler or return pipes. When steam flows through the radiators and into returns, water hammer can occur. Steam traps generally last three to six years and when some traps fail, the resulting water hammer can ruin the remaining traps.

Steam radiator orifices are an option for replacing steam traps. Orifices regulate the steam flow to an amount that can condense in the radiator as fast as the steam enters. The orifices don't fail because they are a simple metal disc with a hole in the center.

Thermostatic radiator valves (TRVs), installed at the radiators entrance, can reduce overheating and increase the steam system's efficiency. Air vents on steam mains can improve the heating performance of radiators farther away from the boiler.

Steam boiler replacement — Replacing a steam boiler often requires changes to the steam distribution system. It takes a bona-fide steam expert to anticipate problems, make distribution-system design changes, and troubleshoot the new system after the boiler is installed.

When the boiler water level changes, the critical "A" dimension changes, which can allow steam and condensate to contact each other in the lower reaches of the condensate return lines connected to the new boiler. New boilers have smaller steam domes than old boilers. The new boiler may produce wet steam or even push water into the steam mains. Owners and operators avoid these problems by good design and expert installation.

Water Treatment for Boilers

Dirt reduces the efficiency of hot-water and steam-heating systems. Technicians or boiler operators should check combustion for CO, dirt, and soot. The tubes or sections and other fire-side surfaces should be cleaned as often as necessary. Residents should dust radiators once a year to improve room heat transfer.

Steam-boiler operators put chemical additives into boilers and drain water out regularly to remove sediment — a process called blow-down. Blow-down removes dirt, rust, and scum from the boiler. Water treatment makes the water less corrosive and also helps keep particulates in suspension so they can be removed from the system by regular blow-down. Water treatment also reduces foaming, which delivers wet steam — less effective for heating than dry steam — into the pipes. Water treatment is a fairly complicated subject. Since water characteristics vary greatly from place to place, local experts are the best source of information on water treatment.

Steam Traps and Vents: Open Versus Closed

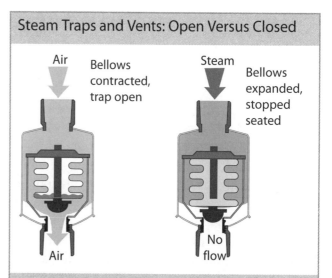

The steam trap's bellows operate a stopper that traps steam when the steam boils the alcohol solution in the bellows.

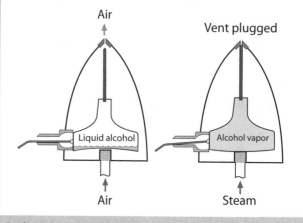

Radiator air vents operate on the same principle as the steam trap, passing air and stopping steam.

Hot-water systems shouldn't need blow-down or water treatment beyond their initial filling. Before the initial filling, the installer should fill the system with a cleaning solution, which then circulates for several hours to remove grease, oil, and chemicals from solder and flux. If the city water is corrosive, an initial charge of water treatment may sometimes be necessary. After the initial fill, a properly designed and correctly functioning hot-water system should operate indefinitely without needing cleaning or additional water.

New Energy-Efficient Combustion Furnaces and Boilers

The most important advances made by newer energy-efficient heaters over older conventional models are control of combustion air and elimination of dilution air. Draft inducer fans or high-pressure, forced-draft fans ration combustion air to the heat exchanger. This forces combustion by-products through tighter spaces, where more heat is removed compared to older heaters. Dilution air — which exhausts heated air from the home — is eliminated because a small blower controls the chimney draft instead of the dilution device.

High-efficiency furnaces and boilers have AFUEs of 80% to 97%, compared to conventional furnaces and boilers with AFUEs of 65% to 78%. The high-efficiency furnaces and boilers contain a number of important improvements over older models:

♦ Electronic ignition (no pilot light).

♦ Heat exchangers that restrict combustion gases, squeezing more heat out of them.

♦ Fans to move the combustion air through the smaller flues.

♦ Water condensed from flue gases in a corrosion-resistant heat exchanger for extra efficiency.

♦ Compact size and lighter weight, reducing off-cycle losses.

When replacing a furnace or boiler, do the following:

♦ Insist on proper installation.

♦ Be sure that deficiencies in ducts, piping, chimney, gas service, and electrical supply be corrected as part of the installation.

♦ Confirm that parts and service will be available in the future.

♦ Compare the competing warranties of the furnaces or boilers.

♦ Establish a maintenance schedule for the new furnace or boiler.

Characteristics of Gas Furnaces

AFUE	SSE	Operating characteristics
60+	70+	Category I chimney, draft diverter, no draft fan, standing pilot, non-condensing, indoor combustion and dilution air.
78+	80+	Category I chimney, no draft diverter, draft fan, electronic ignition, indoor combustion air, no dilution air.
90+	90+	Category IV chimney, no draft diverter, draft fan, low-temperature plastic venting, positive draft, electronic ignition, condensing heat exchanger, outdoor combustion air is strongly recommended.

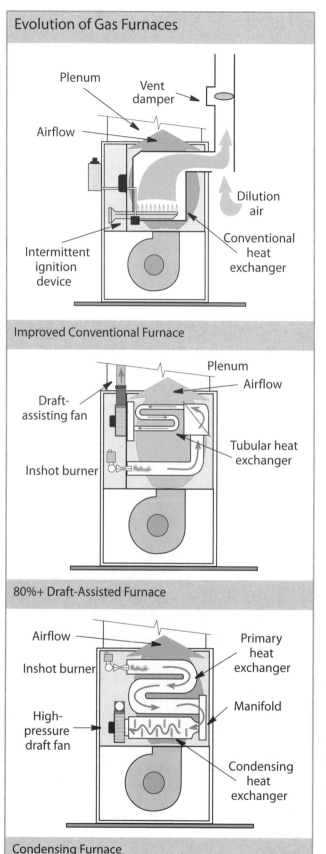

Evolution of Gas Furnaces

Improved Conventional Furnace

80%+ Draft-Assisted Furnace

Condensing Furnace

Modern Wall-Hung Boiler

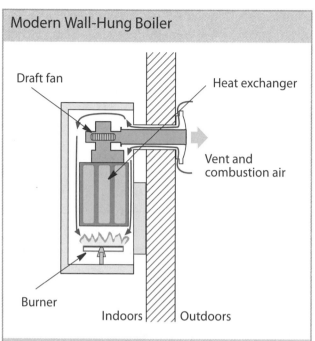

Wall hung boilers are very popular in Europe and becoming more popular in the U.S. The best European models, now available in North America, provide precise control of both gas flow and combustion air.

Energy-efficient Oil Furnaces and Boilers

Energy-efficient oil furnaces and boilers can reach AFUEs of almost 90% without condensing water out of the flue gases. They achieve this by employing a flame retention head oil burner (FRHOB), which gives nearly perfect combustion with very low excess air.

The delayed-action solenoid valve on many new units greatly reduces sooting at start-up, and oil dribble from the nozzle on shutdown. The solenoid valve allows the oil and air pressure to build before releasing the stream of oil from the nozzle.

Solid-state igniters have replaced transformers in newer oil burners, and some of these igniters are interruptible — they turn off after initial ignition — saving considerable electrical energy. Many newer oil burners have permanent split-capacitor motors, which provide electrical savings over conventional motors.

Some new oil heaters eliminate the barometric draft control, and its inefficient dilution air, using a horizontal vent with a power venter or a high pressure burner that doesn't need the barometric control. Eliminating dilution air saves up to 10% over a furnace with just a flame retention head burner.

Condensing oil heaters are available, but their market share is very small. Oil combustion doesn't produce as much water vapor to condense as natural gas. Also, the condensate is very acidic and may corrode parts of the flue and heat exchanger.

See "Modern oil burners" on page 156 and "Oil safety and efficiency checklist" on page 155.

Energy-efficient Gas Systems

There are two modern choices of furnaces and boilers: mid-efficiency and high-efficiency condensing. Both of these technologies have electronic ignition, no draft diverter, and improved heat-exchanger design.

Mid-efficiency heaters have a draft-assisting fan in the flue downstream of the heat exchanger. The draft fan forces exhaust gases out at a controlled rate, pulling combustion air into the heat exchanger at the same time. The draft fan reduces excess air, compared to older furnaces with draft diverters. Mid-efficiency furnaces and boilers also eliminate dilution air — a large energy-waster in older furnaces and boilers. The savings for a mid-efficiency furnace compared to a conventional unit, is 10% to 20%, assuming an AFUE of around 80%. Mid-efficiency heaters are vented vertically into existing chimneys or horizontally, through an exterior wall.

See "Intermittent Ignition Device (IIDs)" on page 151.

Natural gas combustion produces large amounts of water vapor. About 12% of the total heat in the gas is tied up in that water vapor's latent heat. This accounts for the high-efficiency heaters' dramatic increase of AFUE from 82% to 95% and savings over an older gas furnace of 20% to 30%. The water vapor condenses in a stainless steel portion of the heat exchanger and flows to a drain. The combustion gases exit at 100°F through corrosion-resistant plastic pipe, horizontally or vertically.

See "Sealed-Combustion Plastic Venting" on page 147.

Mid-efficiency furnaces and boilers have had problems with condensation in their chimneys and heat exchangers. Condensing furnaces have the advantage of being designed to use the latent heat from condensing flue gases and to resist corrosion.

Both mid-efficiency and high-efficiency furnaces are available in two-stage models. The two-stage heating is accomplished by a two-stage gas valve, a two-speed draft fan, and a two-speed blower. The first stage is about half the heating capacity of the second stage. The two-stage strategy reduces cycling and improves comfort. However, two-stage furnaces are probably no more efficient than single-stage ones. The imprecise control of combustion air continues to prevent the heating industry from supplying more efficient and clean-burning furnaces.

Integrated Heating Systems

A new generation of packaged HVAC units may provide a solution to combustion air and excessive chimney losses. Powered by a small boiler, these units provide space heating, water heating, ventilation, and air conditioning if necessary. Using a single efficient boiler with a single vent for both space heating and water heating increases space-heating efficiency and water-heating efficiency over having separate vents for each. Hopefully, the new boiler features the kind of precise combustion-air control and clean combustion of the best German boilers of today.

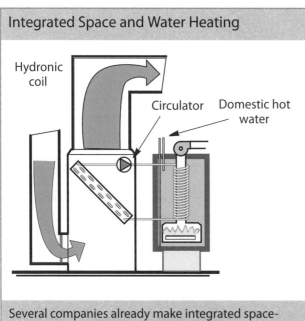

Integrated Space and Water Heating

Hydronic coil

Circulator

Domestic hot water

Several companies already make integrated space-and-water heating systems with air handlers.

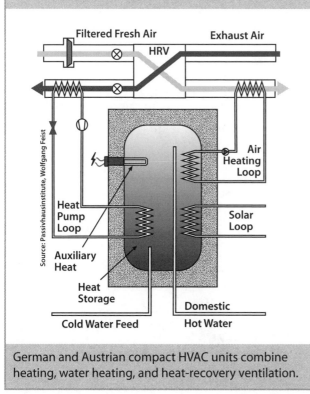

Filtered Fresh Air

Exhaust Air

HRV

Source: Passivhausinstitute, Wolfgang Feist

Air Heating Loop

Heat Pump Loop

Solar Loop

Auxiliary Heat

Heat Storage

Cold Water Feed

Domestic Hot Water

German and Austrian compact HVAC units combine heating, water heating, and heat-recovery ventilation.

The Germans and Austrians have designed compact heating and water-heating units for installation into energy-efficient homes. These units feature a variety of possible heating inputs including gas, heat pump, and solar. Hot-water storage

is often incorporated into the same cabinet as the heating and ventilating equipment. The packaged unit also often contains a heat-recovery ventilator.

Combustion Room Heaters

Combustion room heaters are very common in older residential buildings and buildings in mild heating climates. Wood stoves saw a resurgence in the 1980s, but declined through the 1990s. Pellet stoves and gas fireplaces replaced wood stoves as room heaters in many homes. Then wood stoves surged again after oil prices rose after the turn of the 21st century.

Gas Room Heaters

Gas room heaters have steady-state efficiencies of between 60% and 75%. There are four common types of gas room heaters.
1. Freestanding room heater.
2. Floor furnace.
3. Recessed wall furnace.
4. Direct-vent wall furnace.

The first three models are older designs that may have obsolete flame-safety controls. The oldest existing units may have no flame-safety control, but only manual control of the pilot valve and the main gas valve. Units with obsolete or absent flame-safety controls should be replaced or retrofitted with modern combination gas valves equipped with flame-safety control.

The first three types of heaters are open-combustion — their combustion chamber and chimney are open to the room. The fourth, direct-vent wall furnaces are sealed-combustion heaters with horizontal vents. Older models use atmospheric draft to draw combustion air and exhaust combustion gases. Newer models have a draft fan.

Room heaters with draft or combustion problems are particularly dangerous because they are located within the living space. Floor furnaces often have backdrafting problems due to the long horizontal run of vent connector they require because of their typical location in the center of a room. Heating professionals should test room heaters for CO and draft to ensure that they don't pose an immediate danger.

Most gas room heaters have integral thermostats with numbered dials. The numbers are for reference and don't relate to temperature. Some floor furnaces and wall furnaces have wall-mounted thermostats that give better room comfort than integral thermostats.

New Efficient Gas Room Heaters

New energy-efficient gas room heaters look very similar to the older models. However, they use a variety of efficiency improvements to achieve steady-state efficiencies between 78% and 82%. These improvements include:

♦ Lighter metal heat exchangers.

♦ Blowers to circulate room air.

♦ More restrictive flow of combustion gases, leading to less excess air.

♦ Intermittent pilot lights.

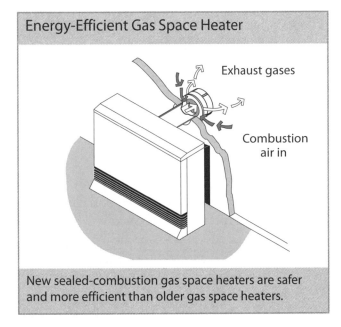

Energy-Efficient Gas Space Heater

Exhaust gases

Combustion air in

New sealed-combustion gas space heaters are safer and more efficient than older gas space heaters.

The safest and most efficient space heaters also have a draft fan and are sealed combustion. These include the console model shown in the illustration and a baseboard model resembling an electric baseboard heater.

Condensing room heaters aren't yet commercially available.

Unvented Gas Room Heaters

Unvented room heaters can deplete oxygen and produce unsafe quantities of CO, water vapor, and oxides of nitrogen. Oxygen depletion and CO are serious health hazards that can be life-threatening. Newer models have oxygen-depletion sensors that shut the unit off when the room becomes depleted of oxygen. However, the safe use of unvented gas room heaters requires one or more wide-open windows, which can interfere with the room's heating and comfort level.

Gas Fireplaces

Gas burning fireplaces and fireplace inserts are very popular. They are valued for their visual appeal, but their annual fuel utilization efficiencies are only 40% to 60%.

Fireplace inserts, consisting of a ceramic log and gas burner inserted into a standard fireplace, are both dangerous and inefficient. The fireplace's chimney draft is unpredictable, because the chimney is a custom-built assembly. A vacuum in the home — caused by exhaust fans or other gas appliances — can easily backdraft the fireplace, polluting the home.

Wood Stoves

Wood stoves burn wood more efficiently than fireplaces, by moving the fire into the center of the room and surrounding the firebox with room air. Air traveling through the combustion chamber is roughly controlled by a manual damper.

The western states and the Environmental Protection Agency established air pollution limits and boosted efficiency of manufactured wood stoves.

Wood Stove Installation

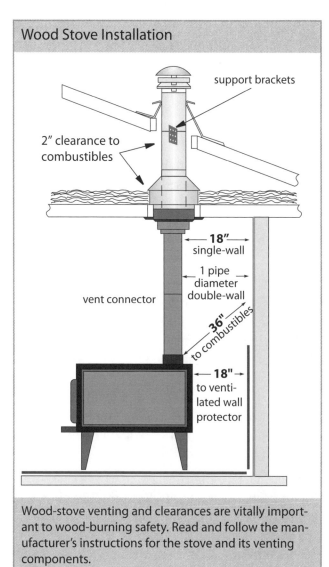

support brackets

2" clearance to combustibles

18" single-wall

1 pipe diameter double-wall

vent connector

36" to combustibles

18" to ventilated wall protector

Wood-stove venting and clearances are vitally important to wood-burning safety. Read and follow the manufacturer's instructions for the stove and its venting components.

New wood stoves are tested for efficiency by the EPA. The efficiency of new wood stoves is between 63% and 78%.

Many new stoves use catalytic converters — a honeycombed tube surfaced with a platinum catalyst that burns most of the unburned hydrocarbons from the fire. Non-catalytic, high-efficiency wood stoves use other methods to improve combustion including these.

♦ Heated combustion air.

♦ Insulated combustion chamber.

♦ Secondary combustion air above the flame.

♦ Secondary heat exchanger for combustion gases.

The habits of wood-burning users can greatly affect the emissions and efficiency of wood burning. Hot fires pollute less and are more efficient than smoldering fires. Feeding the stove more often helps efficiency and reduces emissions, too. It's important to get the right size wood stove. Larger stoves encourage wood burners to smolder their fires to control heat. Smoldering maximizes emissions and minimizes fuel-burning efficiency.

Wood stoves are a potent fire hazard, if installed improperly. The following safety precautions are recommended by most local fire codes:

♦ Use triple-wall pipe or insulated double-wall chimney and maintain 2 inches clearance to combustibles.

♦ Keep single-wall metal vent connectors 18 inches away from combustible walls.

♦ Keep double-wall metal vent connectors one pipe diameter away from combustible walls.

♦ Single-wall stoves must be 36 inches away from combustible walls.

♦ Stoves installed closer than 36 inches must be double wall, or walls must be protected by ventilated wall protectors.

♦ Stove clearances of less than 36 inches must be specified by the manufacturer and printed on a metal tag attached to the stoves.

♦ Bring combustion air from the outdoors to reduce negative pressure around stoves.

Pellet Stoves

Pellet stoves burn pelletized wood waste at higher efficiency than wood stoves burn wood. The best pellet stoves have over 80% SSE. Pellet stoves have draft inducers that control draft and excess air more precisely than wood stoves' atmospheric draft. Pellets are more uniform and drier than average wood, giving these stoves an added efficiency advantage. However, pellet stoves and their fuel are more expensive than wood stoves.

Electric Heat

Electric heaters are usually 100% efficient at converting the electricity to heat in the room where they are located. However, fossil-fuel-generated electricity converts only about 30% of the fuel's potential energy to electricity.

Electric Furnaces

An electric furnace heats air moved by its fan over several electric-resistance heating elements. Electric furnaces have three to six elements — 3.5 to 7 kW each — that work like the elements in a toaster. The 24-volt thermostat circuit energizes devices called sequencers that bring the 240-volt heating elements on in stages. The multiple-speed fan switches to a higher speed as more elements engage to keep the air temperature stable.

While electric furnaces are 100% efficient, they often suffer large heat losses due to duct leakage. Duct leakage can be responsible for wasting up to 30% of electricity used by the furnace. Many electric furnaces have been replaced by fuel-burning furnaces because electric furnaces are the most expensive way to heat a home.

Replacing air filters at regular intervals is vital to the efficient operation of electric furnaces. The electric heating elements should be dusted and vacuumed if they get dirty. Cleaning the heating elements won't be necessary if residents change the air filters regularly.

Electric furnaces can be a peak-load problem for utility companies if they are using more 5-kW heating elements than are necessary to heat the home. The utility experiences a higher peak demand than it would if only the minimum number of elements were used. During mild weather in most climates, only a couple elements are needed. As the temperature gets lower, the other elements become necessary.

Some control systems allow fewer elements to be used during mild weather and more during cold weather. Either a two-stage heating thermostat or a standard heating thermostat, combined with an outdoor thermostat, can accomplish the different levels of heat for different weather.

Baseboard Electric Heaters

Electric baseboard heaters are zonal heaters controlled by thermostats within the zone they heat. Baseboard heaters contain electric resistance heating elements encased in metal pipes. These pipes extend the length of the unit and are surrounded by aluminum fins to aid heat transfer. As air within the heater is heated, the air rises into the room. This draws cooler air into the bottom of the heater.

There are two kinds of built-in electric baseboard heaters, strip-heat and liquid-filled. Strip-heat units are less expensive than liquid-filled, but they don't heat as well. Strip-heat units release heat in short bursts, as the temperature of the heating elements rises to about 350°F. Liquid-filled baseboard heaters release heat more evenly over longer time periods, as the element temperature rises only to about 180°F.

The line-voltage thermostats, used with baseboard heaters, sometimes don't provide good comfort because they allow the temperature in the room to vary by 2°F or more. Newer, more accurate thermostats are available. Automatic setback thermostats for electric baseboard heat employ timers or a resident-activated button that raises the temperature for a time and then automatically returns to setback.

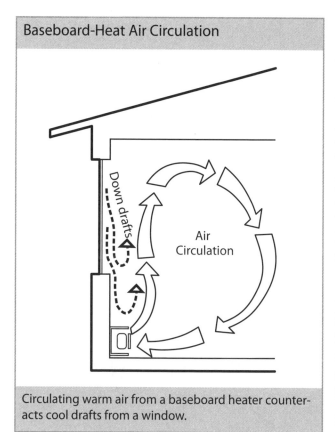

Baseboard-Heat Air Circulation

Down drafts

Air Circulation

Circulating warm air from a baseboard heater counteracts cool drafts from a window.

Electric Radiant Heat

Most electric heating systems distribute heat through air circulation. Radiant heat is different — the heat radiates from a warm surface. Radiant heat can be zoned, with rooms being heated by their own electric radiant heating units.

There are several types of electric radiant heat. Electric heating cables embedded in concrete plaster, or gypsum board are common. Heating cables are sometimes installed above plaster or gypsum-board ceilings.

Electric radiant panels attach to the ceiling. These panels are probably the quickest-recovery heating devices commonly used in residential buildings. If occupants turn the radiant panels on and off as they enter and leave rooms, this may result in the lowest energy use of any electric heating system.

Radiant heat offers draft-free heating that is easily zoned. Unlike other heating systems, radiant heat occupies little or no interior space — allowing complete freedom to place furniture without

impeding air flow. Its proponents claim that radiant heat can provide similar comfort to other systems at lower indoor temperatures, saving significantly heating costs compared to baseboard electric heating or heat pumps.

Radiant heat does have numerous disadvantages, too. Some occupants complain about their heads being too warm and about excessive room temperature fluctuations. And supplying heat at the ceiling or floor — bordering outdoors or unheated spaces — may result in higher heat losses. If there are any insulation flaws, a significant percent of the heat may be lost.

Electric Thermal Storage

Some electric utility companies structure their rates like phone companies, charging more during daytime and less at night. They do this in an attempt to reduce their total necessary generating capacity, or peak demand.

Customers of these utilities can benefit from storing electric heat during nighttime hours, when rates are lower. This is called electric thermal storage. Electric thermal storage doesn't save energy, but it does save money by utilizing lower rates.

Stored heat can be from electric resistance or from a heat pump. The most common type of electric thermal storage heater is a room-size resistance heater, with elements encased in a substantial amount of heat-storing ceramic. Other methods of electric thermal storage include using electric resistance heat or a heat pump to heat water in an insulated storage tank.

Electric Room Heaters

Electric room heaters can save energy by keeping a person warm in a localized area of the home. When you're home alone, use room heaters and a low thermostatic setting on the central heating system for up to 20% energy savings.

There are three types of electric room heaters: strip heaters, radiant heaters, and liquid-filled heaters. The liquid-filled heaters are the most comfortable, since they release heat gradually.

Ceiling Radiant Heat

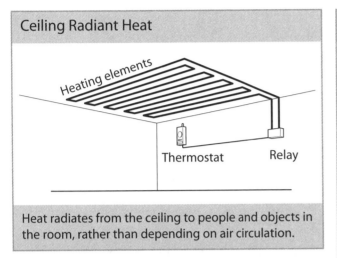

Heat radiates from the ceiling to people and objects in the room, rather than depending on air circulation.

Electric Thermal Storage Heater

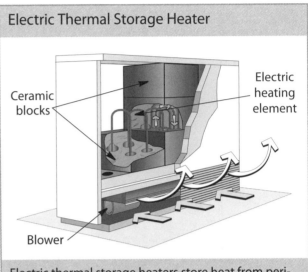

Electric thermal storage heaters store heat from periods of low demand for use in high-demand periods. This type of electric heat qualifies users for lower rates.

Electric Zone Heating

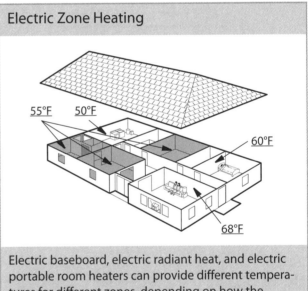

Electric baseboard, electric radiant heat, and electric portable room heaters can provide different temperatures for different zones, depending on how the home's occupants are using them.

The problem with zone heating is that many common zone heaters aren't safe. Many cheaper and older portable electric room heaters aren't safe because their red hot elements and lack of safety features are a safety hazard. Electric room heaters can be safe, depending on the type you choose and the way you use them. Use the following guidelines when employing portable electric room heaters:

♦ Make sure that you have a properly functioning smoke detector.

♦ Use a safe room heater.

♦ Don't overload circuits.

If you decide to use a portable room heater, select one that has the safety features described below:

♦ Tip-over switch: Tip-over switches shut the portable electric heater off automatically if the heater falls over.

♦ Protective grille: All electric elements that glow must be protected by a grille. A grille or other protection is essential to keep fingers and fabrics from touching the hot elements.

♦ Sealed heating elements: The heating elements must be sealed or otherwise inaccessible. Young children might push objects through the protective grille, so having sealed heating elements reduces the risk of electric shock.

Heat Pumps

Heat pumps are difficult to classify because they provide both heating and cooling for the home. Heat pump compressor systems use a refrigerant to move heat from the outdoors to indoors during the heating season, and from the indoors to outdoors during the cooling season. A reversing valve changes the direction of the refrigerant flow depending on the need for heating or cooling.

See "The Refrigeration Cycle" on page 42 for information on principles of operation.

Heat pumps are the most efficient type of electric heat, particularly for the southern United States. Heat pumps can deliver one-and-a-half to four times more heat energy to a home than they consume because heat pumps move heat rather than converting heat from a fuel. Unfortunately, the superior energy efficiency of heat pumps' is often reduced by poor installation, distribution losses, and neglected maintenance.

See "Heat-pump Efficiency Ratings" on page 184

Heat pumps are controlled by two-stage thermostats for heating. The first stage is the compressor of the heat pump; then, if the compressor fails to keep up with the home's heat loss, electric resistance coils (the second stage of heat), come on to assist the compressor. Heat pumps should have an outdoor thermostat that prevents the less efficient electric resistance heat from coming on until the outdoor temperature is below 40°F.

Classifying Heat Pumps

There are two common types of heat pumps, air-source heat pumps and geothermal heat pumps. Air-source heat pumps transfer heat between the home and the outdoor air. Geothermal heat pumps transfer heat between the home and the ground or an outdoor water source.

Another way to classify heat pumps is by their heat source and their heat sink. The heat source is where the heat-pump collects the heat. The heat sink is the indoor heat-distribution medium (water or air) that accepts the heat pump's collected heat. For example, an air-source heat pump that uses a forced-air distribution system would be classified: air-air (source = air; sink = air).

Types of Heat Pumps by Source and Sink

Source-Sink	Typical System Description
Air-Air	Outdoor air-heated evaporator with indoor condenser fan-coil (ductless mini-split)
Air-Water	Outdoor air-heated evaporator with indoor radiant slab
Water-Water	Ground coil (closed or open-loop) with indoor radiant slab
Water-Air	Ground coil (closed or open-loop) with forced-air ducts

Air-source heat pumps — Air-source is the most common type of heat pump, comprising more than 85% of residential heat pumps. Air-source heat pumps employ two coils, one outdoors and one that conditions indoor air. Both coils are made of copper tubing with aluminum fins to aid heat transfer. Fans blow air through these coils.

Electric heat pumps work like mechanical air-conditioning systems. In fact, a heat pump is almost identical to an air conditioner, except for a reversing valve that permits the reversal from heating to cooling.

In the heating mode, the outdoor coil refrigerates the air to harvest heat. The refrigerant brings the collected heat to the indoor coil and releases the heat to the circulating indoor air. In cooling mode, the process is reversed. The indoor coil collects heat from indoor air, and the outdoor coil releases the heat to outdoor air.

Like air conditioners, air-source heat pumps are available as centralized units with ducts or as room units. Most residential heat pumps are split systems with indoor and outdoor units. Room heat pumps are more efficient than central units because they have no ducts and are factory-charged with refrigerant. Mini-split heat pumps are a centralized air-source heat-pump system without ducts. One outdoor unit serves the mini-split system, which has one or several indoor fan-coil units.

See "Air Conditioners" on page 212.

Geothermal heat pumps — Geothermal heat pumps use the refrigeration cycle to transfer heat between the home and the ground or an outdoor body of water to heat or cool the home. Geothermal heat pumps, like air-source heat pumps, work best in well-insulated and airtight homes because they provide heat at a relatively low temperature. Geothermal heat pumps are considerably more efficient than air-source heat pumps because of the ground's moderate and consistent temperatures. But they're also considerably more expensive to purchase and install than air-source heat pumps.

The two most common types of geothermal heat pumps are ground-source heat pumps (also called closed-loop geothermal heat pumps or ground-coupled heat pumps), and water-source heat pumps (also called open-loop ground-source heat pumps, or groundwater heat pumps).

Closed Versus Open Loops — Closed-loop heat pumps collect the earth's heat with a looped ground coil — a buried, sealed loop of pipe circulates a water-antifreeze solution between the ground and the heat pump. During the heating cycle, the heat pump removes heat from the circulating water and uses it to heat the home. The cooled water recirculates through the warmer ground, collects more heat, and then returns again to the heat pump to deliver its collected heat to the home. This process is reversed for the cooling cycle.

Open-loop geothermal heat pumps use water as their heat source. A pump moves water from a well or nearby water source and circulates the water through the heat pump, where the water is refrigerated, removing some of its heat. The cooler water is returned to the source as more water is drawn from the source.

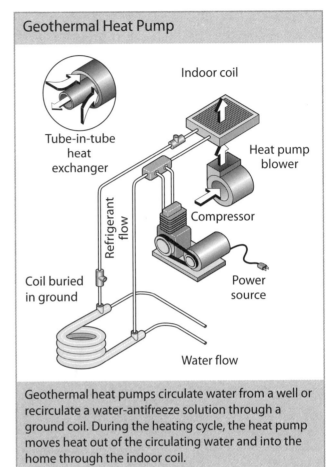

Geothermal Heat Pump

Indoor coil

Tube-in-tube heat exchanger

Heat pump blower

Refrigerant flow

Compressor

Coil buried in ground

Power source

Water flow

Geothermal heat pumps circulate water from a well or recirculate a water-antifreeze solution through a ground coil. During the heating cycle, the heat pump moves heat out of the circulating water and into the home through the indoor coil.

Closed-loop ground-source heat pumps collect the earth's heat with a ground coil — a buried, sealed loop of pipe with water circulating to and from the heat pump. During the heating cycle, the heat pump removes heat from the circulating water. The cooled water recirculates through the warmer ground, collects more heat, and then returns again to the heat pump to deliver its collected heat.

Heat-pump Efficiency Ratings

Heat-pump efficiency is rated in a number of ways. The most common are Coefficient of Performance (COP), Heating Seasonal Performance Factor (HSPF), Energy Efficiency Ratio (EER), and Seasonal Energy Efficiency Ratio (SEER).

COP is oldest and most common rating. COP tells you how many times more efficient a particular heat pump is compared to electric resistance

(100%). Heating COPs range from 1.5 to 4, depending on climate, design, and installation. A COP of 1.6 corresponds to 160% efficiency, and means that the heat pump delivers 1.6 kilowatt-hours (kWh) of heat for every kWh of electricity it consumes. An air-source heat pump's COP is less in the northern U.S. compared to the southern U.S. because air closer to the equator contains more usable heat.

The HSPF rates the heating efficiency of a heat pump and is listed on the Energy Guide label of every heat pump sold in the United States. The HSPF includes both the very efficient heating done by the compressor and the less efficient heating done by the electric resistance elements. The HSPF gives the number of British thermal units (BTUs) that the heat pump delivers for each watt-hour of electricity it consumes. The most efficient heat pumps have an HSPF of around 10.

EER rates the cooling efficiency heat-pumps at specific temperature and humidity conditions. SEER is similar to EER but is measured over a range of outdoor temperatures to account for seasonal variations. EER and SEER are measured in roughly the same way as HSPF, but they rate the number of BTUs removed from the home for each watt-hour of electricity they consume.

See "Air-conditioner Efficiency" on page 214.

Use heat-pump efficiency ratings to compare the efficiency between different units. Because of the wide variety of operating conditions, efficiency ratings aren't useful to estimate the actual amount of energy the unit consumes.

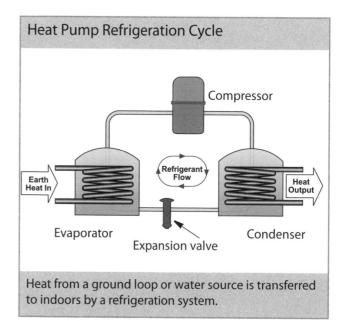

Heat Pump Refrigeration Cycle

Compressor

Refrigerant Flow

Earth Heat In

Heat Output

Evaporator

Expansion valve

Condenser

Heat from a ground loop or water source is transferred to indoors by a refrigeration system.

Heat-Pump Performance Enhancements

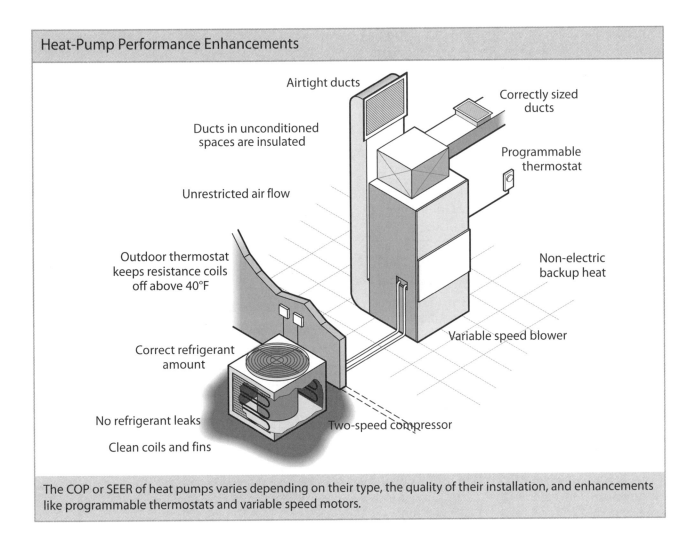

The COP or SEER of heat pumps varies depending on their type, the quality of their installation, and enhancements like programmable thermostats and variable speed motors.

This chapter discusses lighting and home appliances. Lighting and appliances account for 10% to 50% of residential energy use, depending on climate and the energy efficiency of the home. A home with an efficient shell in a mild climate uses a larger percent of its energy for lighting and appliances than one with an inefficient shell in a severe climate.

Annual Electrical Energy: Kilowatt-Hours

Appliance	Low Estimate	High Estimate
Lighting	200	2000
Refrigerator	500	2000
Clothes Dryer	300	1500
Clothes Washer*	100	1000
Television	100	600
Well pump	250	750
Hot tub / spa	1000	2500
Computer	50	400

* Includes water heating.

Energy Information Administration, Lawrence Berkeley Laboratory, and utility sources.

See "Analyzing Annual Energy Costs" on page 277 and "Annual Average Household Energy Cost by Region (1997)" on page 14 for more information on percentage of energy used for lighting and appliances.

Lighting

Homes are the setting for various visually-intensive tasks such as sewing, office work, crafts, and cooking. More people are working at home and need lighting suited for their vocation. Lighting also provides outdoor security and night time visibility. Retrofits consist mainly of replacing the existing lamps or fixtures with more efficient models.

To choose the best lighting options, it helps to understand basic lighting principles and terminology.

Efficacy (efficiency)

Lighting efficiency is known as *efficacy* and is measured in lumens per watt.

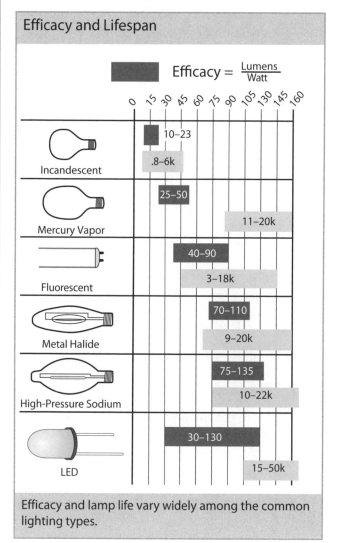

Efficacy and Lifespan

$$\text{Efficacy} = \frac{\text{Lumens}}{\text{Watt}}$$

0 15 30 45 60 75 90 105 130 145 160

Incandescent 10–23 / .8–6k

Mercury Vapor 25–50 / 11–20k

Fluorescent 40–90 / 3–18k

Metal Halide 70–110 / 9–20k

High-Pressure Sodium 75–135 / 10–22k

LED 30–130 / 15–50k

Efficacy and lamp life vary widely among the common lighting types.

Illumination

A lumen measures light output from a lamp. All lamps are rated in lumens. For example, a 100-watt incandescent lamp produces about 1750 lumens. Dividing a lamp's number of lumens by its watts gives efficacy — a measurement of lighting efficiency.

The distribution of light on a horizontal surface is called its illumination. Illumination is measured in footcandles. A footcandle of illumination is a lumen of light distributed over one square foot of area.

The amount of light required, measured in footcandles, varies according to the difficulty of a visual task. Ideal illumination is the minimum footcandles necessary to comfortably perform a task at the maximum practical rate of speed without eyestrain.

In the past, illumination of 100 footcandles was thought to be minimum for visual tasks in the workplace. Now, the Illuminating Engineering Society says that 30 to 50 footcandles is adequate for most home and office work. Difficult and lengthy visual tasks, like sewing for extended periods of time, requires 200 to 500 footcandles. Where no seeing tasks are performed, the lighting system needs to provide only security, safety, or visual pleasure — from 5 to 20 footcandles.

Lighting Uses

Three categories of lighting by function are ambient lighting, task lighting, and accent lighting.

Ambient lighting provides security and safety, as well as lighting for tasks that occur throughout the lighted space.

Task lighting provides light at the work area. Illumination levels should be high enough for accurate task execution in task areas — not throughout the entire lighted space.

Accent lighting illuminates walls so that their brightness contrasts less with brighter areas, like ceilings and windows. Accent lighting is also used to make the space more visually comfortable.

Lighting Color

Lamps are assigned a color temperature depending on their "coolness" or "warmness." People perceive colors at the blue-green end of the color spectrum as cool and those at the spectrum's red end as warm. Morning light from the north is more bluish than southwest evening light.

Cool light sources are preferred for visual tasks, since they produce better contrast at the printed page, workbench, or other task. Warm light sources are preferred for living spaces, because they are more flattering to people's skin and clothing.

Color Rendering Index

Lighting Type	Color Rendering Index
Incandescent	97–100
Fluorescent (Standard)	52–62
Fluorescent (T-8 & CFL)	81–90
Mercury vapor	22–52
Metal halide	60–90
High-pressure sodium	25–65

Color rendering — The color of light from a lamp and that light's ability to render correct color are separate and independent characteristics.

Artificial light sources vary widely in what is called the color rendering index (CRI). Incandescent lamps are rated at CRI of 100 — nearly equal to sunlight — while some high-pressure sodium lamps have a CRI of 22.

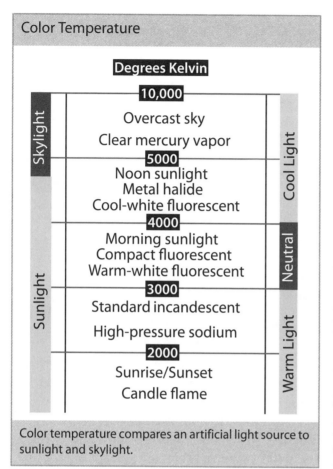

Color Temperature

Degrees Kelvin

Skylight		Cool Light
	10,000	
	Overcast sky	
	Clear mercury vapor	
	5000	
	Noon sunlight	
	Metal halide	
	Cool-white fluorescent	
	4000	Neutral
	Morning sunlight	
	Compact fluorescent	
	Warm-white fluorescent	
Sunlight	3000	
	Standard incandescent	Warm Light
	High-pressure sodium	
	2000	
	Sunrise/Sunset	
	Candle flame	

Color temperature compares an artificial light source to sunlight and skylight.

Light's color rendering ability is not related to its color temperature. Blue north skylight, white noon sunlight, and a red sunset all have perfect color rendering (a CRI of 100), because our eyes are designed to read the colors of objects illuminated by sunlight.

Light Quality

Light quality describes how well people in a lighted space can see to do visual tasks, and how visually comfortable they feel in that space. High lighting quality is characterized by fairly uniform brightness and the absence of glare. Light quality is important to energy efficiency because spaces with higher lighting quality need less illumination.

For example, direct intense sunlight streaming through windows of a room with chocolate brown carpets and dark wall paneling will likely give too much contrast in brightness. The eye's

pupil will have to constantly adjust its diameter as the eye wanders through the differing brightness of contrasting areas. Making this area visually comfortable would involve a high illumination level and many electric lights.

Now consider a room bathed in soft light. You can hardly tell where the light is coming from because no area of the room appears much brighter than another. The walls, ceiling, floor, and work surfaces are light colored. People can perform tasks faster and with fewer mistakes with this type of high-quality lighting. Lighting this area requires far less electric lighting than the previous example because of its superior lighting quality.

Glare — Eliminating glare is essential for good lighting quality. Glare comes in at least three varieties: direct glare, reflected glare, and veiling reflections.

Direct glare is strong light from a window or bright lamp shining directly into your eyes. Reflected glare is strong light reflected off a shiny surface into your eye. Veiling reflection is glare from a work surface like a printed page or computer screen.

Types of Lighting

There are four basic types of lighting: incandescent, fluorescent, high-intensity discharge, and low-pressure sodium.

Incandescents dominate residential lighting, fluorescents dominate commercial indoor lighting, and high-intensity discharge lighting dominates outdoor lighting. These lighting types vary widely in their construction, efficacy, color characteristics, and lamp life.

Incandescent — Incandescent lamps are the oldest, most common, and most inexpensive lamps. Incandescent light is produced by a white-hot coil of tungsten wire that glows when heated by electrical current. The type of glass enclosure surrounding this tungsten filament determines its light beam's characteristics.

Incandescent Lamps

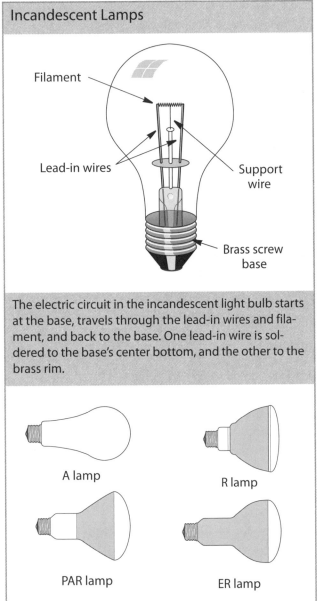

The electric circuit in the incandescent light bulb starts at the base, travels through the lead-in wires and filament, and back to the base. One lead-in wire is soldered to the base's center bottom, and the other to the brass rim.

Choosing the right type and wattage of incandescent lamp is essential to getting the most light out of an incandescent fixture for the electricity it consumes.

Incandescent Quartz Reflector

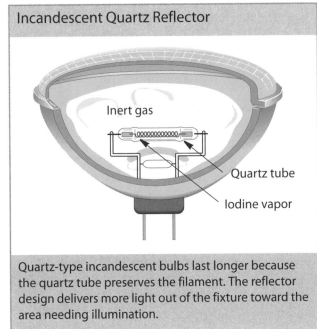

Quartz-type incandescent bulbs last longer because the quartz tube preserves the filament. The reflector design delivers more light out of the fixture toward the area needing illumination.

Incandescent lamps have the shortest service life of the common lighting types. All incandescents are relatively inefficient compared to other lighting types. However, significant savings are possible — if you select the right incandescent lamp for its purpose.

Referred to by lighting experts as the A-type light bulb, these lamps are the most common and the most inefficient light source available. Larger wattage bulbs are more efficient than smaller wattage bulbs. Long-life bulbs, with thicker filaments and lower efficacy, are a common variant.

Tungsten halogen lamps are considerably more expensive than standard incandescents and are primarily used in commercial applications. This newer type of incandescent lighting achieves better efficacy than standard A-type bulbs. Its gas filling and heat-reflective inner coating recycle heat to keep the filament hot with less electricity. Tungsten halogen lamps can replace larger standard reflector lamps in stage/theater, store, and outdoor lighting systems.

Reflector lamps (Type R) are used for flood lighting, spot lighting, and down lighting. The lamps are specifically designed to spread light over a specific area. Reflectors are used mainly indoors for stage/theater, store, flood lighting, spot lighting, and down lighting.

Parabolic reflectors (Type PAR) are used for outdoor flood lighting. Ellipsoidal reflectors (Type ER), which focus the light beam about 2 inches in front of their enclosure, are designed to project light down, out of recessed fixtures. ERs are twice as efficient as PARs for these fixtures.

Fluorescent — The glow of a fluorescent tube is caused by electric current conducting through mercury gas. Fluorescent lighting is used mainly for indoor lighting. Fluorescent lights need controlling devices, called ballasts, for starting and circuit protection. Ballasts also consume energy.

Fluorescent lights are approximately three to four times as efficient as incandescents, and their lamp life is about ten times greater.

Energy savings for existing fluorescent lighting are achieved by relamping, replacing ballasts, and replacing fixtures with more efficient models.

Tubular fluorescent lamps are the next most popular lamps after A-type incandescents. The two most common types of tubular lamps are 4-foot-long 40-watt lamps and 8-foot-long 75-watt lamps.

Tubular fluorescent fixtures and lamps are preferred for ambient lighting in large indoor areas, because they create less direct glare than incandescent bulbs. Long, narrow fluorescent lamps distribute light better than small round lamps. Improved fluorescent lighting features include: electronic ballasts; thinner, energy-efficient tubes known as T-8s; improved coatings for better efficacy and color rendition; and dimmable ballasts.

Compact fluorescents (CFLs) are the most significant recent lighting advance for homes. They combine the efficacy of fluorescent lighting with the convenience and universality of incandescent fixtures. Recent advances in CFL design also provide more natural color rendition and less flicker than older designs.

CFLs can replace incandescents roughly three to four times their wattage. When introduced in the early-to-mid 1980s, CFLs were bulky, heavy, and too big for many incandescent fixtures. But newer models, with lighter electronic ballasts, are only slightly larger than the incandescents they replace.

CFLs come in integral and modular designs. Integral CFLs combine ballast and lamp as a single disposable unit. Modular designs feature a separate ballast that will survive several lamp replacements before it wears out.

Fluorescent Lamp Operation

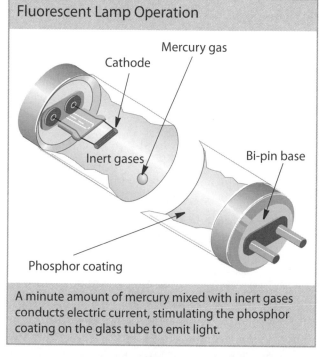

A minute amount of mercury mixed with inert gases conducts electric current, stimulating the phosphor coating on the glass tube to emit light.

Compact Fluorescents

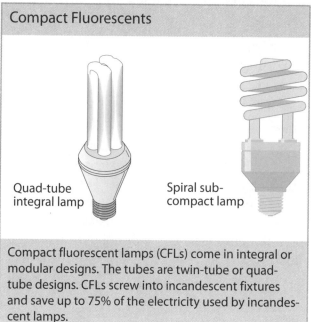

Compact fluorescent lamps (CFLs) come in integral or modular designs. The tubes are twin-tube or quad-tube designs. CFLs screw into incandescent fixtures and save up to 75% of the electricity used by incandescent lamps.

High-intensity discharge — High-intensity discharge (HID) lamps sport the highest efficacy and longest lives of any lighting type. They are used for outdoor lighting and for large indoor areas, like arenas.

HIDs use a very intense light-emitting electric arc to produce their light. HID lamps require ballasts. They don't come on immediately when switched because their ballast needs time to establish the electric arc.

HID fixtures can save 75% to 90% of lighting energy when they replace incandescent fixtures. Significant energy savings are also possible by replacing old mercury vapor lamps with newer metal halide or high pressure sodium lamps.

Mercury vapor — the oldest type of HID lighting — was used primarily for street lighting. Mercury vapor lamps provide about 50 lumens per watt. Their light is very cool — a blue/green white. Mercury vapor light renders colors poorly. Most mercury vapor lighting has been replaced by metal halide lighting.

Metal halide lamps are similar in construction and appearance to mercury vapor. The addition of metal halide gases to mercury gas within the lamp results in higher light output, more lumens per watt, and better color rendition than mercury vapor.

Metal halide lamps are used where color rendition is important: for indoor lighting of large areas like gymnasiums and sports arenas, for example, or for outdoor areas like car sales lots.

High-pressure sodium lighting provides 90 to 150 lumens per watt, the highest of common light sources. High-pressure sodium lamps are reliable and have a very long service life. Their color is a warm white. Their poor color rendering makes high-pressure sodium limited in its application to outdoor lighting where color rendering isn't important.

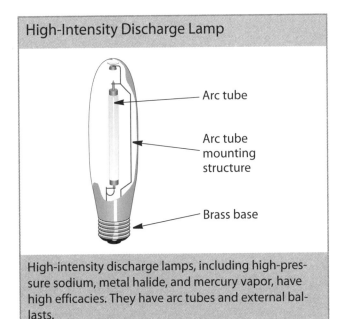

High-Intensity Discharge Lamp

— Arc tube

— Arc tube mounting structure

— Brass base

High-intensity discharge lamps, including high-pressure sodium, metal halide, and mercury vapor, have high efficacies. They have arc tubes and external ballasts.

Light emitting diodes — Light emitting diodes (LEDs) are the newest type of lighting. Commonly available LED lamps provide light with efficacies of 25-100 lumens per watt, similar to fluorescent lamps. However, some architects and lighting designers achieve 130 lumens per watt in custom applications. In early 2014 LED manufacturers achieved efficacies of up to 200 lumens per watt.

Unfortunately, the efficacy of LEDs varies widely depending on the design of the lamp, the design of the LED luminaire or fixture, the fixture's proximity to what it is lighting, and other factors. Also, there aren't many highly efficient LED products available for common light fixtures. Also, the initial cost of LED lighting is high compared with other lighting systems.

The future for LEDs looks hopeful, but the choices of products and applications may require too much design and investment to make LEDs a practical choice for the general public, except for custom applications.

Lighting Energy Efficiency

Lighting accounts for 20% to 25% of all American energy consumption. An average household dedicates 5% to 10% of its energy budget for lighting, while commercial establishments consume 20% to 30% of their total energy use for lighting.

In a typical residential or commercial lighting installation, 50% or more of the energy is wasted because:

♦ Illumination levels are too high.

♦ Lamp size and type are not optimized for their use.

♦ Lights remain on too long because of carelessness or inadequate control.

♦ The lighting system is dirty, antiquated, or inefficient.

Saving lighting energy requires either reducing electricity consumed by the light source or reducing its on-time:

♦ Lowering wattage by replacing lamps (called relamping) or replacing entire fixtures.

♦ Reducing the light source's on-time by improving lighting controls and educating lighting users to turn off unneeded lights.

♦ Replacing electric lights with natural light (daylighting).

♦ Allowing lower initial illumination levels and preserving illumination and light quality by simple lighting maintenance.

Relamping — Relamping means substituting one lamp for another to save energy. You can decide to make illumination higher or lower when relamping. The new lamp's lumen output should fit the tasks performed in the space.

Many incandescent lamps are mismatched to their tasks. Some have excessive wattages — creating unnecessarily high illumination. This can be corrected by smaller-wattage lamps.

Other existing incandescent lamps are not the best type of lamp for their application. A-type light bulbs can often be replaced with improved lamp designs, like reflectors or tungsten halogen lamps.

When used in recessed fixtures, standard A-type bulbs and reflector lamps waste energy because their light gets trapped. For big energy savings, a 75-watt ellipsoidal reflector (ER) will replace a 150-watt standard reflector. ER lamps are designed to force light out into the room by focusing it in front of their lens. However, ER lamps are less efficient at delivering light out of shallower fixtures, so only use reflectors or parabolic reflectors in shallow fixtures.

For energy savings of 60% to 75%, standard A-type bulbs can be replaced with CFLs. A standard 18-watt CFL replaces a 75-watt, A-type lamp. Some CFLs also are packaged in the same glass diffuser shells as incandescents. As with incandescents, use CFLs packaged as ERs for recessed fixtures. Use reflector or parabolic reflector CFLs for flood and spot lighting.

Energy-saving fluorescent lamps incorporate better electrodes and coatings than older fluorescent lamps. They produce approximately the same lumen output with substantially lower wattage.

The two most common energy-saving fluorescent lamps correspond to the two most common standard fluorescent lamps. Common 40-watt, 4-foot lamps and 75-watt, 8-foot lamps can be replaced with energy-saving lamps of 34 watts and 60 watts, respectively. Energy-saving lamps for less common fluorescent fixtures are also available.

Fluorescent Torchieres Replace Halogens

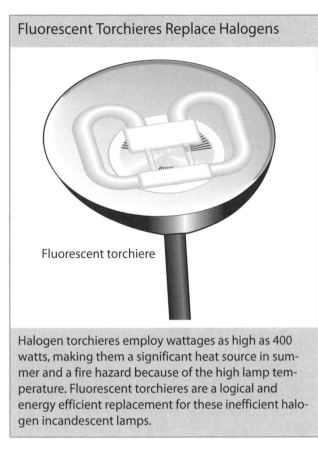

Fluorescent torchiere

Halogen torchieres employ wattages as high as 400 watts, making them a significant heat source in summer and a fire hazard because of the high lamp temperature. Fluorescent torchieres are a logical and energy efficient replacement for these inefficient halogen incandescent lamps.

Replacing fixtures — Matching new replacement lamps to existing fixtures and ballasts can be tricky, especially with older fixtures. Buying a new fixture gives the buyer matched parts that can produce superior energy savings, reliability, and longevity over relamping.

Much has been learned about fixture design since the energy crises of the 1970s. Many common indoor fixtures trap a significant portion of light inside the fixture, while many outdoor fixtures tend to spray much of their light beyond the intended area, causing light pollution.

New incandescent fixtures are designed to push more of their light out into the room. Others use smaller tungsten halogen lamps.

Advances in indoor fixture design include brighter reflectors and better reflecting geometry. New fluorescent fixtures feature more efficient electronic ballasts and thinner tubes.

New high-intensity discharge outdoor fixtures are designed to push all their light towards the ground, where it's needed. Replacing old mercury-vapor fixtures with new high-pressure sodium or metal halide fixtures is a popular and cost-effective energy retrofit.

Improving lighting controls — Lighting controls are devices for turning lights on and off or for dimming them. The simplest type of lighting control is a standard snap switch. Other controls are photocells, timers, occupancy sensors, and dimmers.

Some specific applications of lighting controls are summarized here.

♦ Snap switches encourage people in large shared spaces to extinguish lights in unused areas.

♦ Mechanical or electronic time clocks automatically light and extinguish indoor or outdoor lights for security, safety, and tasks like janitorial work.

♦ Crank timers, spring driven timers similar to old oven timers, limit lights to short durations where the need for light is brief.

♦ Photo cells activate switches or dim lights depending on natural light levels. Photocells switch outdoor lights on at dusk and off at dawn, for example. Advanced photocells gradually raise and lower fluorescent light levels with changing daylight levels.

♦ Occupancy sensors activate lights after sensing a person, and extinguish lights after detecting no human presence for some specific time — 15 minutes for example. They are popular for lightly used areas, like storage areas and outdoor areas. Occupancy sensors offer security advantages over continuous lighting — the abruptly switched lights startle intruders and alert residents and neighbors to motion in the area.

♦ Dimmers reduce the wattage and output of incandescent and fluorescent lamps. Dimmers increase the service life of incandescent lamps significantly. Dimming incandescent lamps reduces their lumens more than their wattage. This makes incandescent lamps less efficient as they are dimmed. Dimming fluorescents requires special dimming ballasts and lamp holders. Dimming fluorescents does not reduce their efficacy.

Daylighting — Daylighting means using daylight for indoor lighting. Modern buildings designed for daylighting typically use 40% to 60% less electricity for lighting than conventional buildings.

Sunlight and daylight are free and readily accessible. However, using sunlight without causing glare and without overheating the building can be difficult. Glare can be avoided by using light shelves, wide window sills, walls, louvers, reflective blinds, and other devices to reflect light deeply into the building. Windows and skylights, carefully located away from the sun's direct rays, minimize overheating. New selective glazings transmit most visible light, while excluding most solar heat.

Lighting maintenance — Maintenance is vital to lighting efficiency. Light levels fall over time because of fixture dirt, room-surface dirt, and lamp aging. Together, these factors can reduce total illumination by 50% or more, while lights continue drawing full power.

Maintenance prevents this costly performance degradation. Follow these basic maintenance suggestions:

♦ Clean fixtures, lamps, and lenses every 6 to 24 months.

♦ Replace lenses if they appear yellow.

♦ Room dirt collects on surfaces reducing the amount of light they reflect. Clean or repaint small rooms every year and larger rooms every 2 to 3 years.

♦ Consider replacing all the lamps in a lighting system at once. This is called group relamping. Common lamps, especially incandescent and fluorescent lamps, lose 20% to 30% of their light output over their service life. Group relamping saves labor, keeps illumination high, and avoids straining fluorescent ballasts with dying lamps.

Optimization of Lighting

When making energy-efficient lighting changes, it often pays to redesign the building's entire lighting system. Optimizing utilization and efficiency will improve lighting quality, make visual tasks easier, and save 50% or more on energy costs.

You can often reduce light levels without reducing light quality by the following procedures:

♦ Redesign visual tasks. For example, begin using a better printer with darker lettering, or install light-filtering shades to reduce glare.

♦ Reduce light levels where there are no visual tasks. Provide minimum light necessary for safety, security, and aesthetics.

♦ Reduce light levels for visual tasks where those levels are currently excessive.

If you want to cut lighting energy consumption, while enhancing light quality, consider the following:

♦ Paint and decorate, using light colors.

♦ Establish ambient illumination at minimum acceptable level.

♦ Provide task lighting at optimal level, depending on the difficulty of visual tasks — for example, sewing requires more light than cooking.

♦ Increase the efficiency of lamps, ballasts, and fixtures.

♦ Improve light quality by reducing glare and brightness contrast.

♦ Use daylighting.

Appliances

Refrigerators, washers, and dryers use more than 80% of the appliance energy in most homes.

Dishwashers

Most of the energy (80% to 90%) used by dishwashers is actually consumed by the water heater. Your dishwasher may dictate the temperature setting of the water heater. Many older dishwashers require a water supply of at least 130°F to get dishes clean. Most newer dishwashers have a small water heater to boost water temperature to about 140°F. This saves water heating energy by reducing the required water temperature and standby losses of the water heater.

Like clothes washers, dishwashers conserve energy and water when using their low and medium cycles. Water usage varies from a low of 7 gallons to a high of 14 gallons per wash, from the light wash cycle to the heavy one.

See Chapter 9 Water Heating for more information.

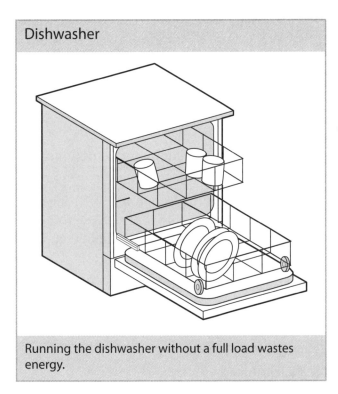

Dishwasher

Running the dishwasher without a full load wastes energy.

Earning the ENERGY STAR®

CHANGE FOR THE BETTER WITH ENERGY STAR

ENERGY STAR guidelines created by the Environmental Protection Agency and the Department of Energy are now a well-known indicator of energy efficiency.

Clothes Washers

The efficiency of clothes washers in using water and energy has increased dramatically since the mid-80s. Horizontal-axis clothes washers use far less energy and water than vertical axis machines. In fact, horizontal-axis machines save 50–75% of both energy and water, compared to most vertical-axis models. The horizontal-axis washers cost considerably more than vertical-axis ones, but will repay this initial investment in 7 years or less through reduction in energy and water costs.

The Department of Energy used to rate clothes washers using an *Energy Factor* (EF). Energy Factor rates clothes washers by comparing the amount energy used to run the machine and heat the water, to the laundry capacity of the machine.

Now the DOE rates clothes washers using a *Modified Energy Factor* (MEF) and a Water Factor (WF). MEF and WF account for energy consumption like EF foes, but they also account for the cost of adding and removing water from the laundry.

♦ MEF: Cubic feet of clothes washed and dried per kilowatt-hour of energy used.

♦ WF: Amount of water used per washing cycle, divided by the capacity of the clothes washer.

MEF gives higher ratings to washers that leave washed clothes drier than for washers that leave more water in the clothes. WF gives lower ratings for washers that use less water per cycle. As of

February 1, 2013, the DOE ENERGY STAR criteria for clothes washers is 2.0 or greater, and a WF of 6.0 or lower.

Unfortunately, no one is suggesting any way of converting from energy factor to modified energy factor. However, comparing existing EFs and MEFs suggests that multiplying MEF by 1.6 or multiplying EF by 0.6 would provide approximate conversions to the other unit.

The Energy Guide Label, required on all new washers by the Federal Trade Commission, lists the cost of 416 loads, but this gives smaller machines an unrealistic advantage over larger ones. The Energy Guide Label may not list EF, MEF, or WF. These values are available from the manufacturer, American Home Appliance Manufacturers Association (AHAM), or the American Council for an Energy Efficient Economy (ACEEE).

Most of the energy used by the American clothes washer originates in the water heater. Clothes washers often perform as well with cold water as with warm or hot water, especially with lightly soiled clothes. For best results, use an enzymatic detergent designed for cold water. Suds-saving cycles are also energy savers for lightly soiled clothes. Full clothes washers use energy most efficiently. With partial loads, experts recommend using the water-level controls that describe the load's size — small, medium, normal, or large. Some new washers have automatic controls to optimize water level.

Clothes Dryers

Line-drying laundry is the most effective way to save energy on clothes drying.

Gas clothes dryers operate more economically than electric clothes dryers. At average prices for electricity and gas, electric clothes drying costs 30–40¢ per load versus gas at 15–20¢ per load. Currently there isn't much difference in consumption between models of gas and electric clothes dryers.

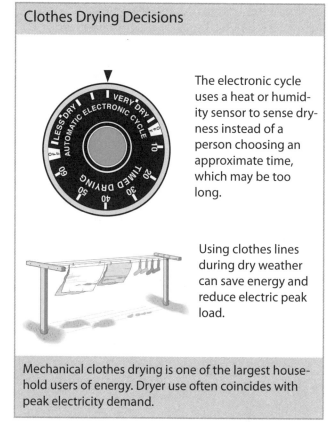

Clothes Drying Decisions

The electronic cycle uses a heat or humidity sensor to sense dryness instead of a person choosing an approximate time, which may be too long.

Using clothes lines during dry weather can save energy and reduce electric peak load.

Mechanical clothes drying is one of the largest household users of energy. Dryer use often coincides with peak electricity demand.

Temperature-sensing or humidity-sensing dryer controls may save 5–15% over timed drying. When working correctly, these controls prevent over-drying. Controls that sense humidity are the most efficient.

Cleaning the dryer lint filter after each cycle minimizes drying time. Over time, lint collects in the vent, elements, and air passageways reducing airflow and increasing cycle time. Every few years, a dryer and its vent should be thoroughly cleaned.

Piping the dryer vent in smooth metal pipe, sealed at joints with silicon caulking, reduces drying time over piping with flexible vent.

Refrigerators and Freezers

Refrigerators are large energy consumers, accounting for 9% to 15% of a household's total energy consumption. A refrigerator runs day and night, 365 days a year. Refrigerator energy efficiency has improved tremendously in the past 15 years. Better insulation and weatherstrip, more effective controls, bigger coils, and better motors improve efficiency.

Compare the energy guide labels of different models when purchasing a new refrigerator or freezer. Appliances that have earned the ENERGY STAR qualification have better-than-average energy efficiency. The most efficient standard refrigerators use less than 500 kW-hours of electricity per year. However, you can special-order refrigerators that use half that much electricity.

The way individuals and families use refrigerators and freezers can make a significant difference in energy consumption. Follow these recommended practices:

♦ Keep freezers as full as possible.

♦ Defrost the freezer when $1/4$ inch of frost has accumulated.

♦ Minimize refrigerator or freezer door openings.

♦ Clean the coils on refrigerators and freezers with a soft brush once a year.

When selecting a new refrigerator, consider the following:

♦ Automatic defrost models waste energy. Choose a manual defrost model, if available in the size you want.

♦ Side-by-side refrigerator/freezers use more energy than units that have the freezer compartment on the top or bottom.

♦ Upright freezers use more energy than chest freezers.

♦ Operating two refrigerators uses far more energy than one larger model.

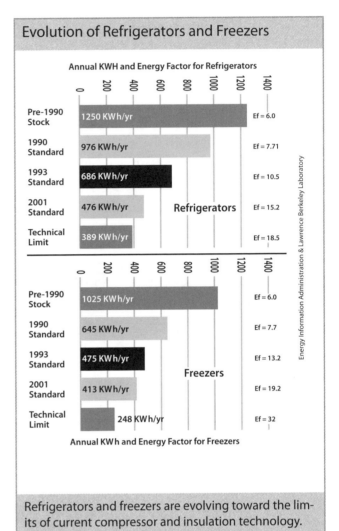

Evolution of Refrigerators and Freezers

Refrigerators and freezers are evolving toward the limits of current compressor and insulation technology.

Refrigerator energy consumption — Refrigerators more than 10 years old typically consume 1000 and 2000 kilowatt-hours per year. It is now common to measure or estimate refrigerator and freezer electricity consumption during an energy audit or comprehensive energy retrofit. The most common methods are measuring a couple hours of electricity consumption or consulting a comprehensive list of refrigerators published by the Association of Home Appliance Manufacturers (AHAM).

Refrigerators have defrost controls that can interfere with accurate measurement of energy consumption. The defrost control should be reset so that it will not activate a defrost cycle while the test is underway.

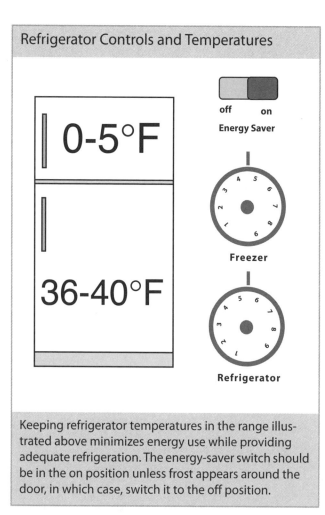

Refrigerator Controls and Temperatures

0-5°F

36-40°F

off   on
Energy Saver

Freezer

Refrigerator

Keeping refrigerator temperatures in the range illustrated above minimizes energy use while providing adequate refrigeration. The energy-saver switch should be in the on position unless frost appears around the door, in which case, switch it to the off position.

Pools and Spas

Pools and spas use energy for heating water and circulating the water through filters and chemical dispersion systems. Conservation for pools and spas focuses on making water heating more efficient, insulating the water surface to reduce evaporation, and improving pumping efficiency.

A spa's or pool's temperature setpoint is directly related to its water-heating consumption. Pools should be kept at 78°F or less, and spas or hot tubs at 102°F or less. Every degree beyond these recommended values increases pool-heating costs significantly. The efficiency of the pool's water heater is also an important factor to remember when buying a new water heater or replacing an old one. Utility customers in warm climates use up to 400 therms to heat an average-sized pool to 78° during a winter month.

Solar pool heating has become quite common. In the southern regions, solar collectors for pools tend to be less expensive than collectors for general water heating. Since they are used only in the summer, many pool-heating solar collector designs don't even use a glass covering.

For more information on solar water heating, see "Solar Water Heaters" on page 231.

More than 90% of pool heat loss occurs by evaporation from the pool's surface. Insulating pool covers can reduce pool-heating energy costs by 50–70%. Solar pool covers are designed to collect solar heat in addition to insulating the pool. Covers for spas should be at least R-12 and the tub itself should be insulated with foam insulation to R-12.

Pumping represents another large energy consumer. Water is circulated for two reasons: to mix germ-killing chemicals and to filter out particles. Many pool owners leave their pumps running 24 hours per day, which is far beyond the requirements of chemical mixing and filtering. Pump run-times of as little as 3 hours per day may be adequate to keep chemicals mixed and to remove those particulates that can be removed by filtering. Filters can't remove leaves from the top or pebbles from the bottom, nor can it scrub algae from the walls. Pool maintenance requires using a skimmer to remove large particles and using a brush to brush the pool walls, especially at the water line. Pool covers help to keep pools clean and reduce the need for filtering.

Pumps can operate more efficiently when their piping takes gradual bends instead of abrupt ones. Replacing 90° elbows with 45° elbows or flexible pipe can reduce resistance and pump horsepower. A smaller pump motor should reduce pumping energy even though the smaller pump runs longer to achieve the same daily circulation rate.

Annual Kilowatt-Hours for Pumping Options

Pumping option	Wh/gal	kWh/yr
Old bronze 1 hp	.45	4060
Standard new 1 hp	.40	3660
High efficiency 1 hp	.36	3260
High efficiency 3/4 hp	.33	3040
2-speed Hi: 1hr/day, Lo: 7 hr/day	.29	2640

Data provided by Pacific Gas & Electric, Energy Training Center. Interpreted and rounded by the author. Assumes 25,000 gallons per day and 365 days per year. First four options run 5.5 hours/day.

See "Household Appliance Electrical Usage" on page 298 for more information on appliance energy consumption.

This chapter contains a mixture of information about the building shell, landscaping, windows, and mechanical cooling systems. This mixture of topics is necessary to develop an energy-efficient cooling strategy.

How Cooling is Different than Heating

Cooling is the most variable type of energy consumption in American homes. Two similar homes in the same neighborhood could differ by a factor of 50 for cooling costs. For example, an inefficient home with air conditioning could use $500 worth of electricity in a hot month, while a neighbor in a well-designed home—with no mechanical air conditioning—might spend only $10 per month on electricity to operate room fans and evaporative coolers.

The most effective strategies for improving cooling efficiency are different from the strategies to improve heating efficiency. For example:

◆ Shade trees and nighttime ventilation will reduce the need for air conditioning, but they won't reduce heating consumption.

◆ Window glass with a low solar heat gain coefficient (SHGC) will reduce cooling load, but heating efficiency is improved by windows with a low U-factor.

◆ Low humidity helps reduce cooling energy consumption but not heating consumption.

A home's cooling energy consumption depends on its shading, insulation, reflectivity, and the heat-tolerance of its residents. Shading the home, making it as reflective as possible, and using nighttime ventilation can reduce air-conditioning costs or eliminate the need for air conditioning altogether.

See "Analyzing Annual Energy Costs" on page 277 and "Annual Average Household Energy Cost by Region (1997)" on page 14 for information on cooling energy consumption.

Annual Air-Conditioning Energy Use (kWh/yr)

Region & A/C Type	Single Family	Multi-family	Mobile Home
North	kWh/yr	kWh/yr	kWh/yr
Room	200–500	100–300	300–600
Central	900–1400	400–600	1200–1800
South	kWh/yr	kWh/yr	kWh/yr
Room	1100–1500	300–600	1000–1400
Central	3000–4600	1000–1600	2600–3400

From: Lawrence Berkeley National Laboratory, Energy Information Administration, and utility sources. For U.S. households.

Solar Radiation: Winter and Summer

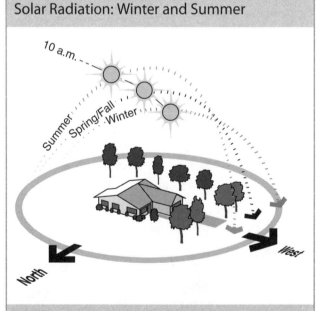

The angle of impact of the sun's rays on the earth changes between seasons. The changes become more extreme farther away from the equator.

Summer Comfort Principles

The combination of air temperature, radiant temperature, humidity, and air movement determine comfort. Air temperature and radiant temperature determine the rate that a human body can lose heat by convection and radiation, which are the body's preferred cooling mechanisms. The relative humidity determines the rate that a human body can reject heat by evaporation of sweat, the body's last-resort cooling system.

Air temperature and radiant temperature have a combined effect on human comfort. Air temperature is widely recognized as a comfort determinant, but radiant temperature is equally important. Absorbed summer sunlight raises wall and ceiling temperatures, making these surfaces radiant heaters.

Relative humidity is the percent at which air at any temperature is saturated with water vapor. Air at 100% relative humidity is saturated and can hold no more water vapor. Dew point is the temperature at which condensation begins. At 100% relative humidity the dew point is the same as the air temperature. Below 100% relative humidity, the dew point is less than the air temperature.

Humidity affects the choice of a cooling strategy during hot weather. At low relative humidity and low dew point, evaporative cooling and ventilation are effective cooling methods. Ventilation works well up to about 70% relative humidity (or a dew point in the high 60's). Most Americans use air conditioning during hot weather—when the dew point is above 68°F or when the relative humidity outdoors is over 70%.

At 70% relative humidity or above, the air feels either hot and sticky, or cold and clammy, and is not comfortable to most people. Air conditioners must remove moisture from indoor air to achieve comfort.

Convection, Radiation, and Evaporation

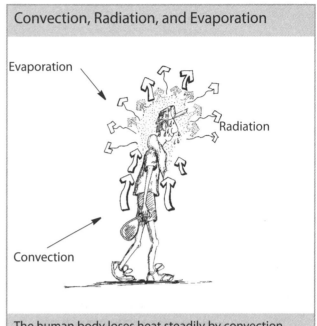

The human body loses heat steadily by convection, radiation, and evaporation. Summer comfort is often defined as staying cool with a minimum of sweat.

Dew Point

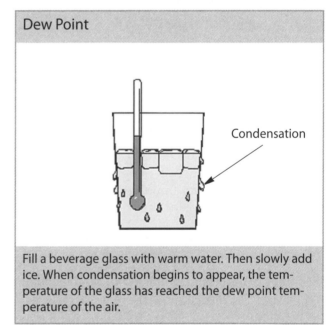

Fill a beverage glass with warm water. Then slowly add ice. When condensation begins to appear, the temperature of the glass has reached the dew point temperature of the air.

Moving air always makes you feel cooler, because it carries heat away from the skin and increases the evaporation of sweat. Circulating air inside your home is the key element to staying comfortable during hot weather. Rapidly moving air works well by itself, and can be combined with air conditioners, evaporative coolers, and whole-house fans to further improve comfort.

Humidity's Effect on Cooling Strategies

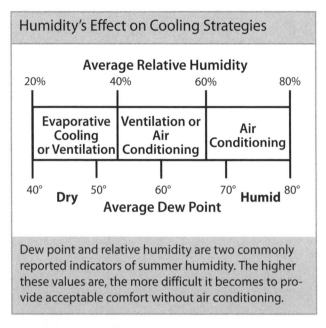

Dew point and relative humidity are two commonly reported indicators of summer humidity. The higher these values are, the more difficult it becomes to provide acceptable comfort without air conditioning.

Four Types of Heat Gains

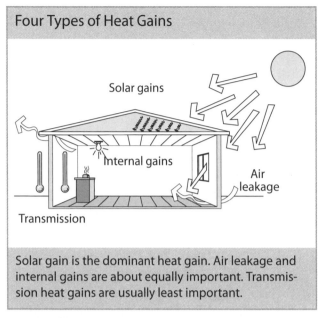

Solar gain is the dominant heat gain. Air leakage and internal gains are about equally important. Transmission heat gains are usually least important.

Whenever the outdoor air temperature and humidity are comfortable, ventilating with outdoor air will carry heat away from the home and reduce air-conditioning costs.

See "Energy, Comfort, Climate" on page 38 for more information on human comfort.

Heat Gain

During the cooling season, unwanted indoor heat is called *heat gain*. There are four types of heat gain in the home: solar heat, internal heat, air leakage, and temperature-driven heat transmission.

Solar Gain — In most climates, solar heat is the largest heat gain, contributing about 50% of the heat accumulating indoors. Solar energy falling on the roof and coming through the windows accounts for most of this. Walls are less important as a source of solar heat.

Internal Gains — Internal gains include the waste heat from lighting, refrigeration, water heating, and other appliances, as well as the body heat from people inside the home. Efficient appliances produce less waste heat, and so contribute less to summer overheating. Internal gains usually account for around 20% of summer heat gain.

Air Leakage — Air leakage allows hot outdoor air to leak into the home, and cold indoor air to leave. Air sealing helps reduce both summer heat gain and winter heat loss. Air leakage contributes about 20% to summer heat gain.

Heat transmission — Heat transmission through the shell of the home is the least important summer heat gain because the temperature difference between indoors and outdoors is much smaller in summer than in winter. Heat transmission typically represents around 10% of the total cooling load.

Percent of Total Heat Gain for Components

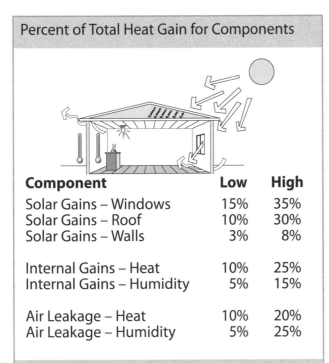

Component	Low	High
Solar Gains – Windows	15%	35%
Solar Gains – Roof	10%	30%
Solar Gains – Walls	3%	8%
Internal Gains – Heat	10%	25%
Internal Gains – Humidity	5%	15%
Air Leakage – Heat	10%	20%
Air Leakage – Humidity	5%	25%

Every home and homesite has a different distribution of heat gains. For example, homes with little shade have high solar gains while shaded homes have lower solar gains. Homes in humid climates have large humidity heat gains while those in dry climates don't. Homes with awnings have low window solar gain.

Reflectivity

Solar energy falling on the roof and coming through the windows accounts for most of the solar heat accumulating indoors. Walls are less important as a source of solar heat.

Just as insulation levels (R-values) are the most important characteristic for low-energy heating, a well-shaded or reflective home enables low-energy cooling.

The most important places to use shading and reflectivity are on the roof and windows. Energy conservation measures that block the sun before it strikes the roof or windows are the most effective. Trees and other plants that provide shade are the best long-term investment for reducing cooling costs.

See "Temperature and Heat" on page 30 , "Sensible and Latent Heat" on page 30, and "Radiation" on page 35 for principles involved in heat gain.

Energy-Saving Landscaping

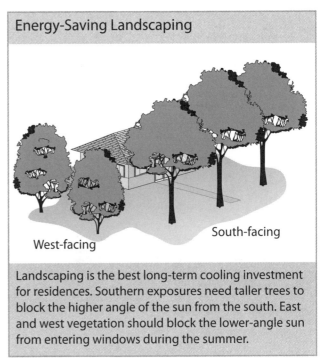

West-facing

South-facing

Landscaping is the best long-term cooling investment for residences. Southern exposures need taller trees to block the higher angle of the sun from the south. East and west vegetation should block the lower-angle sun from entering windows during the summer.

Cooling with Landscaping

A well-planned landscaping program can reduce an unshaded home's summer air-conditioning costs by 15% to 50%.

You may have noticed the coolness of parks and forests when compared to nearby city streets. This is because trees and shrubs create a cool microclimate, reducing the shaded area's temperature and absorbed solar heat.

A tree can produce daily cooling effects similar to five average-sized air conditioners running 20 hours per day. Shading and *evapotranspiration* (the process by which a plant releases water vapor) from trees can reduce air temperatures as much as 9°F compared to unshaded areas. Since cool air falls toward the ground, temperatures directly under trees can be up to 25°F cooler than air temperatures above nearby blacktop.

Studies by the Lawrence Berkeley Laboratory found summer daytime air temperatures 3°F to 6°F lower in neighborhoods with mature tree canopies compared to newly developed areas with no trees. Large urban parks are up to 7°F cooler than surrounding neighborhoods. A 25% increase in tree cover will decrease a city's average mid-afternoon July temperature by 6°F to 10°F according to U.S. Department of Energy simulations for Sacramento, California.

Planting trees is ten times more cost-effective than building new power plants for summer cooling. Lawrence Berkeley Laboratory (LBL) estimates that increasing peak-load electrical supplies costs an average of $1.00 per kW-hour, while planting trees decreases peak-load consumption and is estimated to cost ratepayers only $0.10 per kW-hour.

Homeowners can reap big dividends from their landscaping. Studies by real estate agents and professional foresters estimate that the presence of trees raises a home's resale value 7% to 20%.

Shading Windows

Single-pane, unshaded windows transmit about 85% of the solar heat striking them. This can account for up to 40% of a home's accumulated heat.

Consider these factors when deciding which windows to shade:

♦ Direction the windows face. South windows transmit the most solar heat. West windows contribute solar heat in the afternoon, just when you want it least. East windows begin heating the home early in the morning, causing more hours of discomfort.

♦ Location of natural shade from trees, overhangs, and other objects. If windows are already shaded by trees, nearby buildings, or large overhangs, additional shading is unnecessary.

♦ Total surface area of your windows. Shading devices for larger windows are generally more cost-effective than for smaller windows.

After considering these factors, utilize the following options to block 60% to 90% of the solar heat that currently enters your windows.

Sun Screens

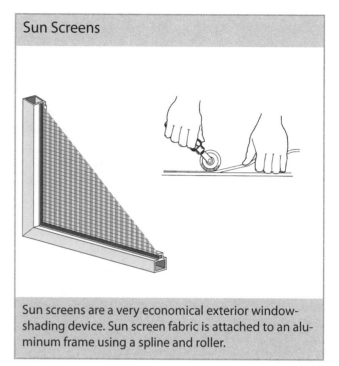

Sun screens are a very economical exterior window-shading device. Sun screen fabric is attached to an aluminum frame using a spline and roller.

Sun screens — Sun screens are often the least expensive window-shading option to retain a view through the window. A sun screen is fabric stretched over an aluminum frame and resembles an insect screen. The fabric absorbs 65% to 70% of the solar heat before it enters the home.

Sun screens must be installed on the exterior of a window to be effective. Therefore, they are not practical for outwardly opening windows, such as awning or casement windows, unless attached to the movable sash.

Reflective films — Metallized plastic window films (similar to those applied to automotive windows) can block 50% to 75% of the solar heat on single-pane glass. A microscopic layer of metal on the film repels solar radiation. Installed on the interior side of single-pane glass, reflective window films repel solar heat, cut glare, and reduce fading. To be most effective, the film must look like a mirror when viewed from outdoors during the daytime. Tinted films that merely color the glass are not as effective in blocking the sun as metallized films.

Exterior Window Shading Devices

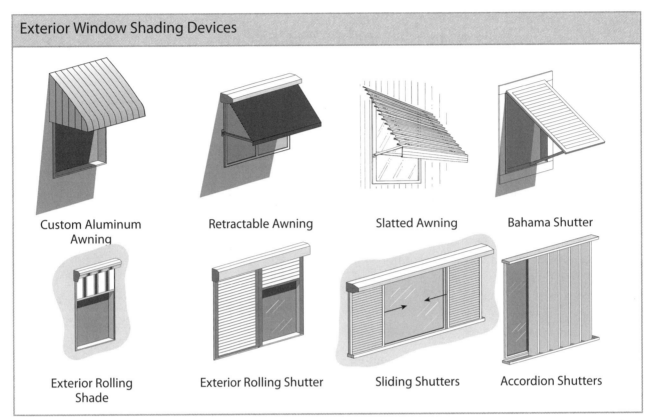

Custom Aluminum Awning

Retractable Awning

Slatted Awning

Bahama Shutter

Exterior Rolling Shade

Exterior Rolling Shutter

Sliding Shutters

Accordion Shutters

Consumer acceptance of reflective window films has been slow because they block daylight in addition to solar heat. Newer films, recently introduced to the marketplace, transmit more light, while blocking most of the heat.

Installing reflective window film is a moderately difficult do-it-yourself project. These films—manufactured with removable protective layers—require careful installation to an absolutely dirt-free glass surface. Unlike sun screens and awnings, reflective window films do not obstruct the operation of any kind of window.

Awnings — Awnings are popular in hot, sunny climates, since they intercept solar heat before it gets to the window. In general, however, awnings are not as good an investment as trees, sun screens, and window films because they are more expensive.

The most important considerations in selecting and designing awnings are:

♦ Amount of shade desired. The shade an awning produces is closely related to how far the awning drops down over the window. This distance is known as the "drop" of the awning.

♦ Importance of maintaining a view out the window. Depending on their drop, awnings can cut off a significant portion of a window's view.

♦ Cost of the awning. Custom-made aluminum or canvas awnings are more expensive than do-it-yourself awning kits or mass-produced awnings.

Awnings on a home's south side need a drop measuring 45% to 60% of the window height to block solar radiation from high in the sky. Awnings on the east and west need to drop 60% to 75% to block solar radiation emanating from lower in the sky in the morning and afternoon, respectively.

Interior window treatments — Interior window treatments with reflective surfaces—metallized or bright white—can block solar heat effectively. An opaque roller shade, with a white surface facing the exterior, rejects about 80% of the solar heat entering the window. Roller shades block most of the light and all the view. White venetian blinds and white slim shades (a smaller-scale venetian blind) reject 40% to 60%. Venetian blinds and slim shades block most of the light and view.

If you want to retain some light or view, install roller shades made with metallized plastic window film. Like reflective films applied directly to glass, metallized plastic roller shades can preserve the view and transmit some light, while blocking most of the heat.

Exterior shutters and shades — Exterior
shutters are not as popular as the window treatments described previously and are generally more expensive. But they can provide security and storm protection in addition to solar control.

Bahama shutters hinge at the top of the window. Sliding shutters slide horizontally to cover the window during the heat of the day. The traditional vertically hinged shutters—popular all over Europe—can also be used to block solar heat. Inexpensive exterior bamboo rolling shades are also popular in some warmer regions.

These movable exterior shading methods require a greater daily commitment by the owner than other window-shading devices. Exterior rolling shutters and shades, controlled indoors by motors or manually, are very expensive, but offer very good security and convenience.

Replacement windows — Replacement windows are not a cost-effective measure for reducing cooling costs. But if the windows are being replaced for other reasons, the added cost of low-e insulated glass is well worth the price in almost all U.S. climates. Multifamily buildings in southern climates should have reflective glass and/or architectural shading features, like overhangs and built-in solar screens.

The most important window glass characteristics for cooling are:

♦ *Solar Heat Gain Coefficient (SHGC)* is the ratio of solar heat passing through the glass to solar heat falling on the glass at a 90° angle. SHGC includes radiant heat transmitted, and also the solar heat absorbed and reradiated indoors. Single pane glass has a SHGC of 0.87.

♦ *Visible transmittance* measures how much visible light is admitted by the window glass. Visible transmittance is important because the window's main job is to give view and admit light. Special coatings—some of which cut visible light to 30%—may be unacceptable in some applications, such as when windows are small and few in number.

♦ *Shading coefficient* is a decimal number, like 0.55, that compares the transmittance of a window glass with clear glass. Clear glass has a shading coefficient of 1.00. A reflective glass window with a 0.55 shading coefficient would transmit 55% of the solar energy of clear glass.

See "Windows and Doors" on page 125 for a complete discussion of windows.

Conservation Measures for Roofs

Homes with reflective roof coatings, at least R-19 insulation, and good attic ventilation, may experience two-thirds less solar heat gain than those homes with darker roofs, little insulation, and poor ventilation. Homes with shaded, reflective, insulated, and ventilated roofs will absorb minimum solar energy.

The most effective measures for blocking solar heat through roofs are shading the roof with trees and giving the roof a reflective coating. Either trees or a reflective surface can block most of the solar heat streaming toward the roof and reduce cooling costs 10% to 40%, depending on climate and R-value of attic insulation.

Compared to poorly ventilated roofs, good roof ventilation helps to keep attic temperatures lower. But expect less savings from improving attic ventilation compared to radiant barriers and other sun-blocking measures, because attic heat gain is dominated by heat radiation.

Radiant barriers — A radiant barrier is composed of aluminum foil bonded to kraft paper or roof sheathing. Radiant barriers have easier consumer acceptance than reflective roofs, given the preference of many consumers for dark roof colors. Expect 2% to 10% savings from radiant barriers depending on climate and insulation level. Radiant barriers are fastened to the bottom of rafters or roof sheathing.

Radiant barriers reflect heat radiation coming toward them. They also impede the heat flow by being poor emitters of heat radiation. Radiant barriers must face an air space with their shiny surface to be effective.

Air spaces bordered by radiant barriers have higher R-values than those bordered by common building materials. For example, a vertical air film bordered by a radiant barrier has double the R-value of one bordered by common materials (R-1.35 versus R-0.68). All surfaces not exposed to high winds have relatively still air films near their surfaces.

However, it's important to note that an air film's R-value drops dramatically with air convection, and this fact presents a practical problem in using radiant barriers as insulation. For the radiant barrier to be an effective insulator, it must face a calm air space—one without air convection. In practice, this so-called "dead" air space is difficult to achieve.

Internal Heat

People contribute heat to the air by shedding body heat (sensible heat) and by sweating (latent heat). Each occupant of the home contributes about 300 BTUs per hour of sensible heat and about 150 BTUs per hour of latent heat.

Internal heat also includes the heat from the refrigerator, lights, cooking, entertainment, and housekeeping. This internal release of heat varies widely, in the range of 1500 BTUs per hour to 7500 BTUs per hour, from one house to another.

Reducing internal heat — Because they release less heat into the indoors, energy-efficient appliances and lights pay a second dividend to the buyer during the cooling season.

Other measures to reduce internal heat require the participation of residents:

♦ Limiting the use of hot water.

♦ Using exhaust fans to remove moisture.

♦ Reducing cooking during the heat of the day.

Air Leakage

Air leakage can be a very costly problem for air-conditioned homes, especially in humid climates. Air conditioners remove moisture from the air to cool it and to provide adequate comfort.

The most severe air-leakage problems have been noted in homes with air conditioning duct work in the attic. Duct leakage wastes cooling energy by:

♦ Allowing cooled air to escape the supply ducts.

♦ Allowing hot, humid air to enter the return ducts.

♦ Creating pressure differences between indoors and outdoors that drive air leakage through the building shell.

Measuring air leakage with a blower door or tracer-gas testing is essential to effective air sealing.

See Chapter 3 Air Leakage.

Reducing air leakage — Sealing ducts to stop duct leakage pays the fastest dividends for reducing air-conditioning costs. However, duct leakage can be difficult to diagnose and the leaks themselves difficult to find. Part of the duct repair procedure should include the elimination of pressure differences caused by air leakage and poorly designed duct systems. Where ducts are leaky, savings of 10% to 25% on air-conditioning costs are possible from an effective air-sealing job.

Besides ducts, technicians should find and seal large, hidden air leaks before worrying about smaller ones around windows and doors.

Humidity — Humid air suppresses evaporation of sweat from the skin, which causes that sticky discomfort so characteristic of humid weather. Humidity also contributes to the cooling load because humid air contains more heat than dry air at the same temperature.

The latent heat contained in outdoor air leaking into the home is an important heat gain in humid climates because the air conditioner works hard to remove excess moisture and provide adequate comfort. Moisture sources, especially the ground, contribute to poor summer comfort and high cooling costs.

See "Controlling Water Vapor" on page 247 for information on moisture in buildings.

Transmission

Transmission of heat through ceiling, walls and windows usually amounts to less than 10% of the cooling load. Transmission through the roof and ceiling is driven more by heat radiation than by indoor-outdoor temperature difference.

Dark-colored roofs and walls should have high insulation levels to retard solar heat's transmission through wall and roof assemblies. Attic insulation, to at least R-38, is cost-effective when both heating and cooling are important energy costs.

Cooling with Ventilation

Ventilation can remove accumulated heat from homes by circulating cool outdoor air through the home. Ventilation works best in areas that have hot days and cool nights. Natural or fan-powered nocturnal ventilation flushes out internal and solar heat that builds up during the day.

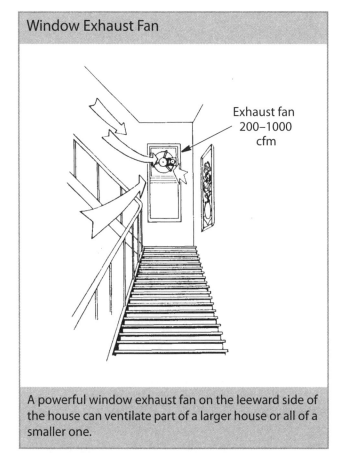

Window Exhaust Fan

Exhaust fan 200–1000 cfm

A powerful window exhaust fan on the leeward side of the house can ventilate part of a larger house or all of a smaller one.

The effectiveness of ventilation for cooling depends on:

♦ The temperature and humidity of evening and morning air.

♦ The amount of shade around the building.

♦ Participation of the residents in opening and closing windows and blinds at the proper time.

♦ Residents turning fans on at the proper time.

Natural Ventilation

Residents of homes and multifamily buildings can use natural ventilation for cooling by paying attention to wind intensity and daily variation of wind direction and outdoor temperature. Windows, closed against the heat of the day, are opened at night to flush heat out.

Whole-House Fan

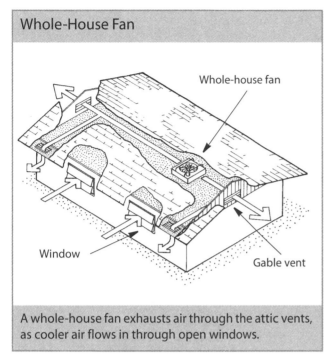

Whole-house fan

Window

Gable vent

A whole-house fan exhausts air through the attic vents, as cooler air flows in through open windows.

Fan-powered Ventilation

Fan-powered ventilation, when combined with shading and other low-cost cooling measures, can provide adequate cooling for most of the northern United States.

Powerful window fans and whole-house fans are the best to accomplish power ventilation. Smaller floor, table, and ceiling fans are best used to create a wind chill indoors, and are less effective as whole-house ventilators.

Powerful fans can create strong house pressures that can cause backdrafting or flame roll-out in water heaters. Provide adequate window openings to avoid excessive house pressure.

Attic Ventilation

Homes with well-ventilated attics may have comfort and energy-conservation advantages over homes with poorly ventilated attics. However, attic ventilation is less important than roof reflectance, radiant barriers, and attic insulation in retarding solar heat migrating through the roof and attic. The solar heat migrates mainly by radiation, and attic ventilation can't do much to retard radiation heat transfer.

Circulation Fans

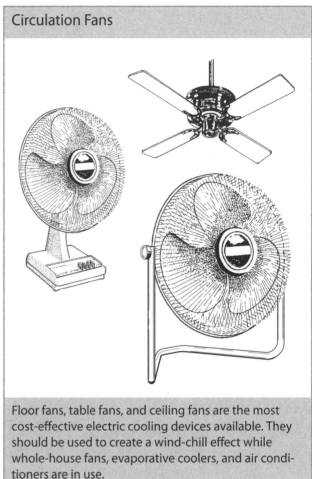

Floor fans, table fans, and ceiling fans are the most cost-effective electric cooling devices available. They should be used to create a wind-chill effect while whole-house fans, evaporative coolers, and air conditioners are in use.

Air Movement

Air circulation creates a wind chill within the home, helping to cool residents directly. Smaller air-circulating fans are inexpensive to operate compared to larger fans, evaporative coolers, and air conditioners. When residents use air circulation effectively, they save energy and stay more comfortable.

Ceiling fans, floor fans and table fans cool your skin; they don't cool the air. Moving air increases bodily heat loss by convection and sweat evaporation.

Circulating fans can save a significant amount of energy by improving comfort when air-conditioning systems are in use, or in moderate weather they can help occupants reduce air conditioner use altogether. Moving air is more comfortable than calm air; 4° to 8°F of perceived comfort can be achieved from air speeds of 100 to 350 feet per minute. The faster the air speed the greater the cooling effect. The general limit for air speed is somewhere above 350 feet per minute, when paper begins rustling on table tops.

Evaporative Coolers

Evaporative coolers can provide adequate cooling for nearly all homes in hot, dry regions, if used together with shading, reflectivity, and air circulation. Evaporative coolers employ different principles than air conditioners because they reduce air temperature without removing heat from the air. They work well only in climates where the summertime relative humidity remains less than 50%.

Evaporative coolers reduce the temperature of outdoor air moving through them. A large blower sucks outdoor air in through the cabinet of the cooler and blows it into the home. The outdoor air passes through water-soaked pads that reduce air temperature and humidify the air. Partially opened windows allow warmer house air to escape as air from the cooler enters the home. Evaporative coolers cost about half as much to install as central air conditioners. They are 2 to 3 times more efficient in providing summer comfort than the most efficient central air conditioners.

An evaporative cooler can be mounted on a roof, through a window or wall, or on the ground. The cooler can discharge directly into a room or hall, or it can be connected to ducts for distribution to numerous rooms.

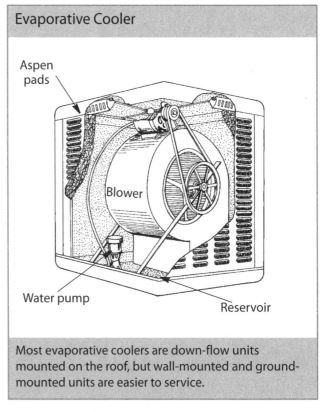

Evaporative Cooler

Aspen pads

Blower

Water pump

Reservoir

Most evaporative coolers are down-flow units mounted on the roof, but wall-mounted and ground-mounted units are easier to service.

Evaporative Cooler Operation

Evaporative coolers must be operated with open windows or special vents called up-ducts. Up-ducts are dampered square openings in the ceiling that let hot air out of the home into the ventilated attic. Coolers may be operated as whole-house fans at night by running the blower without the water pump.

Opening windows in occupied rooms, and closing windows in unoccupied rooms, concentrates cooling where residents need it. Open the windows or vents, preferably on the leeward side of the home, to provide approximately 1 to 2 square feet of opening for each 1,000 cfm of cooling capacity. Experiment to discover the best windows to open and how wide to open them. If the windows are open too wide, hot air will enter. If the windows aren't open far enough, humidity rises and the air feels sticky.

When the cooler has been idle for a few days, it is wise to let the pump run for a while before starting the fan to wash dust out of the pads. Modern cooler controls allow for separate pump and blower operation. The best controls are programmable thermostats, designed for controlling evaporative coolers.

Coolers that are functioning properly should produce air temperatures close to those listed in the following table.

Air Temperature Exiting Evaporative Coolers

Outdoor Temperature	Outdoor Relative Humidity %										
	2	5	10	15	20	25	30	35	40	45	50
75	54	55	57	58	59	61	62	63	64	65	66
80	57	58	60	62	63	64	66	67	68	71	72
85	61	62	63	65	67	68	70	71	72	73	74
90	64	64	67	69	70	72	74	76	77	78	79
95	67	68	70	72	74	76	78	79	81	82	84
100	69	71	73	76	78	80	82	83	85	87	88
105	72	74	77	79	81	84	86	88	89		
110	75	77	80	83	85	87	90	92			
115	78	80	83	86	89	91	94				
120	81	83	86	90	93	95					
125	83	86	90	93	96						

Routine Maintenance

Aspen and cellulose cooler pads collect a lot of dirt from the air. Airborne dirt that sticks to the cooler pads washes into the reservoir. Most evaporative coolers have a bleed tube or a separate pump that changes the reservoir water during cooler operation to drain away dirty water. A cooler may still need regular cleaning, depending on how long the cooler runs and how well the dirt-draining system is working. Be sure to disconnect the electricity to the unit before servicing or cleaning it.

Older cooler sumps were lined with an asphaltic paint and flexible asphaltic liners, but the newer ones have factory powder coatings that are far superior and less environmentally harmful.

Evaporative coolers need yearly maintenance at a minimum. The following is a list of important maintenance tasks for evaporative coolers:

◆ Aspen pads can be soaked in soapy water to remove dirt and then rotated to distribute the wear, dirt, and scale, which remain after cleaning. Replace the pads when they become unabsorbent, thin, or loaded with scale and dirt.

◆ Drain and clean reservoir.

◆ Test the operation of the drip tube or dump pump, whichever system is used to maintain water quality.

◆ Clean fan blades.

◆ Clean louvers in the cooler cabinet.

◆ Oil fan motor and check belt tension.

Air Conditioners

Air conditioners employ the same principles as your home refrigerator. An air conditioner cools your home with a cold indoor coil, called the *evaporator*. A hot outdoor coil, called the *condenser*, releases the collected heat outdoors. The evaporator and condenser coils are actually serpentine copper pipes surrounded by aluminum fins, similar to a car radiator. Fans move air through these coils.

A fluid, called the *refrigerant*, collects heat at the evaporator coil and releases it at the condenser coil. The compressor forces the refrigerant through the circuit of coils and pipes. Heat pumps and air conditioners are almost identical in operation except that heat pumps are reversible for winter heating.

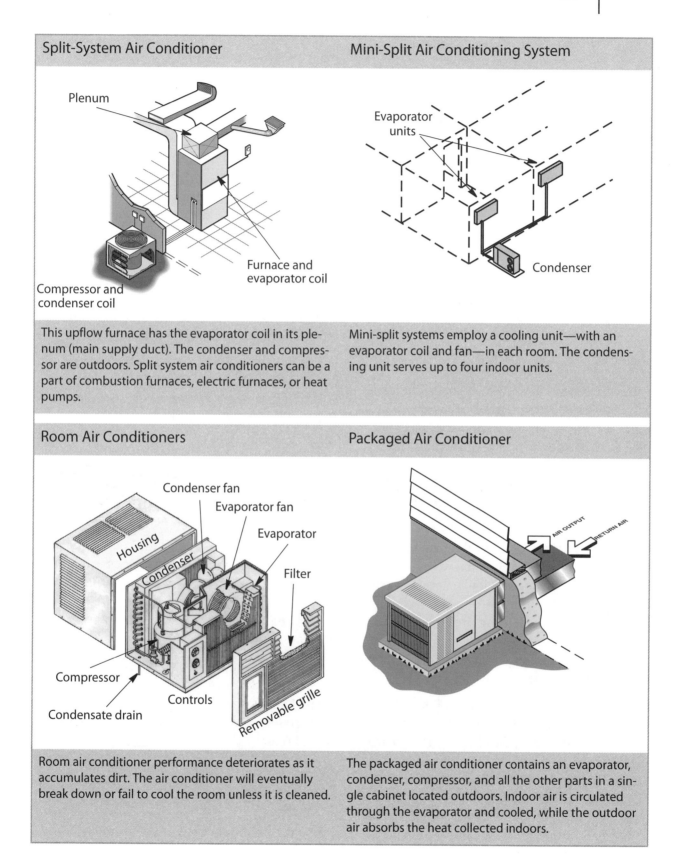

Split-System Air Conditioner

Plenum

Furnace and evaporator coil

Compressor and condenser coil

This upflow furnace has the evaporator coil in its plenum (main supply duct). The condenser and compressor are outdoors. Split system air conditioners can be a part of combustion furnaces, electric furnaces, or heat pumps.

Mini-Split Air Conditioning System

Evaporator units

Condenser

Mini-split systems employ a cooling unit—with an evaporator coil and fan—in each room. The condensing unit serves up to four indoor units.

Room Air Conditioners

Condenser fan

Evaporator fan

Evaporator

Filter

Housing

Condenser

Compressor

Controls

Condensate drain

Removable grille

Room air conditioner performance deteriorates as it accumulates dirt. The air conditioner will eventually break down or fail to cool the room unless it is cleaned.

Packaged Air Conditioner

AIR OUTPUT

RETURN AIR

The packaged air conditioner contains an evaporator, condenser, compressor, and all the other parts in a single cabinet located outdoors. Indoor air is circulated through the evaporator and cooled, while the outdoor air absorbs the heat collected indoors.

Power Draw and Hourly Cost for Cooling

Cooling Device	Watts	Cost (¢/Hour)
Central air conditioner	2000–5000	16–40
Room air conditioner	500–3000	4–24
Evaporative Cooler	400–1800	3–15
Whole-House Fan	300–600	2–5
Circulating/Exhaust Fan	25–200	0.2–1.6

The ranges of watts and hourly cost represent the different sizes of the cooling devices. The hourly cost assumes 8¢ per kilowatt-hour.

Types of Air Conditioners

Central air conditioners have supply and return ducts that connect to a central air handler. The condenser unit is outside and releases heat collected from inside the house. Most central air conditioners are *split-systems*—that is, they have the evaporator coil indoors and the condenser coil outdoors. *Packaged air conditioners* have both coils outdoors.

Room air conditioners work well for smaller homes or homes in mild climates, where residents use air conditioning occasionally. Room air conditioners install in a window or a hole in the wall—wall installations being preferable for appearance. Room air conditioners save energy by cooling only the home's occupied areas, rather than the entire house.

Mini-split system air conditioners combine features of room air conditioners and central split-system air conditioners. Mini-splits, as they are called, use an evaporator coil and fan in each room with a single condensing unit outdoors. They have no ducts. This new type of air conditioner is more expensive than standard room air conditioners, and it may even cost more than a conventional central air-conditioning system. Designers and contractors use them when there is no space to install ducts. Mini-splits can save energy over central air conditioners when used for spot cooling occupied rooms instead of the whole house—a conservation measure not practical with conventional central air conditioners.

Each of these types may be purely an air conditioner or a heat pump. Heat pumps are reversible air conditioners that move heat in or out of the home, depending on the season.

See "Heat Pumps" on page 182.

Air-conditioner Efficiency

The energy ratings of air conditioners are based on how many BTUs (heat) per hour the unit can remove for each watt of power it draws.

For central air conditioners, the efficiency rating is called the *Seasonal Energy Efficiency Ratio*, or SEER. For room air conditioners, it is called *Energy Efficiency Ratio*, or EER.

$$\text{SEER or EER} = \frac{\text{BTUs per hour heat removed}}{\text{Watts of electrical power drawn}}$$

Air conditioners with higher EER or SEER generally cost more, but the energy savings will return the higher initial investment several times during the air conditioner's life. The Energy Guide Label, listing EER or SEER, must remain on the air conditioner until it is sold.

The most efficient air conditioners are listed by size and efficiency in the *Consumer Guide to Home Energy Savings*, published by the American Council for an Energy-Efficient Economy. See Bibliography.

Buy the most efficient air conditioner you can afford, especially if you live in a hot climate, or if your air-conditioning costs are high.

Room air conditioner sizes range from 5500 BTUH to 14,000 BTUH. National appliance standards require room air conditioners built after January 1, 1990, to have an EER of 8.5 or greater.

An EER of 10 is considered very energy-efficient. If you live in a mild cooling climate, select a room air conditioner with an EER of at least 9.0. Select one with an EER over 10 if you live in a hot climate.

National appliance minimum standards for central air conditioners require a SEER between 8.9 and 10.0, depending on when the unit was manufactured. There is a wide selection of units available with SEERs up to almost 17. Before 1979, the SEERs of central air conditioners ranged from 4.5 to 8.0. Replacing a 1970's vintage central air conditioner that has a SEER of 6 with a new unit that has a SEER of 12 will cut air-conditioning costs in half.

To determine the approximate SEER of an existing central air conditioner, find the model number and manufacturer from the nameplate on the outdoor unit. Contact a local dealer of that manufacturer's equipment and ask them to look up the efficiency rating for you. If they can't give you the efficiency rating, ask them if they know of a local manufacturer's representative who can estimate the efficiency.

New Energy-efficient Air Conditioners

The efficiency of today's air conditioners is much greater than air conditioners made in the mid-1970s. This improvement in efficiency has resulted from technical advances such as:

♦ Variable-speed or two-speed blowers.

♦ Copper tubing grooved inside to increase surface area.

♦ Aluminum fins spaced closer together and perforated to improve heat transfer to air.

♦ Improved electric motor design.

♦ Dual-speed compressors.

♦ Time-delay relays controlling evaporator fans.

Sizing and Selecting Air Conditioners

Size is a very important consideration to achieve comfort and minimize energy cost when selecting new air-conditioning equipment. Oversized air conditioners cycle more than correctly sized ones. With each cycle, the air conditioner has to heat the condenser, cool the evaporator, and cool the ductwork before beginning to cool the home. This start-up energy is wasted at the end of the cycle, so more cycles waste more energy.

When selecting air conditioners, consider cooling, moisture removal, and energy efficiency. The amount of heat gain during the hottest (and most humid) weather is used to determine the air conditioner's *capacity*. This capacity is measured in BTUs per hour, or "tons" of cooling. Each ton equals 12,000 BTUs per hour (1 ton = 12,000 BTUs/hour).

Reputable contractors size air-conditioning systems accurately, using hand calculations or computer programs. The Air Conditioning Contractors of America publishes a calculation procedure called Manual J, the standard method for sizing central air conditioners. Several air-conditioning manufacturers and others have developed computer programs based on Manual J or on other calculation methods.

"One ton per 400 square feet of floor space" is an archaic rule-of-thumb used to estimate the size of central air conditioners in older, less efficient homes. However, sizing the system smaller to provide one ton per 700 to 1200 square feet of floor space will provide better efficiency and humidity control in energy-efficient homes.

Contractors normally oversize air conditioners by 30% to 100% to ensure they are big enough to cool the home. However, properly sized air-conditioning systems are more efficient and more effective at removing moisture than oversized systems.

Variation in Cooling Load

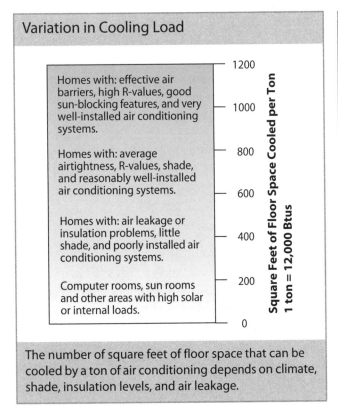

Homes with: effective air barriers, high R-values, good sun-blocking features, and very well-installed air conditioning systems.

Homes with: average airtightness, R-values, shade, and reasonably well-installed air conditioning systems.

Homes with: air leakage or insulation problems, little shade, and poorly installed air conditioning systems.

Computer rooms, sun rooms and other areas with high solar or internal loads.

The number of square feet of floor space that can be cooled by a ton of air conditioning depends on climate, shade, insulation levels, and air leakage.

Variation in Fan Speed

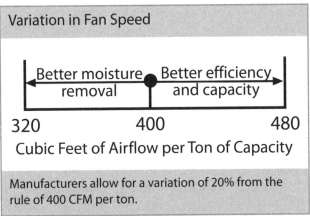

Manufacturers allow for a variation of 20% from the rule of 400 CFM per ton.

Moisture removal capacity of the system—measured by *sensible heat factor (SHF)*—is an important consideration for selecting a central air-conditioning system. The SHF rates the air conditioner on its ability to remove moisture. The SHF is a decimal number between 0.5 and 1.0. The lower the SHF, the more moisture the unit will remove from the air. The SHF depends on the size and construction of the evaporator coil, and on the fan speed.

Cooling comfort is provided by reducing air temperature and removing humidity. The air conditioner must run for long enough at a cold enough evaporator-coil temperature to remove necessary moisture. The moisture condenses on the cold coil and is piped away through a drain. Oversized air conditioners cycle frequently, remove less moisture, and waste energy. Long cycles are good for energy efficiency and moisture control. However, an air conditioner that runs all the time isn't necessarily sized correctly. It could be oversized, and straining to overcome maintenance, repair, or adjustment problems. Or, it could be undersized.

Homeowners in dry and moderate climates should select a high SHF because they need less moisture removal, and air conditioners with high SHF are more efficient. However, air-conditioning systems for humid climates normally require an SHF between 0.67 and 0.77 to reduce humidity. A relative humidity of less than 40% discourages biological pests linked to respiratory problems.

See "Biological Particles" on page 244.

Proper sizing and equipment selection are especially important with new higher efficiency air conditioners. These new energy-efficient units must have a low enough SHF to provide adequate moisture removal for a particular climate. An oversized new air conditioner or one with mismatched parts—evaporator, condenser unit, and blower—won't reach its potential high efficiency, nor will it remove enough moisture to provide adequate comfort.

Air Conditioner Installation

Many air conditioners fail to achieve their rated efficiency because of faulty installation. The most common problems are low airflow, incorrect refrigerant charge, and duct air leakage. The roots of these problems lie in inadequate planning, installation space, and technician training compounded by the selection of low bid contractors.

Air-conditioning systems in new homes should be planned and designed into the home's blueprints and specifications. A heating, ventilation, and air conditioning (HVAC) contractor should be consulted about the physical sizes and clearances of equipment and ducts, so that adequate space is provided for them. Ducts merit special consideration because they are large and need to connect to all main rooms. The HVAC contractor should work with carpenters, plumbers and electricians to ensure that pathways for ducts are not obstructed.

Replacing an air-conditioning system also requires planning. Undersized ducts are so common that provision should be made for correcting inadequate airflow. Increasing duct sizes, reducing the air conditioner's capacity, or replacing the ducts are possible options.

All new systems should be checked for correct charge and airflow. Ducts should be checked for leakage.

Thermostatic Control of Air Conditioners

Turning the thermostat past the desired temperature will not make the air conditioner cool your home any faster, and it will waste energy. Dueling managers—residents who move the thermostat setting back and forth to suit their different comfort demands—also cause air-conditioning systems to operate erratically and inefficiently.

The location of a thermostat can cause problems in controlling cooling systems. Thermostats should be shaded from direct sunlight. A thermostat located on a warm outside wall may cause the air conditioner to operate erratically.

Residents who leave and return at regular times every day can save money and increase the comfort and convenience of both cooling and heating by using automatic setback heating/cooling thermostats.

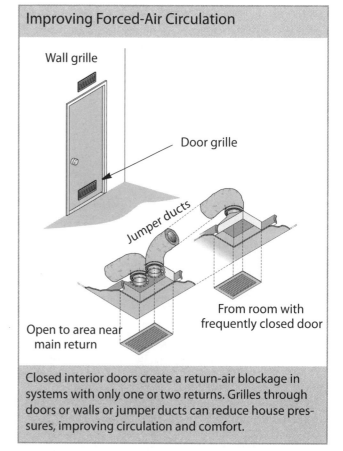

Improving Forced-Air Circulation

Wall grille

Door grille

Jumper ducts

From room with frequently closed door

Open to area near main return

Closed interior doors create a return-air blockage in systems with only one or two returns. Grilles through doors or walls or jumper ducts can reduce house pressures, improving circulation and comfort.

Thermostats often do not provide good comfort control in very humid climates. Manufacturers have developed air-conditioning controls that respond to both temperature and humidity, and have developed variable-speed blowers that are more flexible in providing both cooling and humidity control.

See "Thermostats" on page 158.

Airflow and Performance in Central Air Conditioners

The cooling capacity and the efficiency of the system depend on adequate airflow. There should be about 400 cubic feet per minute (CFM) airflow in the system for each ton of air-conditioning capacity. A designer may specify more airflow for drier climates to increase efficiency or less airflow for more humid climates to increase moisture removal. Central air conditioners are designed to cool the whole house; closing registers in unused rooms will not usually save energy.

Service technicians measure the airflow in the air-conditioning system in a variety of ways. The duct blower is often a more accurate tool for measuring system airflow. Using a flow plate, especially designed for measuring system airflow may also be fairly accurate. Flow hoods can also give a reasonably accurate value for system airflow if used according to the manufacturer's instructions and calibrated with a duct blower. Measuring pressure drop or temperature difference across the coil or across the air handler can indicate whether airflow is adequate. Duct sealing should precede airflow measurements to increase their accuracy.

When the air-conditioning system is operating, the temperature drop between supply and return air should be 15° to 21°F dry bulb or 8° to 12°F wet bulb temperature. *Wet-bulb temperature* accounts for the heat carried by the air's humidity. A reading outside these ranges could indicate a problem with airflow or refrigerant charge.

These temperature change measurements can also estimate cooling rate and coefficient of performance (COP). Technicians can calculate COP by determining the airstream's change in enthalpy (energy content) across the indoor coil by measuring temperature drop. The enthalpy change is divided by the system's electrical input to obtain COP. An air conditioner or air-source heat pump should have a COP of between 2 and 3. A measured COP of between 1 and 2 indicates poor performance, likely due to airflow or refrigerant problems.

Improving airflow — Technicians increase the airflow by cleaning the evaporator coil, increasing fan speed, or enlarging the ducts—especially return ducts. Enlarging ducts may seem drastic, but in some cases might be the only remedy for poor cooling efficiency and high cooling costs.

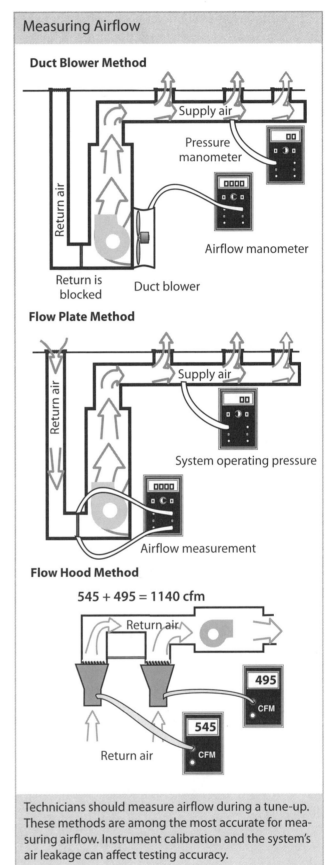

Measuring Airflow

Duct Blower Method

Supply air
Pressure manometer
Return air
Airflow manometer
Return is blocked
Duct blower

Flow Plate Method

Supply air
Return air
System operating pressure
Airflow measurement

Flow Hood Method

545 + 495 = 1140 cfm

Return air
495 CFM
545 CFM
Return air

Technicians should measure airflow during a tune-up. These methods are among the most accurate for measuring airflow. Instrument calibration and the system's air leakage can affect testing accuracy.

Maintaining Evaporator Coils

Gain access from side or bottom to clean coils.

Access the a-coil from the side or underneath in up-flow systems. Clean the fins by brushing, then spraying with cleanser and rinse water, if necessary.

Fin combs are available in various "fins/inch" models.

If the evaporator or condenser fins are bent, they can be combed back into original condition with a fin comb.

Air from every supply register must have an unobstructed airway back to a return register. Blockage of supply or return air ducts and registers can pressurize or depressurize portions of the home, resulting in poor air-conditioning performance and increased air leakage through the building shell. Remedies may include cutting off the bottoms of doors or installing louvered grilles through walls or doors. Installing more return ducts or ducts between rooms are also options for improving air circulation.

Obstructions in the supply air ducts include dents, debris inside the ducts, and bent or dirty registers. Supply registers can have severe blockages if the fins have been flattened by foot traffic or if they are dirty.

Insulated flexduct, as installed in many modern homes, is often kinked or crushed, causing a significant airflow problem. Fiberglass duct board has far less structural strength than galvanized-steel ducts. Crushed or damaged duct board can be an airflow problem. Fiberglass duct liner (installed inside metal ducts) may deteriorate over time from moisture and vibration, partially blocking the duct's airway.

Supply registers closest to the air handler sometimes deliver too much or too little cool air to the rooms. Change the room airflow by moving the balancing dampers at the duct's takeoff, adjustable vanes in registers, or by sealing off portions of the over-supplied registers. It is not usually a good idea to block off registers altogether, because this reduces airflow and cooling efficiency.

See "Duct Airflow Problems" on page 165.

Sealing Leaky Ducts

Testing ducts for air leakage, finding duct air leaks, and sealing ducts are discussed in "Duct Air Leakage" on page 89 and "Duct Leakage Comparisons" on page 67.

Refrigerant Charge

Room air conditioners and packaged air conditioners are charged with refrigerant at the factory. Split-system air conditioners and heat pumps are charged in the field and many of these have too much or too little refrigerant. Split systems that have the correct refrigerant charge and airflow usually perform very close to manufacturer's specifications for SEER and COP. Manufacturers say that a technician must measure airflow prior to checking charge because the charge measurements aren't accurate unless airflow is verified at 400 CFM (±80 CFM) per ton of cooling capacity.

For satisfactory performance and efficiency, a residential central system should be within an ounce of the correct charge as specified by the manufacturer. When the charge is correct, the system will have specific refrigerant temperatures listed by the manufacturer. Two commonly listed measurements are *superheat* and *subcooling*, which are the number of degrees the refrigerant is heated or cooled from its saturation temperature. Saturation temperature is the point between liquid and vapor that exists in both the evaporator and the condenser. The vapor needs superheat to dry it in preparation for compression. The liquid from the condenser needs subcooling to insure that it doesn't flash into a gas before it reaches the evaporator.

See "The Refrigeration Cycle" on page 42 to review air-conditioner operating principles.

Superheat, subcooling and other charge tests must typically be done during the cooling season. New air conditioners and heat pumps, installed or serviced during the heating season, are charged by weight. Refrigeration systems should be leak-checked at installation and every service call. Refrigerant must be added and withdrawn carefully and according to standards specified by the Environmental Protection Agency (EPA).

Maintenance and Service

Air-conditioner efficiency is dependent upon routine maintenance. The difference between the energy consumption of a well-maintained air-conditioning system and a severely neglected system ranges from 10% to 30%. The following routine maintenance tasks could be performed by a skilled technician or homeowner:

♦ Clean or replace filters regularly (depending on operating time, every 1 to 4 months).

♦ Clean supply and return registers and straighten their fins (dirt and damage are visible).

♦ Clean the blower's fan blades.

♦ Clean evaporator coil and condensate pan every 2 to 4 years.

♦ Clean condenser coils each year or two (dirt may or may not be visible).

♦ Remove debris from around condenser.

♦ Straighten bent fins in evaporator and condenser coils.

Professional Service and Commissioning

Adjustments and repairs to air conditioners are strictly for professionals. Even many professionals don't know how to install and service air-conditioning systems correctly. So there is no guarantee that basic operating requirements—correct sizing, airtight ducts, the correct amount of refrigerant, and adequate airflow—are present in existing air-conditioning systems. When a heating and cooling contractor is hired to measure performance and make necessary changes and repairs, this extensive service call is called *commissioning*.

An expert professional service technician might perform the following procedures to service or commission a central air conditioner:

♦ Checks ducts, filters, blower, and indoor coil for dirt and other obstructions.

♦ Verifies correct electric control, especially that heating is locked out when the thermostat calls for cooling and vice versa.

♦ Diagnoses and seals duct leakage.

♦ Verifies adequate airflow by measurement.

♦ Verifies correct refrigerant charge by measurement.

♦ Inspects electric terminals—cleans and tightens connections and applies non-conductive coating, if necessary.

♦ Oils motors and checks belts for tightness and wear.

♦ Checks thermostat operation.

Checking Refrigerant Charge

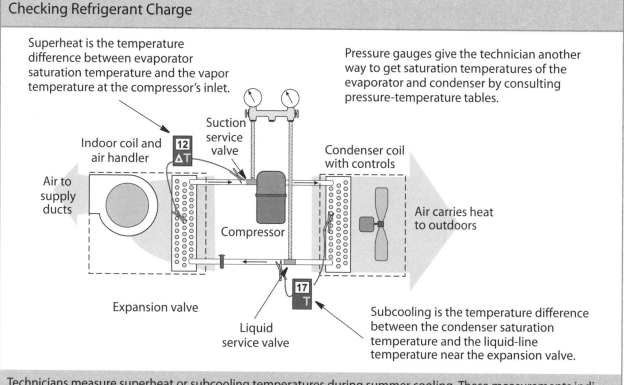

Superheat is the temperature difference between evaporator saturation temperature and the vapor temperature at the compressor's inlet.

Pressure gauges give the technician another way to get saturation temperatures of the evaporator and condenser by consulting pressure-temperature tables.

Suction service valve

Indoor coil and air handler

Condenser coil with controls

Air to supply ducts

Air carries heat to outdoors

Compressor

Expansion valve

Liquid service valve

Subcooling is the temperature difference between the condenser saturation temperature and the liquid-line temperature near the expansion valve.

Technicians measure superheat or subcooling temperatures during summer cooling. These measurements indicate whether or not the refrigerant charge is correct.

Pressure and Temperature Differences Across the Indoor Coil

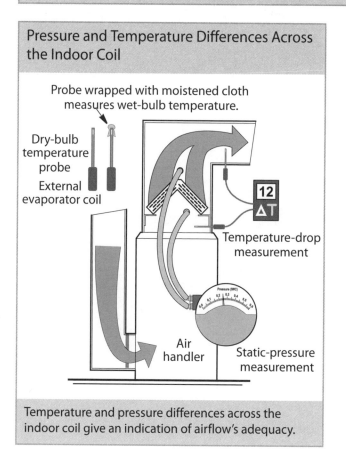

Probe wrapped with moistened cloth measures wet-bulb temperature.

Dry-bulb temperature probe

External evaporator coil

Temperature-drop measurement

Air handler

Static-pressure measurement

Temperature and pressure differences across the indoor coil give an indication of airflow's adequacy.

This chapter explores types of water-heating systems along with energy-efficiency and maintenance issues related to water heating.

A *domestic hot-water system* consists of: a heat source, a heat exchanger, a piping system, and plumbing fixtures like showers and sinks. Most domestic hot-water systems also have storage tanks. The heat source is a gas or oil burner, electric heating elements, a heat pump, or a solar collector. Heat exchangers usually consist of metal tanks or pipes.

A vast majority of North Americans use storage water heaters consisting of a tank, insulation, and a heating device which uses gas, oil or electricity. Recent improvements in water heaters include more and better tank insulation and improved combustion systems.

Water-heating Energy Use

The average household uses around 3500 kilowatt-hours of electricity or 230 therms of natural gas to heat water annually. Water heating consumes approximately 15% of the electricity and 25% of the natural gas used in residences. Water heating is the most variable class of energy consumption among families and varies according to water-heater capacity, climate, economic status, work schedule, and age.

Water heaters use energy in three ways: demand, standby, and distribution. *Demand* means energy is used for heating incoming cold water up to the temperature setpoint as hot water in the tank is used. Demand energy depends on water heater efficiency, occupant behavior, and consumption of fixtures like shower, clothes washer, and dishwasher.

Standby energy accounts for heat lost through the storage tank's walls. Standby losses amount to 20% to 60% of the total water-heating energy. Households using less hot water have a higher percent of standby losses.

Distribution losses consist of heat escaping through the pipes and fixtures. Pipes near the water heater lose heat even when water isn't flowing because hot water rises out of the tank, cools off in the nearby pipes, then falls back down into the tank.

Typical Consumption According to Family Size

Number of Residents	Annual kWh	Annual Therms	Gallons Per Day
1	2700	180	25
2	3500	230	40
3	4900	320	50
4	5400	350	65
5	6300	410	75
6	7000	750	85

Author's interpretation of single-family house data from Energy Information Administration, Lawrence Berkeley Laboratory, *Home Energy Magazine*, and others.

Water-heating Capacity

Americans use 15 to 40 gallons of hot water per day per person. Designing or selecting a water heater involves consideration of the first-hour rating and the storage capacity.

Hourly peak hot-water flow rate in gallons per hour is known as the *first-hour rating* or *recovery capacity*—an important design consideration for water-heating systems. The size of heating equipment, capacity of storage tanks, and design of piping systems is determined by recovery capacity needed by a building.

Water-heating systems are designed for recovery capacities of 3 to 20 gallons per hour per resident. Multifamily buildings—especially large ones—need less recovery capacity per resident or dwell-

Water-Heating Efficiency

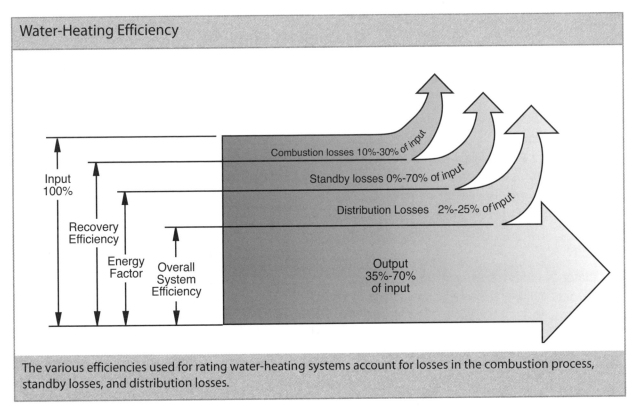

The various efficiencies used for rating water-heating systems account for losses in the combustion process, standby losses, and distribution losses.

ing unit because of residents' differing schedules. Suggested recovery capacities for multifamily range from 3 to 10 gallons per hour per resident.

Storage capacity, the amount of water in the storage tank, relates to the number of occupants or number of dwelling units in a building. Storage capacity typically varies from 8 to 20 gallons per person or 30 to 65 gallons per living unit. Most single-family homes have 40-gallon or 50-gallon storage tanks.

Water-heating Efficiency

There are several types of efficiencies used to rate water-heating systems. The DOE ENERGY STAR program sets criteria for residential electric and gas water heaters using several efficiency ratings; *Energy factor* (EF), *First-Hour Rating* (FHR), and *Gallon-per-Minute* (GPM).

Energy Factor—a number between 0.50 and 2.0 or more— is a ratio of useful water heating energy output to the total energy consumed by the water heater. Heat pump water heaters are able to reach higher EFs of 2.0 or more. *First-Hour Rating* esti-

mates the gallons of hot water a storage water heater can deliver once the water heater is fully heated. *Gallons-per-Minute* is how many gallons per minute that an instantaneous water heater can continuously supply.

See "Heat Pumps" on page 182 for information on heat pump operation.

Energy Factor Requirements for ENERGY STAR

Water Heater	EF	FHR/GPM
Electric	≥ 2.0	≥ 50 FHR
Gas Storage	≥ 0.67	≥ 67 FHR
Gas Instantaneous	≥ 0.82	≥ 2.5 GPM

Recovery efficiency accounts for just the losses during the water-heating process. A storage water heater's energy factor is less than its recovery efficiency. For demand water heaters without pilot lights, recovery efficiency is the same as their energy factor because they have no storage losses.

Overall system efficiency includes all losses and measures the efficiency of the water heater and its distribution system in providing heated water to points of use.

The American Council for an Energy Efficient Economy lists the most efficient storage water heaters in their annual guide, The *Consumer Guide to Home Energy Savings*. See "Bibliography" on page 309.

Water-heater Design Types

Design of water-heating systems is based on three interrelated factors: *recovery capacity* (gallons per hour), *energy input* (BTUs per hour), and *storage capacity* (gallons). These are determined by occupancy, number of plumbing fixtures, and per capita use.

Fuels for water heating include: fossil fuel, electricity, solar energy, and waste heat recovery. Each of these fuels can be used directly or indirectly. Direct water heating applies the fuel's heat to only one heat exchanger—a tank or pipes containing domestic hot water. Indirect water heating applies heat collected by water or air in a remote area to heat the domestic hot water. This remote heat comes from a boiler, solar collector, or waste heat exchanger. Indirect water heaters employ two or more heat exchangers.

Storage Water Heaters

Most single-family homes use direct storage water heaters that combine the heating device, heat exchanger, and storage tank into one unit. Single-family storage water heaters hold 30 to 80 gallons of water. Their tanks are insulated with fiberglass or plastic foam insulation and covered with outer jackets of painted sheet metal. Hot water exits the top of the tank, and cold water enters through a tube extending to the tank's bottom.

Older storage water heaters, insulated with fiberglass, have a thermal resistance (R-value) of R-3 to R-6, while newer models have R-7 to R-25. The extra cost of the better insulated water heaters will be returned to the buyer in energy savings in a year or less. Improved insulation is the only significant, recent improvement to electric storage water heaters.

A thin layer of glass, mineral, or plastic coats the steel tank's inside for corrosion resistance. A metal rod attached to the top of the tank, called the sacrificial anode, also protects the tank's steel parts from corrosion.

Storage water heaters with better warranties incorporate features like improved tank coatings, auxiliary sacrificial anodes, and curved dip tubes that make flushing more effective at removing sediment.

A pressure-and-temperature-relief valve mounted on the tank opens to expel hot water or steam if the pressure or temperature in the tank becomes dangerously high.

Since May 1980, all new storage water heaters sold in the United States must have an Energy Guide Label. The *Energy Guide Label* is intended for comparison shopping and not as a table for actual operating cost and performance. It features an estimated yearly operating cost, a bar scale comparing operating costs for similar models, and a table to allow the buyer to estimate the operating costs.

Gas Storage Water Heaters

A gas water heater and a propane water heater are nearly identical except for burner orifice, gas valve, and pilot orifice. Storage capacities are 30 to 80 gallons for single-family and 40 to 100 gallons for multifamily buildings. Larger multifamily buildings are often zoned and have a water heater for each zone. Or, the water heaters can be staged—one or two units supply hot water for average demand with more heaters coming on at peak demand.

Standard Gas Storage Water Heater

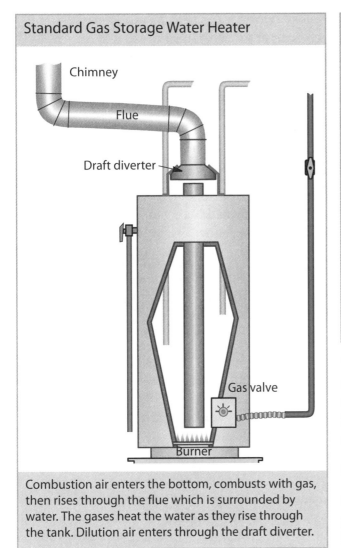

Combustion air enters the bottom, combusts with gas, then rises through the flue which is surrounded by water. The gases heat the water as they rise through the tank. Dilution air enters through the draft diverter.

Function of a Draft Diverter

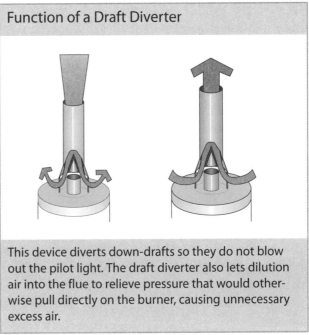

This device diverts down-drafts so they do not blow out the pilot light. The draft diverter also lets dilution air into the flue to relieve pressure that would otherwise pull directly on the burner, causing unnecessary excess air.

A gas burner located under the tank heats water. A thermostat opens the gas valve as the water temperature falls, and closes it when the temperature rises to the thermostat's setpoint. A pilot light—a miniature burner and flame—lights the main burner which heats the water in the storage tank.

The metal flue takes the hot combustion gases up through the center of the tank, using them to heat the water further. Multifamily units have multiple flues. The pressure (called draft) drawing the combustion by-products up the flue comes from the difference in temperature between the combustion by-products and the outside air.

Where the flue and chimney join is an opening called the draft diverter. The draft diverter moderates strong updrafts by allowing indoor air into the flue, and diverts strong down-drafts so they don't extinguish the pilot light.

Oil-fired Storage Water Heaters

Oil-fired water heaters are similar to gas and propane water heaters. However, they have power burners that mix oil and air in a vaporizing mist, ignited by an electric spark. The flue has a barometric damper that performs the same function as a draft diverter, but provides more precise draft regulation. For a fairly airtight residential structure, the oil-fired water heater should have a draft inducer to minimize the indoor air it consumes and to provide more reliable draft than the barometric draft control.

Heat-Pump Water Heaters

Heat pump water heaters can heat water at up to 2.3 times more efficient than electric-resistance storage water heaters. Heat pump water heaters use heat from surrounding air to heat water stored in the tank. They cost much more than conventional electric water heaters but are far less costly to operate.

Heat-Pump Water Heater

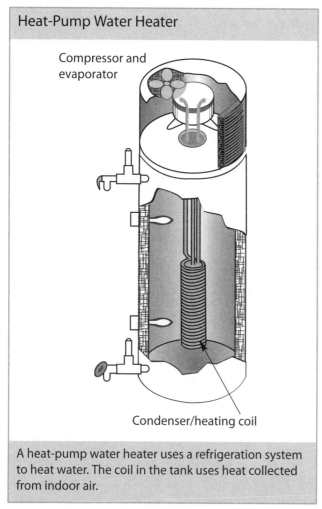

Compressor and evaporator

Condenser/heating coil

A heat-pump water heater uses a refrigeration system to heat water. The coil in the tank uses heat collected from indoor air.

Electric Water Heater Operation

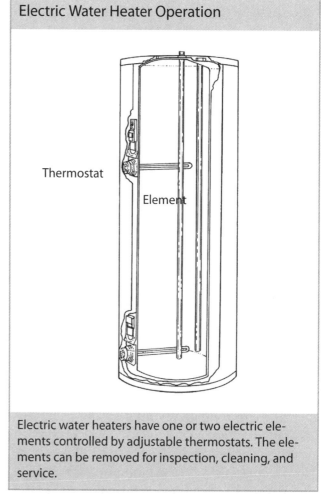

Thermostat

Element

Electric water heaters have one or two electric elements controlled by adjustable thermostats. The elements can be removed for inspection, cleaning, and service.

Electric Storage Water Heaters

Electric water heaters have lower standby losses and higher energy factors than similar gas, propane, and oil water heaters because they don't have flue pipes running up the center of their tanks like combustion units do. However, electric water heating is typically 1.5 to 2 times more expensive than natural gas, reflecting electricity's generation and distribution losses. Because of the higher cost of electricity, electric water heaters tend to have thicker insulation—3 inches of plastic foam in the best new models.

Electric water heaters don't need a chimney, so they can be easier to install than gas water heaters. However, since electricity is more expensive than gas, propane, or oil, many people choose combustion water heaters over electric.

Electric storage water heaters have higher energy factors and lower recovery capacities than fuel-fired water heaters. They tend to have higher storage capacities to compensate for their slower recovery.

An electric water heater is usually wired for 240 volts and has one or two electric elements, each with its own thermostat. In two-element water heaters, the element at the bottom of the tank is the standby element that maintains the minimum setting on its thermostat. The standby element adds heat to replace the tank's heat losses and maintain the minimum thermostat setting. The upper demand element heats water at the top of the tank to provide quick recovery of usable hot water during times of high demand. The elements are wired so they can't operate simultaneously.

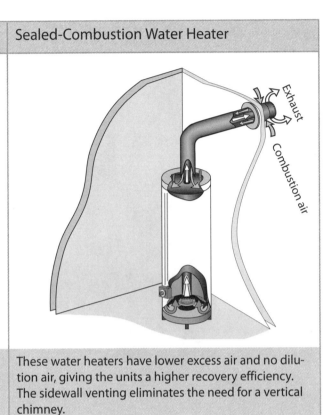

Fan-Assisted Gas Water Heater	Sealed-Combustion Water Heater
The draft-inducer fan controls the draft and reduces excess air to a minimum, increasing efficiency. These improved water heaters are vented through a sidewall.	These water heaters have lower excess air and no dilution air, giving the units a higher recovery efficiency. The sidewall venting eliminates the need for a vertical chimney.

Demand control is an important water-heating issue in multifamily buildings because they may be charged for peak demand by the utility company. Automatic controls should ensure that most of the water heating is done during off-peak hours.

Combustion Water Heater Safety

Most residential combustion water heaters are the open-combustion, atmospheric type. Their combustion efficiency and recovery efficiency haven't improved in decades. The combustion chamber and flue are open to the surrounding indoor air, and the combustion by-products flow up the chimney because they're lighter than surrounding air. This simple combustion system becomes a safety problem if the burner produces carbon monoxide (CO) and the chimney backdrafts—a common occurrence.

See "Combustion By-products" on page 241 and "Combustion-safety Issues" on page 150.

These safety problems are most dangerous when air from the living space has a direct connection with air near the water heater. Testing draft and CO should be part of installation and maintenance of all combustion water heaters. The same testing should accompany all weatherization, heating, and air-conditioning work.

Improved Combustion Water Heaters

Conventional gas water heaters waste a greater percentage of energy than electric water heaters do because of the design of the burner and venting system. Besides standby and distribution losses common to all storage water heaters, the wasted energy specific to gas and oil water heaters can be classified into three different types: excess air, dilution air, and off-cycle air circulation.

About 15 cubic feet of air is required to completely burn a cubic foot of gas. Every molecule of air flowing out the chimney carries wasted heat with it. Some waste is unavoidable, but the more excess air that flows through the burner, the more energy is wasted. Dilution air enters the flue at the draft diverter during combustion. Some or all of this dilution air is heated air from the home.

The third type of waste occurs when the burner is off. Surrounding indoor air circulates through the burner and flue, carrying heat away from the water and up the chimney.

Improved gas and oil water heaters reduce these venting-related losses by restricting the airflow through the flue and chimney and by eliminating the draft diverter or barometric draft control. Restricting airflow through the flue and chimney reduces air circulation, carrying heat away from the tank. Eliminating the atmospheric draft control and closing that hole in the venting system allows far less heated indoor air to pass through the venting system to the outdoors.

An *induced-draft water heater* uses a fan to pull the combustion gases through the flue in the center of the tank. The draft fan regulates the air that passes through the burner—minimizing the amount of excess air during combustion and limiting airflow through the flue during the off cycle.

Draft inducers—small fans for providing a steady and predictable draft—make these water heaters safer. The draft inducer makes the water heater safer by eliminating the draft diverter, using far less indoor air, and providing a more reliable draft.

A *sealed-combustion water heater* uses a combustion and venting system that is totally sealed from the house. Sealed-combustion water heaters draw combustion air from outdoors through pipes connecting to sealed burner compartments. They don't have draft diverters, and they may or may not have draft inducers. Sealed-combustion water heaters are designed for safety in tight homes. They are used routinely in mobile homes when installed in the living space.

Alternatives to Storage Water Heaters

Storage water heaters dominate the market, but indirect water heaters are common in multifamily buildings. Demand water heaters offer an attractive alternative when hot-water use is moderate, space is limited, and fuel is expensive. Solar water-heating equipment is expensive, but its competitive in life-cycle cost with storage water heating in warm climates or where hot-water demand is high.

Integrated space and water heating may be the choice of the future because the combined efficiency of a single heater providing both space and water heating is higher than the efficiency of heaters doing these tasks separately.

Tankless Water Heaters

Tankless water heaters heat water as it flows through the heater; there is no storage tank. Tankless water heaters are also called demand water heaters or instantaneous water heaters. The absence of a storage tank eliminates standby losses through the walls of the tank. Tankless water heaters can provide a continuous flow of hot water at a specific flow rate and temperature. They are available with recovery efficiencies ranging from 78 to 95 percent.

Tankless heaters are more expensive than conventional water heaters. The largest of them provides about 5 gallons of hot water per minute at 140°F. Taking a hot shower and running the automatic dishwasher at the same time stretches a tankless water heater to its limit.

The better gas-fired tankless water heaters have modulating gas valves that vary gas input depending on the demand for hot water. This modulation is necessary if the unit is serving two plumbing fixtures at once.

Sealed-Combustion Tankless Water Heater

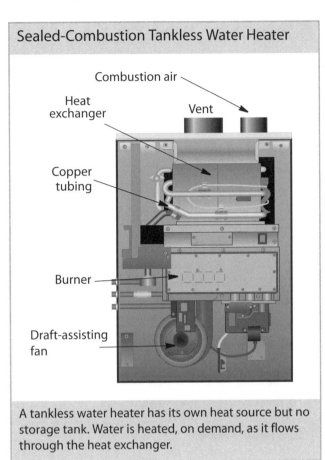

A tankless water heater has its own heat source but no storage tank. Water is heated, on demand, as it flows through the heat exchanger.

Immersed Coil with Tank

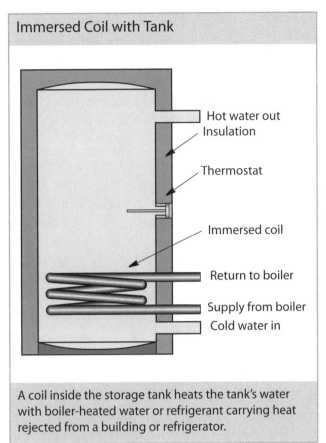

A coil inside the storage tank heats the tank's water with boiler-heated water or refrigerant carrying heat rejected from a building or refrigerator.

There are a variety of gas tankless water heaters available. Be sure to specify sealed combustion or direct vent (they mean the same thing). The old tankless water heaters are inefficient and unsafe because they have natural draft and open combustion. Don't specify or install a tankless water heater equipped with a draft diverter. The 80+ and 90+ efficiency units have draft-assisting fans which make venting safer. The sealed-combustion or direct-vent units are the best choice for both efficiency and safety.

Tankless electric water heaters generally serve just a single fixture like a shower or sink. They are a problem for utility companies because of their very large power draw. The largest electric tankless water heater, which draws up to 20 kW, will produce 2 gallons per minute with a 70°F temperature rise. New, heavily insulated storage electric water heaters have energy factors as high as 0.95, and that doesn't leave much room for improvement by tankless models.

Water Heating Integrated with Space Conditioning

An *indirect water heater* is a heat exchanger that derives its heat from a boiler, a solar collector, a heat pump, or an air conditioner. A boiler is the most common heat source for indirect water-heating systems. Boilers are generally more durable and efficient than combustion storage water heaters. The efficiency of indirect water heaters depends on the boiler's efficiency and how closely the boiler is matched to its water-heating and space-heating loads.

Well-engineered, indirect water heaters may have significant advantages over direct water heaters. First, they eliminate the need for a chimney with its heat losses. They're safer because they don't burn fuel or need combustion air. An indirect water heater can beat a direct water heater's efficiency, if it is well-insulated and coupled to a boiler which also provides space-heating.

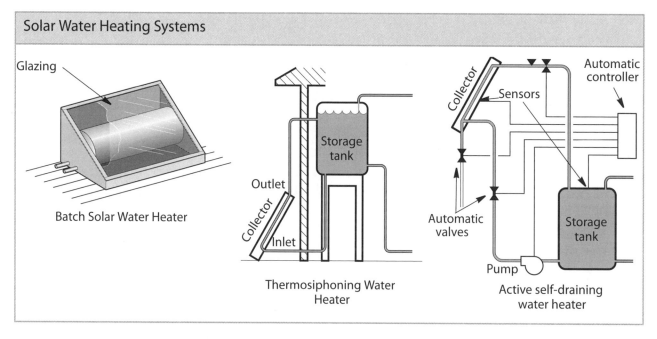

Solar Water Heating Systems

Glazing

Batch Solar Water Heater

Collector

Outlet

Inlet

Storage tank

Thermosiphoning Water Heater

Collector

Sensors

Automatic controller

Automatic valves

Pump

Storage tank

Active self-draining water heater

The two most common types of indirect water heaters are the immersed coil and the tankless coil. *Immersed-coil water heaters* use coils immersed in a tank of water. Boiler water or solar-heated water circulates through the coil, heating the water in the tank.

Tankless coils are heat exchangers installed inside a large boiler for heating domestic water. Tankless coils usually heat water for a separate storage tank near the boiler. A boiler's tankless coil may waste significant energy when it forces the operation of a large boiler during the summer months. Instead, it is better to install a separate water heater which is matched to the building's water-heating load. This allows the large boiler, which is used in the winter for both space-heating and water-heating, to remain idle during warmer months.

See "Boilers" on page 166 for a thorough discussion of boiler efficiency.

Two types of appliances are designed to heat water with hot refrigerant (waste heat) from a heat pump or air conditioner. They are the heat pump water heater and the de-superheater. A *heat pump water heater* is a small air conditioner attached to a tank with an immersed coil that is

the air conditioner's condenser. A *de-superheater* is an exterior heat exchanger that transfers heat from compressed refrigerant to domestic water before it goes to the condenser.

Other indirect water heaters use tanks inside other tanks, tubes inside tubes, or narrow chambers separating the heating water, steam, hot refrigerant, or other hot gases from the water being heated.

See "Integrated Heating Systems" on page 176 for more on integrated space and water-heating systems.

Solar Water Heaters

Solar water heaters are classified as active or passive depending on whether they use a pump to circulate water. *Batch solar water heaters* are just a black painted tank inside a partially glazed and partially reflective box. *Thermosiphoning solar water heaters* are also passive solar water heaters. They move water from the collector to a storage tank on top of the collector using only the buoyancy of hot water.

Active solar water-heating systems circulate water using pumps. They need freeze protection in temperate climates because their collectors become even colder than the outdoor air due to radiation losses into the night sky. Solar water heaters that circulate domestic hot water through the collector employ an automatic valve to drain the water back to the storage tank. Other solar water-heating systems circulate a water-antifreeze mix through the collectors for protection from freezing. Antifreeze systems circulate the water-antifreeze mixture through the collector, then through a heating coil inside a water storage tank—identical to an immersed-coil water heater, as described later.

Solar water heaters are usually connected to backup water heaters in case of cloudy weather.

Increasing Water-Heating Efficiency

Energy-efficient retrofits to water-heating systems follow three strategies:

♦ Reducing the use or waste of hot water.

♦ Reducing standby losses from storage tank and pipes.

♦ Reducing distribution losses through pipes and fittings.

Fixing all leaks, using pressure reducing valves, or installing low-flow shower heads and sink strainers minimizes waste of the hot-water supply. Tank insulation, pipe insulation, heat traps, automatic controls, and reducing water temperature all minimize standby and distribution losses. Designing the system to minimize the length and diameter of piping is the most effective way to minimize distribution losses in new water-heating systems.

Fixing Leaks

Repair leaks in fixtures or pipes before doing any other hot-water energy-conservation measures. If the water heater tank leaks, it needs to be replaced.

Flow Controls

Low-flow shower heads save energy by limiting hot-water use and are one of the most cost-effective energy conservation projects for homes. Shower heads with a maximum flow rate of 2 to 3 gallons per minute will save considerable energy if existing flow rate exceeds 4 gallons per minute.

There are two general types of low-flow shower heads—aerating models and laminar-flow models. The aerating models mix air with water coming out of small holes in the shower head, forming a misty spray.

Laminar-flow shower heads do not mix water and air at the nozzle, but instead, form individual streams of water. The laminar-flow models are recommended for damp climates because aerating shower heads create a lot of steam and may put too much moisture in the air. Many bathrooms don't need any additional moisture.

Approximate Savings: Hot-Water Retrofits		
Retrofit	Electricity (kWh)	Gas (Therms)
Reduce tank temperature	100–200	4–8
Exterior insulation blanket	150–450	4–16
Water-saving shower head	200–400	8–14
Heat traps	100–250	4–10
Home Energy Magazine, Oak Ridge National Laboratory, Pacific Northwest Laboratory, and others.		

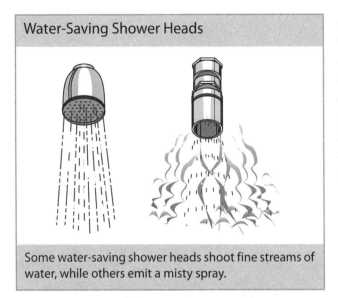

Water-Saving Shower Heads

Some water-saving shower heads shoot fine streams of water, while others emit a misty spray.

Low-flow faucet strainers are cost-effective and practical when delivery pressure is high and when the hot water is circulated. Some large homes and many multifamily buildings use pumps to circulate hot water, so it's available at every tap instantly when residents turn on the water. Faucets that are distant from the water heater can take a long time to receive hot water through a low-flow aerator.

In multifamily buildings, *pressure-reducing valves* can reduce hot-water flow rate. Lower water pressure reduces maintenance on valves and plumbing fixtures. Storing hotter water in smaller, highly insulated tanks is often an effective energy-saving strategy. *Mixing valves* combine cold water with the hot water stored at temperatures above 120°F. The skillful application of pressure-reducing valves, mixing valves, low-flow shower heads, and low-flow faucet strainers can provide adequate flow, comfortable temperature, low maintenance, and low energy costs.

Tank Insulation

Storage water heaters and other hot-water storage tanks rarely have an economically optimal level of insulation. The total R-value for any type of hot-water storage tank should be R-15 to R-35, depending on the cost of fuel. If possible, the insulation should completely surround the tank. Usually the tank already has some insulation.

Standard storage water heaters have a few inches of fiberglass between the tank and outer steel shell, amounting to R-3 to R-6. New standard models use foam insulation for higher R-values.

Technicians commonly use vinyl-faced fiberglass insulation (3 to 6 inches thick) to insulate storage water heaters. The insulation is often strapped or wired to the outside of the tank, with the seams in the vinyl covering taped. The tape alone may not hold the insulation's weight permanently, so plastic straps are often used for support. Technicians don't insulate the tops of gas-fired storage water heaters, since the vinyl facing is combustible and the insulation might interfere with the draft diverter.

When installing or replacing electric storage water heaters, placing them on top of an insulated platform made of 2-inch foamboard and plywood is especially cost-effective.

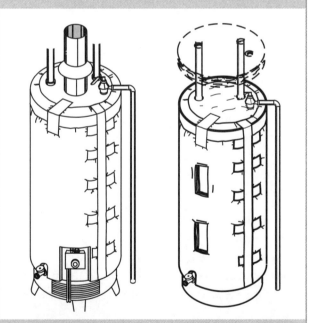

Water-Heater Insulation and Temperature

The external insulation of a gas water heater should not cover the top. Leaving the top uncovered avoids interference with the draft diverter and the hot flue. The insulation should have adequate clearance near the controls and the access door to the burner. Insulation for electric water heaters covers the top of the tank. Provide access to the cover plates for the electric elements and thermostats.

Commercial insulation suppliers offer a variety of insulating systems for larger storage tanks in multifamily buildings. Fiberglass or mineral wool are usually chosen because they are heat-resistant. However, many new storage tanks employ polyurethane insulation. Small uninsulated protrusions from the tank create heat loss. Experts in water-heating efficiency recommend covering all pipes and fittings near the water heater with insulation.

Pipe Insulation

Pipe insulation can reduce heat losses in three ways:

♦ First, it slows the direct conduction of heat through the distribution pipes.

♦ Second, it reduces the loss of convected heat through the hot and cold water pipes near the tank.

♦ And third, insulated pipes deliver water 2°F to 4°F hotter than uninsulated pipes, allowing a lower tank temperature setting.

Insulating exposed water pipes can reduce standby losses 50 to 150 kW-hour per year in single-family homes.

Pipe insulation is particularly cost-effective in larger water-heating systems with pumps that circulate the hot water (so tenants don't have to wait for hot water). In these systems, every exposed foot of pipe should be insulated.

Polyethylene- or neoprene-foam pipe sleeves are most commonly used to insulate pipes. Pipe sleeves should be taped, wired, or clamped with a cable tie every foot or two to secure them to the pipe. Pipe sleeves can be mitered together at 90° bends.

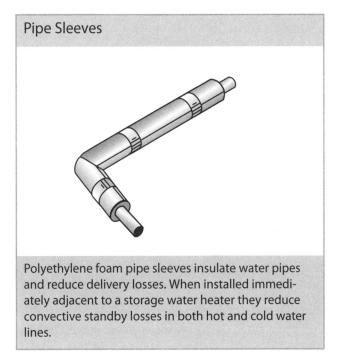

Pipe Sleeves

Polyethylene foam pipe sleeves insulate water pipes and reduce delivery losses. When installed immediately adjacent to a storage water heater they reduce convective standby losses in both hot and cold water lines.

Matching the pipe sleeve's inside diameter to the pipe's outside diameter is important for a snug fit. Most copper pipe is one-eighth of an inch larger in outside diameter than its nominal size. For example, $1/2$-inch copper pipe has an outside diameter of $5/8$ inch. Galvanized steel pipe is $1/4$ inch larger in outside diameter than its nominal size — for example, $3/4$-inch galvanized steel pipe has an outside diameter of 1 inch.

If the pipes are within 8 inches of a flue, fiberglass pipe-wrap, without a facing and wired into place, is the safest choice. The thickness of the fiberglass wrap should be at least 1 inch.

Heat Traps

Heat traps are specially designed valves or loops of pipe that stop convection of hot water into the hot and cold water pipes above the storage water heater or external storage tank. The special valves come in pairs and are designed differently for installation in either the hot or the cold water line. Heat traps have floating ball valves or delicate rubber check valves to stop convection.

Heat Traps

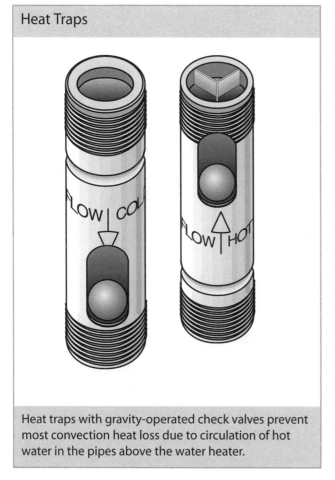

Heat traps with gravity-operated check valves prevent most convection heat loss due to circulation of hot water in the pipes above the water heater.

Automatic Controls

Automatic controls for water-heating systems vary from simple mechanical time clocks to sophisticated electronic controls that chart a large system's demand schedule and change water temperature accordingly.

A time clock controller turns the bottom element of a storage electric water heater off during periods when hot water is not used. The time clock controller saves energy by reducing the standby losses from the tank. Time clocks also save energy unintentionally, by reducing the average tap water temperature. Time clocks are most effective on uninsulated water heaters with high water temperatures, and without heat traps or pipe insulation. These inefficient water heaters cool faster to a temperature where standby losses are negligible. The maximum savings for a time clock is less than 4%, without counting the savings from lower delivery temperature, which is more easily achieved by setting back the tank's thermostat. A better solution for reducing standby losses is to insulate the water heater or buy a new one that is insulated with 3 inches of polyurethane.

Time clocks aren't very effective on well-insulated, storage electric water heaters with heat traps because they lose heat so slowly that the temperature of the water remains high for many hours. Well-insulated, storage electric water heaters have few standby losses for the time clock to save.

Electronic controllers typically save 10% to 25% on larger water-heating systems by reducing the storage temperature during periods of light demand. Usually, a multifamily building's heavy hot-water demand occurs during predictable morning and evening hours. The electronic control learns when the high-demand times occur and increases storage temperature to accommodate high demand.

Electric water heating poses a particular challenge to multifamily building operators in avoiding high electric demand charges. The priority to minimize electric demand requires demand controllers, or at least time clocks, that confine water heating to off-peak hours. This often requires increasing storage capacity.

The word *staging* means activating multiple boilers based on the size of the water-heating load. Staging multiple storage or demand water heaters is an effective control strategy for multifamily buildings, but the system's engineering is very critical to avoid scalding and shortages.

Maintenance and Operation

Water-heating systems are expensive to operate and replace. Nevertheless, most owners neglect inexpensive maintenance and just wait for the tanks to fail. Regular maintenance can minimize operating costs and extend the life of a water heater. Minimizing the water temperature setting is important to both maintenance and energy efficiency because lower temperatures mean less scale, sediment, and corrosion as well as lower standby losses.

Setting Hot Water Temperature

High water temperatures waste energy and threaten occupants with scalding. High water temperatures also speed the buildup of calcium and magnesium deposits in the tank and pipes. These minerals become less soluble as water temperature increases and precipitate out of the high temperature water. A high water temperature also speeds up corrosion, which is the death of many water heaters. Reducing water temperature to around 120°F minimizes mineral buildup, protects residents from scalding, reduces corrosion, and decreases energy consumption.

The storage temperature of a home's hot water is influenced by the presence or absence of a dishwasher. Most dishwashers have small water heaters (called boosters) inside that will boost the temperature about 20°F or more. If the dishwasher has a booster, set the water-heater storage temperature to 120°F. If the dishwasher doesn't have a booster, the setting should be between 130° to 140°F to get clean dishes.

Electric water heaters have a thermostat that is adjusted by turning a setscrew or knob. Gas and propane water heaters have a temperature dial located near the bottom of the tank on the gas valve. Marking the beginning temperature and adjusted temperature on the dial of the thermo-stat will provide a future reference. Several adjustments may be necessary before the water temperature is right.

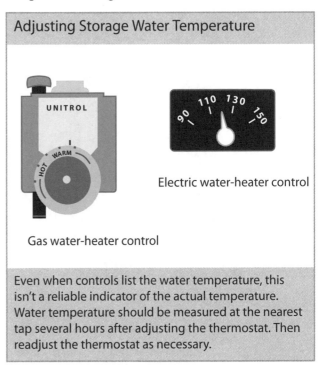

Adjusting Storage Water Temperature

Gas water-heater control

Electric water-heater control

Even when controls list the water temperature, this isn't a reliable indicator of the actual temperature. Water temperature should be measured at the nearest tap several hours after adjusting the thermostat. Then readjust the thermostat as necessary.

Setting water temperature in multifamily buildings is trickier. Finding the lowest adequate storage temperature usually involves turning the temperature down gradually. Day by day, the temperature is reduced to observe the threshold where complaints begin. Then the temperature is slightly elevated until complaints disappear. Tap delivery temperature should be around 120°F.

Preventing Tank Corrosion

The sacrificial anode is a metal rod that gives water something to corrode instead of the tank. The sacrificial anode is made of a magnesium alloy. Most steel storage tanks, regardless of size, have sacrificial anodes.

When the anode has corroded or disintegrated, water attacks the tank. A tank will normally corrode and fail within 2 or 3 years after the anode fails. With softened water, replace the sacrificial anode every 2 to 3 years; with hard water, every 4 to 5 years. Inspecting the anode every 2 to 5 years and replacing it, if necessary, could extend the average 8-to-10-year life of a water heater another 10 years.

Anodes for standard storage water heaters are 30 to 40 inches long and fit into a threaded fitting at the top of the tank. The anode can be replaced or another installed through an additional threaded port. Anodes come in a wide variety of sizes for larger tanks.

New tanks with improved coatings and auxiliary anodes have longer warranties and longer life expectancies. Plastic tanks offer longevity advantages and are increasing their market share.

Removing Sediment

Sediment is waterborne dirt and scale that settles to the tank's bottom. *Scale* is dissolved minerals that precipitate from hot water. Scale flakes settle in the tank's bottom or cling to electric elements. The bottom electric element burns out when sediment builds and surrounds it. Sediment in gas water heaters wastes energy by insulating the tank bottom from the burner. Sediment also overheats the steel tank, shortening its life.

Water hardness—the concentration of scale-producing minerals—is measured in grains per gallon. Expect scale to collect in the tank when your water has a hardness level greater than 10 grains per gallon. Hard water at 160°F can deposit eight to ten times as much scale as 120°F hard water. Reducing the temperature to 120°F helps to control mineral buildup and decreases the water heater's energy consumption.

Water softening reduces scale, but the salt medium that captures scale must be rinsed as often as once a month to recharge it. Water softening adds salt, which may be a health problem for persons with high blood pressure. Salt-softened water corrodes anodes two to three times as quickly as non-softened water.

Signs of sediment include: noise in gas water heaters, bottom-element burnout in electric water heaters, and odors in both types.

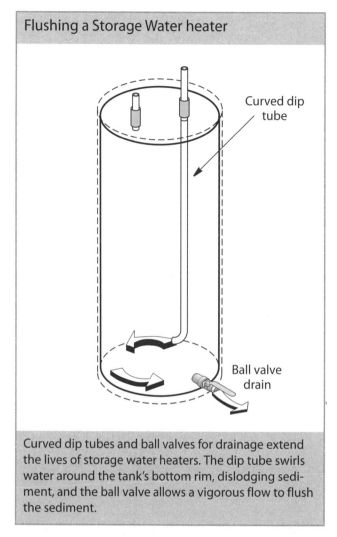

Flushing a Storage Water heater

Curved dip tube

Ball valve drain

Curved dip tubes and ball valves for drainage extend the lives of storage water heaters. The dip tube swirls water around the tank's bottom rim, dislodging sediment, and the ball valve allows a vigorous flow to flush the sediment.

The typical cold-water dip tube discharges water straight down, keeping the tank's area directly underneath it sediment-free. Instead, sediment collects around the edge of the domed bottom of the tank. When the sediment builds up to 2 inches or more, flushing under pressure with the existing drain valve can partially remove it.

Most drain valves, however, won't allow adequate flow for flushing because their opening is too small. A $3/4$-inch ball valve works well as a replacement drain because its large opening permits more flow. Newer dip tubes are curved at the bottom or discharge water sideways to swirl incoming water around the bottom edge of the tank, dislodging sediment. Curved dip tubes, combined with more effective drain valves, remove most sediment.

When a thick layer of sediment has accumulated at the bottom of the tank, it may be difficult to get it all out through the drain valve. A pump with a filter called a muck vac can suck sediment out of a tank through a threaded port.

Plumbers remove scale by pouring a cleaning solution into an emptied tank to dissolve it. They use white vinegar or mild acid solution formulated for cleaning water heaters. A plumber may also remove the elements of electric water heaters and soak them in the same cleaning solution, brushing gently to remove scale.

Large systems with dirty or very hard water will benefit from water treatment. It's easier to change or clean filter elements and maintain water softeners than to clean the various tanks, boilers, fittings, and plumbing fixtures, or to cope with their failure.

More complete instructions on removing sediment, replacing anodes, and other water-heater maintenance tasks are found in *The Water Heater Workbook* by Larry and Suzanne Weingarten.

See "Bibliography" on page 309.

Hot Water Choices: Advantages and Disadvantages

System	Advantages	Disadvantages
Gas/propane storage water heater	Very low first cost Easy to install Available in sealed combustion models	Low energy factor Requires separate chimney or venting for combustion gases
Gas storage condensing water heater	Very high recovery efficiency EF = 0.86 Sealed combustion	Much more expensive than conventional gas storage Requires natural gas service or expensive propane
Instantaneous gas/propane/ oil water heater	High efficiency and low annual cost Easy to install Available in sealed combustion models	Much more expensive than storage models Requires additional venting for combustion gases
Electric storage water heater	Available with very thick foam insulation EF 0.95 units are affordable No chimney or combustion vent	Electricity is relatively expensive Recovery not as quick as combustion water heaters
Electric heat-pump water heaters	Delivers up to 2.2 EF May use waste heat from a central heating system	Expensive Cools the room where they're installed
Indirect water heater	Avoids an additional combustion vent when coupled to a boiler Efficient if powered by an efficient boiler	May be powered by an over-sized boiler operating inefficiently Causes oversized boiler to operate during the summer
Solar water heaters	Fuel is free Integrates well with boilers and ground-source heat pumps	Expensive and seasonal Year round systems are impractical or very expensive

"First, do no harm." This statement has been an admonition to many a service provider and is particularly relevant to home performance and weatherization. Unless a service provider recognizes existing problems and the potential for new ones, calamity eventually occurs.

Weatherization work often interacts with a building's pre-existing hazards. When this interaction occurs, we want to remove, or at least mitigate, the hazard, and never aggravate it. The job site presents a series of hazards that workers must recognize and avoid.

Carbon monoxide from combustion appliances, for example, is frequently encountered during weatherization work. Moisture and fire also present major hazards to human health and safety, and they are the leading causes of building damage. Energy technicians should take the opportunity to add extra value to their work by reducing the danger of these hazards.

Exposure to toxic substances in the home and at work is probably the greatest long-term health hazard we face. Accidents are the fourth leading cause of death in the United States and constitute the greatest short-term hazard in our lives.

Home energy conservation modifications can create health and safety hazards if workers and occupants are not aware of the potential problems. Educating workers and occupants about the hazards at home and at the work site reduces the chances of accidents and exposure to toxic substances.

Indoor Pollutants

Air pollution is the most serious long-term health hazard in the indoor environment. By-products from combustion appliances and environmental tobacco smoke are the biggest contributors to indoor air pollution. Both of these sources contain multiple toxins, including carbon monoxide (CO), nitrogen oxides, volatile organic compounds (VOC), and fine dust particles, which are inhaled deeply into the lungs.

Dust also results from construction and other activities. Smaller and lighter dust particles are more dangerous than larger, heavier particles because they remain airborne for longer periods of time, and they settle more deeply in the lungs. The sharpness and chemical activity of dust particles affects the danger they present. A dusty environment also magnifies radon's danger by providing a transport mechanism that carries radon into the lungs.

See "Ventilation and Air Leakage" on page 83 and Appendix A-21 Indoor Air Pollutants for more information on indoor air quality.

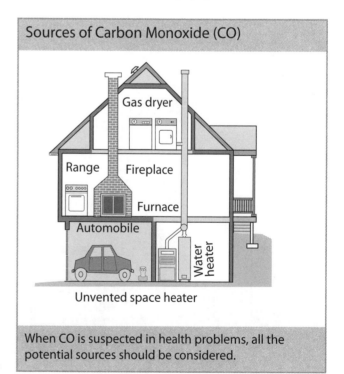

Sources of Carbon Monoxide (CO)

Gas dryer

Range Fireplace

Furnace

Automobile

Water heater

Unvented space heater

When CO is suspected in health problems, all the potential sources should be considered.

Combustion By-products

The most common sources of combustion by-products in indoor air of residential buildings are unvented combustion space heaters, gas ranges, vented combustion space heaters, central heating systems, and tobacco smoke. Unvented space heaters and gas ranges release all their combustion by-products into the indoor air. Vented space heaters may spill combustion by-products, temporarily or continuously, while they are operating. Continuous spillage from the vent of a combustion appliance is called *backdrafting*. Spillage from wood stoves can be particularly dangerous because wood smoke contains numerous toxins in high concentrations.

The chief causes of backdrafting and spillage in central heating systems and vented space heaters are: blocked chimneys; chimney air leaks; cracked heat exchangers; improperly designed or installed venting; and a depressurized zone near a furnace, water heater, or room heater. Furnace fans, exhaust fans, clothes driers, and chimneys can depressurize this combustion zone. Chimneys that are backdrafting or spilling should be inspected for blockage, leaks, and depressurization.

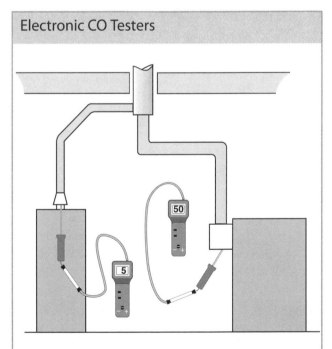

Electronic CO Testers

Electronic CO testers give a digital readout of CO in parts per million. You should test combustion gases as they leave the heat exchanger before they are diluted.

Technicians should test chimneys to ensure that they have proper draft and little or no carbon monoxide. Chimney testing is especially important as part of air sealing work, which may alter the home's pressure conditions. Draft in atmospheric-draft appliances should be negative 1-to-5 pascals (0.004-to-0.020 inches of water) depending on the outdoor temperature — colder outdoor temperatures should produce higher chimney draft. Measured pressure differences between outdoors and the combustion zone should not exceed 4-to-5 pascals, with exhaust fans and furnace fan running during a worst-case depressurization test. The combustion heater should spill for no longer than 30 seconds under these worst-case test conditions.

See "Combustion Safety and Efficiency" on page 150.

Carbon monoxide (CO) — Carbon monoxide (CO) is released by combustion appliances, automobiles, and cigarettes as a product of incomplete combustion. CO is the largest cause of injury and death from gas poisoning, resulting in more than 500 deaths per year. Many more people are injured by high concentrations of the gas, or sickened by lower concentrations of 5-to-50 parts per million (ppm). The symptoms of low-level CO exposure are similar to the flu, and may go undiagnosed.

CO blocks the oxygen-carrying capacity of the blood's hemoglobin, which carries vital oxygen to the tissues. At low concentrations (5-to-50 ppm), CO reduces nerve reaction time and causes mild drowsiness, nausea, and headaches. Higher concentrations (50-to-3000 ppm) lead to severe headaches, vomiting, and even death, if the high concentration persists. The effects of CO poisoning seem to be largely reversible, except for exposure to very high levels, which can cause brain damage.

The EPA's suggested maximum 8-hour exposure is 9 ppm in room air. Room levels of CO at or above 9 ppm are usually associated with the use of malfunctioning combustion appliances within the living space. These include: unvented combustion space heaters, gas ranges, leaky wood stoves, and backdrafting vented space heaters. Backdrafting furnaces and boilers may also lead to high levels of CO. CO is a common problem in low-income housing, affecting 20% or more of residential buildings in some regions.

The most common CO-testing instruments are electronic sensors with digital readouts in parts per million (ppm). Unvented combustion appliances should operate with virtually no CO production and vented appliances should produce no more than 100 ppm of CO in the flue gas, measured before the dilution device. CO is normally tested near the flame or at the exhaust port of the heat exchanger. CO is usually caused by one of the following:

♦ Flame interference from a part of the heating device (a pan over a gas burner on a range top, for example).

♦ Flame interference from dirt and debris.

♦ Misalignment of the burner.

♦ Inadequate combustion air.

♦ Backdrafting of combustion by-products onto the flame.

Environmental tobacco smoke — Tobacco smoke contains more than 3800 chemicals, which include carbon monoxide, ammonia, formaldehyde, and nicotine. According to the EPA, cigarette smoke is responsible for 39% of all exposure to indoor air pollutants.

An estimated 1000 Americans die every day from smoking-related diseases such as lung cancer, emphysema, bronchitis, and heart disease. The EPA estimates that 3,000 nonsmokers die each year from cancer brought about by secondhand smoke. The American Heart Association estimates that 37,000 people die annually in the U.S. from heart disease related to secondhand smoke. Cigarettes are responsible for more deaths than all accidental and environmental causes combined.

Nitrogen oxides, hydrocarbon dust, and volatile organic compounds — Nitrogen oxides are created naturally by the combustion of hydrocarbons in air, which is about 80% nitrogen. Nitrogen dioxide stunts pulmonary development and increases respiratory ailments in children. In healthy adults, nitrogen dioxide causes impaired respiratory function at 2 ppm, and sometimes less.

Wood stoves, unvented kerosene space heaters, and cigarette smoke release fine hydrocarbon dust and volatile organic compounds (VOCs) into the indoor air. The fine particles in smoke can penetrate deeply into the lungs and contribute to a variety of respiratory illnesses.

Other common sources of VOCs are: solvents and cleaners; paints and varnishes; and furniture, carpeting, and draperies. The VOC formaldehyde is particularly prevalent in new homes, because so many new home components — from plywood and drywall to cabinets and carpet — contain formaldehyde. Formaldehyde is a respiratory irritant, a sensitizer, and a probable carcinogen. The World Health Organization considers formaldehyde levels of 0.10 ppm the limit for continuous exposure. Symptoms of overexposure to formaldehyde include watery eyes and persistent respiratory distress. Formaldehyde levels of new homes and newly renovated buildings sometimes produce these symptoms.

Radon

Radon is a dangerous indoor air pollutant that comes from the ground through rocky soil. Studies predict 16,000 lung cancer deaths per year caused by radon.

Radon is a radioactive gas, whose decay particles cling to dust and can mutate lung tissue. The concentration of radon varies widely, both regionally and within regions. Energy conservation work probably has little effect on radon concentrations. However, all housing specialists should be aware of radon's danger, radon testing procedures, and radon mitigation strategies.

The EPA believes that any home with a radon concentration above 4 pico-Curies per liter (pC/l) of air should be modified to reduce the concentration.

There are several common and reliable tests for radon, which are performed by health departments and private consultants throughout the U.S. The least expensive test equipment is charcoal canisters, which are placed indoors for 2-to-7 days, and then sent to a lab for analysis. Another common test is the alpha-track canister, which is set indoors for 1-to-12 months. A film suspended inside the canister is pierced by alpha particles from decaying radon. A more expensive type of sensor can be analyzed in the field using a special volt meter, after the sensor has been exposed to a suspected area for some days or weeks. The most expensive meters give a continuous reading of radon concentration.

Since radon comes through the soil, mitigation strategies include:

♦ Installing a plastic ground barrier and carefully sealing the seams.

♦ Sealing the walls and floor of the basement.

♦ Ventilating the crawl space or basement to dilute radon.

♦ Depressurizing the ground underneath the basement concrete slab.

The first three mitigation strategies serve the needs of low-level radon mitigation (4-to-20 pC/l). Above 20 pC/l, sub-slab depressurization is preferred by most radon specialists. Radon mitigation strategies may affect moisture levels and could cause an atmospheric-draft heating system to backdraft, if a fan used for radon removal depressurized the area around the combustion heater.

Biological Particles

Many types of nonhuman organisms share our living spaces indoors. Bacteria and viruses cause diseases. Dust mites, cockroaches, cats, and fungi put biological dust particles into the air; they are responsible for most allergy and asthma. High relative humidity, and the moisture condensation it causes, encourages the growth of dust mites, cockroaches, and fungi. People who are especially sensitive to biological dust are called biologically sensitive, allergic, or asthmatic, and biological particles often go unrecognized as the cause of these disorders.

Biological Particles

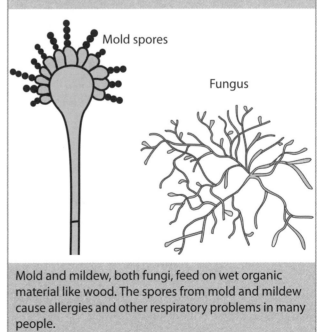

Dust mite populations increase as relative humidity and wetness increase. The feces of dust mites is one of the most powerful allergens known — a major cause of allergy and asthma.

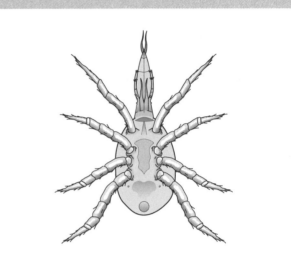

Mold spores

Fungus

Mold and mildew, both fungi, feed on wet organic material like wood. The spores from mold and mildew cause allergies and other respiratory problems in many people.

Biologically sensitive persons must keep biological dust in check. This requires controlling humidity and may even require keeping pets outdoors. Relative humidity, below 50% in winter and below 70% in summer, helps minimize condensation, fungi growth, and dust mite populations.

Asbestos

Asbestos has been a serious health problem to workers in asbestos mines, milling facilities, and certain other industries. Asbestos is classified as a "known carcinogen." Asbestos is found in boiler and steam-pipe insulation, floor tile, siding, roofing, and other building materials. Workers who encounter asbestos in the workplace must be trained to recognize and avoid it. Penalties for mishandling asbestos-containing materials are up to $25,000 per day.

Asbestosis is a disease caused by lung scarring from asbestos dust deposited in the lungs. Mesothelioma is a unique type of tumor linked to Amphibole asbestos — a long fiber with a very small diameter. The risk of lung cancer is increased through exposure to asbestos, particularly among cigarette smokers. These diseases have been documented almost entirely among workers who were exposed to very large amounts of asbestos dust.

Moisture Management

Moisture in American homes causes billions of dollars in property damage and millions of cases of respiratory disease each year. Moisture condensation problems are common during both the heating and cooling seasons. Moisture condensation is an important issue in homes for three reasons:

- ◆ Water leads to building deterioration by biological pests. These pests also create a threat to human respiratory health.
- ◆ Water corrodes metal, dissolves glue, warps wood, and weakens mortar.
- ◆ Water reduces the thermal resistance of insulation and may permanently damage it.

Weatherization work can make moisture problems better or worse, depending on the knowledge and skill of the workers. All necessary steps should be taken to prevent or mitigate moisture condensation, water leakage, and water seepage during energy retrofits.

Liquid flow is the most serious water threat, because it moves large amounts of water rapidly. Capillary seepage can also move liquid water rapidly into a home through damp soil and a porous foundation.

Water vapor movement by *air leakage* occurs mainly when heating or cooling systems are operating. Winter air leakage tends to carry moist indoor air through building assemblies toward the outdoors — drying the indoor air. Summer air leakage tends to bring moist, hotter air into the home — increasing indoor humidity.

Vapor diffusion is the slowest form of moisture movement. An absolute-humidity difference creates vapor pressure, which drives vapor to flow through porous materials. However, vapor diffusion can cause condensation and moisture damage inside building cavities during both the heating and cooling seasons if the water vapor encounters a dew-point temperature or a vapor barrier.

Moisture moves into a building during wet seasons and out during drier seasons. Moisture is a problem when it reaches a level of material saturation that encourages pests — termites, dust mites, dry rot, and fungus.

Sources of liquid water — Problems with water intrusion into the building determine how long the building survives. Rain water leaks in the roof, walls, and foundation — especially roof leaks — are important causes of moisture problems. Snow melting and refreezing on the edge of the roof — known as *ice dams* — can force water underneath the shingles and into the attic and upper walls. Poor site drainage allows capillary seepage into the foundation. Water moves easily as a liquid or vapor from the ground to porous building materials like concrete and wood. Undetected plumbing leaks drip water unnoticed into the building.

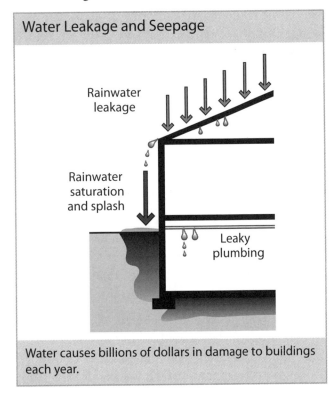

Water Leakage and Seepage

Rainwater leakage

Rainwater saturation and splash

Leaky plumbing

Water causes billions of dollars in damage to buildings each year.

Solutions for foundation water leakage —

Crawl-space and basement moisture problems are common in existing buildings. Consider these solutions to below-grade moisture problems, depending on their severity.

♦ Install or repair gutters and downspouts to lead water drainage to 3 feet away from the foundation.

♦ Correct the slope of soil bordering the foundation walls to drain water away from the foundation.

♦ In areas where surface water must flow near a building, cap the ground next to the foundation with impermeable concrete or clay.

♦ Re-position sprinklers to avoid wetting soil near the foundation.

♦ Install a ground-moisture barrier, sealed at the seams and to the foundation perimeter on crawl-space floors.

♦ Install a basement perimeter drainage system that drains into a sump with a sump pump or into a drain that flows by gravity. Either way, the leaking water should flow to daylight or to a drainage structure.

♦ Excavate the foundation and waterproof it properly if this was neglected during construction. Install exterior perimeter drainage to drain water collecting around the foundation.

Solutions for roof and wall water leakage — Roof and wall moisture problems are also common in existing buildings. Consider these solutions to roof and wall water leakage, depending on their severity.

♦ Repair roof leaks promptly. If you fail to stop the leak, try again, or replace the roof.

♦ Seal air leaks between the indoors and the attic to keep the roof cold in winter and to prevent ice dams. Sealing air leaks also stops humid attic air from entering the home during the air-conditioning season and causing condensation.

♦ Look for areas damaged by splash from the roof, and install gutters, downspouts, diverters, and flashing as necessary to carry water away from the wall and foundation.

♦ Improve attic or roof venting if necessary to keep the roof cold in winter to prevent ice dams.

♦ Add cap flashing to windows if window water leakage is observed.

Preventing Water Damage

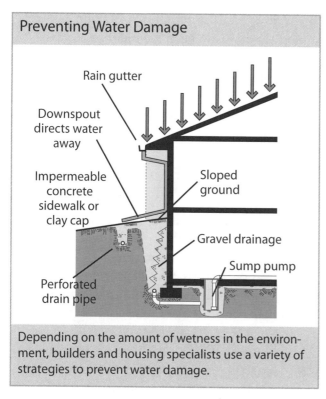

Depending on the amount of wetness in the environment, builders and housing specialists use a variety of strategies to prevent water damage.

Controlling Water Vapor

High relative humidity in indoor air can cause comfort problems in summer and condensation problems in both summer and winter. Experts on cooling say the indoor air should be less than 60% relative humidity for adequate indoor comfort in summer. Experts on winter conditions say that indoor relative humidity in cold climates should be less than 40% to avoid moisture condensation problems.

See "Window Condensation Chart" on page 129 for more information on the relationship between temperature and condensation.

Sources of water vapor — The average person evaporates 4 pints of water into the air daily through respiration or perspiration. Showers, housecleaning, and cooking can add up to another 3 pints per person daily. Water tracked into the home on shoes or clothing evaporates and increases humidity. Moist firewood and house plants put additional moisture into the air.

Air and Vapor Migration

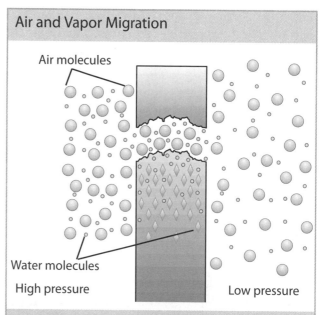

Water vapor travels through most porous materials, because water vapor molecules are small enough to migrate through the interstitial spaces in materials. Air molecules are larger and need a crack to pass through the same relatively porous material.

Relative Humidity

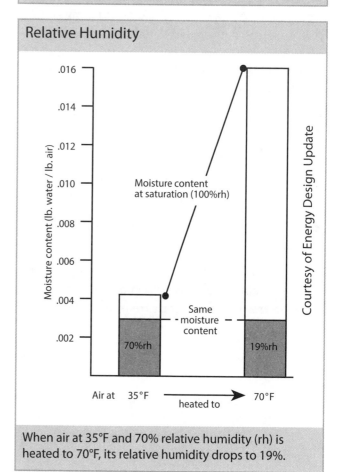

When air at 35°F and 70% relative humidity (rh) is heated to 70°F, its relative humidity drops to 19%.

Dryers and exhaust fans should always be vented outdoors and not into living spaces, crawl spaces, basements, or attics. Humidifiers should be avoided, unless there is a medical reason for their use. Home owners should know that some furnaces have automatic humidifiers that add moisture to the air in the home without occupants being aware of their operation.

Unvented combustion space heaters and gas ranges add moisture and other pollutants to indoor air. Backdrafting furnaces and boilers can also be a source of water vapor and other dangerous combustion by-products.

Moisture condensation problems

Moisture condenses on cold surfaces, such as windows and outside walls, due to a combination of relative humidity and temperature. As air cools, caused by its contact with cool surfaces, the relative humidity of the air increases until it reaches saturation. When that saturated air is cooled, some of its water vapor turns to liquid water and clings to the cold surfaces that cooled the air. Condensation occurs most frequently and plentifully on the room's coldest surfaces. Condensation increases as relative humidity increases and as surface temperatures decrease.

Effective strategies for reducing moisture condensation include these.

- Reducing relative humidity by reducing the moisture sources mentioned previously.

- Equalizing pressure between indoors and outdoors.

- Installing or improving air and vapor barriers to prevent air leakage and vapor diffusion from transporting moisture into building cavities.

- Ventilating with drier outdoor air to dilute the more humid indoor air.

- Removing moisture from indoor air by cooling the air to below its dew point, with refrigerated air conditioning systems and dehumidifiers.

- Adding insulation to the walls, floor, and ceiling of a home to keep the indoor surfaces warmer, and therefore more resistant to condensation. During cold weather, well-insulated homes can tolerate higher humidity, without causing condensation, than poorly insulated homes.

Preventing Moisture Problems

Preventing moisture problems is the best way to guarantee a building's durability, and its occupant's respiratory health. Besides the source-reduction strategies listed in the above sections, air and vapor barriers, ventilation, air conditioning, and dehumidification can mitigate moisture problems.

Air and moisture barriers

Air barriers and vapor barriers stop water vapor from migrating into building cavities and condensing.

It's important to stop the air, because the warm, moist air from the home can carry moisture rapidly from a source into the building cavities. Sealing all penetrations in the interior membrane of the home creates an *air barrier*.

This air sealing would include:

- Identifying and plugging air conduits like plumbing chases, chimney enclosures, and wire holes.

- Installing gaskets on all outlets and switches.

- Sealing window and door frames; patching holes and cracks in ceilings and walls.

- Sealing the floor/wall junction.

The air barrier — achieved with caulking, gaskets, and tight joints between building materials — may be separate from the vapor barrier. Many new homes employ a water-resistive barrier on the outside of the exterior sheathing that also serves as an air barrier. This water-resistive barrier or house wrap is permeable to water vapor, allowing water vapor to escape.

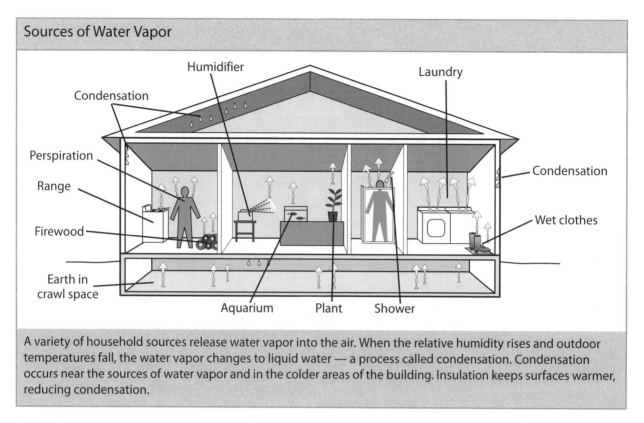

Sources of Water Vapor

A variety of household sources release water vapor into the air. When the relative humidity rises and outdoor temperatures fall, the water vapor changes to liquid water — a process called condensation. Condensation occurs near the sources of water vapor and in the colder areas of the building. Insulation keeps surfaces warmer, reducing condensation.

Vapor barriers are important in cold climates, where the difference in humidity between cold dry outdoor air and warm moist indoor air forces moisture through the walls and ceiling. The vapor barrier in cold climates should face the indoors.

If an impermeable material like polyethylene, installed as a vapor barrier, is attached in an airtight manner to framing lumber, the result is an *air/vapor barrier*. Vapor-barrier paints are often the only practical way to achieve a vapor barrier in existing homes.

In homes with significant air conditioning and heating seasons, moisture travels from outdoors to indoors during the summer and from indoors to outdoors during the winter. In these climates, avoid installing materials that are vapor barriers. Instead allow building cavities to be vapor permeable. This facilitates drying to either the indoors or the outdoors.

The ground under a crawl space or basement can be the major source of water vapor from air migration through the ground and also evaporation from damp ground. *Ground moisture barriers*

stop water vapor rising through the ground and into the home and also prevent evaporation from damp ground. Ground moisture barriers should be installed over dirt floors in crawl spaces and under basement concrete slabs. Reinforced polyethylene plastic makes a durable ground moisture barrier where people access the space.

If the seams of the barrier are sealed with a durable tape and/or sealant, this ground covering can also be an air barrier. Ground-moisture barriers aren't effective in crawl spaces with standing water, unless the ground moisture barrier drains water into a sump.

See "Air-sealing Materials and Application" on page 100 and "Facings and Barriers" on page 114.

Ventilating Attics and Crawl Spaces

Attic and crawl spaces provide a number of benefits related to moisture control.

Attic ventilation — Attic ventilation removes moisture deposited in attics by roof leakage and condensation. Most attic moisture problems come from moist home air leaking through the ceiling in winter. The preferred strategy for attic moisture control is to prevent the moisture intrusion into attics by air sealing the ceiling.

Attic ventilation also prevents uneven snow melt in cold climates. Snow melting in one part of the roof and freezing in another causes destructive ice damming. One goal of attic ventilation in cold climates is to keep the entire roof cold. This requires the entire roof to have outdoor air circulating beneath it in the attic.

The International Residential Code (IRC) recommends one square foot of vent for every 150 square feet of attic with no ceiling vapor retarder at the ceiling. If there is a vapor retarder, the code recommends one square foot of vent for every 300 square feet of attic space area.

During periods of high outdoor relative humidity, when the attic is cooler than the outdoor air, ventilation may cause condensation in an attic. The IRC recognizes this possibility and exempts humid climates with approval from a local building official.

Crawl-space ventilation — The IRC allows crawl spaces to be ventilated by passive vents or exhaust fans. Contractors also condition crawl spaces to include the crawl space within the home's thermal boundary and this option serves the same moisture-control purpose as ventilation. If the crawl space has an airtight ground moisture barrier, the vent openings are only required to be a ratio of 1 square foot of vent for 1500 square feet of crawl space floor.

In cooler and drier climates, the passive ventilation option, which complements floor insulation, is still the best choice. In warmer and damper climates, insulating the crawl space walls seems to work well with crawl-space exhaust ventilation or crawl space conditioning, with exhaust ventilation being preferable in most cases.

Whole-Building Mechanical Ventilation

Whole-building ventilation is one of the most important issues in residential energy efficiency. The two major strategies for whole-building ventilation are: ventilating with air leakage and ventilation with a whole-building mechanical ventilation system. ASHRAE (American Society of Heating, Refrigerating, and Air Conditioning Engineers) publishes household ventilation standards. The current standard 62.2-2013 requires fan-powered ventilation in all homes with the exception of very leaky homes or homes that require little heating or cooling. If you air-seal homes during retrofit work, you are usually required to install whole-building mechanical ventilation or to add capacity to local ventilation in kitchens and bathrooms as needed.

The problem with using air leakage for ventilation is that the air leakage rate is usually either inadequate or excessive, and it is uncontrolled. Air leakage doesn't ventilate all areas of the building equally, leaving some areas drafty and fresh, and others stagnant and polluted. Also, air leakage is highest during severe weather, especially in winter, because it is driven by wind and temperature differences between indoors and outdoors.

The three types of whole-building ventilation systems are: exhaust, supply, and balanced. Exhaust ventilation pulls stale air out of the home with make-up air coming through air leaks. Supply ventilation pushes outdoor air into the home and moves stale air out through air leaks. Balanced ventilation uses one fan to bring fresh air in and another to exhaust stale air out.

The IRC requires exhaust fans in kitchens (100 cfm) and bathrooms (50 cfm). These fans are important for removing moisture and pollutants at their source. Existing exhaust fans tend to be noisy and inefficient and aren't suitable for whole-building ventilation.

ASHRAE Ventilation Standard

Ventilation standards can be a confusing topic because of the lack of standardized terminology.

The current ASHRAE Standard 62.2-2013 specifies ventilation fan size according to floor area and number of bedrooms. The standard describes how to size the ventilation system's fan using either the following formula or table to find the total ventilation rate (TVR).

$$TVR \text{ (CFM)} = (0.03 \times floor\ area) + 7.5 \times (\text{\# bedrooms} + 1)$$

From ASHRAE Standard 62.2-2013

Floor Area (ft^2)	Number of Bedrooms				
	1	2	3	4	5
<500	30	38	45	53	60
501–1000	45	53	60	68	75
1001–1500	60	68	75	83	90
1501–2000	75	83	90	98	105
2001–2500	90	98	105	113	120
2501–3000	105	113	120	128	135
3001–3500	120	128	135	143	150
3501–4000	135	143	150	158	165
4001–4500	150	158	165	173	180
4501–5000	165	173	180	188	195

Fan flow in CFM. From ASHRAE Standard 62.2-2013, Table 4.1a

ASHRAE 62.2-2013 also requires 50 CFM local ventilation in bathrooms and 100 CFM in kitchens. An openable window contributes 20 CFM. If there is a deficit of local ventilation, add 25% of that CFM deficit to the whole-building ventilation fan's capacity to comply with the standard.

When a home is tested with a blower door, an infiltration credit may reduce the required ventilation rate. The procedure for qualifying for the infiltration credit is complicated and beyond the scope of this book. For a free online ASHRAE 62.2-2013 calculator, search for *Residential Energy Dynamics* on the internet.

Exhaust Ventilation

Exhaust ventilation systems use an exhaust fan to remove indoor air, which is replaced by infiltrating outdoor air. Better air distribution is achieved by using a remote fan that exhausts air from several rooms through small (about 3-inch) diameter ducts. In existing homes, install a high-quality ceiling exhaust fan, operating continuously. If you decide to replace a bathroom exhaust fan with an exhaust ventilation fan, the new fan should run continuously on low speed with a high speed to remove moisture and odors quickly. ASHRAE 62.2-2013 requires that new fans be no louder than 1.0 sone during continuous operation.

Exhaust ventilation systems are inexpensive and easy to install, but they don't recover heating and cooling energy or control the source of incoming air. Since most exhaust ventilation systems don't have filters, dust collects in the fan and ducts and must be cleaned out every year or so to preserve the design airflow. Exhaust ventilation systems create negative pressure, so they may not work for homes with fireplaces or other open-combustion appliances.

Exhaust systems create negative pressure within the home, drawing air in through leaks in the building shell. This keeps moist indoor air from traveling into building cavities, reducing the likelihood of moisture accumulation in cold climates.

In hot and humid climates, however, this depressurization can draw outdoor moisture into the home.

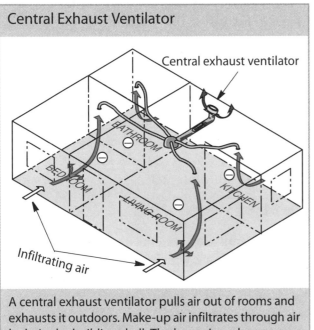

Central Exhaust Ventilator

Central exhaust ventilator

BATHROOM

BEDROOM

LIVING ROOM

KITCHEN

Infiltrating air

A central exhaust ventilator pulls air out of rooms and exhausts it outdoors. Make-up air infiltrates through air leaks in the building shell. The house is under a negative pressure. A central supply ventilator would be installed in a similar manner but with filtered outdoor air delivered to the home and stale air exiting through air leaks.

Supply Ventilation

Supply ventilation uses a fan to deliver outdoor air to the house, which becomes slightly pressurized, forcing indoor air out through air leaks. Using a supply fan makes it possible to filter incoming air, which is distributed to the bedrooms and living areas by ducts. A 5-to-10 inch diameter supply duct admits outdoor air to the air handler's return plenum. This supply duct often has a motorized damper that opens when the air-handler blower operates, bringing outdoor air in, mixing it with return air, and then heating or cooling it.

Ventilation only happens when the air handler operates, so the air handler must operate even when heating and cooling aren't required. An electronic control can activate the blower, timing its cycles to deliver the design ventilation rate.

Using the air handler for ventilation is inefficient because forced-air blowers are designed to move around 10 times more air than needed for ventilation.

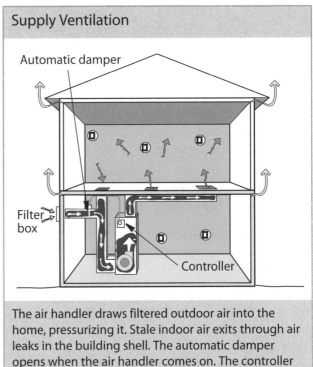

Supply Ventilation

Automatic damper

Filter box

Controller

The air handler draws filtered outdoor air into the home, pressurizing it. Stale indoor air exits through air leaks in the building shell. The automatic damper opens when the air handler comes on. The controller opens and closes the damper and cycles the air handler as needed to ventilate the home.

Supply ventilation doesn't require a large air handler. You can use a correctly sized fan with its own small duct system, which operates continuously. Outdoor air is filtered, keeping most dust out of the duct system, which is an advantage of central supply ventilation over central exhaust ventilation.

Supply ventilation isn't appropriate for very cold climates because it pushes indoor air through exterior walls, where moisture can condense on cold surfaces.

Balanced Ventilation Systems

Balanced ventilation systems exhaust stale air and provide fresh air through a ducted distribution system. Of all the ventilation schemes, they do the best job of controlling pollutants in the home.

Balanced systems move equal amounts of air into and out of the home. Most balanced systems incorporate heat recovery ventilators (HRVs) or energy recovery ventilators (ERVs) that reclaim heat and/or moisture from the exhaust air stream.

Balanced systems, when operating properly, reduce many of the safety problems and moisture-induced building damage that is possible with unbalanced ventilation. They are not trouble-free, however, and there are many homes with "balanced" ventilation systems that experience pressure imbalances and poor air quality due to poor design, installation, or maintenance.

These complicated systems can improve the safety and comfort of home, but a high standard of care is needed to assure that they operate properly. Testing and commissioning is vital during both the initial installation and periodic service calls.

Heat and Energy Recovery Ventilators

The difference between an HRV and an ERV is that HRVs transfer heat only, while ERVs transfer both sensible and latent heat (moisture) between airstreams.

The HRV core is usually a *flat-plate* aluminum or polyethylene air-to-air heat exchanger in which the supply and exhaust airstreams pass one another with minimal mixing.

Heat travels through the core, by conduction, from the warmer to the cooler airstream. In heating climates, this means that heat contained in the exhaust air warms the incoming supply air. In cooling climates, the heat of the incoming fresh air is passed to the outgoing exhaust.

In cold weather, outgoing moisture condenses when it passes the cold incoming air in the HRV core. This condensate is drained. Defrost mechanisms are required in severe climates to thaw frozen condensate in the heat exchanger. The most economical defrost method is periodic recirculation of warm indoor air, though some HRVs with aluminum cores use electric heat strips.

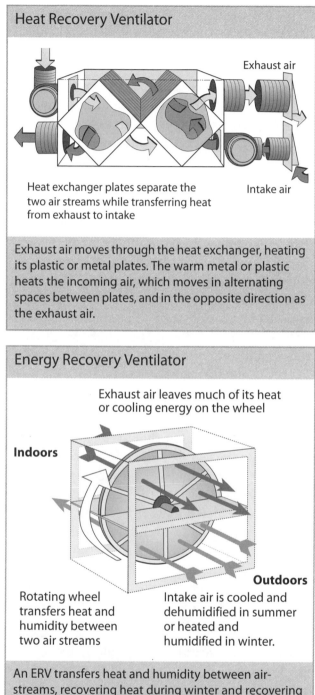

Heat Recovery Ventilator

Exhaust air

Intake air

Heat exchanger plates separate the two air streams while transferring heat from exhaust to intake

Exhaust air moves through the heat exchanger, heating its plastic or metal plates. The warm metal or plastic heats the incoming air, which moves in alternating spaces between plates, and in the opposite direction as the exhaust air.

Energy Recovery Ventilator

Exhaust air leaves much of its heat or cooling energy on the wheel

Indoors

Outdoors

Rotating wheel transfers heat and humidity between two air streams

Intake air is cooled and dehumidified in summer or heated and humidified in winter.

An ERV transfers heat and humidity between airstreams, recovering heat during winter and recovering cooling energy during summer.

ERVs can also be used to ventilate homes during summer in warm climates, where they limit the intake of outdoor humidity. ERVs reduce the costs of conditioning ventilation air, and the greater the difference in temperature and moisture between the air streams, the more energy is recovered. Energy recovery ventilators may improve comfort in winter by transferring moisture as well as heat to cold dry incoming air.

Ventilation-air distribution — Whole-building ventilators are most effective when installed with their own system of supply and return air ducts. Fully ducted systems are popular for buildings with hydronic heating, or for very energy-efficient homes heated by just a few space heaters.

Homes with central forced-air systems often have the ventilator connected to the central duct system. The supply ventilation air comes from outdoors through the ventilator and into a main return duct 4 to 8 feet from the air handler. In a simplified installation, both the supply and exhaust of the ventilator may be connected to the air handler's return ducts. The ventilator's exhaust duct should be connected closer to the air handler and the ventilator's supply duct farther away.

When balanced ventilators use forced-air ducts for distribution, the ducts should be very airtight. The air handler's blower should run at its lowest speed when the ventilator is running to help distribute the air. Running the blower also increases energy use. New electronically commutated blowers, operating at 250 watts or less, make the extended and simplified ventilator installations more practical and energy efficient. Some ventilators connect to forced-air ducts but don't use the air handler's blower, but this strategy results in airflow that is too low to provide adequate ventilation.

Like forced-air heating and cooling systems, many whole-building ventilation systems are installed without measuring system airflow or room airflows. Lack of testing leaves many systems performing inadequately. At minimum, installers should measure supply and exhaust airflow to ensure that they achieve the designed airflow and are balanced with one another.

Humidistats or timers are used with manual switches to control the operation of air-to-air heat exchangers for insuring good air quality. The associated system of ducts is subject to the same problems of leakage, obstruction, and balancing as other forced-air distribution systems.

See "Ventilation and Air Leakage" on page 83.

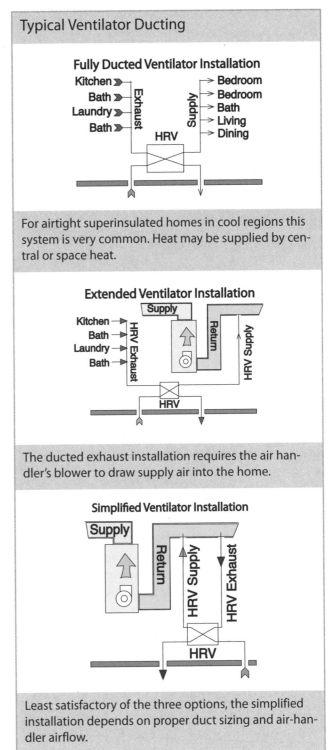

Typical Ventilator Ducting

Fully Ducted Ventilator Installation

For airtight superinsulated homes in cool regions this system is very common. Heat may be supplied by central or space heat.

Extended Ventilator Installation

The ducted exhaust installation requires the air handler's blower to draw supply air into the home.

Simplified Ventilator Installation

Least satisfactory of the three options, the simplified installation depends on proper duct sizing and air-handler airflow.

Air Conditioners and Dehumidifiers

Air conditioners and electric dehumidifiers remove water vapor from the air by refrigerating the air and condensing some of its water vapor. This drying process removes heat from the air. The air conditioner releases this heat outdoors through its outdoor condenser coil. The dehumidifier, on the other hand, reheats the indoor air after refrigerating it, making the dehumidifier somewhat like a space heater. The dehumidifier can be a very efficient space heater, if moisture removal and space heat are needed in the same part of a building.

See "Air Conditioners" on page 212.

Air-conditioning systems should be designed to remove enough moisture to provide adequate comfort, although unfortunately this isn't always the case.

Avoid using dehumidifiers at the same time as air conditioning. The air conditioner and the dehumidifier work in opposition, with the dehumidifier heating the space and the air conditioner cooling it.

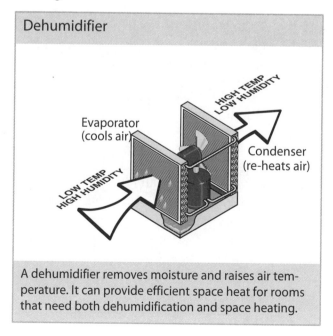

Dehumidifier

Evaporator (cools air)

HIGH TEMP LOW HUMIDITY

Condenser (re-heats air)

LOW TEMP HIGH HUMIDITY

A dehumidifier removes moisture and raises air temperature. It can provide efficient space heat for rooms that need both dehumidification and space heating.

Pollutant Control Strategies

Pollutant	Source Control	Ventilation	Filtration
Ground Source Moisture	Best solution: control surface water, seal foundation, install crawl space moisture barrier.	Partial solution: use after all source control measures have been enacted.	No effect.
Occupant-Generated Moisture	Good solution: duct dryers and fans to outdoors, cover pans when cooking, avoid use of humidifiers.	Good solution: install ventilation equipment with intakes at the sources of pollutants.	No effect.
Biological Contaminants	Partial solution: but only limited effect because of widespread occurrence of organisms.	Best solution: use ventilation to lower humidity levels and discourage growth.	Limited effect.
Formaldehyde And Other Volatile Organic Compounds	Best solution: use low-emission building materials, avoid storing chemicals indoors.	Partial solution: but higher ventilation rates may be required while new materials out-gas.	Limited effect.
Carbon Monoxide and Other Combustion By-Products	Best solution: confirm that combustion appliances are vented properly. Install sealed combustion equipment when possible.	Unsafe option: combustion appliances should never allow spillage into the home.	No effect.
Carbon Dioxide and Other Occupant-Generated Effluents	Not practical: higher occupancy creates more pollutants.	Best solution: install ventilation equipment with exhaust pick-ups near the sources of pollutants.	Not practical.
Asbestos, Lead, and Other Particulates	Best solution: avoid use of these materials. If present, protect from damage.	Not practical.	Not practical.
Radon, Methane, Fertilizers, and Other Soil Gases	Best solution: seal foundation and provide sub-slab ventilation if needed.	Partial solution: but it's expensive at required ventilation rates.	Not practical.
Tobacco By-Products	Best solution: don't smoke indoors.	Partial solution: but it's expensive at required ventilation rates.	Partial solution.

APPENDICES

Glossary

Absolute humidity - Air moisture content expressed in grains (or pounds) of water vapor per pound of dry air. Also called: humidity ratio.

Absorptance - The ratio of a solar energy absorbed to incident solar. Also called absorptivity.

Absorption - A solid material's ability to draw in and hold liquid or gas.

Accent lighting - Lighting that illuminates walls, reducing brightness contrast between walls and ceilings or windows.

Air barrier - Any part of the building shell that offers resistance to air leakage. The air barrier is effective if it stops most air leakage. The primary air barrier is the most effective of a series of air barriers.

Air conditioning - Cooling buildings with a refrigeration system. More generally means both heating and cooling.

Air exchange - The total building air exchanged with the outdoors through air leakage and ventilation.

Air handler - A steel cabinet containing a blower with cooling and/or heating coils connected to ducts.

Ambient lighting - Lighting spread throughout the lighted space for safety, security, and aesthetics.

Ampere - A unit of measurement of electrical current flow. A coulomb per second.

Annual fuel utilization efficiency (AFUE) - A laboratory-derived efficiency rating for heating appliances which accounts for chimney losses, jacket losses, and cycling losses.

Annual return - The yearly savings divided by the initial cost needed to achieve the savings, expressed as a percent.

Approach temperature - The temperature difference between the fluid inside a heat exchanger and the fluid outside it.

Aquastat - A heating control that switches the burner or the circulator in a hydronic heating system.

Asbestos - A material made of brittle mineral fibers that damage lungs and other bodily tissues.

Atmospheric appliance - A combustion appliance that moves combustion air and combustion byproducts through the heat exchanger and venting by the gas buoyancy created by the flame.

Audit - The process of identifying energy conservation opportunities in buildings.

Backdrafting - Continuous spillage of combustion gases from a combustion appliance.

Backdraft damper - A damper, installed near a fan, that allows air to flow in only one direction.

Backer rod - Polyethylene foam rope used as a backer for caulking.

Baffle - A plate or strip designed to retard or redirect the flow of flue gases.

Balance point - The minimum outdoor temperature at which no heating is needed.

Ballast - A coil of wire or electronic device that provides a high starting voltage for a lamp and limits the current from flowing through it.

Band joist - See Rim joist.

Batt - A narrow blanket of fiberglass insulation, often 14.5 or 22.5 inches wide.

Beam - A strong horizontal building support used to carry the weight of a floor or roof.

Bimetal element - A metal spring, lever, or disc made of two dissimilar metals that expand and contract at different rates as the temperature around them changes. This movement operates a switch in the control circuit of a heating or cooling device.

Blow-down - Draining water from a boiler, evaporative cooler, water heater, etc. to remove sediment and suspended particulates.

Blower - The squirrel-cage fan in a furnace or air handler.

Blower door - A device that consists of a fan, a removable panel, and gauges used to measure and locate air leaks.

Boot - A duct section that connects between a duct and a register.

Branch circuit - An electrical circuit used to power outlets and lights within a home.

Brightness - The intensity of sensation resulting from viewing a lit surface. Measured in foot-lamberts. Also called luminance or luminous intensity.

British thermal unit (BTU) - The quantity of heat required to raise the temperature of one pound of water one degree Fahrenheit.

BTUH - British thermal units per hour.

Building cavities - The spaces inside walls, floors, and ceilings between the interior and exterior sheeting.

Building science - Branch of science dealing with construction, maintenance, safety, and energy efficiency of buildings.

Building tightness limit (BTL) - See minimum ventilation guideline (MVG).

Burner - A device that facilitates the burning of a fossil fuel like gas or oil.

Capillary action - The ability of water to move through materials, even upward against gravity, through small tubes or spaces.

Capillary barrier - A material or air space designed to stop capillary action from carrying water into a building.

Carbon dioxide - One of two main products of complete combustion of a hydrocarbon (the other is water vapor).

Carbon monoxide - An odorless and poisonous gas produced by incomplete combustion.

Caulking - A mastic compound for filling joints and cracks.

Cellulose insulation - Insulation, packaged in bags for blowing, made from newspaper or wood waste and treated with a fire retardant.

Celsius - A temperature scale on which water freezes at 0°C and boils at 100°C.

Centigrade - See Celsius

CFM$_{50}$ - The number of cubic feet per minute of air flowing through the fan housing of a blower door when the house pressure is 50 pascals (0.2 inches of water). This figure is the most common and accurate way of comparing the airtightness of buildings that are tested using a blower door.

CFM$_n$ - The number of cubic feet of air flowing through a house from indoors to outdoors during typical, natural conditions. This figure can be roughly estimated using a blower door.

Circuit breaker - A device that disconnects an electrical circuit from electricity when it senses excessive current.

Coefficient of performance (COP) - A heat pump or air conditioner's output in watt-hours of heat moved divided by watt-hours of electrical input.

Coil - A snakelike piece of copper tubing surrounded by rows of aluminum fins that clamp tightly to the tubing in order to aid in heat transfer.

Color-rendering index (CRI) - A measurement of a light source's ability to render colors the same as sunlight. CRI has a scale of 0 to 100.

Color temperature - A measurement of the warmness or coolness of a light source in the Kelvin temperature scale.

Column - A vertical building support usually made of wood or steel.

Combustible - The rating for building materials that will burn under some conditions.

Combustion air - Air that provides oxygen for combustion.

Combustion analyzer - A device used to measure steady-state efficiency of combustion heating units.

Combustion chamber - The area inside the heat exchanger where the flame burns.

Combustion efficiency - Synonymous with fuel-burning efficiency or steady-state efficiency. Usually means the latter.

Commissioning - The process of testing and adjusting building mechanical systems after building construction or as a retrofit measure.

Compressor - A motorized vapor pump that compresses the gaseous refrigerant and sends it to the condenser where collected heat is released.

Condense - When a gas turns into a liquid as it cools, we say it condenses. Condensation is the opposite of evaporation.

Condenser - The coil in an air conditioning system where the refrigerant condenses and releases heat.

Condensate - Liquid formed by condensing vapor.

Condensate receiver - A tank for catching returning condensate water from a steam heating system.

Conditioned - Heated or cooled areas of a building are said to be conditioned, either intentionally or unintentionally.

Conductance - The property of a material to conduct some energy form like heat or electricity.

Conduction - Heat flow from molecule to molecule in a solid substance.

Contrast - Difference in brightness of areas in the lit environment.

Control circuit - A circuit whose work is switching a power circuit or opening an automatic valve.

Convection - The transfer of heat caused by the movement of a fluid like water or air. When a fluid becomes warmer it becomes lighter and rises.

Cooling load - The maximum rate of heat removal required of an air conditioner when the outdoor temperature and humidity are at the highest expected level.

Cost-effective - Having an acceptable payback, return-on-investment, or savings-to-investment ratio.

Cross section - A view of a building component drawn or imagined by cutting through the component.

Cubic foot per minute (cfm) - A measurement of air movement past a certain point or through a certain structure.

Curtain wall - A wall between columns and beams that supports no weight but its own.

Decatherm - One million BTUs or 10 therms.

Decking - The wood material installed under roofing material to support the roofing.

Degree-days - A measure of the temperature element of climate produced by multiplying temperature difference by time.

Demand - The peak need for electrical energy. Some utilities levy a monthly charge for demand.

Demand-side management (DSM) - Electricity conservation and peak-demand reduction guided by utility organizations

Density - The weight of a material divided by its volume, usually measured in pounds per cubic foot.

Depressurize - Cause to have a lower pressure or vacuum with respect to a reference of a higher pressure.

Desiccant - A liquid or solid material used to absorb water or water vapor.

Design temperature - An extreme high or low outdoor temperature used for designing heating and cooling systems.

De-superheater - A heat exchanger that removes the superheat from a compressed refrigerant and transfers that heat to another fluid, usually water.

Dew point - The warmest temperature of an object in an environment where water condensation from the surrounding air would form on that object.

Dilution air - Air that enters through the dilution device—an opening where the chimney joins to an atmospheric-draft appliance.

Dilution device - A draft diverter or barometric draft control on a combustion appliance.

Direct vent - A combustion appliance that draws combustion air from outdoors and vents combustion products to outdoors.

Distribution system - A system of pipes or ducts used to distribute energy.

Dormer - A vertical window projecting from a roof.

Draft - The pressure in a flue or vent that propels combustion gases out of a building.

Draft diverter - A device located in gas appliance chimneys that moderates draft and diverts down drafts that could extinguish the pilot or interfere with combustion.

Draft inducer - A fan that depressurizes the combustion chamber or venting system to move combustion products through the appliance.

Drainage plane - A space that allows water storage and drainage in a wall cavity, adjacent to or part of the water resistive barrier.

Drywall - Gypsum interior wallboard used to produce a smooth and level interior wall surface and to resist fire.

Dry-bulb temperature - Normal ambient air temperature measured by a thermometer.

Duct blower - A blower-door-like device used for testing duct leakiness and airflow.

Efficacy - The number of lumens produced by a watt used for lighting a lamp. Lighting efficiency.

Efficiency - The ratio of output divided by input.

Electro-mechanical - Describes controls where switching is performed by an automatic mechanical device like a bimetal or bulb-and-bellows.

Electronic - Describes controls where switching is performed by transistors and other solid-state devices.

Emittance - The ability of a material to emit radiant energy from its surface. Also called emissivity.

Energy - A quantity of heat or work.

Energy consumption - The conversion or transformation of potential energy into kinetic energy for heat, light, electricity, etc.

Energy efficiency - Term describing how efficiently a building component uses energy.

Energy efficiency ratio (EER) - A measurement of energy efficiency for air conditioners or heat pumps. The EER is computed by dividing cooling capacity, measured in British thermal units per hour (BTUH), by the watts of power.

Energy factor - The fraction of water heater input remaining in 64 gallons of hot water extracted from a water heater.

Energy-recovery ventilator - A ventilator that recovers latent and sensible energy from the exhaust airstream and imparts it to the incoming airstream.

Enthalpy - The internal heat of a material measured in BTUs per pound.

Envelope - The building shell. The exterior walls, floor, and roof assembly of a building. Also sometimes denotes a building cavity or building assembly.

Environmentally sensitive - A person who is highly sensitive to pollutants, often because of overexposure, is said to be environmentally sensitive.

Equivalent length - The length of straight pipe or duct that has equivalent resistance to a pipe or duct fitting. Used for piping and duct design.

Evaporation - The change that occurs when a liquid becomes a gas. Evaporation is the key process in the operation of air conditioners and evaporative coolers.

Evaporative cooler - A device for cooling homes in dry climates that cools the incoming air by humidifying it.

Evaporator - The heat transfer coil of an air conditioner or heat pump that cools the surrounding air as the refrigerant inside the coil evaporates and absorbs heat.

Exfiltration - Air flowing out of a residence from its conditioned space through the shell.

Expansion valve - A valve that meters refrigerant into the evaporator.

Fahrenheit - A temperature scale used in the United States and a few other countries. On the Fahrenheit scale water boils at 212°F and freezes at 32°F.

Fan control - A bimetal thermostat that turns the furnace blower on and off as it senses the presence of heat.

Feeder wires - The wires connecting the electric meter and main switch with the main panel box indoors.

Fenestration - Window and door openings in a building shell.

Fiberglass - A fibrous material made by spinning molten glass.

Fill tube - A plastic or metal tube used for its stiffness to blow insulation inside a building cavity.

Fin comb - A comb-like tool used to straighten bent fins in air conditioning coils.

Finned tube - A length or coil of pipe with heat transfer fins attached for water-to-air heat transfer.

Fire barrier - A tested building assembly, designed to contain a fire for a particular time period: typically 1-to-4 hours.

Fire stop - Framing member designed to stop the spread of fire within a wall cavity.

Firewall - A structural wall between buildings designed to prevent the spread of a fire.

Flame rectification - A modern method of flame sensing, which uses the flame itself as a conductor in the flame-safety circuit.

Flame safety control - A control for avoiding fuel delivery in the event of no ignition.

Flammability - The rating for building materials that will burn readily when exposed to a flame.

Flashing - Waterproof material used to prevent leakage at intersections between the roof surface at walls or penetrations.

Floor joists - The framing members that support the floor.

Flue - A channel within an appliance or chimney for combustion gases.

Foamboard - Plastic foam insulation manufactured most commonly in 4'x8' sheets in thicknesses of $1/4$" to 3".

Footcandle - A measure of light intensity of a surface.

Footing - The part of a foundation system that actually transfers the weight of the building to the ground.

Frost line - The maximum depth of the soil where water will freeze during the coldest weather.

Furring - Wood strips providing a space for insulation.

Fuse - A current carrying element that melts if too much current flows in an electric circuit.

Gable - The triangular section of an end wall formed by the pitch of the roof.

Gasket - Elastic strip that seals a joint between two materials.

Glare - Any brightness or brightness relationship that annoys, distracts, or reduces visibility.

Glass load factor - A number combining glass' solar heat transmission and its heat conduction. Used for cooling load calculations.

Glazing - Glass installation. Pertaining to glass assemblies or windows.

Gusset - A metal or wood plate added to the surface of a joint to strengthen the connection.

Head - Foot pounds of mechanical energy per pound of fluid created by a pump to overcome gravity or friction.

Heat anticipator - A very small electric heater in a thermostat that causes the thermostat to turn off before room temperature reaches the thermostat setting, so that the house doesn't overheat.

Heat capacity - The quantity of heat required to raise the temperature of 1 pound of a material 1°F.

Heat gains - Heat that accumulates in homes; this is desirable during the heating season and undesirable during the cooling season.

Heat loss - The amount of heat escaping through the building shell during some period of time like an hour, month, or year.

Heat-recovery ventilator - A central ventilator that transfers heat from exhaust to intake air.

Heat transmission - Heat flow through the walls, floor, and ceiling of a building. Does not include air leakage.

Heat-transfer coefficient - See U-factor.

Heating degree day - Each degree that the average daily temperature is below the base temperature (usually 65°F) constitutes one heating degree day.

Heating load - The maximum heating rate needed by a building during the very coldest weather.

Heating seasonal performance factor (HSPF) - Rating for heat pumps describing how many BTUs they provide per watt-hour of electricity consumed.

High limit - A bimetal thermostat that turns the heating element of a furnace off if it senses a dangerously high temperature.

Home heating index - The number of BTUs of energy used by a home divided by its floor area in square feet, then divided by the number of heating degree days.

House pressure - The difference in pressure between the indoors and outdoors measured by a manometer.

Humidistat - An automatic control that switches a fan, humidifier, or dehumidifier on and off to control relative humidity.

Humidity ratio - The absolute amount of air's humidity measured in pounds of water vapor per pound of dry air or grains of water vapor per pound of dry air.

Hydronic - An ambiguous term meaning either hot-water space heating or both hot water and steam space heating.

Ignition barrier - A material installed to prevent another material, often plastic foam, from catching fire.

Illumination - The light level measured on a horizontal plane in footcandles.

Incandescent lamp - TA bulb that produces light by running electricity through a thin filament.

Inch of water column - Small air pressure differences are measured in inches of water column (IWC) in the American measurement system.

Infiltration - The inflow of outdoor air into the indoors, which is accompanied by an equal outflow of air from indoors to the outdoors.

Infrared - Pertaining to heat rays emitted by the sun or warm objects on earth.

Input rating - The rate at which an energy-using device consumes electricity or fossil fuel.

Insolation - The amount of solar radiation striking a surface.

Insulated glass - Two or more glass panes spaced apart and sealed in a factory.

Insulation - Material with relatively high thermal resistance.

Intermittent-ignition device - A device that lights the pilot light on a gas appliance when the control system calls for heat, thus saving the energy wasted by a standing pilot.

Intermediate zone - A zone located between the building's conditioned spaces and outdoors, like a crawl space or attic.

Internal gains - The heat generated by bathing, cooking, and operating appliances, that must be removed during the summer to promote comfort.

Jamb - The side or top piece of a window or door frame.

Joist - A horizontal wood framing member that supports a floor or ceiling.

Kilowatt (kW) - A unit of electric power equal to 1000 joules per second or 3412 BTUs per hour.

Kilowatt-hour (kWh) - A unit of electric energy equal to 3600 kilojoules or 3412 BTUs.

Kinetic energy - Energy in transition or motion.

Lamp - A light bulb.

Latent heat - The heat absorbed or released by a substance when it changes state. For instance, from a liquid to a gas.

Lath - Perforated base or furring strips for plaster or stucco, made from wood, metal, or plastic.

Light quality - Good light quality is characterized by absence of glare and low brightness contrast.

Low-e - Short for low emissivity, which means the characteristic of a metallic glass coating to resist the flow of radiant heat.

Low-water cutoff - A float-operated control for turning the burner off if a steam boiler is low on water.

Lumen - A unit of light output from a lamp.

Luminaire - A light fixture.

Main panel box - The service box containing a main switch, and the fuses or circuit breakers located inside the home.

Make-up air - Air supplied to a space to replace exhausted air.

Manifold - A section of pipe with multiple openings.

Manometer - A pressure-measuring instrument.

Masonry - Construction of stone, brick, or concrete block.

Mastic - A thick creamy substance used to seal seams and cracks in building materials.

Metabolic process - Chemical and physiological activities in the human body.

Metering device - In refrigeration, an orifice or capillary tube that meters refrigerant into an evaporator

Microclimate - A very localized climatic area, usually of a small site or habitat.

Minimum ventilation guideline (MVG) - The measured blower door air-leakage value below which mechanical ventilation is necessary. Same as minimum ventilation level (MVL) or building tightness limit (BTL).

Minimum ventilation level - See minimum ventilation guideline.

Mortar - A mixture of sand, water, and cement used to bond bricks, stones, or blocks together.

Natural ventilation - Ventilation using only natural air movement, without fans.

Net free area - The area of a vent after that area has been adjusted for insect screen, louvers, and weather coverings. The net free area is always less than the actual area.

Nozzle - An orifice for spraying a liquid like oil.

Open-combustion heater - A heater that takes its combustion air from the surrounding room.

Orifice - A small hole in piping where gas or oil exits to be mixed with air before combustion.

Output - The useful energy that a device produces after accounting for waste involved in the energy transfer.

Oxygen depletion sensor (ODS) - A safety device for unvented combustion heaters that shuts gas off when oxygen is depleted.

Packaged air conditioner - An air conditioner that contains the compressor, evaporator, and condenser in a single cabinet.

Pascal - A unit of measurement of air pressure. (See Inch of water.)

Payback period - The number of years that an investment in energy conservation will take to repay its cost in energy savings.

Perlite - A heat-expanded mineral used for insulation.

Perm - A measurement of how much water vapor a material will let pass through it per unit of time.

Photoresistor - Electronic sensing device used to sense flame, daylight, and artificial light.

Plate - A piece of lumber installed horizontally to which the vertical studs in a wall frame are attached.

Plenum - The piece of ductwork that connects the air handler to the main supply duct.

Polyethylene - Polymer plastic used for vapor barriers, air barriers, and foam backer rod.

Polyisocyanurate - A plastic foam insulation sold in sheets, similar in composition to polyurethane.

Polystyrene insulation - A rigid plastic foam insulation, usually white or blue in color.

Polyurethane - A versatile plastic foam insulation, usually yellow in color.

Potentiometer - A variable resistor used as a controller or sensor.

Potential energy - Energy in a stored or packaged form.

Power vent - A combustion appliance that uses fan-powered draft for venting combustion byproducts.

Pressure - A force encouraging flow by virtue of a difference in some condition between two areas.

Pressure boundary - An air barrier or plane where the largest blower-door-induced pressure is found.

Pressure diagnostics - The practice of measuring air pressures and flows in buildings.

Pressure pan - A device used to block a duct register, while measuring the static pressure behind it, during a blower door test.

Pressuretrol - A control that turns a steam boiler's burner on and off as steam pressure changes.

Psychrometrics - The science of the relationship between air, water vapor, and heat.

Purlins - Framing members that sit on top of rafters, perpendicular to them, designed to spread support to roofing materials.

R-value - A measurement of thermal resistance.

Radiant barrier - A foil sheet or coating designed to reflect heat rays or retard their emission.

Radiant temperature - The average temperature of objects in a home like walls, ceiling, floor, furniture, and other objects.

Radiation - Heat energy, which originates on a hot body like the sun, and travels from place to place through the air.

Radon - A radioactive gas that decomposes into radioactive particles.

Rafter - A roof beam that follows the roof's slope.

Rain screen - The combination of a water resistive barrier and a space, used to keep wall assemblies dry in climates with high rainfall.

Rater - A person who performs energy ratings.

Recovery efficiency - A water heater's efficiency at actually heating incoming water.

Reflectance - The ability of a material's surface to reflect radiant heat. Also called reflectivity.

Refrigerant - A special fluid used in air conditioners and heat pumps that heats air when it condenses and cools air when it evaporates.

Register - A grille covering a duct outlet.

Relamping - The replacement of an existing lamp with a lower wattage lamp.

Relative humidity - The percent of moisture absorbed in the air compared to the maximum amount possible. Air that is saturated has 100% relative humidity.

Relay - An automatic, electrically-operated switch.

Reset controller - A device that adjusts fluid temperature or pressure in a central heating system according to outdoor air temperature.

Resistance - The property of a material resisting the flow of electrical energy or heat energy.

Retrofit - An energy conservation measure that is applied to an existing building. Also means the action of improving the thermal performance or maintenance of a building.

Return air - Air circulating back to the furnace from the house, to be heated by the furnace and supplied to the rooms.

Rim joist - The outermost joist around the perimeter of the floor framing.

Room air conditioner - A unitary air conditioner installed through a wall or window, which cools the room by removing heat from the room and releasing it outdoors.

Room heater - A heater located within a room and used to heat that room.

Sash - A movable or stationary part of a window that frames a piece of glass.

Saturation - Describing vapor and liquid at the phase-change point.

Savings-to-investment ratio (SIR) - Measures how many times an energy retrofit pays for itself during its lifetime.

Scale - Dissolved minerals that precipitate inside boilers and storage tanks.

Sealed-combustion - A combustion appliance that draws combustion air from outdoors and has a sealed exhaust system. Same as direct vent.

Seasonal energy efficiency ratio (SEER) - A measurement of energy efficiency for central air conditioners. The SEER is computed by dividing cooling capacity, measured in BTUH, by the watts.

Sensible heat - The heat absorbed by a substance, which raises its temperature.

Sequencer - A bimetal switch that turns on the elements of an electric furnace in sequence.

Service equipment - The electric meter and main switch, usually located outside the building.

Service wires - The wires coming from the utility transformer to the service equipment of the building.

Shading coefficient (SC) - A decimal describing how much solar energy is transmitted through a window, compared to clear single glass, which has an SC of 1.0.

Sheathing - A structural sheeting, attached on top of the framing, underneath siding and roofing of a building.

Sheeting - Any building material used for covering a building surface.

Shell - The building's exterior enclosure—walls, floor, and roof of a building.

Short circuit - A dangerous malfunction in an electrical circuit, where electricity is flowing through conductors without going through an electric load, like a light or motor.

Sill - The bottom of a window or door frame.

SIR - See savings-to-investment ratio.

Sling psychrometer - A device holding two thermometers that is slung through the air to measure relative humidity.

Soffit - The underside of a roof overhang or a small lowered ceiling, as above cabinets or a bathtub.

Solar gain - Heat from the sun that is absorbed by a building and contributes to the need for cooling.

Solar heat - Radiant energy from the sun with wavelengths between 0.7 and 1 micrometers.

Solar heat-gain coefficient (SHGC) - The ratio of solar heat gain through a window to incident solar heat. Includes both transmitted heat and absorbed and reradiated heat.

Solar transmittance - The percent of total solar energy transmitted by a material.

Solenoid - An electro-magnetic device that moves a switch or valve stem.

Space conditioning - Heating, cooling, or ventilation of an indoor space.

Space heating - Heating the living spaces of the home.

Specific heat - The ratio of a material's heat storage capacity to the heat storage capacity of water.

Spillage - Temporary flow of combustion gases from a dilution device.

Spline - A strip that, when inserted into a groove, holds a screen or plastic film in place on a frame.

Split-system air conditioner - An air conditioner that has the condenser and compressor outdoors and the evaporator indoors.

Stack effect - The draft established in a building from air infiltrating low and exfiltrating high.

Standing losses - Losses from a hot water storage tank through its shell.

State point - Air at a particular temperature and humidity occupies a single point on the psychrometric chart called a state point.

Static pressure - Measurement of pressure in a fluid filled chamber at a specific location. Use of a static pressure probe allows measuring pressures in forced air duct systems without regard to pressure changes due to movement of air in the system.

Steady-state efficiency - The efficiency of a heating appliance, after an initial start-up period, that measures how much heat crosses the heat exchanger. The steady-state efficiency is measured by a combustion analyzer.

Steam trap - An automatic valve that closes to trap steam in a radiator until it condenses.

Steam vent - A bimetal-operated air vent that allows air to leave steam piping and radiators, but closes when exposed to steam itself.

Stop - A thin trim board for windows and doors to close against or slide against.

Strike plate - The metal plate attached to the door jamb that the latch inserts into upon closing.

Stucco - Plaster applied to the building's exterior walls.

Stud - A vertical framing member used to build a wall.

Subcooling - The number of degrees Fahrenheit that a condenser and nearby piping cools the liquid refrigerant below its saturation temperature.

Subfloor - The sheathing over the floor joists and under the flooring.

Substrate - A layer of material to which another layer is applied.

Superheat - The number of degrees Fahrenheit that an evaporator and nearby piping heats gaseous refrigerant above its saturation temperature.

Supply air - Air that has been heated or cooled and is then moved through the ducts and out the supply registers of a home.

Task lighting - Lighting provided at the area where a visual task is performed.

Temperature rise - The number of degrees of temperature increase that air is heated as it is blown over the heat exchanger. Heat rise equals supply temperature minus return temperature.

Therm - A unit of energy equaling 100,000 BTUs or 29.3 kilowatt-hours. Ten therms equal one decatherm (dkt).

Thermal barrier - A material that protects materials behind it from reaching 250° F during a fire. Drywall is a 15-minute thermal barrier.

Thermal boundary - A line or plane where insulation and air barrier(s) exist in order to resist thermal transmission and air leakage through or within a building shell.

Thermal break - A piece of relatively low conducting material between two high conducting materials.

Thermal bridging - Rapid heat conduction resulting from direct contact between very thermally conductive materials like metal and glass.

Thermal conductance - General term referring to K-value, meaning conduction heat-flow rate.

Thermal envelope - Insulated and air-sealed building assemblies that surround the conditioned space of a building.

Thermal resistance - Same as R-value, expressing ability to retard heat flow.

Thermal transmittance - Expressed as U-factor, thermal transmittance is heat flow by conduction, convection, and radiation through a non-uniform layered building component like a wall.

Thermistor - An electronic resistor used to sense temperature.

Thermocouple - A bimetal-junction electric generator used to keep the safety valve of an automatic gas valve open.

Thermodynamics - The study of work, heat, and energy in a system.

Threshold - The raised part of a floor underneath a door that acts as an air and dust seal.

Tracer gas - A harmless gas used to measure air leakage in a building.

Transformer - A double coil of wire that reduces or increases voltage from a primary circuit to a secondary circuit.

Truss - A lightweight, rigid framework designed to be stronger than a solid beam of the same weight.

U-factor - The amount of heat that will flow through a square foot of building cross-section experiencing a temperature difference of 1° F.

U-value - See U-factor. An older term for U-factor.

Ultraviolet radiation - Solar radiation having wavelengths just shorter than visible light.

Unconditioned space - An area within the building shell that is not intentionally heated or cooled.

Underlayment - Sheeting installed to provide a smooth, sound base for a finish material.

Vapor barrier - A material that resists the flow of water vapor to less than 0.1 perms.

Vapor diffusion - The flow of water vapor through a solid material.

Vapor retarder - A material that resists the flow of water vapor between 0 and 10 perms.

Vaporize - Change from a liquid to a gas.

Veiling reflection - Light reflection from an object or task that obscures details.

Vent connector - The vent pipe carrying combustion gases from the appliance to the chimney.

Vent damper - An automatic damper powered by heat or electricity that closes the chimney while a heating device is off.

Ventilation - The movement of air through an area for the purpose of removing moisture, air pollution, or unwanted heat.

Venting - The removal of combustion gases by a chimney or other type of combustion vent.

Vermiculite - A heat-expanded mineral used for insulation. Sometimes contains asbestos.

Visible transmittance - The percent of visible light transmitted by a glass assembly.

Volt - The energy contained in each unit of charge in joules per coulomb.

Water resistive barrier - A material that prevents water from wetting the building assembly.

Watt - A unit of electrical power equivalent to one joule per second or 3.4 BTUH.

Watt-hour - A unit of electrical energy equivalent to 3600 joules or 3.4 BTUs.

Weatherization - The process of reducing energy consumption and increasing comfort in buildings by improving energy efficiency of the building.

Weatherstripping - Flexible gaskets, often mounted in rigid metal strips, for limiting air leakage.

Webbing - A reinforcing fabric used with mastics and coatings to prevent patches from cracking.

Weep holes - Holes drilled for the purpose of allowing water to drain out of an area in a building where it has collected.

Wet-bulb temperature - The temperature of a dampened thermometer of a sling psychrometer used to determine relative humidity, dew point, and enthalpy.

Window films - Plastic films, coated with a metalized reflective surface, that are adhered to window glass to reflect heat rays from the sun.

Window frame - The sides, top, and sill of the window which forms a box around window sashes and other components.

Worst-case depressurization test - A safety test, performed by specific procedures, designed to evaluate the probability of chimney backdrafting.

WRT - Acronym meaning "with reference to" used to show that the air pressures between two areas are being measured and compared.

Zone - A room or portion of a building separated from other rooms by an air barrier—not usually an effective air barrier.

A-1 Energy Related Formulas

Transmission heat flow

There are two common forms of the transmission heat flow equation. The first equation is for heating load in BTUH. The second equation is heat loss in BTU.

$$q = U \times A \times \Delta T$$

q is heating load in BTUs per hour.
U (BTU/hr•ft²•°F) is the conduction heat transfer coefficient.
A is the surface area of the building component under consideration.
ΔT is the temperature difference between the design temperature and 65°F.

$$Q = U \times A \times HDD \times \frac{24hrs}{day}$$

Q is BTUs of heat crossing the building shell annually.
HDD (°F•day) is the number of heating degree days.

Sensible heat

When a mass of material changes temperature, the mass has gained or lost heat. To calculate how much, the concept of specific heat is used.

$$q = m \times c \times \Delta T$$

q is heat in BTUs
m is mass in pounds.
c (BTU/lb•°F) is specific heat.
ΔT is temperature change in degrees F.

Latent heat

When a material changes phase, its latent heat of fusion or evaporation is absorbed or released.

$$q = m \times L$$

q is heat in BTUs
m pounds is the material's mass.
L (BTU/lb) is the latent heat of fusion or evaporation.

Bags of Insulation

The following equation estimates the number of bags of insulation needed for an insulation job. It can also be used to determine whether the proper amount and proper density of insulation were installed in a particular area depending on the number of bags installed.

$$B = \left(\frac{D \times A \times T}{P} \right)$$

B is bags of insulation.
D is desired density of insulation (lbs./ft³).
A is surface area to be insulated (ft²).
T is thickness (ft).
P is pounds of insulation per bag.

Area-weighted average R-value

Calculating wall U-factor and R-value requires considering the surface area of the insulated cavity and also the surface area of framing members. Wood-framed walls have 0.15 to 0.40 of their surface area in framing lumber which has a higher U-factor and lower R-value than the insulated cavity. The area-weighted average estimates the U-factor of the whole wall. The area-weighted R-value is the inverse of the area-weighted U-factor.

$$U = (A_1 \times U_1) + (A_2 \times U_2)$$

$$R = 1 \div U$$

U is area-weighted average U-factor.
A_1 is the decimal fraction of wall represented by framing.
U_1 is the U-factor of the framing section.
A_2 is the decimal fraction of wall represented by insulation within the cavity.
U_2 is the U-factor of the insulated section.
R is the area-weighted R-value of the wall.

Air leakage/ventilation heat transfer

Infiltration and ventilation heat transfer have two components: sensible heat and latent heat. These two equations are both for hourly heat transfer. The first is sensible heat and the second is latent heat. To find annual heat transfer, substitute HDD X 24 hr/day for ΔT.

$$q = \frac{1.08 \times ACH \times V \times \Delta T}{60}$$

q is rate of sensible heat transfer (BTU/hr).
ACH is number of natural air changes per hour.
V is volume of air (ft³/air change).
ΔT is the temperature difference between outdoor and indoor air (°F).

$$q = \frac{0.68 \times ACH \times V \times \Delta F}{60}$$

q is rate of latent heat transfer (BTU/hr).
ΔF (grains/lb) is difference in moisture content between outdoor and indoor air.

See "Deciphering Common Pressures" on page 299.

Air exchange factors from CFM$_{50}$

Measuring CFM$_{50}$ with a blower door allows the energy specialist to estimate other useful values relating to airflow in a home. The first equation gives air changes per hour at 50 pascals—a sometimes-used standard for home air leakage. The second equation converts that air change rate to air changes per hour at natural conditions. The third equation is for estimating the annual cost of air leakage.

$$ACH_{50} = \frac{CFM_{50} \times (60)}{V}$$

ACH$_{50}$ is air changes per hour at 50 pascals house pressure.
CFM$_{50}$ is measured airflow through the blower door.
V is house volume.

$$ACH_n = \frac{CFM_{50} \times 60}{n \times V}$$

ACH$_n$ is natural air change rate in air changes per hour.
n is the LBL correlation factor (see See Appendice A-12   Air-Sealing Economic Limits.)

$$ALH = \frac{26 \times HDD \times Fuel\ Price \times CFM_{50}}{n \times heating\ efficiency}$$

ALH is annual air-leakage heating cost.
HDD is annual heating degree days.
n is the LBL correlation factor
The number 26 combines the heating capacity of air (0.018) with the factors 24 and 60 for relating CFM to HDD.

Cost effectiveness

Cost effectiveness of energy retrofits is usually expressed as payback, return on investment, or savings-to-investment ratio. The simple formulas are listed below. In life-cycle costing, the future savings are often adjusted to reflect their present value, which is less than their future value.

$$PB = \frac{IC}{AS}$$

PB is simple payback in years.
IC is initial cost in dollars.
AS is annual savings in dollars per year.

$$ROR = \frac{AS}{IC} \times 100$$

ROR is annual rate of return on investment in percent.

$$SIR = \frac{AS \times L}{IC}$$

SIR is savings-to-investment ratio, a dimensionless number.
L is lifespan of the measure.

Home heating index

Home heating index (HHI) can be used to compare the energy efficiency of homes in cold climates. HHI can also be used to estimate the input capacity of heating systems.

$$HHI = \frac{q}{A \times HDD}$$

HHI is home heating index in BTUs/sf/HDD
q is actual BTUs of the main heating fuel converted within the home during the chosen time period.
A is the heated floor area.
HDD is the number of heating degree-days recorded over the chosen time period.

$$I = \frac{HHI \times A \times \Delta T}{24}$$

I is estimated design input of a replacement heating system in BTUH.
HHI is the home energy factor in BTUs/ft²/ HDD.

ΔT is the balance point temperature minus the desired indoor temperature.
24 is hours per day.

Heating input from gas meter

The heater's input is often measured by clocking the gas meter. All other gas appliances must be off. Count the number of revolutions of $^1/_2$, 1, or 2 cubic foot dials on the gas meter in 60 seconds. That number of cubic feet per minute becomes F in the following equation.

$$I = F \times Q \times 60$$

I is the heater's input in BTUH.
F is the gas flow rate in cubic feet per minute.
Q is the energy content of local gas, typically 850-to-1100 BTUs/ft³
60 is the number of minutes per hour.

Electrical input from electric meter

Make sure all electric loads that you don't want to measure are off. Count the time required for the electric meter's dial to make 10 revolutions. For multiple-stage furnaces or heat pumps, repeat this procedure for each stage.

$$I = \frac{36 \times k_h \times CTR \times PTR}{t}$$

I is the input in kW.
k_h is the meter constant, often 7.2.
CTR is the meter's current transformer ratio.
PTR is the meter's potential transformer ratio.
t is the time required for the electric meter's dial to make 10 revolutions (seconds).
Note: the values of kh, CTR, and PTR may be indicated on the meter or obtained from the utility company.

Heating improvement savings

If you have a reasonable, accurate comparison of the steady-state efficiencies (SSE) or annual fuel utilization efficiencies (AFUE) of two heating systems, use the formula below to find annual savings from the more efficient system. The same formula is used for replacement or improvement.

$$AS = \left(1 - \frac{Ef_b}{Ef_a}\right) \times HC$$

AS is annual savings in dollars per year.
Ef_b is existing efficiency (before).
Ef_a is improved efficiency (after).
HC is the annual heating cost for the existing system.

Cost of ventilation

Home ventilation involves costs for both moving air into and out of the home, and for heating the incoming air. The first formula computes ventilation's heating cost, and the second computes the electrical cost of the ventilation fan(s).

$$V_\$ = \frac{1.08 \times CFM \times HDD \times T \times C}{\text{heating efficiency}}$$

$V_\$$ is annual space-heating cost in dollars.
CFM is the flow rate of the ventilator.
T = hours per day fan(s) operate.
HDD is the number of heating degree days.
C = cost of fuel per BTU.

$$VC = FP \times T \times D \times K \times 0.001$$

VC is the annual electricity cost of ventilation.
FP = fan power in watts.
T = hours per day fan(s) operate.
D = days per year of fan operation.
K is the cost per kilowatt-hour.

A-2 Geometry

Plane Geometry

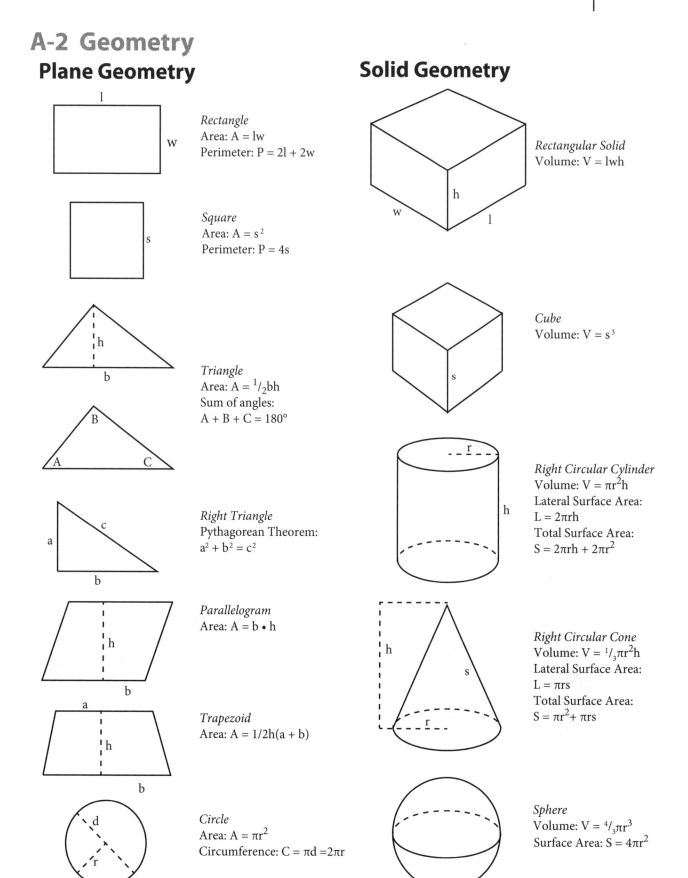

Rectangle
Area: $A = lw$
Perimeter: $P = 2l + 2w$

Square
Area: $A = s^2$
Perimeter: $P = 4s$

Triangle
Area: $A = {}^1/_2bh$
Sum of angles:
$A + B + C = 180°$

Right Triangle
Pythagorean Theorem:
$a^2 + b^2 = c^2$

Parallelogram
Area: $A = b \cdot h$

Trapezoid
Area: $A = 1/2h(a + b)$

Circle
Area: $A = \pi r^2$
Circumference: $C = \pi d = 2\pi r$

Solid Geometry

Rectangular Solid
Volume: $V = lwh$

Cube
Volume: $V = s^3$

Right Circular Cylinder
Volume: $V = \pi r^2 h$
Lateral Surface Area:
$L = 2\pi rh$
Total Surface Area:
$S = 2\pi rh + 2\pi r^2$

Right Circular Cone
Volume: $V = {}^1/_3\pi r^2 h$
Lateral Surface Area:
$L = \pi rs$
Total Surface Area:
$S = \pi r^2 + \pi rs$

Sphere
Volume: $V = {}^4/_3\pi r^3$
Surface Area: $S = 4\pi r^2$

A-3 Conversion Factors

Energy Conversions

Existing Unit	Desired Unit					
	BTU	Wh	kWh	cal	ft-lb	J
British thermal unit (**BTU**)	–	0.293	0.000293	252	778.2	1055
Watt-hour (**Wh**)	3.412	–	0.001	860	2656	3600
Kilowatt-hour (**kWh**)	3412	1000	–	860,000	2,656,000	3,600,000
Calorie (**cal**)	0.00397	0.001163	0.0000012	–	3.085	4.184
Foot pound (**ft-lb**)	0.001286	0.0003765	0.00000038	0.3241	–	1.353
Joule (**J**)	0.0009479	0.0002778	0.0000003	0.2390	0.7393	–

Power Conversions

Existing Unit	Desired Unit					
	BTUH	ft-lb/min	hp	boiler hp	tons	kW
British thermal unit/hour (**BTUH**)	–	12.97	0.00039	0.0000298	0.000083	0.0002929
Foot-pounds/minute (**ft-lb/min**)	0.0771	–	0.00003	0.0000023	0.0000064	0.0000226
Horsepower (**hp**)	2546	33,000	–	0.07605	0.2121	0.7457
Boiler horsepower (**boiler hp**)	33,520	433,880	13.15	–	2.793	9.808
Tons of refrigeration (**tons**)	12,000	155,640	4.715	0.358	–	3.516
Kilowatts (**kW**)	3412	44,260	1.341	0.102	0.2844	–

Pressure Conversions

Existing Unit	Desired Unit						
	Pa	psi	kPa	mm-Hg	IWC	In-Hg	Bar
Pascals (**Pa**)	–	0.000145	0.001	0.0075	0.00401	0.0003	0.0001
Pounds/square inch (**psi**)	6895	–	6.895	57.1	27.68	2.036	0.0689
Kilopascals (**kPa**)	1000	0.145	–	7.503	4.014	0.2952	0.01
Millimeters of mercury (**mm-Hg**)*	133.3	0.0193	0.1333	–	0.5352	0.0394	0.001333
Inches of Water (**IWC**)	249.1	0.0361	0.2491	1.868	–	0.0735	0.002491
Inches of mercury (**In-Hg**)	3388	0.4912	3.387	25.4	13.60	–	0.03387
Bar	100,000	14.5	100	750.2	401.4	29.53	–

* 1 micron = 0.001 millimeters of mercury; 1000 microns = 1 millimeter of mercury

Flow Conversions

Existing Unit	Desired Unit			
	cfm	gpm	l/s	m³/s
Cubic feet/minute (**cfm**)	–	7.482	0.4719	0.0004719
Gallons/minute (**gpm**)	0.1337	–	0.06309	0.0000631
Liters/second (**l/s**)	2.119	15.85	–	0.001
Cubic meters/second (**m³/s**)	2119	15,850	1000	–

Weight/Mass Conversions

Existing Unit	Desired Unit				
	lbs	oz	gr	g	kg
Pounds (**lbs**)	–	16	7000	453.6	0.4536
Ounces (**oz**)	0.0625	–	437.5	28.35	0.02835
Grains (**gr**)	0.000143	0.00229	–	0.0648	0.0000648
Grams (**g**)	0.00221	0.0353	15.432	–	0.001
Kilograms (**kg**)	2.205	35.27	15,432	1000	–

Length Conversions

Existing Unit	Desired Unit					
	in	ft	m	mm	mi	km
Inches (**in**)	–	0.083	0.0254	25.4	0.0000158	0.0000254
Feet (**ft**)	12	–	0.305	304.8	0.000189	0.0003048
Meters (**m**)	39.37	3.281	–	1000	0.0006214	0.001
Milimeters (**mm**)	0.0394	0.00328	0.001	–	0.0000006	0.000001
Miles (**mi**)	63,360	5,280	1609.34	1,609,344	–	1.6093
Kilometers (**km**)	39,370	3,281	1000	1,000,000	0.6214	–

Temperature Conversions

	Conversion formula
Fahrenheit to Celsius	C=(F-32) x 0.55
Celsius to Fahrenheit	F=(1.8 x C) + 32
Equivalents	0 degrees Celsius = 32 degrees Fahrenheit
	100 degrees Celsius = 212 degrees Fahrenheit

A-4 Conversion Charts

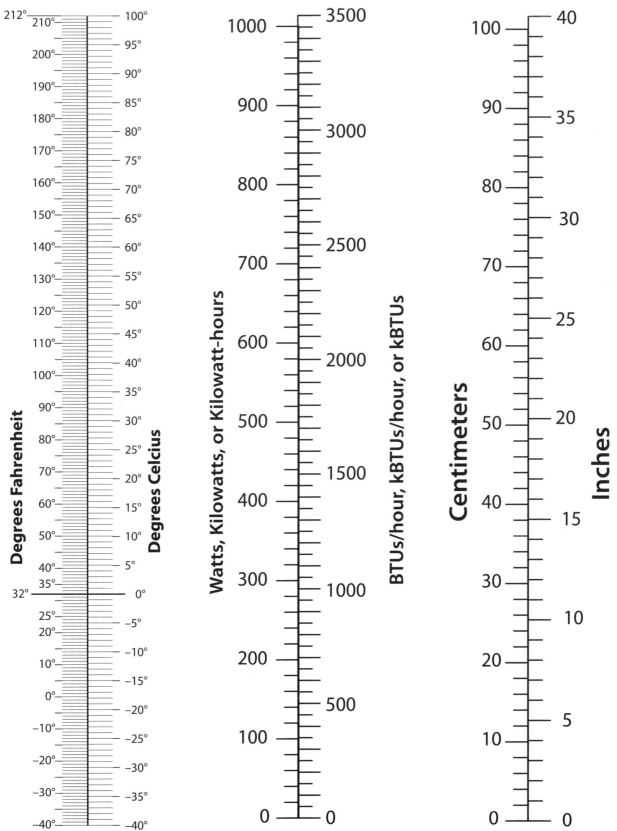

A-5 Analyzing Annual Energy Costs

The method outlined here allows you to analyze the consumption data for a home by 1) separating the baseline usage from the heating and cooling usage, and 2) comparing this consumption to other homes. First, retrieve 12 months of gas and electricity costs as shown below. Next, list the home's characteristics as shown. Then separate gas costs into heating and domestic hot water (DHW), and separate electricity costs into baseload and cooling, as shown. Finally, calculate the energy indexes using the home's characteristics and energy consumption; compare these values to the scales shown "Home Heating Index" on page 25 and "Energy Indexes for Buildings (Total Energy)" on page 26.

12-Month Electricity and Gas Costs

Month	1	2	3	4	5	6	7	8	9	10	11	12	Total
kWh	380	382	379	372	837	1066	1271	1308	877	361	381	421	8035
therms	195	177	99	47	26	24	22	23	50	90	163	211	1127

Home Characteristics	Value
Floor area: sq. ft.	1590
Heating degree days	5035
Family size	4
Elec. cost per kWh	$0.10
Gas cost per therm	$1.20
Electric cost/yr	$803.50
Gas cost/yr	$1352.40
Total energy cost/yr	$2155.90

Separating Gas into Heating and Domestic Hot Water (DHW)

DHW (therms) = 12 X 1.1 (adj. factor) X (avg. of 3 lowest months' therms)

$$= 12 \text{ X } 1.1 \left(\frac{22 + 23 + 24}{3} \right) = 304 \text{ therms}$$

Explanation of adjustment factor: Though DHW usage doesn't vary much throughout the year, the highest demand is in the winter when incoming water is coolest and hot-water usage is highest. Because this high water-heating demand can be masked by the winter heating energy consumption, we multiply by a correction factor of 1.1 to account for this variation. This factor will vary depending on family size, timing of long vacations, temperature of incoming water, climate, etc.

Heating (therms) = Total (therms) – Water heating (therms)

$$= 1127 - 304 = 823 \text{ therms}$$

Separating Electricity into Baseload and Cooling

Baseload (kWh) = 12 X 1.1 (adj. factor) X (average of 3 lowest months' kWh)

$$= 12 \text{ X } 1.1 \left(\frac{361 + 372 + 379}{3} \right) = 4893 \text{ kWh}$$

Explanation of adjustment factor: Baseload electricity consumption is typically highest in the winter months (residents use more lighting and spend more time at home) and lowest in the summer. In cooling climates, air conditioning usage may mask the lower summer baseload consumption. We multiply by a correction factor of 1.1 to account for the additional time most families spend at home in winter, and to adjust for the slightly higher use of lighting and electric appliances.

Cooling (kWh) = Total (kWh) – Baseload (kWh)

$$= 8035 - 4893 = 3142 \text{ kWh}$$

1 kWh = 3412 BTUs
1 therm = 29.3 kWh

Energy Consumption Summary from Calculations

Energy Breakdown	Amount	Cost $	% of Cost
Heating	823 therms	$987.6	45.8%
Water heating	304 therms	$364.8	16.9%
Air conditioning	3142 kWh	$314.2	14.6%
Appliances and other	4893 kWh	$489.3	22.7%

Home Energy Indexes

Energy Index	Value
BTU/ft²/HDD (heat only)	10.3
BTU/ft²/yr (total energy)	88,100
kWh/ft²/yr (total energy)	25.8
$/ft²/yr (total dollars)	$1.25

A-6 Materials/Building Assembly R-Values

Material / Description	Per inch thickness hr•sf•°F/BTU	For listed thickness hr•sf•°F/BTU
Building Shell (Framing members, boards, panels)		
Wall stud 3.5 inches	1.25	4.38
Wall stud 5.5 inches	1.25	6.88
Asbestos-cement board	0.25	
Gypsum or plaster board	0.9	
Plywood or wood panels	1.25	
Fiber Board	2.6	
Particleboard (low to high density)	0.85–1.4	
Flooring Materials		
Carpet 0.25 inch thick		1.3
Carpet 0.50 inch thick		2.0
Cork tile, 0.125 in		0.25
Terrazzo	0.08	
Tile-asphalt, linoleum, vinyl, rubber		0.05
Wood, hardwood finish, 0.75 in		0.68
Insulation		
Blanket and Batt		
Fiberglass batts, 0.4–2.0 lb/ft^3 [a]	2.6–4.2	
Low-density batts and blankets, 0.4 lb/ft^3	2.6–2.8	
3.5 inch standard density		11
3.5 inch medium density		13
3.5 inch high density		15
5.5 standard density		19
5.5 inch medium density		21
9-10 inch standard unfaced batt		30
12-13 inch standard unfaced batt		38
Board and Slabs		
Glass fiber, organic bonded, 3.8-4.2 lb/ft^3	4.0–4.4	
Mineral fiber 4.0-5.0 lb/ft^3	4.0–4.4	
Extruded polystyrene, 1.6-2.0 lb/ft^3	5.0	
Expanded polystyrene, molded bead, 1.4-2.0 lb/ft^3	3.6–4.4	
Cellular polyisocyanurate (foil faced, glass fiber-reinforced core)	5.6–7.6	
Loose Fill		
Cellulose insulation, 1.2-2.0 lb/ft^3 horizontal application, open blow	3.2–3.6	
Cellulose insulation, 3.0-4.0 lb/ft^3 vertical wall application	3.0–3.4	
Perlite, expanded, 2.0-3.0 lb/ft^3	2.4	
Mineral wool, 0.6–1.2 lb/ft^{3}0.6-1.2 lb/ft^3, horizontal application, open blow	2.6–3.6	
Fiberglass: chopped batt waste,0.4-0.8 lb/ft^3, horizontal application, open blow	2.4–3.0	
Fiberglass virgin fiber, 0.4-0.8 lb/ft^3, horizontal application, open blow	2.6–3.0	
Fiberglass virgin fiber, 1.0-2.5 lb/ft^3, vertical wall application	3.6–4.4	
Vermiculite, exfoliated	2.1	
Field Applied		
High-density polyurethane foam	6.0–7.0	

Material / Description	Per inch thickness hr•sf•°F/BTU	For listed thickness hr•sf•°F/BTU
Low-density polyurethane foam	3.5–3.8	
Spray-on cellulose, included wetted cavity fill	3.0–3.6	
Spray-on fiberglass, included wetted cavity fill	3.2–3.8	
Masonry Materials[b]		
Concrete, stucco, cement plaster, cement mortar	0.10–0.20	
Brick, common	0.15–0.30	
8-inch concrete block		1.1
with vermiculite fill in cores	-	2.1
12-inch concrete block		1.2
with vermiculite fill in cores	-	2.9
Roofing		
Asbestos-cement shingles	-	0.21
Asphalt roll roofing	-	0.15
Asphalt shingles	-	0.44
Built-up roofing, 0.375 in	-	0.33
Slate, 0.5 in	-	0.05
Wood shingles	-	0.94
Siding		
Asbestos-cement	-	0.20
Asphalt roll siding	-	0.15
Asphalt insulating siding (0.5 in bed.)	-	1.5
Wood siding over sheathing	-	
Hardboard siding, 0.4375 in	-	0.7
Wood, drop, 1 • 8 in	-	0.8
Wood, bevel, 0.5 • 8 in, lapped	-	0.8
Wood, bevel, 0.75 • 10 in, lapped	-	1.0
Wood, plywood, 0.375 in, lapped	-	0.6
Aluminum or Steel, over sheathing		
Hollow-backed	-	0.6
Insulating-board backed nominal 0.375 in	-	1.8
Insulating-board backed nominal 0.375 in, foil backed	-	2.9

a. This wide variability of R-values per inch is due to density and installation, which are highly variable. Small air gaps and channels within and around the insulation can lead to significant reductions in R-value.

b. When installed with exterior insulation or in very thick walls to achieve a high R-value, the effective R-value may be 1.2–2.6 times as high as expected due to the thermal mass factor, depending on climate.

Mass Factors for 6-inch Concrete Walls Insulated Interior or Exterior for Six Locations

R-value	Insulation Location	Atlanta	Denver	Miami	Minneapolis	Phoenix	Washington
R-13–R-17	interior	1.3	1.4	1.1	1.3	1.4	1.3
R-13–R-17	exterior	2.1	1.8	2.3	1.5	2.5	1.8
R-9	interior	1.3	1.4	1.1	1.2	1.5	1.3
R-9	exterior	2.0	1.8	2.1	1.4	2.6	1.7
R-5	interior	1.1	1.1	0.7	0.9	1.3	1.1
R-5	exterior	1.5	1.4	1.5	1.1	2.1	1.3

Condensed from research reports by Oak Ridge National Laboratory, Building Technology Center from testing using the guarded hot box apparatus together with computer simulations. Multiply these factors times the R-value determined from a conventional calculation approach to estimate a more accurate R-value, which considers the effects of thermal mass on the wall's seasonal heat transmission.

Approximate R-Values of Wall Assemblies from Guarded Hot Box Testing

Wall Type	C-W R	W-W R	W-W R / C-W R
Standard wood 2x4, R-11 Fiberglass-batt insulated	10.5	9.7	92%
Standard wood 2x6, R-19 Fiberglass batts, installed perfectly	15.4	12.8	83%
Standard wood 2x6, R-19 Fiberglass batts, installed typically	14.1	11.7	83%
Standard wood 2x6, R-19 Fiberglass batts, installed poorly	13.2	11.0	83%
Steel frame wall C-stud, Fiberglass batts, installed typically	7.3	5.6	78%
Steel frame wall, Fiberglass batts, 1-inch EPS sheathing	14.0	10.5	75%
Steel frame wall Fiberglass batts, 0.5 inch EPS sheathing	10.9	8.0	73%
Steel frame wall with cavity-sprayed polyurethane and fiberglass batts	11.3	8.2	73%
Structural insulated panel, 6 inches of EPS foam	24.7	21.6	87%
Concrete block 12-inch, insulated with EPS inserts into cores[a]	4.2	3.9	93%
Light-weight EPS-bead concrete block, insulated with EPS inserts[a]	19.2	14.7	82%
Straw insulated panels[b]	16.5	15.7	95%
Stuccoed 19-inch straw-bale wall[c]	–	16-28	–
Insulating concrete form[d]	11.8	11.1	94%
Autoclaved concrete block[e]	9.4	8.6	91%

These values are calculated using data from guarded hot-box tests of 8-foot by 8-foot square wall sections. Tests performed by scientists at Oak Ridge National Laboratory's Building Performance Center. C-W R is an average of R-value of the cavity between the framing members. W-W R is whole-wall R-value, which considers the lower R-value of the framing material. In some cases, test results are averaged from two similar tests by the author.

a. Averages two test walls, insulated with slightly different methods. Mass factor not available but may be significant.
b. Effective R-value, including thermal mass, is 16.8 to 23.5 depending on climate.
c. Test results vary widely according to spaces within the wall. Mass factor not available but may be significant.
d. Effective R-value of ICF, including thermal mass and airtightness, is between 26 and 44 depending on climate.
e. Effective R-value of the concrete block is 12.1 to 16.8 depending on climate.

A-7 Water Vapor Permeability

Material	Thickness (in.)	Permeance (Perm)[a]	Permeability (Perm-in.)
Materials used in construction			
Concrete (1:2:4 mix)			3.2
Brick masonry	4	0.8[b]	
Concrete block (cored, limestone aggregate)	8	2.4[b]	
Tile masonry, glazed	4	0.12[b]	
Asbestos cement board	0.12	4-8[c]	
Asbestos cement board with oil-base finishes		0.3-0.5[c]	
Plaster on metal lath	0.75	15[b]	
Plaster on wood lath		11[e]	
Plaster on plain gypsum lath (w/studs)		20[b]	
Gypsum wall board (plain)	0.375	50[b]	
Gypsum sheathing (asphalt impregnated)	0.5		20[c]
Structural insulating board (sheathing quality)			20-50[b]
Structural insulating board (interior, uncoated)	0.5	50-90[b]	
Hardboard (standard)	0.125	11[b]	
Hardboard (tempered)	0.125	5[b]	
Built-up roofing (hot mopped)		0.0	
Wood, sugar pine			0.4-5.4[d]
Plywood (Douglas fir, exterior glue)	0.25	0.7[b]	
Plywood (Douglas fir, interior glue)	0.25	1.9[b]	
Acrylic, glass fiber reinforced sheet	0.056	0.12[c]	
Polyester, glass fiber reinforced sheet	0.048	0.05[c]	
Thermal insulations			
Mineral wool (unprotected)			116[e]
Expanded polyurethane (R-11 blown) board stock			0.4-1.6[c]
Expanded polystyrene - extruded			1.2[c]
Expanded polystyrene - bead			2.0-5.8[c]
Phenolic foam (covering removed)			26
Unicellular synthetic flexible rubber foam			0.02-0.15[c]
Plastic and metal foils and films[e]			
Aluminum foil	0.001	0.0[c]	
Aluminum foil	0.00035	0.05[c]	
Polyethylene	0.002	0.16[c]	
Polyethylene	0.006	0.06[c]	
Polyethylene	0.010	0.03[c]	
Polyvinyl chloride, unplasticized	0.002	0.68[c]	
Polyvinyl chloride plasticized	0.004	0.8-1.4[c]	
Polyester	0.0032	0.23[c]	

This table gives the water vapor transmission rates of some representative materials. The data are provided to permit comparisons of materials, but in the selection of vapor retarder materials, exact values for permeance or permeability should be obtained from the manufacturer or independent lab tests. A range of values shown in the table indicate variations among mean values for materials that are similar but of different density, orientation, lot, or source. The values are intended for design guidance, and should not be used as design or specification data.

a. Permeance and permeability are given in the following units:

Permeance Perm = $gr/hr \cdot ft^2 \cdot in.$ Hg

Permeability Perm-in. = $gr/hr \cdot ft^2 \cdot (in.$ Hg/in.)

b. Other than dry- or wet-cup method.

c. Dry-cup method.

d. Depending on construction and direction of vapor flow.

e. Usually installed as vapor retarders but sometimes used as an exterior finish and elsewhere near cold side, where special considerations are then required for warm side barrier effectiveness.

A-8 Climatic Data for U.S. Cities

State and City	Average Winter Temp.	Winter Design Temp.	Heating Degree Days[a]	Summer Design Temp.	Summer Mean Daily Range
Alabama					
Birmingham	54.2	19	2823	94/75	21
Huntsville	51.3	13	3262	93/74	23
Mobile	59.9	26	1681	93/77	16
Montgomery	55.4	22	2194	95/76	21
Alaska					
Anchorage	23.0	-25	10470	68/58	15
Fairbanks	6.7	-53	13980	78/60	24
Juneau	32.1	-7	8574	70/58	15
Nome	13.1	-32	13674	62/55	10
Arizona					
Flagstaff	35.6	0	8340	82/55	31
Phoenix	58.5	31	1125	107/71	27
Tucson	58.1	29	1578	102/66	26
Winslow	43.0	9	4992	95/60	32
Yuma	64.2	37	782	109/72	27
Arkansas					
Fort Smith	50.3	9	3437	98/76	24
Little Rock	50.5	19	3084	96/77	22
Texarkana	54.2	22	2421	96/77	21
California					
Bakersfield	55.4	31	2120	101/69	32
Burbank	58.6	36	1575	91/68	25
Eureka/Arcata	49.9	32	4403	65/59	11
Fresno	53.3	28	2447	100/69	34
Long Beach	57.8	36	1211	80/68	22
Los Angeles	57.4	41	1274	80/68	15
Oakland	53.5	35	2400	80/63	19
Sacramento	53.9	30	2666	98/70	36
San Diego	59.5	42	1446	80/69	12
San Francisco	55.1	42	2862	77/63	20

State and City	Average Winter Temp.	Winter Design Temp.	Heating Degree Days[a]	Summer Design Temp.	Summer Mean Daily Range
Santa Maria	54.3	32	2783	76/63	23
Colorado					
Alamosa	29.7	-17	8736	82/57	35
CO Springs	37.3	-1	6480	88/57	30
Denver	37.6	-2	6128	91/59	28
Grand Junct.	39.3	8	5489	94/59	29
Pueblo	40.4	-5	5598	95/61	31
Connecticut					
Bridgeport	39.9	4	5466	84/71	18
Hartford	37.3	1	6104	88/73	22
New Haven	39.0	5	5897	84/73	17
Delaware					
Wilmington	42.5	12	4888	89/74	20
D.C, Washington	45.7	16	4925	91/74	18
Florida					
Daytona Beach	64.5	32	815	90/77	15
Fort Myers	68.6	38	302	92/78	18
Jacksonville	61.9	29	1354	94/77	19
Key West	73.1	55	62	90/78	9
Lakeland	66.7	35	489	91/76	17
Miami	71.1	44	149	90/77	15
Miami Beach	72.5	45	154	89/77	10
Orlando	65.7	33	580	93/76	17
Pensacola	60.4	29	1498	93/77	14
Tallahassee	60.1	25	1604	92/76	19
Tampa	66.4	36	591	91/77	17
W. Palm Beach	68.4	40	246	91/78	16
Georgia					
Athens	51.8	17	2861	92/74	21
Atlanta	51.7	18	2827	92/74	19
Augusta	54.5	20	2525	95/76	19
Columbus	54.8	23	2154	93/76	21
Macon	56.2	23	2364	93/76	22

State and City	Average Winter Temp.	Winter Design Temp.	Heating Degree Days[a]	Summer Design Temp.	Summer Mean Daily Range
Rome	49.9	16	3510	93/76	23
Savannah	57.8	24	1799	93/77	20
Hawaii					
Hilo	71.9	59	0	83/72	15
Honolulu	74.2	60	0	86/73	12
Idaho					
Boise	39.7	4	5727	94/64	31
Lewiston	41.0	6	5220	93/64	32
Pocatello	34.8	-8	7109	91/60	35
Illinois					
Chicago	37.5	-4	6498	89/74	20
Moline	36.4	-7	6415	91/75	23
Peoria	38.1	-2	6097	89/74	22
Rockford	34.8	-7	6933	89/73	24
Springfield	40.6	-1	5596	92/74	21
Indiana					
Evansville	45.0	6	4617	93/75	22
Fort Wayne	37.3	0	6205	89/72	24
Indianapolis	39.6	0	5521	90/74	22
South Bend	36.6	-2	6294	89/73	22
Iowa					
Burlington	37.6	-4	5948	91/75	22
Des Moines	35.5	-7	6436	91/74	23
Dubuque	32.7	-11	7270	88/73	22
Sioux City	34.0	-10	6900	92/74	24
Waterloo	32.6	-12	7348	89/75	23
Kansas					
Dodge City	42.5	3	5037	97/69	25
Goodland	37.8	-2	6023	96/65	31
Topeka	41.7	3	5225	96/75	24
Wichita	44.2	5	4765	98/73	23
Kentucky					
Covington	41.4	3	5265	90/72	22

State and City	Average Winter Temp.	Winter Design Temp.	Heating Degree Days[a]	Summer Design Temp.	Summer Mean Daily Range
Lexington	43.8	6	4713	91/73	22
Louisville	44.0	8	4352	93/74	23
Louisiana					
Alexandria	57.5	25	1908	94/77	20
Baton Rouge	59.8	25	1689	93/77	19
Lake Charles	60.5	29	1546	93/77	17
New Orleans	61.0	32	1417	92/78	16
Shreveport	56.2	22	2251	96/76	20
Maine					
Caribou	24.4	-18	9560	81/67	21
Portland	33.0	-5	7318	84/71	22
Maryland					
Baltimore	43.7	12	4720	91/75	21
Frederick	42.0	7	4430	91/75	22
Massachusetts					
Boston	40.0	6	5630	88/71	16
Pittsfield	32.6	-5	7578	84/70	23
Worcester	34.7	-3	6831	84/70	18
Michigan					
Alpena	29.7	-5	8274	85/70	27
Detroit	37.2	4	6422	88/72	20
Escanaba	29.6	-7	8584	83/69	17
Flint	33.1	-1	7005	87/72	25
Grand Rapids	34.9	2	6896	88/72	24
Lansing	34.8	2	7098	87/72	24
Marquette	30.2	-8	8272	81/69	18
Muskegon	36.0	4	6943	84/70	21
Sault St. Marie	27.7	-12	9224	81/69	23
Minnesota					
Duluth	23.4	-19	9724	82/68	22
Minneapolis	28.3	-14	7876	89/73	22
Rochester	28.8	-17	8308	87/72	24
Mississippi					

State and City	Average Winter Temp.	Winter Design Temp.	Heating Degree Days[a]	Summer Design Temp.	Summer Mean Daily Range
Jackson	55.7	21	2401	95/76	21
Meridian	55.4	20	2352	95/76	22
Vicksburg	56.9	23	2089	95/78	21
Missouri					
Columbia	42.3	2	5177	94/74	22
Kansas City	43.9	4	5249	96/74	20
St. Joseph	40.3	-1	5345	93/76	23
St. Louis	43.1	4	4758	94/75	18
Springfield	44.5	5	4602	93/74	23
Montana					
Billings	34.5	-10	7006	91/64	31
Glasgow	26.4	-25	8560	89/63	29
Great Falls	32.8	-20	7828	88/60	28
Havre	28.1	-22	8250	90/64	33
Helena	31.1	-17	7975	88/60	32
Kalispell	31.4	-7	8193	87/61	34
Miles City	31.2	-19	7620	95/66	30
Missoula	31.5	-7	7622	88/61	36
Nebraska					
Grand Island	36.0	-6	6385	94/71	28
Lincoln	38.8	-4	6242	95/74	24
Norfolk	34.0	-11	6766	93/74	30
North Platte	35.5	-6	6766	94/69	28
Omaha	35.6	-5	6311	91/75	22
Scottsbluff	35.9	-8	6742	92/65	31
Nevada					
Elko	34.0	-13	7181	92/59	42
Ely	33.1	-6	7561	87/56	39
Las Vegas	53.5	23	2239	106/65	30
Reno	39.3	2	5600	93/60	45
Winnemucca	36.7	1	6271	94/60	42
New Hampshire					
Concord	33.0	-11	7478	87/70	26

State and City	Average Winter Temp.	Winter Design Temp.	Heating Degree Days[a]	Summer Design Temp.	Summer Mean Daily Range
New Jersey					
Atlantic City	43.2	14	5113	89/74	18
Newark	42.8	11	4843	91/73	20
Trenton	42.4	12	4980	88/74	19
New Mexico					
Albuquerque	45.0	14	4281	94/61	27
Raton	38.1	-2	6356	89/60	34
Roswell	47.5	16	3332	98/66	33
Silver City	48.0	14	3705	94/60	30
New York					
Albany	34.6	-5	6860	88/72	23
Binghamton	36.6	-2	7237	83/69	20
Buffalo	34.5	3	6692	85/70	21
New York	42.8	11	4947	89/73	17
Rochester	35.4	2	6728	88/71	22
Schenectady	35.4	-5	6860	87/72	22
Syracuse	35.2	-2	6803	87/71	20
North Carolina					
Asheville	46.7	13	4326	87/72	21
Charlotte	50.4	18	3162	93/74	20
Greensboro	47.5	14	3848	91/73	21
Raleigh/Durham	49.4	16	3465	92/75	20
Wilmington	54.6	23	2429	91/78	18
Winston-Salem	48.4	14	3070	91/73	20
North Dakota					
Bismarck	26.6	-24	8802	91/68	27
Devil's Lake	22.4	-23	9424	88/68	25
Fargo	24.8	-22	9092	89/71	25
Williston	25.2	-21	9044	88/67	25
Ohio					
Akron-Canton	38.1	1	6154	86/71	21
Cincinnati	45.1	8	4883	90/72	21
Cleveland	37.2	2	6121	88/72	22

State and City	Average Winter Temp.	Winter Design Temp.	Heating Degree Days[a]	Summer Design Temp.	Summer Mean Daily Range
Columbus	39.7	2	5492	90/73	24
Dayton	39.8	0	5690	89/72	20
Mansfield	36.9	1	6364	87/72	22
Toledo	36.4	1	6460	88/73	25
Youngstown	36.8	1	6451	86/71	23
Oklahoma					
OK City	48.3	11	3663	97/74	23
Tulsa	47.7	12	3642	98/75	22
Oregon					
Astoria	45.6	27	5056	71/62	16
Eugene	45.6	22	4786	89/66	31
Medford	43.2	21	4539	94/67	35
Pendleton	42.6	3	5321	93/64	29
Portland	45.6	21	4400	85/67	23
Roseburg	46.3	25	4018	90/66	30
Salem	45.4	21	4784	88/66	31
Pennsylvania					
Allentown	38.9	3	5830	88/72	22
Erie	36.8	7	6243	85/72	18
Harrisburg	41.2	9	5201	91/74	21
Philadelphia	41.8	11	4759	90/74	21
Pittsburgh	38.4	5	5829	86/71	22
Reading	42.4	6	5395	89/72	19
Scranton	37.2	2	6234	87/71	19
Williamsport	38.5	1	6063	89/72	23
Rhode Island					
Providence	38.8	6	5754	86/72	19
South Carolina					
Charleston	57.9	26	2005	91/78	18
Columbia	54.0	20	2594	95/75	22
Florence	54.5	21	2524	92/77	21
Greenville	51.6	18	3272	91/74	21
Spartanburg	51.6	18	3080	91/74	20

State and City	Average Winter Temp.	Winter Design Temp.	Heating Degree Days[a]	Summer Design Temp.	Summer Mean Daily Range
South Dakota					
Huron	28.8	-16	7834	93/72	28
Rapid City	33.4	-9	7211	92/65	28
Sioux Falls	30.6	-14	7812	91/72	24
Tennessee					
Bristol-Tri City	46.2	11	4445	89/72	22
Chattanooga	50.3	15	3427	93/74	22
Knoxville	49.2	13	3690	92/73	21
Memphis	50.5	17	3041	95/76	21
Nashville	48.9	12	3677	94/74	21
Texas					
Abilene	53.9	17	2659	99/71	22
Amarillo	47.0	8	4318	95/67	26
Austin	59.1	25	1648	98/74	22
Corpus Christi	64.6	32	950	94/78	19
Dallas	55.3	19	2370	100/75	20
El Paso	52.9	21	2543	98/64	27
Galveston	62.2	32	1008	89/79	10
Houston	61.0	28	1525	95/77	18
Laredo	66.0	32	931	101/73	23
Lubbock	48.8	11	3508	96/69	26
Port Arthur	60.5	29	1447	93/78	19
San Antonio	60.1	25	1494	97/73	19
Waco	57.2	21	2164	99/75	22
Wichita Falls	53.0	15	3024	101/73	24
Utah					
Salt Lake City	38.4	5	5631	95/62	32
Vermont					
Burlington	29.4	-12	7665	85/70	23
Virginia					
Lynchburg	46.0	15	4354	90/74	21
Norfolk	49.2	20	3368	91/76	18
Richmond	47.3	14	3919	92/76	21

State and City	Average Winter Temp.	Winter Design Temp.	Heating Degree Days[a]	Summer Design Temp.	Summer Mean Daily Range
Roanoke	46.1	15	4284	91/72	23
Washington					
Olympia	44.2	21	5531	83/65	32
Seattle	46.9	28	4797	80/64	22
Spokane	36.5	-2	6820	90/63	28
Walla Walla	43.8	12	4882	94/66	27
Yakima	39.1	6	6104	93/65	36
West Virginia					
Charleston	44.8	9	4644	90/73	20
Elkins	40.1	1	6036	84/70	22
Huntington	45.0	10	4446	91/74	22
Parkersburg	43.5	8	4966	90/74	21
Wisconsin					
Green Bay	30.3	-12	7963	85/72	23
La Crosse	31.5	-12	7340	88/73	22
Madison	30.9	-9	7493	88/73	22
Milwaukee	32.6	-6	7087	87/73	21
Wyoming					
Casper	33.4	-11	7571	90/57	31
Cheyenne	34.2	-6	7388	86/58	30
Lander	31.4	-16	7790	88/61	32
Sheridan	32.5	-12	7680	91/62	32

Reprinted by permission of the American Society of Heating, Refrigerating and Air-Conditioning Engineers, Atlanta, Georgia, from the ASHRAE Handbook: 1985 Fundamentals.

a. Heating Degree Day data courtesy of National Climatic Data Center; averages for period 1971-2000. HDD data represents mean average daily values below a balance point of 65° F. For example, an average outdoor temperature of 45° F over a 24-hour period equals 20 HDD.

A-9 Solar Radiative Properties for Materials

Description/Composition	a *	e *	t *
Aluminum			
polished	0.09	0.03	
anodized	0.14	0.84	
foil	0.15	0.05	
Asbestos, felt	0.25	0.50	
Asphalt pavement		0.85-0.93	
Brick, red (Purdue)	0.63	0.93	
Concrete	0.60	0.88	
Concrete, rough	0.60	0.97	
Galvanized sheet metal			
clean, new	0.65	0.13	
Oxidized, weathered	0.80	0.28	
Glass, 1/8 inch thick			
float or tempered			0.79
low iron oxide type			0.88
Gypsum or plaster board		0.90-0.92	
Ice, with sparse snow cover	0.31		
Marble, polished	0.5-0.6	0.9	
Mylar, 3/64 inch thick			0.87
Paints			
black (Parsons)	0.98	0.98	
green, oil base	0.50	0.90	
grey	0.75	0.95	
red, oil base	0.74	0.90	
white, acrylic	0.26	0.90	
white, on aluminum	0.20	0.91	
white, zinc oxide	0.16	0.93	
Plexiglas, 1/8 inch thick			0.90
Snow, fine particles, fresh	0.13	0.82	
Snow, ice granules	0.33	0.89	
Water		0.94	0.95-0.96
Wood		0.82-0.92	
White plaster	0.07	0.91	

* Alpha (a) -absorptance; epsilon (e) -emittance; tau (t) -transmittance

A-10 Equalized Heating Energy Cost Chart

This chart's purpose is to compare different heating fuels by their equalized energy cost in dollars per therm (left side of graph) or decatherm (right side of graph). The costs determined by this chart are approximate and assume that the heating system is 100% efficient. To compare two fuels, divide the fuel's equalized energy cost by its respective delivered heating efficiencies.

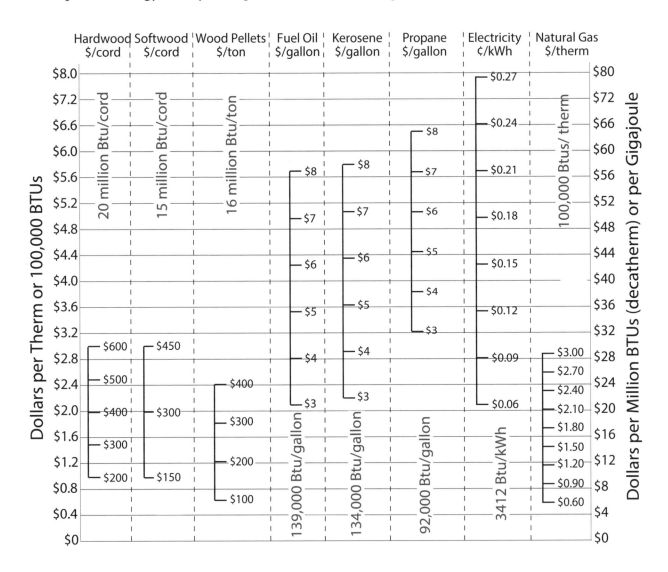

How to use this chart.
1. Find the fuel type at the top of the chart and look at the yardstick in the column below it.
2. Find your unit cost for the fuel on this yardstick in dollars per unit.
3. Draw a horizontal line directly across—to either left or right—to the column of numbers indicating cost per therm or decatherm.

4. Divide this cost per therm or decatherm by the estimated seasonal efficiency of the heating system. For heat pumps, divide by the COP (coefficient of performance) instead of dividing by the seasonal heating efficiency.

A-11 Embodied Energy of Building Materials

Material	Megajoules per kilogram	BTUs per pound	Megajoules per cubic meter	BTUs per cubic foot
Aggregate	0.10	43	150	4020
Stone (local)	0.79	340	2030	54404
Concrete block	0.94	404	2350	62980
Concrete (30Mpa)	1.30	559	3180	85224
Concrete precast	2.00	860	2780	74504
Brick	2.50	1075	5170	138556
Cellulose insulation	3.30	1419	112	3002
Steel (recycled)	8.90	3827	37210	997228
Steel	32.00	13760	251200	6732160
Plywood	10.40	4472	5720	153296
Glass	15.90	6837	37550	1006340
Fiberglass insulation	30.30	13029	970	26996
Zinc	51.00	21930	371280	9950304
Brass	62.00	26660	519560	13924208
PVC	70.00	30100	93620	2509016
Copper	70.60	30358	631164	16915195
Paint	93.30	40119	117500	3149000
Linoleum	116.00	49880	150930	4044924
Polystyrene Insulation	117.00	50310	3770	101036
Carpet (synthetic)	148.00	63640	84900	2275320
Aluminium (recycled)	8.10	3483	21870	586116
Aluminium	227.00	97610	515700	13820760

From Canadian Architect, Designing for Disassembly, January 2001

Conversions: 1 megajoule per kilogram = 430 BTUs per pound; 1 megajoule per cubic meter = 26.8 BTUs per cubic foot

A-12 Air-Sealing Economic Limits

The numbers in the body of this table represent the number of therms saved per 100 CFM_{50} reduction to achieve a one-year payback. By knowing your fuel cost per therm (See page 292) and the simple payback you desire, you can find your unique cost-effectiveness limit using the formulas printed below the table. If you prefer to use savings-to-investment ratio (SIR), the second option gives you the cost-effectiveness limit, but you need to estimate the lifespan of your air-sealing measures — generally 8-to-30 years.

Therms saved/ 100 CFM_{50} Air-Sealing Reduction

Heating Degree Days

LBL Factor (n)	4000	4500	5000	5500	6000	6500	7000	7500	8000	8500	9000	9500	10,000
10	6.24	7.02	7.80	8.58	9.36	10.14	10.92	11.70	12.48	13.26	14.04	14.82	15.60
11	5.67	6.38	7.09	7.80	8.51	9.22	9.93	10.64	11.35	12.56	12.76	13.47	14.18
12	5.20	5.85	6.50	7.15	7.80	8.45	9.10	9.75	10.40	11.05	11.70	12.35	13.00
13	4.80	5.40	6.00	6.60	7.20	7.80	8.40	9.00	9.60	10.20	10.80	11.14	12.00
14	4.46	5.01	5.57	6.13	6.69	7.24	7.80	8.36	8.91	9.47	10.03	10.59	11.14
15	4.16	4.68	5.20	5.72	6.24	6.76	7.28	7.80	8.32	8.84	9.36	9.88	10.40
16	3.90	4.39	4.88	5.36	5.85	6.34	6.83	7.31	7.80	8.29	8.78	9.26	9.75
17	3.67	4.13	4.59	5.05	5.51	5.97	6.42	6.88	7.34	7.80	8.26	8.72	9.18
18	3.47	3.90	4.33	4.77	5.20	5.63	6.07	6.50	6.93	7.37	7.80	8.23	8.67
19	3.28	3.70	4.11	4.52	4.93	5.34	5.75	6.16	6.57	6.98	7.39	7.80	8.21
20	3.12	3.51	3.90	4.29	4.68	5.07	5.46	5.85	6.24	6.63	7.02	7.41	7.80
21	2.97	3.34	3.71	4.09	4.46	4.83	5.20	5.57	5.94	6.31	6.69	7.06	7.43
22	2.84	3.19	3.55	3.90	4.26	4.61	4.96	5.32	5.67	6.03	6.38	6.74	7.09
23	2.71	3.05	3.39	3.73	4.07	4.41	4.75	5.09	5.43	5.77	6.10	6.44	6.78
24	2.60	2.93	3.25	3.58	3.90	4.23	4.55	4.88	5.20	5.53	5.85	6.18	6.50
25	2.50	2.81	3.12	3.43	3.74	4.06	4.37	4.68	4.99	5.30	5.62	5.93	6.24
26	2.40	2.70	3.00	3.30	3.60	3.90	4.20	4.50	4.80	5.10	5.40	5.70	6.00
27	2.31	2.60	2.89	3.18	3.47	3.76	4.04	4.33	4.62	4.91	5.20	5.49	5.78
28	2.23	2.51	2.79	3.06	3.34	3.62	3.90	4.18	4.46	4.74	5.01	5.29	5.57
29	2.15	2.42	2.69	2.96	3.23	3.50	3.77	4.03	4.30	4.57	4.84	5.11	5.38
30	2.08	2.34	2.60	2.86	3.12	3.38	3.64	3.90	4.16	4.42	4.68	4.94	5.20

Thanks to Rick Karg

$$\text{Economic Limit} (\$/100\ \text{CFM}_{50}) = \begin{cases} \textbf{Option 1: } \text{Therms saved/100 CFM}_{50} \times \text{Desired Payback (years)} \times \text{Energy cost (\$/therm)} \\ \\ \textbf{Option 2: } \dfrac{\text{Therms saved/ 100 CFM}_{50} \times \text{Energy cost (\$/therm)} \times \text{Lifespan (years)}}{\text{Desired SIR}} \end{cases}$$

A-13 Air Leakage at Various House Pressures

The chart below is designed to estimate the air-leakage rate for houses under pressure from leaky ducts, unbalanced ducts, or other sources of house pressure. The diagonal lines represent airflows at various house pressures. When this page is turned 90°, the left-hand vertical axis gives leakage in CFM for the measured blower-door readings on the bottom horizontal axis. If you measure a house's CFM_{50} and its house pressure, you can estimate the air leakage caused by its house pressure using this chart.

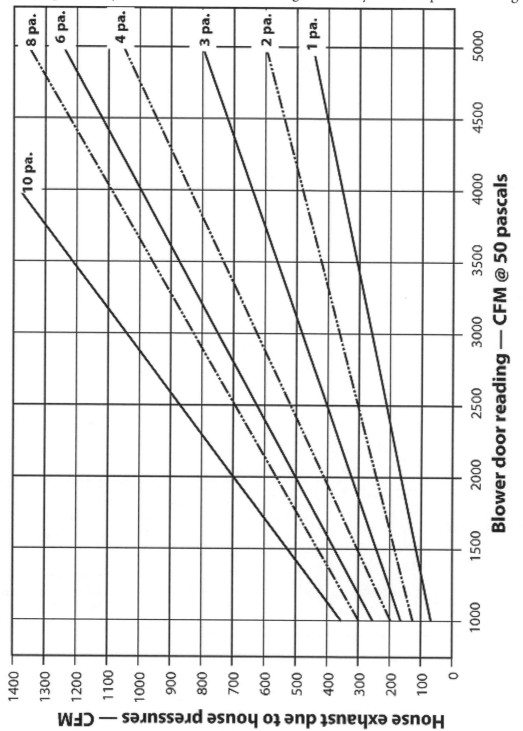

Thanks to Neil Moyer

A-14 Insulation Characteristics

Material	Product type	R-value per inch	Density Lb/ft^3	Temperature, toxicity, and fire characteristics
Fiberglass	Batts Dense pack Rigid board	2.6–4.3 3.6–4.4 4.0–4.4	0.4–1.6 1.0–2.5 4.0	Flame spread 15 or less. Airborne particles are a respiratory irritant. Considered combustible because of organic binders. Organic binders vaporize at temperatures above 350°F. 180°F maximum with kraft or foil face. 750°F maximum without organic binders.
Mineral Wool	Batts Loose fill Rigid board	3.0–3.6 2.6–3.4 4.0–4.4	1.5–4.0 1.5–2.5 4.0–5.0	Non-combustible. Airborne particles are an irritant. Organic binders vaporize above 350°F. 180°F maximum with kraft or foil face. 750°F maximum without organic binders.
Cellulose	Loose fill Dense pack Spray on	3.2–3.6 3.0–3.4 2.9–3.4	1.2–2.5 3.5–4.5 2.8–3.8	Flame spread is less than 15; smoke developed is 0. Water can carry away fire retardant. Maximum temperature 200°F.
Vermiculite **Perlite**	Loose fill	2.1 2.1	2–5 4–8	Non-combustible. Maximum temperature over 500°F. Dust may contain toxic, inorganic particles such as asbestos or silica.
Polyisocyanurate	Rigid board	5.6–7.6	1.6–2.0	Maximum temperature 160°F. Flame spread is less than 15; smoke developed is 60 to 130 depending on thickness.
Polyurethane Spray	Hi-density Lo-density	6.0–7.0 3.5–3.8	2.0–2.5 0.5	Maximum temperature is 160°F to 350°F, depending on formulation. Flame spread is 25 or less. Smoke developed 100-to-400 depending on thickness and formulation.
Polystyrene	Rigid board Expanded Rigid board Extruded	3.6–4.2 5.0	0.9–2.0 1.6–2.0	Flame spread less than 15. Maximum temperature 165°F. Melts at around 300°F. Spontaneously combusts at 600°F. Smoke developed as high as 400.

Moisture considerations	Advantages	Disadvantages
Absorbs 1% water by weight. Very permeable to water vapor.	Inexpensive and readily available. Excellent fire and moisture resistance. Loose fill produces less dust than cellulose.	Installation of blowing wool requires better equipment than cellulose. Tends to fluff when blown into attics. Poor air infiltration resistance unless tightly packed.
Absorbs up to 5% water by weight. Very permeable to water vapor.	Non-combustible and suitable for high-temperature applications. Fairly inexpensive.	Heavier and more compressible than fiberglass. More difficult to blow than cellulose.
Absorbs up to 130% water by weight. Very permeable to water vapor.	Inexpensive and easy to install. Very resistant to air infiltration. Installs in attics at appropriate density to resist air penetration. Extremely effective for wall insulation in older homes with high air leakage.	Requires careful chemical treatment to avoid fire hazard. Absorbs water and dries slowly. Flame retardant combined with water may corrode steel and aluminum. Settles and deteriorates after wetting. Density variations cause settling in walls at less than 3.5 lbs./cu. ft. density. Very dusty to blow.
High water absorption and vapor transmission.	Non-combustible. Pours easily into irregular wall cavities, like cores of concrete block.	Low R-value per inch. Expensive. Dusty.
Water absorption negligible. Very low vapor permeability.	Highest R-value per inch of any common insulation. Easy to cut and fit. Versatile and commonly available. Very resistant to moisture especially when coated with sealant. Great adhesion and structural strength. The most versatile insulation material.	Expensive. Codes require covering by fire barrier. R-value decreases slightly over time. Contains fluorocarbons. Expensive. Installation is difficult and sensitive to wind, moisture, and temperature. Degrades with exposure to U.V.
Molded polystyrene absorbs 4% water by weight. Molded EPS available in a variety or vapor permeances. Extruded absorbs 1% water by weight and is a vapor barrier.	High R-value per inch. R-value maintained over time. Expanded polystyrene is the least expensive plastic foam and is widely available. Extruded polystyrene has excellent moisture resistance and is widely used as foundation insulation.	Degrades with exposure to U.V. Shrinks and degrades at temperatures above 165°F. Requires special adhesives. Codes require covering with a fire barrier.

A-15 Household Appliance Electrical Usage

Appliance	Annual kWh	Appliance	Annual kWh
Heating and Cooling		Hot wash, cold rinse	1200–1700
Room air conditioner	500–2000	Warm wash, cold rinse	600–1000
Two-and-one-half ton central air conditioner	2000–8000	Cold wash, cold rinse	70–160
Five ton central air conditioner	4000–12,000	Water cooler with hot water	600–900
Evaporative Coolers	200–2000	**Kitchen Appliances**	
8-foot electric baseboard heater	750–2000	Refrigerator/freezer	
Electric furnace	6000–16,000	20-year-old manual defrost	1300
Furnace fan	300–900	20 year-old side-by-side, frost-free	1400–1900
Hot water circulator	250–700	10-year-old	800–1100
Heat recovery ventilator	400–1100	New ENERGY STAR qualified	400–540
General Appliances		Freezer	
Engine block heater	50–400	20-year-old upright, frost-free	1400–2000
Clothes dryer	400–1500	20-year-old chest, manual defrost	1100–1300
Computer	50–350	10-year-old chest	600–800
Ceiling fan	20–50	New ENERGY STAR qualified	370–430
Whole house fan	60–200	Range (with oven)	200–800
Television, color (solid state)	100–400	Dishwasher	100–600
Television cable box	40–160	Broiler	20–100
Television off-cycle energy	10–40	Coffee maker	80–200
Video cassette recorder	15–40	Microwave oven	100–250
Hair blow-dryer	8–16	Roaster	20–80
Hand iron	10–100	Slow cooker	40–150
Heat lamp	10–25	Toaster	15–50
Lighting (average total)	200–2000	Toaster oven	50–300
Vacuum cleaner	20–80		
Water heater (1–3 people)	2500–6000		
Water heater (3–6 people)	4000–8000		
Water heater (15 gallon)	2000–3500		
Water bed	1000–2000		
Hot tub heating (indoor 300–500 gallons)	1500–3000		
Hot tub heating (outdoor 300–500 gallons)	3000–8000		
Hot tub circulation	1000–2500		
Pool circulator	1100–4000		
Well pump	250–500		
Clothes washers	80–200		

Assembled from utility studies and utility company information sources.

A-16 Deciphering Common Pressures

Inches of Water Column (IWC)

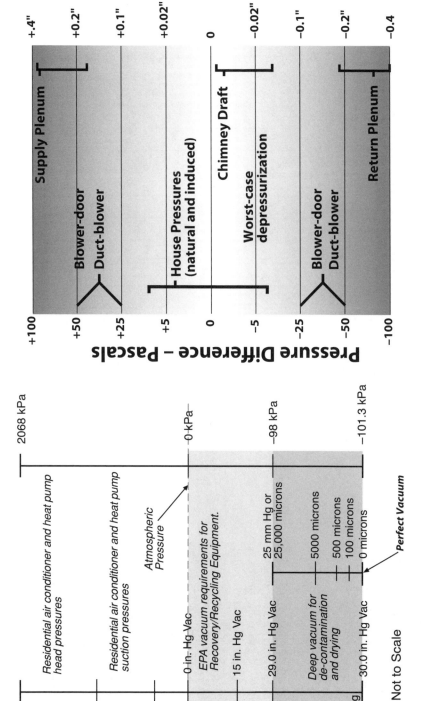

The house-pressure ranges described on this chart are the most common ones. However, house pressures outside these ranges are often found. For example, during windy conditions, chimney draft may be positive. Or a completely blocked filter may give greater negative pressures in the return system of a furnace.

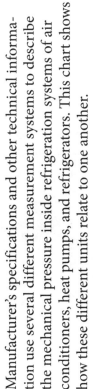

Manufacturer's specifications and other technical information use several different measurement systems to describe the mechanical pressure inside refrigeration systems of air conditioners, heat pumps, and refrigerators. This chart shows how these different units relate to one another.

A-17 Psychrometrics

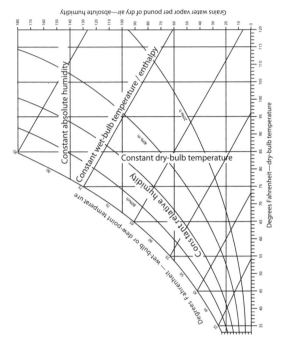

Psychrometrics is the science of air and its properties related to buildings and comfort. Energy specialists use psychrometric charts to understand human comfort and the energy required to produce it. Each point on these charts represents a particular state (or set of properties) of an air mass, called a state point.

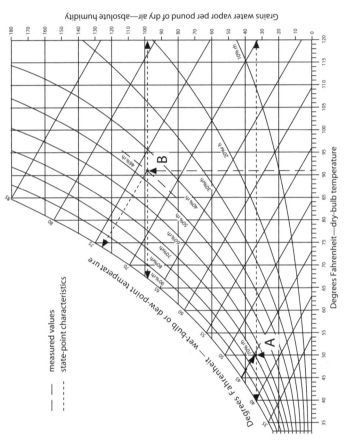

The parallel lines on these charts represent different characteristics of air. The chart to your right shows how each group of lines represents air at some constant value: relative humidity, absolute humidity, dew point, dry-bulb temperature, wet-bulb temperatures, or enthalpy. Dew point and dry-bulb temperature follow the same lines. Wet-bulb temperature and enthalpy follow the same lines. To simplify the explanation, the enthalpy (energy content) scale is not

— — — measured values
- - - - - state-point characteristics

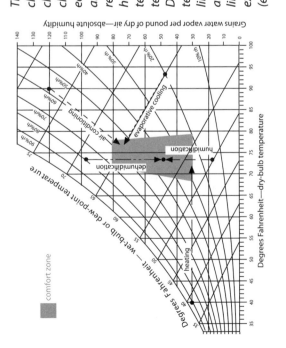

comfort zone

The state-point of any air mass can be determined by measurements. State-point A, on the chart to your right, was determined by a sling psychrometer—a device that measures both dry-bulb (50°) and wet-bulb (45°) temperatures. State-point A's other characteristics—relative humidity (70%), dew point (40°), and absolute humidity (33 grains per pound)—are determined from the chart. State-point B was determined by a thermometer (91°) and a hygrometer, which measures relative humidity (46%). State-point B's other characteristics are: wet-bulb temperature (74°), dew point (64°), and absolute humidity (98 grains per pound). A grain is a very small unit of weight; there are 7000 grains in a pound.

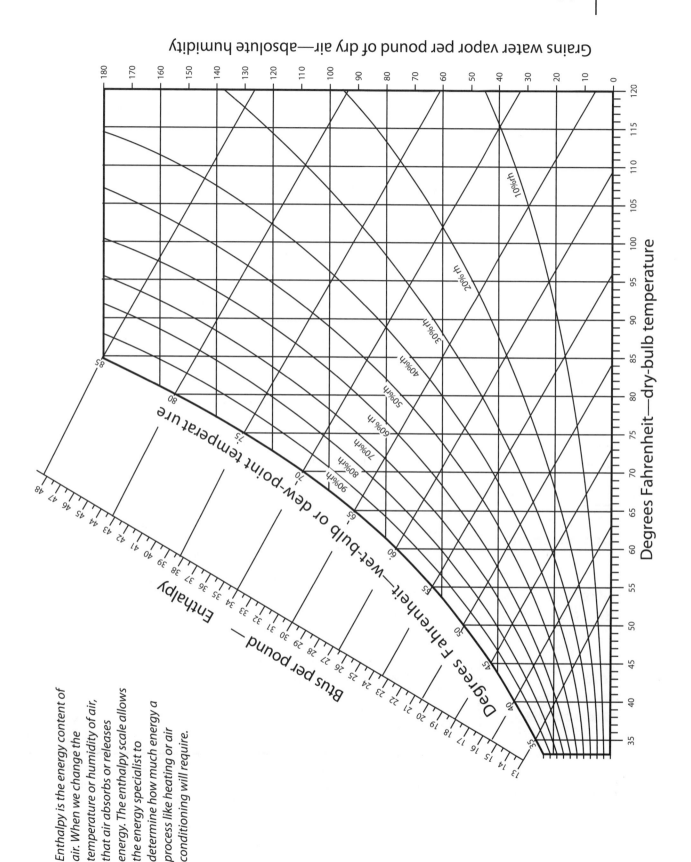

Grains water vapor per pound of dry air—absolute humidity

Degrees Fahrenheit—dry-bulb temperature

Degrees Fahrenheit—wet-bulb or dew-point temperature

Btus per pound — Enthalpy

100% rh
20% rh
30% rh
40% rh
50% rh
60% rh
70% rh
80% rh
90% rh

Enthalpy is the energy content of air. When we change the temperature or humidity of air, that air absorbs or releases energy. The enthalpy scale allows the energy specialist to determine how much energy a process like heating or air conditioning will require.

A-18 Indoor Air Pollutants

	Pollutant	Health effects and victims	Exposure limit
Dust	**Asbestos**	Lung cancer, asbestosis, mesothelioma. Smoking greatly increases risk of asbestos-related lung cancer. *Victims:* Asbestos workers.	No safe level. (EPA) 0.1 fiber/cc (OSHA 8 hr.) 1 fiber/cc (OSHA 30 min.)
	Biological particles	Allergies, asthma, infectious diseases, toxic effects. *Victims:* Occupants of buildings with moisture problems.	No established limits.
	Combustion particles	Decreased lung function, cancer. *Victims:* Smokers, wood stove users, city dwellers.	EPA/ASHRAE Limits 50 µg/m³ (continuous) 150 µg/m³ (8-hr.) 15,000 µg/m³ (8-hr. OSHA)
	Lead	Damage to kidneys, nervous system, and red blood cells. *Victims:* Toddlers who ingest lead dust hand-to-mouth; demolition and renovation workers who breathe lead dust.	1.5 µg/m³ (EPA and ASHRAE 3-month exposure limit)
	Radon progeny	Lung cancer. *Victims:* Long-time occupants of buildings with high radon levels.	4 pCi/l (EPA) 2 pCi/l (ASHRAE)
Gases	**Carbon monoxide**	Decreased reaction time and work capacity; chest pain and exacerbation of existing respiratory problems; headaches, nausea; asphyxiation, brain damage, coma, and death in high concentrations. *Victims:* Occupants of buildings with CO from combustion appliances and tobacco smoke.	9 ppm (EPA 8-hr.) 35 ppm (EPA 1-hr.) 200 ppm (Instantaneous OSHA)
	Formaldehyde	Irritant, allergen, and possible carcinogen. Exacerbates existing respiratory problems. *Victims:* New home occupants, smokers, occupants of recently remodeled buildings.	0.1 ppm (ASHRAE continuous) 1 ppm (OSHA 8-hour)
	Nitrogen dioxide	Retards pulmonary function in children and possibly in adults. Animal studies suggest decreased immune capacity. *Victims:* Occupants of buildings with combustion gases in indoor air.	100 µg/m³ or 0.08 ppm (EPA/ASHRAE continuous)
	Volatile organic compounds	Respiratory irritants. Damages nervous system, cardiovascular system, kidneys, and liver. Many VOCs are carcinogens. *Victims:* New home occupants, workers using solvents, wood stove users, smokers.	Varies according to particular VOC compound.
Mixtures	**Environmental tobacco smoke**	Carcinogen. Irritates mucous membranes. Chronic and acute cardio-pulmonary effects in children. *Victims:* Occupants of buildings with indoor smoking.	Wood and tobacco smoke contain carbon monoxide, nitrogen dioxide, formaldehyde and VOCs. See above for limits.
	Wood smoke	Acute respiratory illness. Chronic lung disease. *Victims:* Residents of wood-heated buildings and towns with many wood stoves.	EPA/ASHRAE Particulate Limits 50 µg/m³ (continuous) 150 µg/m³ (8-hr.) 15,000 µg/m³ (8-hr. OSHA)

Symptoms and sensory detection	Sources
Symptoms: No immediate symptoms. *Sensory detection:* Workers must be able to recognize asbestos and activities that raise asbestos dust.	Asbestos cement; pipe, furnace, and boiler insulation; ceiling and floor tiles; shingles and siding; vermiculite insulation.
Symptoms: Allergies, asthma, fevers, eye irritation, nose and throat irritation, and skin irritation. *Sensory detection:* moldy smell and visual detection.	Plants, animals, and humans; pillows, household dust; damp materials; standing water; humidifiers, evaporative coolers, air conditioners, water heaters.
Symptoms: Respiratory and eye irritation. *Sensory detection:* No odor. Fine black soot collects on horizontal surfaces over time.	Combustion appliances, tobacco smoke.
Symptoms: Decreased coordination and mental abilities. *Sensory detection:* By chemical test only.	Lead-based paint, outdoor lead dust from lead-containing gasoline, lead-using activities like soldering, stained-glass work, handling wheel weights, and lead-acid batteries.
Symptoms: No acute effects. *Sensory detection:* Colorless and odorless. Detection by specialized radon test equipment only.	Soil and rock, well water; some building materials.
Symptoms: Headaches, nausea, breathlessness, dizziness, tiredness, flu-like symptoms, chest pain in cardio-pulmonary disease sufferers. *Sensory detection:* Colorless and odorless, but usually accompanied by other combustion gases that have odor.	Gas cook stoves; unvented gas or kerosene heaters; fireplaces and wood stoves; gas and oil furnaces, boilers, and water heaters; tobacco smoke.
Symptoms: Eye, nose, and throat irritation; respiratory irritation; wheezing; coughing; fatigue; and skin rash. *Sensory detection:* Sharp, pungent odor. Presence of new building materials, paint, varnish, carpet, furnishings, and draperies.	Particle board, plywood, drywall; cabinetry and furniture; carpet and drapery fabrics; tobacco smoke.
Symptoms: Drowsiness; headache; respiratory irritation; eye, nose, and throat irritation; and labored breathing. *Sensory detection:* Odorless, colorless. Detection by chemical or electric device only.	Gas cook stoves; gas or oil heaters and water heaters; wood stoves; fireplaces; unvented gas and kerosene heaters; vehicle exhaust; tobacco smoke.
Symptoms: Eye, nose, and throat irritation; fatigue; weakness; skin rash; depression; irregular heartbeats; muscle twitching and convulsion; poor coordination; memory loss; and headache and nausea. *Sensory detection:* Some VOCs have a solvent smell; also presence of tobacco smoke and wood smoke.	Tobacco smoke; kerosene heaters; wood-burning stoves and fireplaces; perfumes and hair sprays; furniture polish; cleaning solvents; hobby and craft supplies; carpet; glues and adhesives; sealants, paints, varnishes, and stains; wood preservatives; dry-cleaned clothes; moth repellents; air fresheners; automotive products; and plastics.
Symptoms: Eye, nose, and throat irritation; respiratory irritation; headache; nausea; dizziness; appetite loss; and asthma aggravation. *Sensory detection:* Tobacco smoke odor.	Tobacco smoking.
Symptoms: Eye, nose, and throat irritation; respiratory irritation; headache; nausea; dizziness. *Sensory detection:* Wood smoke odor.	Wood-burning stoves, fireplaces.

A-19 Household Moisture Sources

Moisture Source	Estimated Moisture Amount (pints)
Bathing: tub, excludes towels and spillage	0.12/standard size bath
shower, excludes towels and spillage	0.52/5-minute shower
Clothes washing: automatic, lid closed	0+/load (usually nil)
Clothes drying: vented outdoors	0+/load (usually nil)
not vented outdoors, or indoor line drying	4-6/load (more if gas dryer)
Combustion: unvented kerosene space heater	0.5 - 2.0/hour, or 7.6/per gallon
Cooking: three meals (four people)	2.10 (plus 2.84 if cooking over gas)
simmer at 203° F, 10 min., 6 in. pan	0.01 covered, 0.13 uncovered (more if gas)
boil 10 min., 6 in. pan	0.48 covered, 0.57 uncovered (more if gas)
Dish washing: three meals (four people)	1.05/day
Firewood storage indoors (1 cord of green wood)	400-800/6 months
Gas range pilot light (each)	0.37 or less/day
House plants (5 to 7 average plants)	0.86 to 0.96/day
Respiration and perspiration (four people)	0.44/hour average
Refrigerator defrost (per day)	1.03/day average
Saunas, steam baths, and whirlpools	0 to 2.7+/day
Evaporation (desorption) from materials:	
seasonal	6.3 to 16.9/day average
new construction	10+/day average
Ground moisture	0 to 105/day (highly variable)

Adapted from: *Moisture Sources Associated with Potential Damage in Cold-Climate Housing*, University of Minnesota, 1988.

A-20 Commissioning Air Conditioners and Heat Pumps

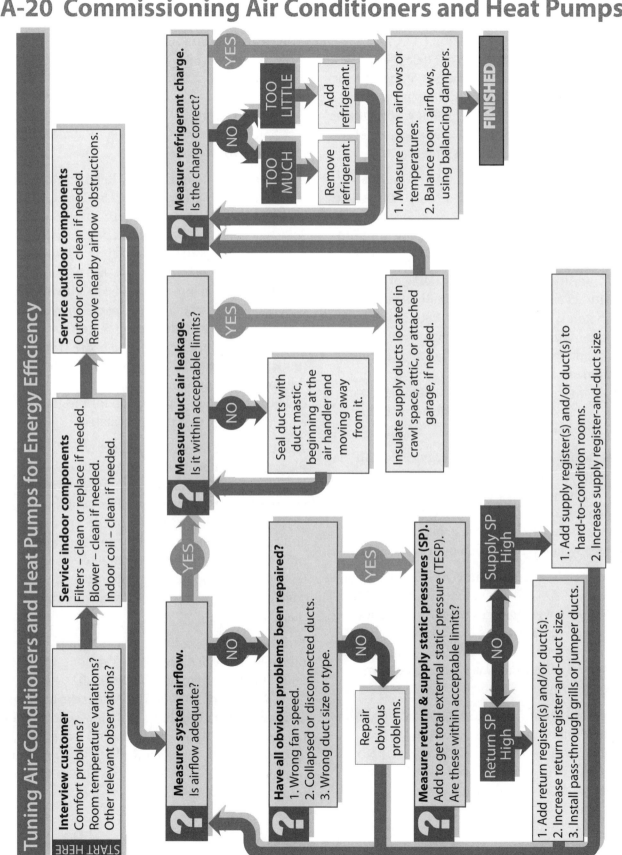

Tuning Air-Conditioners and Heat Pumps for Energy Efficiency

START HERE

Interview customer
Comfort problems?
Room temperature variations?
Other relevant observations?

Service indoor components
Filters – clean or replace if needed.
Blower – clean if needed.
Indoor coil – clean if needed.

Service outdoor components
Outdoor coil – clean if needed.
Remove nearby airflow obstructions.

? Measure system airflow.
Is airflow adequate?

NO → **Have all obvious problems been repaired?**
1. Wrong fan speed.
2. Collapsed or disconnected ducts.
3. Wrong duct size or type.

NO → Repair obvious problems.

YES → **? Measure return & supply static pressures (SP).**
Add to get total external static pressure (TESP).
Are these within acceptable limits?

NO → Return SP High / Supply SP High

Return SP High →
1. Add return register(s) and/or duct(s).
2. Increase return register-and-duct size.
3. Install pass-through grills or jumper ducts.

Supply SP High →
1. Add supply register(s) and/or duct(s) to hard-to-condition rooms.
2. Increase supply register-and-duct size.

YES →

? Measure duct air leakage.
Is it within acceptable limits?

NO → Seal ducts with duct mastic, beginning at the air handler and moving away from it.

YES → Insulate supply ducts located in crawl space, attic, or attached garage, if needed.

? Measure refrigerant charge.
Is the charge correct?

NO → TOO MUCH → Remove refrigerant.
NO → TOO LITTLE → Add refrigerant.

YES →

1. Measure room airflows or temperatures.
2. Balance room airflows, using balancing dampers.

FINISHED

A-21 Energy-Efficiency Organizations

Advanced Energy Corporation (AEC), 909 Capability Drive, Raliegh, NC 27606. 919-857-9000. www.advancedenergy.org. A nonprofit corporation that provides utility companies with information about energy efficiency. Specializes in energy-efficient installation and service of residential heating and cooling systems.

Air Conditioning Contractors of America (ACCA), 2800 Shirlington Rd., Suite 300, Arlington, VA 22206. 703-575-4477. www.acca.org. The most active and widely recognized organization representing contractors in the HVAC industry.

Air Conditioning, Heating & Refrigeration Institute (AHRI), 2111 Wilson Blvd, Suite 500 Arlington, VA 22201. 703-524-8800. www.ahri-net.org. Association representing manufacturers of air conditioning, refrigeration, and heating equipment. Provides a variety of services including an information center for dissemination of general information on the industry and the industry's products.

American Council for an Energy-Efficient Economy (ACEEE), 529 14th Street N.W, Suite 600 Washington D.C, 20045-1000. 202-507-4000. www.aceee.org. ACEEE collaborates with other groups on research into the benefits of energy efficiency, and publishes many reports.

American Gas Association (AGA), 400 N. Capitol St. NW #450, Washington, DC 20001. 202-824-7000. www.aga.org. The AGA publishes reports on gas efficiency in restaurants, chain stores, cogeneration, gas-fired HVAC, gas-fired heating, cooling, and water heating equipment, and numerous case studies.

American Solar Energy Society, Inc. (ASES), 4760 Walnut Street, Suite 106. Boulder, CO 80301. 303-443-3130. www.ases.org. ASES is a nonprofit educational organization that encourages the use of solar energy technologies. ASES publishes *Solar Today*.

American Lighting Association, 2050 N. Stemmons Freeway, Unit 100. Dallas, TX 75207-3206. 1-800-605-4448. www.americanlightingassoc.com. Offers information, products, services to general public, educational events and technical assistance to members regarding residential lighting energy conservation.

American Society of Heating, Refrigerating and Air Conditioning Engineers (ASHRAE), 1791 Tullie Circle NE, Atlanta, GA 30329. 404-636-8400. www.ashrae.org. Dedicated to the advancement of heating, refrigeration, air conditioning, and ventilation technology and theory. Sponsors research and develops standards documents that help establish acceptable levels of performance for buildings and mechanical equipment. The ASHRAE Handbooks, technical texts on energy fundamentals and systems, and ASHRAE Journal, the Society's monthly magazine, are considered essential sources of information for mechanical engineers. Large publications catalog.

Association of Energy Engineers (AEE), 4025 Pleasantdale Road, Suite 420, Atlanta, GA 30340. 770-447-5083. www.aeecenter.org. Membership organization of engineers, architects, and other professionals with an interest in energy efficiency and energy-related product manufacturers. Promotes scientific and educational interests of professionals engaged in energy management, cogeneration, and overall efficiency improvements.

Building Enclosure Council, c/o National Institute of Building Sciences, 1090 Vermont Ave. NW, Suite 700, Washington, DC 20005. 202-289-7800. www.nibs.org/betechm.html. Assists the building community with building regulations; encourages the acceptance of new products and technology, and provides relevant technical information. Publications include many research reports and conference proceedings.

Building Performance Institute, 107 Hermes Road, Suite 210, Malta, NY 12020. 518-899-2727. www.bpi.org. Certifies technicians working in the weatherization and home performance fields. Manages both classroom and field testing of technicians.

Building Science Corporation, 30 Forest Street. Somerville, MA 02143. 978-589-5100. www.buildingscience.com. Consulting and publishing on building science and sustainable building construction. Website has great information on building science.

Building Research Council, University of Illinois At Urbana-Champaign, One East St. Mary's Road, Champaign, IL 61820. 217-333-1801. brc.arch.illinois.edu. Established by the University of Illinois as an agency for research, publication, education, and public service in the area of housing and building. Publishes Council Notes, which are fact sheets about home remodeling, maintenance, and building.

California Energy Commission (CEC), Media & Public Communications Office 1516 Ninth Street, MS-29 Sacramento, CA 95814-5512. 916-654-4287. www.energy.ca.gov. The CEC's publications catalog lists many written information resources on building technology and building energy standards.

Canada Mortgage and Housing Corporation (CMHC), 700 Montreal Road, Ottawa, Ontario K1A OP7, Canada. 613-748-2367. www.cmhc-schl.gc.ca/en/index.cfm. Produces many valuable research reports, booklets, and fact sheets on a wide variety of topics relating to single-family and multifamily buildings.

Electric Power Research Institute (EPRI), 3420 Hillview Avenue Palo Alto, CA 94304. 650-855-2000. www.epri.com. The electric power industry's research institute. Its publications and research reports may be searched on-line through EPRINET and the EPRI data base on DIALOG. Reports span energy-efficiency, renewable-energy, and waste-management topics related to electric power. Publishes the EPRI Journal, which summarizes EPRI research activities, eight times a year.

Energy Efficiency and Renewable Energy (EERE). Mail Stop EE1 Department of Energy Washington, D.C, 20585800-363-3732. www.eere.doe.gov. EREC provides free general and technical information to the public on many topics and technologies pertaining to energy efficiency and renewable energy.

Energy Efficient Building Association (EEBA), 6520 Edenvale Boulevard, Suite 112. Eden Prairie, MN 55346. 952-881-1098. www.eeba.org. Dedicated to the development, dissemination and acceptance of information on the design, construction, and operation of efficient buildings. EEBA offers professional and technical publications and conference proceedings.

Florida Solar Energy Center (FSEC), 1679 Clearlake Rd., Cocoa, FL 32922. 321-638-1000. www.fsec.ucf.edu. For anyone building in hot, humid climates, FSEC is a necessary information resource. Publications cover topics such as passive cooling, radiant barriers, moisture control in hot climates, shading techniques, air leakage, air-conditioner performance, and more.

HUD User, P.O. Box 23268, Washington, DC 20026-3268. 800-245-2691. www.huduser.org. HUD User is the information source for research reports and other information generated with HUD funding and through HUD programs. Supplies a great variety and number of reports.

International Code Council (ICC), 4051 W. Flossmoor Rd. Country Club Hills, IL 60478 888-422-7233. http://www.iccsafe.org/ Writer and publisher of the International Building Code (IBC), International Residential Code (IRC), and the International Energy Conservation Code (IECC).

Lawrence Berkeley National Laboratory, 1 Cyclotron Road. Berkeley, CA 94720. 510-486-4000. http://eetd.lbl.gov/bt.html. Conducts research in energy analysis, energy-efficient windows, and lighting systems. Pioneered end-use planning and continues to monitor and inventory cost-effectiveness of energy-saving technologies in residential and commercial buildings.þ

National Association of Home Builders (NAHB), National Research Center (NRC), 1201 15th Street, N.W., Washington, DC 20005. 800-368-5242. www.nahb.com. Sells many books and publications on energy-efficient buildings and all other aspects of the building industry.

National Center for Appropriate Technology (NCAT), P.O. Box 3838, Butte, MT 59702. 406-494-4572. www.ncat.org. NCAT is a good source of information on residential energy efficiency programs operated by utility companies and states.

National Fenestration Rating Council (NFRC), 6305 Ivy Lane, Suite 140. Greenbelt, MD 20770. 301-589-1776. www.nfrc.org. A collaboration between industry, government, and public interest groups working to establish a viable and economical fenestration rating system that will be used by product manufacturers in marketing windows.

National Renewable Energy Laboratory (NREL), 1617 Cole Blvd., Golden, CO 80401-3305. 303-275-3000. www.nrel.gov. The DOE's solar and renewable energy laboratory. Performs many kinds of building energy research. Produces residential energy standards for the DOE.

Oak Ridge National Laboratory (ORNL), Buildings Technology Center, Battelle, UT, P.O. Box 2008, Oak Ridge, TN 37831. www.ornl.gov/sci/btc/index.shtml. Under contract to the U.S. Dept. of Energy, its building research facility performs thermal testing on full size building components. The results of the lab's research are published and available to the public for a nominal price.

Residential Energy Services Network (RES-NET). P.O. Box 4561, Oceanside, CA 92052. 760-806-3448. www.resnet.us. National organization of energy raters and rating organizations. Mis-

sion: To develop a national market for home energy rating systems and energy efficient mortgages.

Southface Energy Institute, 241 Pine St. NE, Atlanta, GA 30308. 404-872-3549. www.southface.org. Nonprofit educational institute focuses on energy-efficient building for the southern states. Website has a good question-and-answer section.

Sustainable Buildings Industry Council, 1090 Vermont Ave. NW, Suite 700 Washington D.C, 20005. 202-289-7800. www.sbicouncil.org. Mission is to advance the design, affordability, energy performance, and environmental soundness of residential, institutional and commercial buildings.

Texas A&M University, Energy Systems Laboratory, 3581 TAMU College Station, TX 77845-3581. 979-845-9213. www-esl.tamu.edu. Performs research and publishes reports on residential and commercial air conditioning and other topics related to comfort in buildings in hot and humid climates.

U.S. Green Building Council (USGBC), 2101 L Street, NW Suite 500. Washington, D.C, 20037. 1-800-795-1747. www.usgbc.org. Administers Leadership in Energy and Environmental Design (LEED), an educational and rating system for green buildings.

Bibliography

2002 Buildings Energy Databook: U.S. Department of Energy, Office of Energy Efficiency and Renewable Energy, Washington, DC. 2002.

ASHRAE Handbook: 2005 Fundamentals: American Society of Heating, Refrigerating and Air-Conditioning Engineers, Inc. Atlanta, GA. 1993.

Combustion Efficiency: Fact or Fallacy: Davis, Jim. Covington, KY. 1985.

Consumer Guide to Home Energy Savings: Wilson, A, Thorne J. & Morrill, J. American Council for an Energy-Efficient Economy, Washington, DC. 2003.

Cooling Our Communities, A Guidebook On Tree Planting and Light-Colored Surfacing: United States Environmental Protection Agency; Policy, Planning and Evaluation. Lawrence Berkeley Laboratory Report. Washington, DC. 1992.

Cooling With Ventilation: Chandra, Sobrato; Fairey, P.W., III. M.M. Solar Energy Research Institute. Golden, CO. 1986.

Efficient Residential Oil-Heating Systems: Canadian Combustion Research Laboratory. Energy, Mines and Resources, Canada. Ottawa, ON. June, 1983.

Energy Data Sourcebook for the U.S. Residential Sector, Energy Analysis Program, Lawrence Berkeley Laboratory, Berkeley, CA. 1997.

Guide to Oil Heat: Beckett Corporation, Elyria, OH. 1997.

HVAC Installation Procedures: Carrier Corporation, Syracuse, NY. 1997.

HVAC Maintenance Procedures: Carrier Corporation, Syracuse, NY. 1997.

HVAC Service Procedures: Carrier Corporation, Syracuse, NY. 1995.

Hydronic Heating: A Practical Overview: Krigger, J. Electric Power Research Institute. Palo Alto, CA. 2000.

Introduction to Indoor Air Quality: Environmental Protection Agency. Washington, DC. 1991.

Landscape Design That Saves Energy: Moffat, Anne Simon; and Schiler, Marc. William Morrow & Company, Inc. New York, NY. 1981.

Landscape Planning For Energy Conservation: Robinette, G.; and McClennon, C. Van Nostrand Reinhold Company, Inc. New York, NY. 1983.

Landscaping for Energy Conservation: Girgis, Magdy. Florida Solar Energy Center. Cape Canaveral, FL. February, 1985.

Lost Art of Steam Heating, The: Holohan, Dan. Holohan Associates, Bethpage, NY. 1992.

Manual J: Load Calculation for Residential Winter and Summer Air Conditioning: Air Conditioning Contractors of America. Washington, DC. 1986.

MWX90: Minnesota Low Income Weatherization Procedure for the 1990s: Underground Space Center, University of Minnesota. December, 1993.

Modern Hydronic Heating: Siegenthaler, J. Delmar, Albany, NY. 1995.

Moisture Control For Homes. Energy Design Update: Nisson, J.D. Cutter Information Corp. 1989. (report)

Moisture Control Handbook: Principles and Practices for Residential and Small Commercial Buildings: Lstiburek, J., and Carmody, J. Nan Nostrand Reinhold. Oak Ridge, TN. 1993.

No Regrets Remodeling: Home Energy Magazine, Energy Auditor and Retrofitter, Inc. Berkeley, CA. 1997.

Passive Cooling and Human Comfort: Fairey, Phillip W. Florida Solar Energy Center. Cape Canaveral, FL. 1981.

Quiet Indoor Revolution, The: Konzo, S.; and MacDonald, M. Small Homes Council-Building Research Council, University of Illinois, College of Fine and Applied Arts. Champaign, IL. 1992.

Refrigeration and Air Conditioning Technology: Whitman, W, Johnson, W, Tomczyak, J. Delmar, Albany, NY. 2000.

Residential Controls For Heating and Cooling. First Edition: Honeywell, Inc. St. Paul, MN.1985.

Residential Windows: A Guide to New Technologies and Energy Performance: Carmody, J., Selkowitz, S. Heschong, L. WW Norton & Co. New York, NY 1996.

Shading Our Cities: Moll, G.; and Ebenreck, S., eds. Island Press. Washington DC. 1989.

Specification of Energy-Efficient Installation Practices for Residential HVAC Systems: Karg, R. and Krigger, J. Consortium for Energy Efficiency. Boston, MA. 2000.

Water Heater Workbook, The: Weingarten, Larry and Suzanne. Elemental Enterprises, Monterey CA. 1992.

Water Heaters for Superinsulated Homes: Energy Design Update. New York, NY. 1988.

Windows and Energy Efficiency: Energy Design Update. New York, NY. 1986.

Your Home Cooling Energy Guide: Krigger, J. Saturn Resource Management. Helena, MT. 1992.

Your Mobile Home: Energy and Repair Guide For Manufactured Housing: Krigger, J. Saturn Resource Management, Helena, MT. 1998.

Periodicals

Energy Design Update: Aspen Publishers, 1185 Avenue of the Americas, New York, NY 10036. 800-638-8437. www.aspenpublishers.com.

Journal of Light Construction: 186 Allen Brook Lane, Williston, VT. 802-879-3335. www.jlconline.com.

Home Energy: PMB 95, 2124 Kittredge St., Berkeley, CA 94704. 510-524-5405. www.homeenergy.org.

INDEX

Natural lighting, 195
Neutral pressure plane, 80

O

Occupancy sensors, 194
Occupant education. See Customer education.
Oil
  water heating, 226
Oil burners
  excess air, 156
  performance indicators, 156, 157
Oil heating, 155
  burners, 144
    flame retention, 156
Oil pressure, 156, 157
Open-loop, 184

P

Parallel circuits, 44
Payback
  calculating, 74
Payback period, 26
Pellet stoves, 179
Photo cells, 194
Photocell heating control, 151
Photoresistors, 47
Pilot light, 143
Pipe insulation, 234
Platform-frame construction, 53
Polyethylene film
  for air sealing, 100
Polyisocyanurate
  insulation, 113
  R-value decrease with time, 113
Polystyrene
  extruded insulation, 113
  molded insulation, 112
Polyurethane
  sprayed on, 119
Pools and spas, 199
Porches
  thermal flaws of, 95, 96
Potentiometers, 47
Power
  and energy, 32
  definition, 32
  electrical, 44
Power bills. See Utility bills.
Power burner, 144
Power circuits, 48
Power venters, 147, 155
Pressure
  See also House pressure.
  and flow, 33
  examples of, 33

in high-rises, 98
  wind effect, 80
Pressure balancing. See Pressure diagnostics.
Pressure boundary. See Air barrier.
Pressure controller
  for steam, 171
Pressure diagnostics, 86, 86-88
  for ducts, 91
Pressure pan, 91
Pressure-reducing valves, 233
Primary air, 143
Propane. See Natural gas.
Pumps
  swimming pool, spa, 199

R

Radiant barriers, 208
  savings, 208
Radiant electric heat, 181
Radiant temperature, 38
Radiation
  absorptance, 35
  emittance, 37
  spectrum, 36
  types of, 35
Radiator temperature controls, 172
Radiators, 168
  air vents, 173
Radon, 243
Rain screen
  weep screed, 114
Rain screens, 114
  masonry cladding and, 114
  pressure-equalized, 114
Rates
  utility, 23
Recovery capacity, 223
Reflectance, 37
Reflective films, 206
Refrigerant charge, 220
Refrigeration cycle, 42
  principles, 43
Refrigerator, 197-198
  energy consumption, 198
  selecting a new, 198
  See also Freezers.
Relamping, 193
  fluorescents, 193
  incandescents, 193
  with compact fluorescents, 193
Relative humidity, 248
  and comfort, 39
  recommended levels, 39, 247
  saturation, 41
  summer/winter effects, 39
Relays, 46, 169, 171
Reset controllers, 161, 169

Resistance, 33
Return on investment
  calculating, 74
Roof coatings
  reflective, 207
Roofing, 54
Room air conditioners, 214
Room heaters
  combustion, 177
  electric, 181, 181-182
R-value
  clear-wall, 106
  of doors, 138
  whole-wall, 106

S

Sacrificial anode, 236
Safety
  and combustion heating, 150-158
  and combustion water heaters, 228
  fire, 150
  for combustion water heating, 228
  of residents, 245
Saturation
  of air, 39
Savings-to-investment ratio, 27
Sealants, 101
  See also Caulk.
Seasonal cooling load, 73-74
Seasonal energy efficiency ratio, 214
Seasonal energy efficiency ratio (SEER), 184
Seasonal heating load, 73-74
Seasonal loads, 71
Secondary air, 143
SEER. See Seasonal energy efficiency ratio.
Sensible heat factor, 216
Series circuits, 44
Shades
  exterior, 207
Shading coefficient, 70
  of windows, 127
Sheathing, 54
Shell. See Building shell.
Short circuit, 48
Siding, 54
Single-family homes
  construction, 53
  energy weaknesses, 54
SIR, 27
Smoke number, 156, 157
Solar absorptance, 37
Solar gain, 70
Solar heat
  principles, 36
Solar Heat Gain Coefficient, 127, 207
Solar heat gain coefficient, 70
Solar radiation

NOTES